Diary of a Hunger Striker

Diary of a Hunger Striker

Diary of a Hunger Striker

&

Four and a Half Steps

Oleh Sentsov

Translated from the Russian by
Dmytro Kyyan and Kate Tsurkan

DEEP VELLUM PUBLISHING
DALLAS, TEXAS

Deep Vellum Publishing
3000 Commerce St., Dallas, Texas 75226
deepvellum.org · @deepvellum

Deep Vellum is a 501c3 nonprofit literary arts organization
founded in 2013 with the mission to bring
the world into conversation through literature.

Support for this publication has been provided in part by grants from the National Endowment
for the Arts, the Texas Commission on the Arts, the City of Dallas Office of Arts and Culture, the
Communities Foundation of Texas, and the Addy Foundation.

LIBRARY OF CONGRESS CATALOGING-IN-PUBLICATION DATA:

Names: Sentsov, Oleg, author. | Sentsov, Oleg. Khronika odnoho
holoduvannia. | Sentsov, Oleg. Khronika odnoho holoduvannia.
English. | Sentsov, Oleg. 4 z polovinoiu kroki. | Sentsov, Oleg. 4
z polovinoiu kroki. English. | Kyyan, Dmytro, translator. | Tsurkan,
Kate, translator.
Title: Diary of a hunger striker : &, Four and a half steps / Oleh Sentsov
; translated from the Russian by Dmytro Kyyan and Kate Tsurkan.
Other titles: Four and a half steps
Description: Dallas : Deep Vellum, 2024.
Identifiers: LCCN 2024011465 (print) | LCCN 2024011466 (ebook) | ISBN
9781646053162 (trade paperback) | ISBN 9781646053315 (ebook)
Subjects: LCSH: Sentsov, Oleg--Translations into English. | Sentsov,
Oleg--Diaries. | Sentsov, Oleg--Imprisonment. | Political
prisoners--Russia (Federation)--Diaries. | Hunger strikes--Russia
(Federation) | Prisoners' writings, Ukrainian.
Classification: LCC PG3950.29.E58 D53 2024 (print) | LCC PG3950.29.E58
(ebook) | DDC 365/.45092 [B]--dc23/eng/20240525
LC record available at https://lccn.loc.gov/2024011465
LC ebook record available at https://lccn.loc.gov/2024011466

ISBN (paperback) 978-1-64605-316-2 | ISBN (Ebook) 978-1-64605-331-5

Cover art and design by Emily Mahon
Interior layout and typesetting by KGT

The translators gratefully acknowledge the editors at the *New Yorker* for publishing "Anatoly"
in its online edition, and to *Harpers* for publishing the first three days of the *Diary*.

PRINTED IN CANADA

CONTENTS

Introduction

It is a strange feeling when you become close to a person without seeing him once—similar to a relationship you build with a character from a book or a historical figure you admire. This is how I first learned about Oleh Sentsov, and how, for a good five years while he was serving his outrageous and unjust twenty-year sentence in one notorious Russian prison after another, I felt while advocating for his freedom. It is a rare joy for human rights defenders who work in such a difficult region as Eurasia to see a political prisoner released. I experienced this joy. I met Oleh in Kyiv about a week after he was finally released from prison in a prisoner exchange in 2019—just to see him go to the frontline in 2022 to risk his life again defending his country from a bloody, unprovoked Russian onslaught.

As an artist, Oleh has always been interested, both in his texts and his movies, in describing life and its brutality in an honest, uncompromising, and direct way, but with a humor, sometimes even a black humor, that the situation requires. *Diary of a Hunger Striker and Four and a Half Steps* depicts his life in prison, including a hunger strike of 145 days, a duration that still gives me chills when I think about it. I remember vividly how every day during this hunger strike I would come to work thinking, "What else can I do to make him not die?" His post-prison movie *Rhino* is emotionally hard to watch, even for those like me who remember how dangerous the Soviet Union was during the '90s. The way he approaches his writing and his filmmaking is truly unconventional: from meticulously documenting his physical condition during the hunger strike without being sure that these notes will ever see light to hiring nonprofessional actors for his movies. Now, however, Oleh admits that he doesn't want to film movies. He likes to describe himself now as he did in a 2022 interview for Al Jazeera: as a "simple soldier" who is fighting in a fight that is "nothing like you imagine from the movies."

Oleh has always been a hero standing firm against dictatorship. A tall and broad-shouldered freedom-fighter, you picture him in "a four-and-a-half-step prison cell" as an anomaly, a plaguy misconception that needs to be corrected as soon as possible. The year 2019 was a time when the prisoner exchange of a cultural figure like Oleh Sentsov was still possible in Russia— this is less and less so now. In 2023, Russia was among top-five jailers of writers around the world according to PEN America's Freedom to Write Index. By the end of 2023, there were seventy-nine Ukrainian artists and seventy journalists who were killed since the start of Russia's full-scale invasion of Ukraine, including writer Volodymyr Vakulenko, who wrote his own diary, a diary that gives us a testimony and record that wouldn't be possible without writers. Victoria Amelina, who discovered this diary after Vakulenko's death, was herself killed by a Russian missile attack.

How many more lives will be ruined by this war? At least I have seen Oleh miraculously survive despite courageously throwing himself into the most dangerous situations. I wish for an end to the war and for Oleh to come home to his wife and little son as soon as possible. In the era of disinformation and lies, we need writers and artists to write books and make movies that are as close to life—real life.

—Polina Sadovskaya
Director, Eurasia & Advocacy, PEN America
2024

Translators' Note

The original published version of this diary presented the text as one continuous stream. For this English edition, we have divided it into three parts.

One

I'VE NEVER KEPT A DIARY, even in my lonely young years when many do. This will be my first and most likely my last. On many levels. Though I would like to keep a diary—or to be more precise, notes regarding a certain affair—in the future. But that affair is still a long ways off, particularly from this cell, so I won't be writing about that. I generally don't like sharing my plans. And not because I'm so private or secretive, but because if what I've announced doesn't pan out, I'll feel awkward—in relation to myself above all—whereas if everything does turn out as I have described, there'll be no surprise in it for anyone else.

I decided to keep a diary on the third day of my hunger strike. It's hard to write the truth and even harder to write about myself, but I'll try. Writing in a way that's simple, true, and, at the same time, interesting has always been my goal. I don't know to what extent I've been successful at it in the past, but there's certainly nothing to get in my way right now. I don't know why I've decided to keep this diary. A thought popped into my head, then a sentence, and it took off from there—new thoughts, and more of them—and I decided to begin writing them down even though I hadn't planned on it. But that's how it always is with me—in my creative work, though likely in my life as well. An author doesn't exist apart from his life. His creative work is just one part of him.

When I made the decision to write, I spent a long time debating whether to hide these pieces of paper or write openly. I decided to be open about it: I have nothing to hide. I'll try to write as little as possible about the penal colony I'm in so that this notebook doesn't get confiscated on the excuse that I'm allegedly describing the camp's safety and security protocols. I'll try to avoid that, though it doesn't really make a difference, as the chances of this notebook someday making it past the walls of this colony and breaking out into the free world are pathetically low. But then, so are my chances of achieving what I'm hunger-striking for. But, we'll see what happens: We both have a chance. I suspect that the writing, while knowing full well that, most likely, no one will read this and also understanding that a hunger strike may have a heartbreaking denouement, will end up being true. As the Soviet rocker Yuri Shevchuk used to sing, "The closer to death people are, the purer they are."

I'll start by recounting the first three days in one go, then sum up each new day in writing. Though there's no guarantee that there'll be anything to write about. There are few events in prison, let alone interesting ones.

DAY ONE

At 6:00 AM, after roll call, I handed a notice about my hunger strike to a prison officer. He grew furious and flung the sheet of paper in the direction of the nightstand. The sheet of paper didn't make it all the way back and landed on the floor. The prison police don't like it when an inmate announces a hunger strike. He dragged me off to the duty officers' unit.

The major on duty initially got worked up as well, but then cooled off and switched into "good cop" mode. For fifteen minutes or so, he engaged with me mostly in monologue—ending inevitably with Ukraine, where he too was from, though he had now become a veritable Putinist. Then he personally escorted me to the exit and said that this type of notice needed to be submitted right before breakfast instead of frightening people at the break of dawn. He, of course, was very distressed that the "emergency incident" had occurred during his shift. They always get distressed in such instances, as if they're going to get graded for it at the end of the year. OK, fine, breakfast is at eight; we can wait.

I was taken off to join the rest of the prisoners, then brought back to the duty unit just before eight. The top brass had arrived and wanted to chat. We chatted. Upon learning that my demands were purely political—and, therefore, unrealizable—they calmed down a bit. They requested that I submit a written statement that I have no complaints against the colony.

I declined. Words aren't enough for them; they need a piece of paper to hide behind too. Here, in this system, they have no trust at all—toward convicts all the more so, though possibly toward one another too.

They proposed waiting for a lawyer to arrive and only then making a definitive decision. I declined, explaining that I had already made my decisions and a lawyer would be irrelevant. Once again, they made sure that I wasn't planning on complaining about the colony. Once again, I confirmed this, then also pointed out that in all my four years behind bars, I hadn't submitted a single complaint. Whether or not they believed me, who knows, but the conversation came to an end.

I was locked up in the so-called "drinking glass," a small cage in the duty unit where you can spend quite some time standing around and waiting. I stood there for four hours. Over the course of that time, practically all of the top brass came in, one after another. The same questions and the same answers. They were polite. They didn't try to scare me, just warned me of the consequences—above all, of the possible damage to my health. Accusations of a conspiracy with other prisoners to engage in some kind of shady dealings were voiced.

They tried to tell me that I was being used. I replied that I was doing everything on my own and that I wasn't easily manipulated. The concluding summary of all these conversations: "We didn't put you in here!" and "You're not the ones I'm fighting against!"

I never saw as many nice cops as I did that morning, even in TV shows about nice cops. After the third hour in the "drinking glass," they even brought me a stool. Obviously, the prison and camp workers are no cops. They're not even law enforcement, but the prisoners continue to occasionally refer to them as *militsiya*—as the Soviet police force used to be called—when we can't use a slang term.

Around noon, I was finally frisked and led off to a separate cell designated for me. I had expected this: Anyone who announces a hunger strike gets put into isolation. So that the prisoner can carry out their hunger strike "properly" and that he's close by, under supervision—and, well . . . so that the stubborn guy can be "worked over" as needed. They won't be working me over, that much is clear. They'll just ignore me and wait for me to give up on my own.

The cell turned out to be one I already knew: I had spent fifteen days of concurrent quarantine and probationary isolation in it when I arrived at the camp. It was in a small, separate building of the operative unit: offices on the second floor, a few cells, and a storeroom below. The cell is spacious even for a double—ten meters or so—and, for one person, it's a total palace. Until now, I had spent my entire time in what were basically one-man cages.

This cell contains the standard setup for an isolation cell: a double bunk, a table and bench, a squat toilet, a sink, and a shelf. But also, of course, a door with extra bars and a little window complete with two grilles and a *fortochka* for ventilation up top. Tucked away in a corner, like a spider, is the all-seeing eye of round-the-clock video surveillance. An all-inclusive correctional getaway. The only drawback—and it's a serious one—is that, though the heater's big, it's not really warm, while the cell itself is a corner one and, therefore, cold. As if the cell were for the overly hot-headed so that they might cool off here.

They changed me into a fresh uniform, which in no way differed from my last one other than that it was older, as well as comparably old thermal underwear. What the point of this was remained unclear, only that it was the rule.

Seeking out any logic in this system is generally difficult, and finding any is practically impossible. This place is governed not by common sense but by the internal regulations of Russia's Federal Penitentiary Service.

It didn't take long for me to settle in. The cell, as I've already noted, was one I knew, but I hadn't yet received any of my things, either mine or replacement items. So, I tried to kill time by warming up—next to the barely warm heater or pacing around the cell. The building's Keeper of the Keys issued me a mattress and bedding before clocking out. We talked for a bit.

This Key Keeper is a convict who works for the administration, a steward and watchman in one. He's got a face with a broken nose and the eyes of an executioner's assistant. He and I last saw each other when I passed through this cell half a year ago. In his thirteen years as a prisoner, he's seen it all. He, too, asked why I was doing this, in search of ulterior motives, conspiracies, and unavoidable consequences. In the end, he delivered the tirade of the day: "You're either very dumb or very intelligent."

The food slot on the door closed, and he clocked out. I got into bed still in my clothes: I was freezing from the day. I had assumed that in a new place, in the cold, with an empty stomach, it would take me a long time to fall asleep, but that's not what happened. I passed out almost immediately.

DAY TWO

The standard 6:00 AM wake-up. Snow was billowing outside the window, but I hadn't frozen over the course of the night, which was good. All I needed was to sleep badly because of the cold . . .

Every two hours, a worker comes by and switches on the video recording device to confirm that I'm still here—that I haven't run off. From the very beginning, all six months that

I've been here, I've had the red mark of a potential fugitive next to my name. My presence is confirmed every two hours.

During the day, your presence is verified by calling out your last name and other details. At night they do it while you sleep, turning on a small flashlight in the process. Some employees shine it at you from a little further away in order to not wake you with the light, while others, conversely, endeavor to poke you in the face with it. Each cop has their own unique way of doing things. In addition to the physical presence check, there's also the inspection.

Here, in my cell, which as an isolation cell is officially labeled a "safe place," it's typically conducted quickly: an employee comes and, in less than a minute, ticks off that you're present twice a day, in the morning and evening. This has its pluses because when you're living in the barracks, you file into the prison yard with the whole camp in advance, to music, and wait as everyone gets checked. It takes almost an hour and is pretty tiring, especially when it's negative twenty degrees Celsius and windy. Below negative twenty-five, the check is conducted in the barracks, which is obviously much more pleasant, but this happens seldom, only during a severe frost.

Another one of the mandatory procedures is the official turning down of food—three times a day, also to be recorded on the video-recording device. Well, and once a day, there's also the mandatory search. And that's theoretically it. All day I'm free to do whatever I like. Mostly I try to keep warm, but sitting and, worse yet, lying down on the bunk isn't allowed. The indefatigable video camera in the corner is vigilantly monitoring this as well. And, of course, the Keeper of the Keys is always close by, on watch. He seems to not be in sight all day, but he's always right on hand in a moment of need.

After the morning check, the supervisor of the penal colony arrived with the human rights ombudsman.* Both were in uniform with colonels' insignia. Which of them was policing me and which was protecting me was hard to figure out. But the supervisor was wearing an Astrakhan fur hat, while the one who was supposedly there to protect me was in an ordinary one. That was the only thing differentiating them.

The one protecting my rights was even more concerned about the camp than the immediate director of this establishment: he said that my hunger strike was a violation of protocol and described artificial feeding to me. I responded artificial feeding that involved being held down and having a spoon shoved down your throat was on par with torture, so we could only talk about medical support for my body as it weakened. We went back and forth on this subject for a bit. It seemed that, among the local cops, the quality of kindness didn't extend higher than the rank of major. And those allegedly protecting my rights didn't even know of their existence. Though the kindness of the former was also highly dubious and quite possibly temporary.

At lunchtime, I was taken to see my lawyer. We had, as he put it, a constructive conversation—a whole two hours. He was flying out today and took my private correspondence with

---

* An official appointed by the government to serve as a public advocate by investigating and resolving complaints, such as those pertaining to human rights issues.

him, as well as an open statement about my declared hunger strike and my explanation of the matter. But the most important thing was a letter to my daughter. Last night I was given a long-awaited letter from her and my mother, and I managed to pass along a response to my daughter with my lawyer because she was leaving soon, and an ordinary letter may not have caught her on time.

I'll write to my mom later this evening and send it by the normal post. She's always at home and will be excited to hear from her son. In all honesty, yesterday evening, receiving these letters and reading them a few times proved rather difficult. I suddenly became distinctly aware that the list of people I had made miserable was very long and filled with names of people I cared about, whereas the column that should've contained those I had made happy was hopelessly empty. It was a very difficult few hours, especially not knowing what to do with these feelings—knowing only that my announced hunger strike wouldn't add names to the second group.

But it's too late to retreat: everything has already been decided, the die has been cast, the Rubicon has been crossed, or whatever it is Caesar said.

This evening has been unusually pleasant so far. They brought me my things, which I had requested, and also a small TV, which I hadn't requested. They also promised to give me a space heater because they took the temperature in the cell, and it turned out to be sixteen point five degrees Celsius. That's half a degree higher than the minimum standard per their requirements, so it should supposedly be fine. But they nonetheless decided to warm me up a little, and that couldn't *not* make me happy. Police kindness on the day your lawyer visits typically hits record highs. I'll let them keep doing their thing in this respect.

After checking the news before lights out—nothing else interesting turned up on the two channels that this little tube caught—I began to get ready for bed. The Key Keeper brought a small heater, and an hour before I fell asleep, the cell had warmed up, but he took it away again for the night. I boiled water in a mug with a handheld electronic kettle and sipped my fill of hot water. Warmed up now, I decided to try to sleep without my uniform, just in my thermal underwear. As the morning would show, this was a mistake.

DAY THREE

The day was a bust from the very beginning, starting off during the night. My uniform was seemingly thin, but the lack of this layer had clearly kept me from sleeping at all peacefully: I was freezing and woke up constantly. For some reason, it didn't occur to me to put the uniform on in the middle of the night. And yet I did get taken by the urge to go to the bathroom.

I don't think I stood up too abruptly, but I grew lightheaded and a large dark blotch appeared before my eyes, as sometimes happens before you get very disoriented. It's been a long time since something like that happened to me, and this time it more or less passed. But it still wasn't a good sign. Moreover, it happened very early on, and I had counted on these kinds of special effects manifesting themselves significantly later.

In the morning, I boiled myself some water and turned on the TV. Yet again, other than the news, there was nothing interesting this early, nor would there be before evening. I had already developed persistent nausea in response to all these vapid series and shows a long time ago. The news couldn't be described as interesting either, unless it was in comparison to the rest of the bullshit on TV. They were showing the same thing as yesterday—Putin driving a KamAZ truck over the new bridge into Crimea; such symbolism! The news on the other channel was identical, as if they were following the same script, only things had been shuffled around in order and spliced a little differently. Still, Putin behind the steering wheel—of course—trumped everything else.

The rest of the montaged exaltations of Russia and chastisement of the west and Ukraine followed in whatever order. Over my four years in prison, I've grown used to sorting out the kernels of truth from this dribble of sludge and lies, but it's exhausting work. Good that I also get a newspaper and letters so that at least something worthwhile and real can be gleaned. How much longer can this mountain of falsehood keep holding out? I had expected it to collapse sooner and finally bury its creators, but no . . . judging by the news, they're all thriving. The only useful information was in the scrolling news ticker—that today was Yuri Shevchuk's birthday. So that's why he and his lyrics had recently come to mind . . . Everything is connected by incomprehensible and invisible threads and nerves. But anyway, Happy Birthday, old man! Thank you for existing! And that's where the good news ended.

After the morning inspections and checks, a furious duty officer showed up—the same one who was first to learn about my hunger strike and had been rather amiable and civil at the time. But the goodness of cops is short-lived, especially after your lawyer leaves.

He took away the TV and some of my things, then secured the bunk to the wall. But the important thing was that he took away my kettle! I parted with the TV and the other stuff with no problem, but the immersion water heater—why that? It had been my only source of warmth and hot water! Judging by everything, I wouldn't be able to count on the heater anymore either. And what about the boiling water?! That too? The explanation arrived through clenched teeth: I wasn't authorized to have a heater because I was on a hunger strike.

There was, as usual, no logic in this, as even the rules affixed to the door of my cell included a kettle in the list of permitted items. But a lot of the police either don't know these rules at all or follow them at their own discretion. Arguing this point was useless. In response, the duty officer's eyes began to roam in search of what else he might snatch up in this already empty cell. I decided to speak to the less idiotic supervisor later, especially since the Keeper of the Keys had been authorized to serve me boiling water on demand. It wasn't very convenient, and I don't like having to ask, even for the littlest things.

But none of this really matters. My heart and the dizziness have been troubling me more. I sense that my motor is giving out—a real nuisance at the start of a marathon.

After lunch I was taken to the med point. The head doctor, with the insignia of a lieutenant colonel, wasn't evil, but an odd duck. Though that's not uncommon among his breed. The check-ups would now be daily. My pulse and blood pressure were OK for now, even if they were near their lower limits.

I gave some samples. The blood barely oozed from my prick-riddled finger. My motor really was only just chugging along. There was acetone in my urine already, and the doctor began narrating horrible stories about how the body begins to process its own protein, about irreversible processes and people's individual critical thresholds—then he smoothly veered from dissuasions to politics and half an hour later, as was to be expected, landed on Ukraine. It had been a long time since I'd engaged in futile polemics around here, so when I was given the floor, I restricted myself to the summary "Time will tell." There was nothing for him to argue, which was why the lieutenant colonel, upon finishing smoking his fifth cigarette, didn't in fact argue, even though his position as a die-hard Russophile with Orthodox imperial leanings could've interested someone. But obviously not me: psychiatry wasn't my field.

In the end, I was weighed. Without clothes, I was eighty-four kilograms. Let's take another kilo for the last three days. Which meant I began the hunger strike at eighty-five kilos. Hmm, that was my minimum weight. That was how much I'd weighed as a famished teenager and occasionally while in prison. I was over ninety kilograms when I was free and ninety-five when I was going to the gym regularly.

I'm generally lean: I've never carried excess weight, let alone fat. For the last month, I prepared for the hunger strike by subsisting only on *balanda*—the prison's default potato stew—so as to more easily transition to complete abstinence from this type of minimal diet. It was really easy. My stomach wasn't protesting, and I barely felt any hunger. But then the dizziness, weakness, and tinnitus began.

Now, I can feel my heart as it beats. Maybe I should've chosen a different strategy and put on a little more weight so that my internal reserves would last longer. Though it's not like there was a nutritionist on hand to turn to for advice. In any case, it's too late now: the die has flowed away with the Rubicon's current, and our troops are already on the other side, but it's still a long ways' march to Rome, and it likely won't fall without a fight...

DAY FOUR

Today's highlight: I was put on bed rest! I got to lie down and sleep on my bunk all day. I knew it would happen eventually, but I didn't expect to be granted it so soon.

This is really helpful on a hunger strike: you can warm up and relax while conserving energy and body heat. It's much better than sitting on your bench and trying to keep warm by huddling up against a lukewarm heater or pacing around your cell.

But I was only granted this privilege around lunchtime. In the morning, I felt how weak I'd become when I had to perform my routine procedure of taking my mattress off the bunk and out of the cell and locking the wooden slats of the bunk back up against the wall. I realized that, with each passing day, I would find it harder and harder to do this. How had I been able to lift a ninety-nine-kilogram barbell before this?

Now, everything is different: it's no longer necessary to take my mattress out or lock my bunk up. I can sleep or loaf around to my heart's content. But I'm trying not to abuse this, otherwise, I won't fall asleep at night or get enough sleep, and

I'll just sleep again during the next day, which would completely disorient my sleep schedule. Even so, I was in bed for several hours and ended up falling asleep earlier this afternoon.

I dreamed that my father was standing next to his red Moskvitch car, and I was in the Peugeot I had owned before my most recent car. My brakes weren't working, and I couldn't park next to him. My father didn't seem to be looking at me and instead talked to someone at a roadside kiosk. This was all happening in my home village, where the road turned off from the garage where he used to work and led toward the kindergarten where my mother worked. In the end, I managed to park the car a little ways up the street, next to some others, instead of on that dangerous turnoff. That was the extent of my dream. Short but vivid, just like reality. They say that communicating with the dead is a sign of an affliction, but we didn't seem to exchange any words with each other—he didn't even look at me.

The deterioration of my health is clearly impending, but today, I feel a little better. My body has begun to adapt to the new conditions of this embargo on nutrition. I feel less dizzy, though my fingernails have started to occasionally turn blue—probably from the cold or because my heart isn't coping too well.

Once again, I was taken to the doctor: he measured my blood pressure and was surprised that I had such cold hands. I told him that his would be just the same as mine if he were in my cell, whereas the doctor's office was a comfortable twenty-one degrees Celsius, and he was sitting at his desk in a navy blue striped tank top. Today, he told me about Tajikistan, his homeland. He himself is Russian, but he was born there. He spoke of the bloody civil war that had been going on there for ten years.

I didn't know anything about it. It was scary but also interesting to hear about it. I also warmed up a bit, so overall, it was a productive visit.

It was snowing outside my window again. Of course, it was strange for me, a southerner, to see snow in mid-May, as the heat would have already reached us in Crimea and the strawberries ripened.

One of the prison officers came, the head of my detachment: he's a captain, a good guy. He was the one who brought me the two letters from my family on my first night here. Today, I gave him a letter to my mother, and he handed me a piece of paper stating that, in case of a medical emergency, I would be force-fed. We read the Criminal Enforcement Code of the Russian Federation together, discussed the issue, and he confirmed what I envisioned force-feeding to involve: IV drips, not stuffing food down my throat. After that, he left. I wanted to tell him that if all policemen were like him, there'd probably be fewer criminals, but we didn't have the time to discuss such things.

No big deal: I'll be sure to tell him next time.

DAY FIVE

I had a bad night. I slept for a couple of hours yesterday afternoon, which meant that I struggled to fall asleep later on. My legs were still very cold. Even though I was wearing socks and lying under a blanket, they didn't warm up during the night, and in the morning they were like ice. It was probably too difficult for my heart to pump blood to them, or maybe it was just the cold. Thankfully, my hands warmed under the blanket and weren't blue anymore. The strain on my body generally seemed to lessen while I was lying down, compared to when I was standing or sitting. During the night, I got up to go to the toilet, and, though I thought I did so carefully, I started seeing stars, like before you faint. I barely made it back to bed. No problem in the end: I slept it off.

I remember when I was very ill as a child, and I had a problem with my heart, I was prescribed three months' bed rest and advised to avoid any physical activity. Now, I'm also trying to rest more—we'll see what happens. This morning, I didn't even manage—as I should have—to enjoy that I wasn't required to get up at six in the morning and make my bed but could instead take it easy in my cell. Now that I'm on bed rest, I can laze around as much as I want to—though it's true that I'm hindered by a large fluorescent lamp, which they switch on in the morning.

At half past six, the next guard on duty came with the slop server, the *balander*, who gave me my rations in my cell. They've already reached a crisis point of dissatisfaction with my ongoing refusal to eat, so they decided to rely on this Jesuit method of persuasion. When I asked them what the point of this charade was, they merely replied: "You were given food. If you don't want it, don't eat it. We'll pick it up in two hours." Well, at least they didn't leave it for two days.

They think the look and smell of food will tempt me, but the slop they try to feed me doesn't smell very appetizing. Besides, the cold has made my nose stuffy, so the smell of the food isn't even a problem.

I moved the tray and placed it onto the upper bunk, right under the surveillance camera, so that it wouldn't distract me on the table where I sit, read, and write.

The bunks, by the way, are very good here: they're long and welded from angle irons, but the bed itself is wooden. This is *very* helpful. I can actually fit on them, and they're not too cold. In all the cells I've been in before, especially in solitary confinement, the iron beds were small and uncomfortable. You couldn't sleep on them properly, and you would freeze no matter what, especially since the mattresses in pre-trial detention and transit centers were complete crap. Here, by comparison, we have almost king-sized beds.

On the second day, after they brought me my possessions, including two books, I started reading Haruki Murakami. I've read most of his work, and it's pretty good. The book I'm currently reading is called *The Windup Bird Chronicle*. Murakami has a unique style; he writes about life and relationships simply, but with a dash of philosophy and mysticism. The result is quite cool. Hemingway also wrote simply, but his simplicity was unique—there was something Spartan about it, like a faded military or hunting jacket. Murakami's simplicity would be more like a student or petty official's shirt.

I wonder if my writing has its own style and, if so, what it's like. It's difficult to evaluate one's own creative output. I'm very skeptical about what I create, but for some reason, I keep writing. I guess I just like it as an exercise. It's like this diary here: I didn't plan to write one, and it seems to be working well. How well—that's difficult to assess and probably not worth thinking about too much. The only question that remains is what to call it: *Diary of a Hunger Striker* or *Chronicle of a Hunger Striker*? The first title is more accurate, but the second one sounds more beautiful. I'll let the editors choose if this text ever manages to reach them. If I make it to the editing process, I won't correct anything myself. It can stay as it is: it'll be more authentic that way.

I went to my daily appointment at the med point. It's only in the next building over, and it takes thirty seconds to walk there. The heat of the sun outside clearly started to grow stronger. The northern winter was gradually coming to an end. Maybe my dungeon would get warmer soon too. The doctor weighed me, then took my pulse, blood pressure, and another urine sample. I weighed eighty-two kilos, and there was acetone and protein in my urine. According to the doctor, all of my stats were normal, as far as hunger strikes went. He asked me why I'd been given a twenty-year sentence. Good question—I'm sometimes curious about that myself.

The duty assistant to the colony head took me there and back. He's the one who checks for escapees every two hours and conducts the solemn process of bringing in my food and taking it out two hours later. Today this procedure began to acquire the characteristics of a ritual. The *balander*, who used to distribute food without even taking off his prison coat, was dressed in a white jacket, like a real chef, and he brought a bowl of food into the cell under the supervision of the guard. It was like a prison feng shui ceremony—or maybe a dressage show.

Since the only person with access to me now is the duty assistant to the colony head, who, in theory, is responsible for the whole prison, it means my situation has taken a serious turn. The prison administration is clearly disgruntled and is turning up the heat.

They started to broadcast a daily hour-long lecture on prison rules and protocol over the radio, which they hadn't done in the preceding days. The saga with the kettle, meanwhile, has continued. In response to my demands over their seizure of this device, the guard merely blamed management protocol, though he knows perfectly well that it was a violation of their own rules.

Their system has a characteristic feature: if one of them ever makes a mistake or commits an outright abuse, they don't admit to it but continue to stand by their decision with all their might, even as the mistakes and examples of idiocy build up, whether the problem has to do with a kettle or a twenty-year prison sentence.

At least the Keeper of the Kettle supplies me with boiling water on a more or less regular basis—though, sometimes, it's just warm water—not realizing that I don't want to drink it as much as I want to warm up with it. I tried to explain this to him, but he was in no hurry to have a conversation with me. He felt that dark clouds had begun to gather over me and quickly went off to hide in his underground vault.

DAY SIX

I slept badly again last night: it took me a long time to fall asleep, and I kept waking up through the night because of the cold. My legs didn't warm up, not even in the morning. Still, my overall condition has stabilized somewhat: my head isn't spinning as much and the ringing in my ears no longer sounds like the roar of a distant plane constantly taking off. My heart, which regularly sends signals to the brain that something is wrong, has now been joined by my kidneys, though they nag at my back more than anywhere else. My feet won't go out of cryogenic mode. My hands regularly do the same. My knees display signs of chronic rheumatism and now complain like an elderly person.

It's not clear what's causing the aching pain in my groin, whether my joints are also inflamed or just my lymph nodes. My stomach periodically mutters something incomprehensible. In response to all this, my brain sends cheerful messages to my organs: Hold on, guys, this is how it's supposed to be, everything's going to be fine! Because of this, my mood is more or less calm. My subconscious begins to play tricks on me, aware its time is coming, knowing that when basic instincts like hunger start to rule over the body, it will take over and push consciousness aside. But all of that's still to come—and no time soon, I hope.

Meanwhile, my scheming subconscious has launched a campaign of food propaganda in my brain, bombarding it with various images of meals my body has consumed or even just seen over its lifetime, sometimes inventing fantastically exquisite dishes of its own. But it hasn't yet succeeded. Deep within each person lurks a whole host of demons that are constantly trying to pull him over to their side. I rid myself of my most destructive horned demons a long time ago and forced the rest to work in my favor. Then again, maybe they'll take advantage of this situation in order to have their revenge. We'll see. At least tempting me with food for the majority of the day isn't working.

The prison officers have resorted to speaking official jargon in their interactions with me, and, on top of this, I barely see anyone beyond the guard on duty. When they lead me around outside, they close off the yard and make sure all the other prisoners are in their cells in such a way that I'm led through an almost empty prison.

I cleaned my cell. I used to do it every day, with a general clear-out once a week, but I've since decided to limit myself to a couple of times a week. Trying to crawl around on all fours with a rag is unpleasant; now, conserving energy is more important than ideal hygiene. While cleaning I opened the window to ventilate the room, which I tend to do several times a day. Fresh air is very necessary, as it's twice as difficult to sit in the cold with stagnant air.

The weather in the morning deteriorated again: fog, mist, and damp. Such is the Russian north. I was recently told by one of the guys from these parts that "the cold weather lasts for three months, then we're freezing our balls off like arctic foxes for the rest of the year . . . "

The thrice-daily process of serving my rations to my cell has finally turned into a proper ritual: the guard on duty opens the door and solemnly announces that it's time to eat. The white-clad *balander* brings the bowls and places them on the table. We politely bid our farewells and my "guests" leave. Then I place the food onto the upper bunk, to keep it away from me and closer to the All-Seeing Eye. Surprisingly, when I pick up the bread and the bowl of porridge or soup, I don't feel like eating it. This is either a sign of a strong sense of resolve or merely the early stages of a hunger strike. We'll see what happens next.

My overall condition has actually stabilized a bit today, reduced to only an unpleasant odor in my mouth. Maybe my stomach is slowly starting to cannibalize itself. At the beginning of the week, I could only fit my thumb behind the waistband of my trousers, and now I can fit my whole fist.

I went to the bathhouse today—not by myself, of course. I was escorted by the guard, but convicts often use "walked" or "rode" to talk about themselves instead of being "driven" or "escorted" somewhere. It gives us the illusion of independence. The word "bathhouse" is also rather generous: in reality, it's a large shower room with a dozen showerheads and benches. There is always some commotion and line here when all of the prisoners wash at the same time.

I was alone, in total isolation. They gave me twenty minutes, which wasn't that bad: in some places, you only got ten or fifteen minutes. Ten minutes of pure bliss from the hot water. I had time to wash both myself and my clothes. My body was grateful, especially my legs. I started feeling bad at the end, to tell the truth, but it wasn't unbearable.

I decided to shave right after I returned. The Keeper of the Blades gave me my razor and shaving cream. He keeps them somewhere with him so that I don't go and slit my wrists. As I shaved, I saw myself in the mirror for the first time this week.

The cell mirror is small: it's built into the wall above the sink but placed low, so you need to crouch down in order to see yourself. Since I'm tall and don't like to look at myself in the mirror, I had yet to see my reflection in this cell, even while brushing my teeth. Despite the virtual absence of plaque, I still brush my teeth twice a day because it's very easy to lose teeth during a hunger strike—something I was able to witness first-hand recently—and you can't grow new teeth.

My reflection wasn't pleasing: my cheekbones had grown sharper and hollow. My eyes looked even more sunken, and the creases on my forehead had deepened; besides now being adorned with bulging veins, my forehead was continuing its advance along my receding hairline, doomed to a slow retreat to become a barren field after its defeat in battle. In short: I saw nothing good, and it would have been better not to have looked at all.

I then called to mind a friend's father back in our village who had cirrhosis of the liver. His whole family came to visit us one holiday. Everyone would talk with and smile at him as if nothing had happened, as if unaware that he didn't have long left. He smiled back at everyone with a toothless grin, and his eyes seemed to bulge out of his skull. Of course, I'm still very far from that physical state, but, by the looks of it, I've already started moving in that direction.

DAY SEVEN

The night passed as badly as expected. I was sleeping in my uniform and thermal underwear, covered in a blanket, but I still felt the cold, especially in my legs. The blanket was more like a thick top sheet, to be honest, but still. At night, I discovered another mild irritant.

The cell's toilet is a standard prison one—a hole in the floor with a plug and a string—but water flows into this system from the sink, which is a lousier set-up than what it would be from the toilet tank via a pipe. That would be more efficient. But the tank is old and its internal piping system is all worn out, and I noticed how it now just emits a sad *plink-plink*, or a cheerier-sounding rumbling.

This is almost inaudible during the day and isn't irritating. You can't hear it in your sleep either. But if it takes you a while to get to sleep at night, then it starts getting on your nerves. Any attempt to repair the tank is rarely crowned with success. After quieting down for about five minutes, it resumes its monotonous song, which is especially loud in the nighttime silence of a prison cell. Sometimes, it stops showing signs of life, but not for long. In any case, I believe that if you can't overcome something, you can get used to it with time. People can get used to anything—especially in prison.

The morning started as usual. My general physical and mental state seemed stable, but a powerful weakness had revealed itself. I could barely make my bunk bed, and I brushed my teeth while sitting down, hoping it would pass during the day and I'd eventually limber up. As I washed myself, something pricked my eye, like a dried-up crust. I looked in the mirror and saw that my right eye was bloodshot. It looked like conjunctivitis had made its own small contribution to the cards I'd been dealt. But where could I have caught it from? I hadn't made physical contact with anyone all week, and I kept on top of my hygiene, no matter what. Oh well, it would pass—no big deal.

The on-duty police have introduced a new element to the end of their ritual of bringing in and taking out meals. The whole process is recorded on video by the prison guard, and when the *balander* carries the untouched rations out of the cell, he zooms his video device on a plate and says, "He hasn't eaten his food"—and "scene."

They brought boiling water, and I warmed up enough to write these lines. I write at different times of the day, sometimes in parts, sometimes all at once. Now, I will forever associate the taste of boiled water with going on hunger strike.

I'm still reading Murakami's *The Windup Bird Chronicle*. I like it a lot—both Murakami's work in general and this book in particular. There are good books you read in one sitting, and others you take your time to read, drawing out the pleasure of it. I've been chewing this one slowly, in mouthfuls. It's quite hefty and I'm already halfway through.

I realized, unexpectedly, that reading this book was what gave me the urge to start keeping a journal. That's why it should be called *Chronicle of a Hunger Striker*, in honor of Murakami. The editors wouldn't have a choice.

In the book, the protagonist spent three days at the bottom of a dried-up well, suffering from thirst and hunger while looking for something he'd lost. Reading it felt very familiar. After this, who could say that things just happen at random, that they're unconnected? Not me. During that time, the protagonist was really suffering from hunger; he had stomach pains, cramps, and so on.

I had nothing like that; my stomach was behaving peacefully. Was it because I had a smooth entry into the hunger strike by preparing for it and reducing my rations beforehand? Or maybe it was for another reason. I'd heard a lot about fasting for health reasons, but I never fasted, though I thought about it. Not before this opportunity came about! Purifying the body, clearing the toxins, and all that jazz. To be fair, none of the toxins have exited my system yet, so we'll just have to wait. On the whole, then, I propose not thinking of this as a political hunger strike, but a medicinal one! Who's with me? I don't see any hands up!

What was noticeable was that, during the day, my legs weren't as cold as they were at night under the blanket, probably because I was still moving, if only a tiny amount. I opened the vent to get a breeze going. The air outside didn't bite like before and no longer gave me a chill, but it was a long way from warm. The fresh snow had been cleared off the paths, and the paltry sun had thawed the snow in patches, but the somber, gray banks still towered in the corners of the yard. They say that snow can last here until July. Here's hoping it doesn't.

That rotten taste in my mouth has intensified. The dryness compounded it; the hot water only helped for so long. I don't want to drink cold water and, besides, it's bad for you.

It's strange that I haven't been searched for the past few days. Ever since I got a red mark on my chest tag for being a runaway risk, I've been frisked every single day for the six months I've been in this joint. They were very committed to it right from the start while I was in this cell: they'd tip everything upside down, strip me down to my underwear—or naked— and search me thoroughly. Afterward, once I was transferred to the penitentiary camp unit of inmates, they didn't search me as aggressively. Now they don't even perform this procedure at all. Strange. But there's no guarantee it'll stay like that.

I remembered my dream last night, or more like a set of dreams involving chaotic, unrelated situations. Some people; cars, buses, trains; I traveled on all of them, sometimes alone, but more often with someone. Stations, platforms, bus stops. I was on the bus, sitting in one of the rear seats, legs up on the headrest. My grandma and my aunt were with me, in different seats. My aunt was eating ice cream, and neither of them looked like any of my relatives. I lowered my feet so as not to be rude.

After that, we were standing on one of the train platforms, and my aunt and grandma wanted to write in their diaries about a boy who'd just pulled off a great feat by grabbing someone out of the way of an oncoming train. The boy stood next to his father, and no one had a pen to write it all down. There were a lot of people around, but I jumped down and over the tracks to the next platform to ask a policeman with captain's shoulder straps walking past with his family for a pen. I ran back to my relatives with the pen. Judging by my actions, I wasn't that old in this dream.

I'm not used to seeing signs and omens in dreams. It seems to me that they're still directed more toward the past. One of those typical mixes of memories, old emotions, hidden beliefs, and desires. Still, dreams can be very interesting.

DAY EIGHT

And thus the eighth day of my hunger strike has come to pass— sounds like something from the Bible or Thornton Wilder.

I awoke from my first restful night feeling almost warm, and my legs even warmed up a little. Though the temperature both in my pressure chamber and outside barely changed. I slept well enough, though it took me a long time to fall back asleep. I was just imagining the meals I'd make with the kids when we'd be together again. An illusion and comfort for the mind and belly. My general physical and mental state also seem fine. Not that all the things bothering me have gone away. The weakness, dizziness, ringing in my ears, and other odds and ends are still there. It's just that my body's stopped reacting to them so much, it's grown used to them. Only new negative sensations or exacerbations of old ones cause a response, and without any of those, I can take a break during a ceasefire.

It's been over a week since the start of the hunger strike. How much longer do I have to go? I believe this issue worries not just the guards, but my supporters on the other side of the barbed wire fence. And myself, of course. We'll see. "We'll see," as D'Artagnan said in the Soviet version of *The Three Musketeers*: "We'll see who kneels before whose *bottes fourrées* at the end of it all!"

Lately, the Keeper of the Music has been blasting some bad pop music nonstop down the prison corridors. It's just unlistenable. Good thing I can't hear it too well; there hasn't been a single decent track played all week. But then I heard some faint, familiar-sounding notes today. I moved closer to the door of my cell and tried to listen. I was right: it was the song "To the Watchmen" by the Ukrainian band Boombox. A classic. I stood there and, of course, didn't move until it was over. Three minutes of pleasure. How can you tell a good song from a bad one? The good ones don't age. In all this time, "To the Watchmen" hasn't aged a single chord.

Music is a very important part of my life—good music,
that is. Viktor Tsoi's songs have probably influenced the formation of my personality more than all other musicians put
together. That's why I really hate it when people play his songs
badly. I remember one time, during a fairly large film festival in Minsk, one particular well-known Russian actor with
Ukrainian roots who was the star of the show decided to show
off his vocal abilities to his adoring audience. His vocal abilities turned out to be not that great, but the people pretended
to like it, the evening was drawing to a close, and the long-
awaited reception buffet was up next. But as soon as I heard
him hit a flat note in the song "Blood Type" I couldn't take it
anymore. I stood up and left. It wasn't easy. I was in a huge hall
with about a thousand people, and I was seated in the middle
of the second row among the other participants, and half of
them had to squeeze up to let me through. The singer didn't
miss a beat (though how much more could he have messed
up?) as I walked down the wide central aisle, and he saw me
off from behind with a few more botched lines of the song. Bad
memories all around.

There were also some good memories—and not only
about Tsoi. The day after the long and sleepless night of my
arrest I sat in the investigator's office in what used to be the
Ukrainian State Security Service's Crimean HQ. The occupi-
ers had just made me a cooperation offer, which I'd refused,
opting instead for twenty years behind bars. The detective
did his routine pronunciation of the charges and my fate as
I sat there handcuffed and waiting to be taken back to a cell.
Meanwhile, the radio was playing quietly. Judging by the

songs, the frequency was still on a Ukrainian radio station and hadn't been shut off yet. The song "Warriors of Light" by Lyapis Trubetskoy came on. This was the unofficial anthem of the Maidan Revolution, and it was playing in what was then occupied Crimea, where I found myself in this tough spot. It was like someone had sent me a sign: "Hang in there, man, everything's gonna be alright." A weight was lifted off my soul. Because I knew I hadn't betrayed anyone. Not myself or anyone else. Not my country, nor the hundred protestors who were shot dead on Institutska Street. The investigator said that I was responsible for destroying my future, but I believed I'd made the only right choice. And the music coming from the radio's speakers only confirmed that.

I went to the doctor. Weight, blood pressure, pulse, body temperature—everything was falling. I didn't weigh much more than seventy-nine kilograms. The thermometer read thirty-six degrees. "Your body is cooling down . . . " the doctor said. We discussed what ambient temperature was best for when you're starving. I said that it was better to be warm because the body didn't need to use extra energy to heat itself. The doctor maintained that a hunger strike would be better tolerated in the cold, something to do with the metabolic processes in the body slowing down, hibernation, and all that. Where the truth lay was anyone's guess. We both stuck to our positions: him in a tank top in his warm office, and me in a cold cell.

The supervisory prosecutor came, took another statement regarding my hunger strike, and examined my living space and medical records. I didn't bother complaining about minor problems and inconveniences. I'm not at war with them. My main battlefield is elsewhere.

DAY NINE

Life has gradually settled down and started flowing along its calm, monotonous course. The days scroll past like pages from a photocopier, each one indistinguishable from the next. This is the way it always happens in the prison system when you get used to a new place. During the day, I feel pretty much fine. Only the weakness gets to me, especially in the morning when I have to use up energy making my cot or brushing my teeth. At night, the cold doesn't bother me as much anymore. Though it took me a while to fall asleep again, and, in my dreams, I went on a hike with my children.

The ritual of bringing in and taking out food doesn't cease to acquire new elements. Now, in addition to the white jacket, the *balander* also wears rubber gloves. During the past six months that I went to the prison mess hall, I never saw them on the hands of his colleagues, whose fingers would meander from plate to plate without much attention to hygiene. But they're trying to keep up appearances here. I look forward to the appearance of a chef's hat or maybe even a beret.

A strong, cold, and sharp wind has picked up outside. The glass in the window frame trembles, and something creaks and groans out on the street. This situation is standard for those who live on the banks of the large northern rivers in Russia. When the ice begins to break and splits open the frozen river, a large mass of cold is released and very strong winds form at the end of spring.

That was what it was like when I was in Yakutsk, by the Lena. It's the same here in Labytnangi, where the Ob flows. This wind lasts for a week or more, then after that finally comes heat. At least, this is how the locals explained the phenomenon to me . . . Which means we're now experiencing the wind and waiting for the heat.

Yet another conversation with yet another supervising officer. It started with the usual formalities. He asked me about my well-being and any complaints about the conditions of my detention, before switching to something simpler: why are you doing this, you can't change anything anyway, you'll just destroy your health in the process, and so on. Afterward, of course, politics also came up: everything's a mess back home, Ukraine will soon fall apart, they're using you, you're needed now, but then suddenly you won't be and everyone will forget about you.

A long time ago I resolved not to enter into such debates, so I sat and waited for the tiresomely conventional flow of words to cease. This man had never set foot in Ukraine, nor was he there on the Maidan or during the seizure of Crimea, but he felt compelled to tell me what happened with an expert's opinion. The classic "knowledge" typical of a Russian policeman, gleaned from watching local TV channels. Even his sentences and word formations were spot-on. I've been hearing the same thing my whole four years in prison. Only everything hasn't fallen apart in Ukraine, and no one has forgotten about me. We ended with a draw. He left.

I went to another doctor's appointment. I hadn't seen him for two days, and he told me that I looked more haggard:

"You're drying up . . . " He advised me to drink more water. How was I supposed to have any more, when I was already drinking six cups of hot water a day? He said that it wasn't enough, but I just didn't have it in me to drink more than that. The doctor was very attentive and caring, right down to the pimple on my forehead.

How infuriating it is that I'm treated with such selectivity and attention to detail by the prison system; here, some people only have only to cluck to get attention, whereas others have to open a vein in order to be taken to a dentist because they can no longer endure the pain. Equality and justice don't exist in prison.

As I was heading back "home," the wind picked up small ice flakes. They flew almost parallel to the ground and hurt my eyes. The people of Labytnangi are probably unaware that people are having May picnics elsewhere.

The Keeper of the Boiling Water appeared with a kettle as soon as I, invoking him, started rattling the bars, so that he knew in advance what I wanted from him. He was polite and smiling but no longer engaged in heart-to-heart conversation—he had new orders, clearly.

I'm finishing up the Murakami book. Of course, reading in a dimly lit cell is bad for the eyes, and I noticed early on during my time in prison that my eyesight was already going downhill. But I haven't stopped reading, and I won't stop for as long as I can still see. A philosophical question has arisen out of this predicament: What's better, to sit, well-read, in the dark, or to remain with sight in the darkness of your ignorance? I've met many people here who only picked up a book for the first time in their lives while in solitary confinement, simply out of boredom, but gave up reading as soon as they left and returned to drinking *chifir*, a strong tea typically brewed in prison, along with smoking and having empty conversations. My choice was already made a long time ago.

I finished the Murakami book. It was really great, one of his best. Somewhat reminiscent of David Lynch in certain parts. But Murakami and his work, of course, were more far-reaching. I always thought that for a good writer or director, all work seemed to grow from one worldview, and the larger, more diverse, and integral it was, the deeper and more powerful the author's talent.

Murakami definitely has his own world, which is unlike any other. I'm into it. I'm thankful to him for this. I closed the book as if I were saying goodbye to a wonderful new friend with whom I had just spent a week and now it was time to leave. Or rather, he went somewhere far away back home, and I stayed here.

DAY TEN

The morning began with the traditional courtesy visit with *balanda*. I decided to go back to sleep after they left when the on-duty officer came back, this time with a thermometer. Not to take my temperature, but the cell's. The thermometer kept showing sixteen point five degrees Celsius. The on-duty officer scratched the back of his head with one hand while squeezing the thermometer in the other. "We need to close the door so there's no draft," he decided. He placed the thermometer on the table once more and closed the outer cell door. In less than a minute, the temperature rose to eighteen degrees. Either he'd warmed it up in his hand, or it really had warmed up in my cell, because after that I stopped feeling so cold at night. The duty assistant to the colony head left content, exuding self-satisfaction mixed with a fraction of care.

The past three nights have gone by relatively calmly in comparison with the established scenario. I filled the "non-sleeping" hours with recollections of all the Simferopol cafés and restaurants I liked to visit or had visited at least once before, imagining their delicious menus. It seemed like the subconscious mind had intertwined with the conscious, and they began to pester me with these images for a while. You might say there was no harm in it, just a little culinary nostalgia. But I understood that these thoughts could gradually make me give in to the soggy pasta on the *balanda* tray. I will be alert from now on and be sure to drive such thoughts away from my mind.

Last night I dreamed of the sea, that I'd gone swimming and diving with some other people. There were jellyfish in the water; one of them was huge. Then I was some kind of handyman chiseling away at asphalt. There were road signs with warnings on them nearby, and some couple was distracting me from my work. Toward the end of my dreams: a partisan detachment, an ambush, a battle, and I was in the prone position with a PPSh-41 submachine gun. As always, my dreams were colorful, overwhelming, and intense.

During the day the restless on-duty officer escorted a female psychologist to my cell. We talked through the bars that form the second door to my cell. This was to keep her "safe" from me.

The conversation was nothing extraordinary since I declared that I didn't need a psychologist. Then she gave me a short lecture, which was as incoherent as one of my dreams. It went along the lines of how only broken people usually take such drastic measures, and that I wasn't broken, I needed to take care of my health, be smarter, and as a creative-minded person I needed to look for other opportunities, along with a whole other bundle of meaningless combinations of words. It reminded me of lectures I'd received from other inmates who believed they were much smarter than me or that I'd been looking for their advice my whole life: why did you actively resist the seizure of Crimea, why didn't you just make a film about it, that would have been a better idea, and so on. Yeah, and when Hitler invaded, instead of blowing up tanks people should have made films about it, then shown them in movie theaters in Siberia because there would've been nowhere else to . . .

I'd already spoken with this psychologist a few months ago or, rather, I'd already refused to speak with her once before. She was surprised: "Don't you want to answer a few question-naires? Aren't you interested in learning more about yourself?"

I replied that I'd already known everything about myself for some time and had figured it out on my own.

"You must be happy," was the reply of this woman who, judging by everything, was far from being in such a state herself.

An event of monumental scale occurred today: they brought me a heater. Not the small electric one they gave me before, but a big oil heater. When it's turned on, it heats up the room really well, much better than a radiator. It means that my cell will see some long-awaited warmth. This is the second real indulgence granted over the past ten days. The first was bed rest. I can hold out for longer while lying down in the warmth. At least I hope so. Looks like I'll have to leave a thank-you note in the visitor's book.

There was almost no wind today, though it did start raining in the evening. I stood by the open window vent and breathed in the fresh air: it always smells so clean and pleasant after rain. It was the first time I'd seen it rain in Labytnangi—they didn't have eternal winter here after all.

DAY ELEVEN

A strong wind has picked up outside once again. The temperature is above zero and there's even some bright sunshine. It's on a doomed mission to melt the snowdrifts that remain in spite of yesterday's rain, but to little avail so far, as they're holding out to the last. The sun of the north is devoid of affection.

When I got up this morning, I felt sick and dizzy; dark spots appeared in my line of vision. Even the on-duty officers who came for the morning inspection seemed to notice, but I refused their help. I lay down for a while.

The heater, as fiery as a Komsomol member at a party meeting, has worked to warm this dank kennel. It managed yesterday with some difficulty, but, by this morning, the room had warmed up noticeably. It felt like the bitter lump at the back of my throat was even drier than usual, but that was probably because of the heater.

Last night I dreamed that I was staying with a five-year-old child after her mother had been knocked off the edge of a cliff by falling rocks. The child wasn't afraid, nor was she looking for her mother, and we walked down a road for a long time. I was talking to her and even managed to teach her a few things, all while collecting large round caramel candies, which she kept dropping because she couldn't hold all of them in her hands. I may have been her father, but I didn't tell her this. She looked like my daughter when she was small, and her name was the same. Dreams have no logic. We entered a town and walked up to a house. I tried to treat another girl, who was standing there next to her mother and grandmother, to some candy, but she wouldn't take it. Then I noticed that she was disabled as they went through an entrance. The entrance turned out to be large and passable, and while I climbed under some sort of pipe-work, my daughter had already slipped out on the other side. I made it out right after her, but she was nowhere to be found. The street, or rather the embankment, was busy and full of people. I called out to a child wearing a similar-looking jacket, but it was no longer her.

I don't reread what I write in this diary, but I realize that I often describe my dreams. It's no surprise: in prison, especially in isolation cells like these, sleep is often the most interesting thing that happens to you. In general, it seems to me that you dream the most vivid dreams either in prison or during your childhood.

The electricity cut out for more than an hour. Maybe because of the wind, or maybe something else. The heater went out too. My little studio flat immediately began to cool down due to a draft, thin walls, and its location at the corner of the block. I noticed that I've begun to walk around the cell less. I'm just spending more and more time sitting—or, well, lying down.

I went to the doctor. The wind outside almost knocked me off my feet. It was stronger today than the day before yesterday.

The doctor wasn't happy with how I looked or my test results. He prescribed an IV drip for a couple of hours. It included one liter of glucose, vitamins, and salts.

The doctor is not just a prison medic—he's the head of an entire medical department and happens to be based here. What's important is that he's a top specialist and a good person. He deals with me like an individual.

As I lay there with the IV in, we talked about our families. He also has two children the same age as mine. Coincidences do happen. Or, rather, they don't.

I received the treatment while he did some paperwork and typed away at his computer. He even arranged for me to have the drip in his office. I lay down on the sofa, and he kindly put a chair under my long, dangling legs before covering me with a blanket. Straight-up VIP service. A relaxing song by Splean resounded from the speakers—turned out we both loved this band. My hand grew pleasantly cold from the IV drip, and my condition started to improve. Plus, I got to listen to some of my favorite music. It was one of the few pleasant moments I've had lately. But the doctor had a particular habit of repeatedly listening to tracks—or more like a single track, which he would listen to on repeat for hours. It was some kind of meditation, listening to the same song nonstop. But he made an exception today since he had a guest and didn't listen to a song more than ten times. After the IV drip was done, the doctor told me I was starting to look better. I was starting to feel better too. At this, we said goodbye.

The wind hadn't subsided by the time I got back, but it didn't blow me over so much either.

DAY TWELVE

Normal night. Normal morning. Normal day. Incoherent dreams without any meaning that seemed to stretch into my waking hours. The differences between them were minor. After yesterday's IV drip, I'm feeling better today, and most importantly, my cell has warmed up. I slept without a uniform, only in thermal underwear, and I didn't freeze! I can barely believe my ice age has come to an end.

My window is neither big nor small, typical for an isolation ward. A small window with a double frame and a grate over it, but something on the outside is still visible. The view is average. Most of it is taken up by a wall and the roof of the prison barracks a few meters off. A piece of the sky above is also visible: today it's light blue with a few white fluffy clouds, not the usual gray-black thunderclouds. It's springtime, after all. If you move to the side, you can make out a small part of the path along which prisoners move in formation, followed by prison employees. There are fences, flower beds that look more like dug-up vegetable patches, and barbed wire. A little further along, there's another small prison barrack, a utility building, and pipes. The remains of the snowdrifts, which thought they would lie there forever, but it turned out they would not, are now melted and blackened. And close behind them, a little further below, lies the town. Wooden houses, the same sheds and fences, and, closer to the horizon, some more modern-looking five-story buildings, boiler pipes, and some kind of masts. You can't see the closed security zone that separates the prison camp from the town behind the furthest barrack, so it almost seems like it's located right in the middle of town. The mind plays tricks and you think, for a moment, that it's enough to step out the door, walk down that path, and find yourself back on the streets among cars and people again.

But it's not possible. It's all an illusion. You can't live with illusions. During my time spent in Russian prisons, I've had my fair share of windows and can't count them all. It was difficult to look out of most of them, but when I could, it was often impossible to see anything through the small dusty glass. There were so many layers of grates on the window in one of the previous cells that even at noon when the summer sun strove to break through and reach me, I saw only four tiny specks of light on the floor.

In the FSB prisons, the windows were also small, and though clean, they were covered with a matte film and located somewhere closer to the ceiling. From them, all you could discern in the yard was whether it was day or night. The window of another cell I was in overlooked the wall of the next building, almost back to back; I spent three months living in twilight, the cell illuminated only by a lightbulb, never quite understanding what time of day it was. But there were rare cases when cells came with normal, almost standard-looking windows.

I remember two of them. From the windows of both, there was a very good view of the city, the surrounding nature, and the sun setting in the distance. I ended up in both after difficult transit periods where I'd found myself in concrete cells that began to erase the memory of what sunshine looked and felt like. There, I spent half the day standing at the window and taking in the landscape. A free man would pay no attention to the dirty suburbs, road, steppe, or withered forest on the horizon. But for me, during those moments, they were more beautiful than all the paintings in the world.

After arriving in my latest cell, I didn't spend long standing at the window. It wasn't very exciting, as I'd just come from an open-air prison camp where you could see the sky; I hadn't been locked up underground like before. Standing by the window, I recited Vladimir Vysotsky's song "It's Not Evening Yet," barely audibly, poetically. My heart twinged and my eyes watered. Vladimir Semyonovich can still pull at your heartstrings even without music—just his verses, unaccompanied by a guitar.

Back when I received many letters, I often came across the word "courage" in them. I don't know how brave I truly am; I find it hard to see myself like that. In one book I came across one of the word's definitions: courage is when someone takes up some cause, even while knowing it's doomed from the very beginning. I don't quite fit that definition. I often, even mostly, have taken on causes that have seemed impossible or even disastrous to others. But I never thought they were doomed, even if I was the only person to hold that opinion. And, surprisingly, sooner or later I would almost always succeed. And it didn't matter what the doubters said afterward. The main thing was that I never felt completely happy, even after achieving my goal. Either I grew very tired from the process, or I quickly got used to the result, or the result wasn't what I'd originally expected. I don't know.

It probably has something to do with my psyche: the desire for something is always sweeter and more pleasant than actually possessing it. Maybe everyone has this complex—or maybe it's just me. People want to be happy, but they don't always know how. When I started this diary, I was worried that there would be nothing to write about. Nothing really seems to happen, but still, I manage to write something every day. A twelve-sheet student notebook ran out in twelve days. Today I'll sew pages for a new one together, the same kind, out of white office paper, as I've run out of notebooks.

It's windy outside again, but now with bright sunshine. My day is marked by the transition point of having shifted to a new weight category: seventy-eight kilograms.

The whole afternoon, Rammstein blasted at full volume down the corridor. This meant that some "difficult" prisoners, or transit prisoners, had been brought to the offices on the second floor "for a frying," as they say here. The loud music drowned out the sound of the physical and psychological processing on this prison conveyor belt. Toward evening, the music abruptly fell silent, and the inspector stomped outside the door, coming for the "processed" who, judging by the noise, tumbled down the stairs to meet him, probably not without the help of others. A short conversation took place on a video recording device between this newly arrived officer on duty and the two beaten-up detainees. A cheerful "Any health problems?" was answered with the strained "None, citizen chief," which is how inmates are always expected to address prison officers. Then the small group left. A clear example of the Russian penitentiary system's psychological conditioning at work.

DAY THIRTEEN

Insomnia is becoming a new problem. Once again, I just couldn't fall asleep. Several times already I'd fantasized about getting together and celebrating the New Year in the Carpathians with my friends, attending several film festivals, but still, sleep wouldn't come.

I got up and turned off the heater, suspecting it of working with excessive zeal, then opened the window for some fresh air. Judging by the fact that the midnight round of patrols had passed a while ago, it must have been nearly one in the morning. Yet, outside, it was as bright as day.

The polar night of the Russian north, where nighttime can last for more than twenty-four hours, isn't easy to endure— just four hours of dim light, and the rest of the time is followed by thick twilight and night. But the constant daylight of the Midnight Sun, by contrast, is much harder to bear. You're never able to sleep enough and are left feeling shattered.

In the morning I got up early after the on-duty officer made his rounds and my morning *balanda* was brought in. I didn't sleep anymore—I couldn't and, well, I didn't really feel like it.

I don't sleep during the day now, I just lie there. My strength is fleeting. Maybe tonight will be easier. I can just about force myself to walk around my cell, even for half an hour a day. I used to do this often, but my legs feel like they're about to give out.

Despite that persistent feeling, I did my best this morning to put my house in order, dusting and mopping the floor. The Keeper of the Bedding came with a fresh set, and I changed my bed sheets. Today's bath day, so I'll hand the dirty sheets over to the laundry.

At night the toilet tank lives its own life—murmuring, whistling, or dripping. Sometimes it falls silent, meaning it can rest too, apparently. It's already getting along in age but never stops its daily grind. Here's an interesting observation: Why is the murmur of a fountain pleasing to our ears, but the murmur of a tank not, even though it's pretty much the same thing?

The smell of fresh soup for lunch gradually has made its way through my stuffy nose, reaching my brain and stomach. It doesn't cause much of an appetite, just gets on my nerves. But it's only one o'clock, so the *balanda* will soon cool down and sit quietly on the side without irritating the olfactory receptors. The on-duty officers know that this method of bringing food in to annoy me is subtle, but it works.

I went to see the doctor. He came to work on a Saturday just for me. My pulse and blood pressure were below normal. He prescribed another IV drip, the same plan as before: two hours of infusions of various liquids. Looking at me, the doctor said that he was pleased to see a direct and effective result of his work with an actual patient and not just bury his head in reports. According to him, my lips have turned pink again and stopped giving off the bluish-purple hue of Soviet delicatessen chickens.

Again, we talked during the procedure. The doctor explained how the kidneys function and how tuberculosis spreads. In response, I briefly told him about my short career as a film director before I was cut down to size. Then we both agreed the best place to live was in your own small house with a simple and cozy yard. The doctor insisted on having a farm and was already fantasizing about owning a goat. I said that I didn't want to go back to such living conditions, since I'd already done so in my past. But the doctor was dreaming about the future. Next month was his birthday; he'd get his colonel's stars and could even go on his pension if he wanted. That was why he was mulling this all over.

He wanted to settle down with his wife and two daughters in a white house with a cherry orchard. But he was also considering the option of remaining in the north. I reminded him that there weren't many cherry trees to be found here. I wanted to propose settling down somewhere in Roussillon, opposite the house of Athos, but then these lofty sakura-themed aspirations were interrupted by an emergency.

The cat who lived at the med point had fallen gravely ill. Two convicts who worked there brought Mr. Cat in because he was no longer able to move on his own. All of his paws were jerking around in an indescribable way. The cat was an ordinary house cat. The two veterinarians reported that he had been like this for half an hour and had just vomited up something purple.

A quick yet thorough investigation was carried out. In the fashion of Nero Wolf, the doctor executed it flawlessly from his chair, going through only two cigarettes. The hypotheses of food poisoning and seasickness were rejected immediately. The main conclusion was that one of the dozen sick prisoners occupying one of the three wards on this same floor had committed sabotage. He reviewed the appointment sheets, checking who had been given psychotropics or substances of a similar effect with a purple casing. The suspicions as to who it was had been immediately aroused in our chief of the investigative bureau; he merely waited for the documentation to prove it. As it turned out, the cat poisoner was some run-of-the-mill scumbag. The doctor immediately canceled all his appointments but said that no one had yet forbidden punitive medicine in his institution, so the would-be cat killer would have to prepare for the worst come Monday. He'd better pray for the cat's recovery, as the dosage of the punishment would depend on the condition of the animal.

Well, the cat didn't get any better. It was proposed to carry out resuscitation or some other support measures. At this, everyone squirmed a little, except for the boss. They were preparing to shave the cat's paw and had already sent for a razor until they realized there was no specialist on hand who could cannulate the cat's vein. It was decided not to carry out a medical intervention for the time being and to keep an eye on any changes in the unfortunate cat's state.

They gave it some water to drink right from their hands and then put it to bed. The doctor was very agitated and upset. The strangest thing about this whole situation was that he didn't actually like cats very much. He was allergic to their fur and tended to avoid them. But he allowed the cat to be at the med point. He was very angry because someone had played a cruel joke on the cat or perhaps even had a worse intent. The doctor loved animals—all of them, including cats—more than people. People were evil.

When they finished with me at the med point, not only was I doing better but the cat as well. He began to gradually get up and even move by himself, supported by the wall.

I came from the bathhouse later feeling tired and out of breath as if I had just run a cross-country race. It wasn't windy today, but not sunny either—only clouds that didn't promise anything good. Except for rain, maybe. But definitely not snow.

DAY FOURTEEN

Again, the night passed marked by insomnia due to the polar day. During the short periods of sleep, I dreamed that I worked at some factory: I arrived there on a bus carrying the next shift of workers, but they didn't take me because I didn't have a hat. Someone had mistakenly put mine on in the locker room. We were all military personnel, apparently, but dressed like in this camp—prison always found a way to squeeze itself into my dreams. Then I bought a tram ticket, which seemed to include a seat, but I still couldn't find it because there were no seats with that number. I even disembarked at the bus stop and searched for it on the benches there. I saw a friend pass by in his truck and I asked him to give me a ride, but he didn't have any free space. So, I idled away till morning at the bus stop before I woke up.

It's still cloudy outside my window. The weather isn't very spring-like. There's no rain, but the wind is picking up again.

The weather in the north is not only cold but very erratic: it can change dramatically several times a day. I would not be surprised to see snow or bright sunlight by evening.

The cell where I'm located is considered part of the isolation ward. The detainees in the isolation ward are always entitled to a slightly larger ration than what they're given in the mess hall in the main residential block. That's why I always got a heaping ladle of *kasha* and the cabbage soup would splash right up to the rim. With my now rarely steady hands, I am often afraid to spill this full bowl of liquid when I move it from the table.

It's not because I'd rather not wash the floor later; the point is that the guards will document the size of the ration on the measurer: if the level of the soup is any lower than when they brought it, they can declare that I've withdrawn from the hunger strike. For that same reason, I don't pour my *balanda* down the drain. That, and because throwing away food is wrong. As a result, I've had to put up with the presence of food in my cell for hours at a time.

The whole morning, I watched from the corner of the window how a dozen prisoners were rolling a huge metal cylinder with a long handle into an area that was closed off, like everything and everyone else here, by a fence. At first, it was impossible to make out what they were doing out there with that improvised asphalt roller. Before that, three unlucky guys armed with shovels had been poking around this site for at least a week, trying to dig it up with varying degrees of success. Everything became clear around dinnertime when the prisoners began to run across the now almost perfectly flat surface with a ball. They'd made a futsal* court. And, judging by the fact that half of the guys running around were wearing tattered red T-shirts over their prison uniforms, a match was about to begin.

Of course, today is Sunday, and according to the camp's plan for prisoner "education," either mass cultural or sporting events are to be held.

I was witnessing sport! True, the match was hard to follow up here. But I knew that the only people playing on the field were a bunch of *kozly*—they're the prisoners actively cooperating with the prison administration to get better conditions and, ideally, parole.

Soon the clouds erupted with some precipitation: light rain turned into light snow then back again to a liquid state. But the match went on without interruption: they couldn't upset the boss. Or maybe these guys had been taken over by some kind of fury, stretching out bodies that had stagnated over the long winter. When the game was finally over, the sun came out. I think that everyone, including the few spectators who had gathered to watch, was pleased with the overall result, even if they were all wet and exhausted.

Taking in the dreary local weather, I can't help but think that, somewhere, there is a place where everything has bloomed and turned green a long time ago. People are eating strawberries, and cherries are ripening on the branches. They have already changed into T-shirts and sneakers, the last school bell

---

* Futsal is a game similar to soccer but played with a smaller, heavier ball and on a small, hard court.

of the year has rung, and my kids have gone to visit their grand-mother. I feel like Stierlitz* haunted endlessly by Tariverdiev's music about his distant and native shores.

Two weeks have passed since the start of the hunger strike. The second week, as expected, turned out to be easier than the first: I'd adapted, and the IV drips definitely helped. But I know that, from now on, it will only get more difficult with each new day. The negative effects on my body will only increase, and it won't get any better. But I'm not going to give up. I'll keep going for as long as my body can bear.

DAY FIFTEEN

Insomnia doesn't let go: it pushes you to the point of exhaus-tion, like a demanding lover. The night brought neither rest nor relief. Again, I fell asleep late and woke before the morning roll call (it makes no sense to write "before dawn," as dawn has dis-appeared here, sunset too).

I hadn't fully reached the surface or even opened my eyes when, for the first time, a little imp awoke in me: he hopped out onto the morning "market square" and incited all the other demons to sink their teeth into their morning *kasha* before the master woke up. The imp's calls were drowned out by other

---

* Max Otto von Stierlitz, born Maxim Isaev, was a Soviet spy who infiltrated the German establishment in 1927, rose through the ranks, and became a Nazi counterintelligence officer. There was a twelve-part TV series *Seventeen Moments of Spring* based on the novel by Yulian Semyonov in the USSR in 1973. Mikael Tariverdiev composed the music for the series.

demons locked behind strong fences. I finally came to and put an end to this attempt at a hungry mutiny, chasing the little devils back into their kennels. I said we would stand fast, like the *Varyag* battleship after the twentieth hit by enemy projectiles. It seemed that my mind was suffering more from hunger than my stomach.

This morning snow fell lightly, not having the gall to fall more heavily, though the wind whistling round the corners was clearly inciting the snow to gather strength. The Keeper of the Tunes turned on some Russian *chanson** music and blasted it down the corridor for the whole day. To me, the *chanson* is one of the worst genres of music—the performers sing mostly about things they haven't tried themselves, and this is obvious, no matter what their hoarse voices and thug-like rhymes try to convince us of.

The only exception is probably Mikhail Krug, who may not have done time, but at least he can understand and transmit what a prisoner is feeling inside. When it comes to other inmates, only older guys over the age of forty listen to *chansons*, whereas the younger generation prefers gangster rap or pop. The *kozel* working in my building is one of those old guys, but he doesn't have the pickiest taste in music, judging by what has been playing from his tape recorder for the past two weeks.

But this is not what I'm struck by. I'm struck by a person who, having departed in reality from the concepts of life as a felon and as a free civilian, is now cooperating with the administration in, to

---

* The chanson ("song," borrowed from French) is a popular genre of music in Russia that romanticizes the lives of criminals.

put it bluntly, the saddest place for any self-respecting inmate—the colony's internal police department. How can he still think of himself as real and righteous to the core, listening to music about criminal fantasies and dirty cops? Yes, people in any situation will find excuses for themselves and, no matter what they do, think they're one of the good guys.

I've been reading Ilf and Petrov. I finished *The Twelve Chairs* yesterday, and today I'm onto *The Golden Calf.* I first read it when I was about thirteen years old, and, back then, it didn't make a lasting impression on me, which is no surprise—it was a little early to read such a book.

The volumes are small, but I read them slowly. I'm not dragging them out, as I did with Murakami—I don't have much strength, not even for reading. *The Twelve Chairs* is a good book, of course, but I liked the movie versions better. Maybe it's because I saw them first and have rewatched them several times since then.

Or maybe it's because film means more to me than literature. There could be another reason. Ilf and Petrov's original literary idiom seemed a little faded to me, like black and white outlines for coloring-in. The screenwriters and movie directors could take out anything unnecessary, like the satire of contemporary events, of which there was a great deal in both books, and single out the main themes. They were so good at reviving the immortal characters and the adventurous plot, they picked the best lines, polishing them to a shine with the help of brilliant actors, in such a way that all three classic Soviet movie adaptations outshone and overshadowed the literary original, at least for me.

I've seen other, post-Soviet and even foreign attempts to put this timeless classic on screen, but they're not worth remembering, especially in comparison to the three golden movies. Of these, I think director Leonid Gaidai's work was the weakest. He didn't get the author's irony. The movie has the signature gags, directorial finds, and the expected Gaidai class, but it missed the mark in some ways. The actor in Bender's role did not look like a master strategist, but a silly, petty swindler.

Mark Zakharov's *Twelve Chairs*, on the contrary, was shot with an unhurried tempo, in his theatrical style that would make him famous later on. It had the worthy and intelligent Andrey Mironov playing the title role, along with his wonderful partner Anatoly Papanov. Despite its multi-part protractedness, guaranteed by being in the television format, this film was closer to Ilf and Petrov—and to me—than Gaidai's version.

But the oldest, black-and-white production of *Antelope*—that was a small masterpiece! Unfortunately, I don't remember the name of the director, but he did everything so well and with such talent that neither I nor anyone else can raise any objections. Maybe that's why, despite almost fifty years passing since the film adaptation of this book, nobody dares to take it on anymore. It's unbeatable! This is where you go to learn how to shoot a movie!

Back at the med point. Tests, examination, IV drip. The cat looked better, but the doctor feared that it might experience negative neuropsychiatric effects from the drug poisoning. The poisoner of the animal repented and confessed. The doctor still hasn't given him up, but changed his mind about pumping him with antipsychotics. The doctor's computer speakers played a song with lines that shuffled: "God save the Tsar . . . " and "The empire is eternal and lives in our hearts."

DAY SIXTEEN

The night passed with surprising calm. I fell asleep faster than usual and even slept well. The sky was covered with clouds in the evening and, by morning, they still hadn't dispersed, having managed to cover the roofs and the ground with fine powdered sugar. The powder crunched pleasantly under the feet of passers-by when I opened the window in the morning to get some air.

No electricity since this morning, but the cell hasn't gotten cold yet. It's nice to shake off that feeling of constant chill. I'm writing these lines in the weak light of the wintry, northern May morning. It's only slightly brighter than the light shining through the window at night, but more than the lights left on inside.

Despite constant weakness, I force myself to walk around the cell. At least a little bit, several times a day. My muscles have weakened, but they still need some exercise. At the same time, there's this feeling of heaviness in my legs, like weights are tied to them. Reminds me of the Gadfly in Ethel Voynich's novel, shuffling along with his ball and chain.

Around lunchtime, the thin layer of snow on the ground melted. Though some paltry support in the form of fine grains rushed to its aid from the sky, it could no longer reconquer its position on the damp surface. The freezing temperature didn't help either. Soon, a group of prisoners was sent out onto the wet

pathway with large brooms. They cleared the remaining precipitation, which was mostly water and dirt at that point. Some of
it was swept up into dustpans, but mostly, they swept it off to
the side. The path's concrete surface was shining afterward.

Officially, it's known as the Main Alley, wide as a two-lane
road and running through the entire camp. This is where prisoners were moved about and checked, with roll call carried out
twice a day. The surrounding buildings and barracks, with their
barbed wire fences and penned-off exercise yards, huddled
around it. Everything's very compact; you never have to go
far. A small little camp town of one street and a dozen houses.
Through my window, I could only see the final segment of this
alley, pretty much a dead end.

The prisoners in the alley were there for their obligatory
two hours of work to improve the camp. Alongside them were
the so-called "volunteers." They were there on their initiative,
not because they were forced to, hoping to gain incentives that
could speed up their parole. Call them part-time "activists," if
you will. Of course, the *kozly* don't work with their hands. They
walk alongside the cleaners, monitoring their work and disci-
pline. Cleaning is done daily, sometimes twice a day. The tools
they use depend on the weather. For snow it can be shovels,
mops, or brooms. Sometimes it makes sense. Other times, like
today, it didn't.

But nobody broke the rules, even when they bordered on
insanity. They swept brooms along a clean alley or chased after
a fleeting water droplet if that's what they were told to do. But
still, the water hid from the mops in the cracks of the road's
concrete slabs.

I was lucky to avoid the sad fate of a rain sweeper. The red stripe of high-risk inmates like myself means I'm let out sparingly. Everything has its upside.

Got my newspapers yesterday! I've been waiting for them for the past two weeks and now, finally, they brought them to me. I subscribed to *Novaya Gazeta*, which I've been reading on and off all four years of my imprisonment. Now, at least, I know what's really happening in Russia, the world, and most importantly, in Ukraine. This is definitely one of the last decent Russian publications in print. They write mainly about politics, economics, people's lives, culture, and sports. It's standard content, but they make it interesting. They do it well, and, more importantly, they're honest. That's enough in modern Russia to be labeled as oppositionists, enemies of the people, and U.S. State Department lackeys. Though the true enemies of the people don't sit in small editorial offices, but in more spacious ones. The newspaper comes out three times a week but arrives here with a one- or two-week delay.

I'm glad that even though they took away my TV, they didn't deprive me of this newspaper. It's better to learn the truth with a two-week delay than to be fed fresh lies daily. One issue was completely devoted to the topic of POWs during the Second World War. Very interesting. That war is probably one of my favorite historical topics—like a huge scorched black hole through all of humanity.

You read all these stories and understand that what has happened to you is not comparable to even a tenth of what any of them experienced. Today's conditions are something else entirely. But still, the main tragedy of Soviet POWs was not even that nearly two-thirds of them died in Nazi captivity, or that they endured extreme physical deprivation and torment, including almost no food and unbearable hard labor. It was that many of them returned to find themselves once again facing Soviet prison and dishonor. Or they were met with dishonor alone, but this hurt them more than any Gulag. At home, they were considered cowards and traitors and treated accordingly. They had to live with this lasting stain on their lives, and most importantly, in their souls. This was the state Stalinist policy toward them, and the Soviet people, devoted to the leader and the party, treated them the same way. That government was cursed. Injustice must be one of the main words used to describe that war.

In one of the articles, I came across a connection to the Murakami book I'd recently read regarding a story about Japanese prisoners who worked and died from the harsh conditions in a camp in the village of Irsha, near Irkutsk. Murakami was deeply troubled by his fellow countrymen's plight, and this natural concern permeated the text. He also briefly mentioned the execution of several Chinese in Japanese-occupied Manchuria. It was all supposedly for a "good cause," yet the junior officer in charge of the executions still struggled with it, as did the author—of course. It's all beautiful, artistic—it makes sense. The only thing is that Murakami forgot to mention how the Japanese treated the British and American prisoners they captured, their poor conditions, and their high fatalities. And as for the millions of Chinese civilians killed, that's a separate and not very pleasant topic for Japan. But every citizen, particularly every patriot, tries to bring their country's and people's accomplishments or suffering to the forefront, ignoring or hiding their crimes, only mentioning them briefly.

Novaya Gazeta wrote about that camp in Irsha, where prisoners from other Axis-allied countries, as well as Soviet prisoners, were put to work alongside the Japanese. The Japanese prisoners perished in greater numbers than the others during that first winter, but not because of the conditions—it was the same for everyone, but the harsh Siberian climate and strange food didn't suit them. And in less than three years, they were all repatriated home to their islands. The Stalinist machine continued to grind up human lives and destinies, not really distinguishing a Russian from anyone else, not even the Japanese.

Meanwhile, the electricity was switched back on and the sun came out. Life goes on.

DAY SEVENTEEN

Tough night. I slept badly again and lay awake long before I had to get up. Waking up with a headache is one of the worst feelings in life. Then I fell back asleep in fits and starts. Again, I felt dizzy with dark spots in my line of vision and ringing in my ears. I'll get another IV drip later today, which is nice; I'll feel better.

The snow only managed to take hold of the barrack roofs overnight, but the soggy morning weather soon drove it away. A couple of particularly resilient veteran snowdrifts, greatly reduced in size, still stubbornly defend their corners under the fences, like the Germans in Berlin.

A whole crowd of the top brass with lots of stars on

their rank insignia came by. They asked if I would be against a video call with some bigwig from Moscow, a member of the Federation Council. I thought a little and decided not to refuse. Negotiations with the enemy still sometimes needed to be conducted, if only to accept their surrender. It was unlikely that it would come to that, and indeed, he was not likely to say anything specific but would be interested, as always, in the conditions of my detention and my well-being. It was unlikely that an official of this level would want to make contact with me on his own initiative without approval or higher command. This, of course, was a good sign, but I decided to hold off on any conclusions until after the conversation itself. The fact that it would happen was significant, rather than whatever was discussed.

They gave me a new prison uniform, slippers, and three pairs of socks from storage. A strange set, considering I didn't need any of it. But that's how it goes in here—whatever you need you don't get, and what you don't need is randomly thrown at you. What's important is that they can report you've been looked after.

I spent almost half the day at the med point. More medical tests, but this time, they also took some blood. It wouldn't flow because of low blood pressure and high viscosity, so they had to puncture my other arm. Another physical exam. My systolic blood pressure was definitely lower than one hundred. The other parameters seemed to be OK; my results weren't the best, but not the worst either. As the doctor said, "So far, so good." He also said it would get harder after the third week. Let's see, I thought it would get harder after the second one.

They did an EKG of my heart, which was still holding out. But that was probably because of the IV drips. I've been feeling better after them and, as the doctor observed, I looked a little rosier too. This time they gave me a liter and a half of infusions.

They'll gradually start increasing the dosage and add something more to it—the body's resources aren't endless.

The doctor warned me that when they ran out or got to a critical point, he would force-feed me and would not let me die. Not for my own sake, but for my children and my mother. Force-feeding doesn't mean IV drips, but a rubber tube that feeds through the nose to the stomach. Very unpleasant stuff. I hope it doesn't come to that. And if it does, I'll hardly be able to resist and get myself out of it. The limit is different for every person. Let's see what mine is.

Then there were appointments with a psychiatrist and an endocrinologist. Everyone's a little anxious and trying to exert some control over what comes next. I didn't have enough patience for the psychologist—I refused. I wasn't in a fit state to lay my cards out once again, answer stupid questions, to look into the eyes of these unfortunate prison psychologists who need help themselves. I'd had enough police attention for today; it was too much. And there's more of it every day, which is alarming.

But the doctor told me some amazing stories from working in the colony* for the past fifteen years—he had a lifetime's worth. I was especially shocked by the story of an elderly single mother and her only son, a former drug addict with HIV,

---

* Penal colonies are the most common kind of prison in Russia, where detention is combined with labor.

who'd been in this exact colony. He was shooting up anything he could get his hands on, and she ran around all the crack-houses looking for him. He got infected, and then he ended up here. By that time, he'd long been in poor health, though he wasn't old. In prison, his health got even worse. The doctor treated him as best as he could and eventually managed to get him released on account of his poor health, even though he hadn't served his term. The doctor would lead him by the arm while the man's other hand gripped a cane because he was already having trouble walking. His mother saw them and, distressed, ran toward them along the entirety of the long fence. They then regularly called each other, and the doctor continued giving medical advice, as medical care on the outside was not always better than in the camp. He no longer shot up—he didn't want to and he couldn't. His condition worsened, and, six months later, his legs completely stopped working. He lived another five years, but he lived them together with his beloved mother. And it was a good life for both of them because, for the first time, they were truly happy.

DAY EIGHTEEN

The night was quite calm. I slept for a long time and slept well. Though I had to get up three or four times in the morning when the ceremonial bringing in and taking out of the prison *balanda* was performed before the checking and marking . . . And today, immediately upon getting up, the duty officer came with a thermometer to measure the temperature in the cell. But I refused this procedure, saying that I was no longer cold.

Despite all these interruptions to my morning dream, it formed into something solid. A prisoner's dream is sensitive in a special way. I wake up not because they wake me up or the door in the cell begins to squeak, but long before, when someone just stops in front of it on the other side or when a faint squeak from the video recorder being turned on is heard after that. Prison teaches a person to always be on the alert, on the "fox," as they say here, even when you sleep.

Before going to bed, during the hours until I can fall asleep, my consciousness feeds my inner demons with pictures of attractive food. For example, yesterday I recalled delicious breakfasts that could be prepared at home and a video of the cooking process to top it off. Hunger is more of a psychological need than a physical one. Training myself to think of other things helps to do away with it. I don't mind as long as no one inside me rebels.

At night, I had a lot of dreams again—short, plot-driven, and, as always, unconnected. I remember one: a huge asteroid was approaching the Earth, and due to the imminent death of all mankind, a general amnesty had been declared. My relatives took me, and we were going somewhere by car with them. We stopped near the store, I went shopping, and as we were leaving the store, in the parking lot, in the dark evening sky, the approaching object appeared. It was hard to see it because of the clouds; we could only make out a piece of it, but its outlines were huge, dozens of times larger than the moon sticking out nearby.

The people next to me also stopped and began to look up at this dark, indistinct body. There was no particular fear or awareness that we were all about to die, but there was some kind of ominous admiration as if it were an unusual rainbow or eclipse. But there was also a kind of depression and doom. Then the light changed slightly and the object disappeared from view, though everyone knew very well that it was still there and implacably approaching. People went about their business, but without haste and fuss, and we drove on. Where we were going wasn't clear: either home to cook dinner or to escape, though it was impossible to escape. It was exactly like the film *Melancholia* by Lars von Trier—both creepy and mesmerizing.

In the morning, the snow didn't last long, and it was only enough to leave a white frost on the roofs; then it melted, but the day was still very cold and windy. My pen can't be convinced to call it spring. They say that as the ice passes along the river, it will get warmer. This is hard to believe. It seems to me more and more that it can't get warmer here. And summer really is coming tomorrow . . .

They took me to the video call announced yesterday with the deputy. There were so many bosses in the small room that there was hardly any place for a chair where I could sit. A few more spectators in uniform stared out the window. This was some kind of a local show. The video call was established not through an official payphone but on a laptop, something more casual. The connection lagged a bit, but overall we could see and hear just fine.

First of all, the official turned out to be a woman— Lyudmila Borisovna, who, second of all, was Ksenia Sobchak's mother. I learned this during the conversation. She was a pretty nice woman, yes, a member of the Russian Duma, but she was calling on her own initiative. She wanted to find out how I felt, my condition, and other standard issues. She asked me once again to voice what I was trying to achieve and whether I was going to stop. I repeated what I had already said to the lawyer when I went on a hunger strike, but with a little more detail.

At first, the conversation, though supposedly official, as I expected, was conducted in a confidential and sympathetic tone. A little later, Ksenia herself announced her participation in the conversation. First, there were her remarks out of frame, then she began to appear in it: her hair first, glasses, eyes, then I saw her completely, she started sharing the air with her mother, and, in the end, as expected, began to lead the conversation. Words of support, requests to stop, something about solidarity actions. We all started talking at the same time. The constantly lagging Skype didn't help much. Ksenia showed off her T-shirt with the inscription "Free Sentsov." I showed the "victory" sign with my fingers and shouted "Slava Ukraini!"* The formal conversation quickly turned into a joyful circus, but the three of us were satisfied. I told them that my mother's name was also Lyudmila, and it turned out they knew that. I just can't get used to the fact that strangers often know so much about me. We said goodbye happily as if we'd become relatives.

When the session ended, I looked at the faces of the bosses—they were all discontent, no questions for me either. I said goodbye to those gathered for this viewing and went with the attendant to my cell. The degree of kindness that the bosses

* "Glory to Ukraine!" is a Ukrainian patriotic slogan that is like the boogeyman for Russians, who falsely claim it is a "Nazi" slogan.

have been trying to wrap around me has reached the point that they sometimes call me not by my last but first name. I wonder if this trend will continue after the current video conversation or if it will only be a semblance of friendship that lasts for an hour.

By evening, a blizzard broke out outside the window: wind, snow, dampness, and fog.

DAY NINETEEN

Everything was blanketed in snow on the first summer morning in Labytnangi—from the roofs to the windows, the central path, and even the field where inmates were recently playing soccer. The wind howled like a hungry she-wolf. My window was also covered with snowflakes, and only half of the outside world was visible.

In the early morning, two supervisors arrived with a large thermometer and finally measured the temperature in the cell. It turned out to be above twenty degrees Celsius. They left satisfied. I'd grown content even earlier, shortly after they'd provided me with an electric heater. Meanwhile, the degree of police kindness and attention toward me following the deputy's call yesterday was rapidly approaching the level of absurdity. I had mentioned in our conversation that I had lost two teeth during these past six months up north, and it sparked general concern among various levels of authorities. They started plaguing the doctor with calls, fretting over my health and reports about the state of my two teeth.

The doctor spent half a day grinding his teeth and responding as patiently as he could to those calls, diligently sending a uniform report to his superiors. The gist of the report was that the patient's teeth were gone but that there was nothing that could be done about it. Moreover, the overall condition of their dear patient appeared to be more or less normal, though it couldn't be described as completely normal, let alone good, given the patient's hunger strike. Examinations, analyses, and medical assistance were practically a daily routine, and the superiors needed to concentrate on their own duties while the doctor attended to their patient, just as they would with their regular medical responsibilities, which had been momentarily disrupted due to the ongoing commotion.

They brought in a cardiologist to examine me, and he said that everything was fine—for now. It was reassuring, except for that final phrase. But there's no need to dwell on it. When they began setting up the IV drip, my vein burst, causing the medication to seep under my skin, forming a blister. They switched to my other arm. The swelling, the nurse said, would subside. As a precaution, she used a smaller needle for the next attempt, which prolonged the process to four hours instead of the usual two. I could barely endure the drip before, let alone the extended one—it's pretty draining.

Another superior from the doctor's team arrived, along with a lieutenant colonel. He'd come on a business trip to deal with his own matters, but, of course, also to see me. Soon, all the prison management would be focused on just one patient. He also reviewed the test results. Naturally, mine were not entirely good, but not entirely bad either, considering the length of the hunger strike.

A comprehensive commission of nearly a dozen doctors

has been scheduled for Monday. They won't be prison doctors—they'll be from the outside. So, the first day of the following week promises to be eventful, with a scheduled trip through the city in a paddy wagon, walks through the civilian hospital escorted by armed guards, and the scattering of staff and visitors due to their intimidating appearance. Our circus is going on a one-day tour. Why they need to do this remains unclear, but it's all part of an escalated care strategy that's becoming quite tiresome.

Meanwhile, outside the window, the summer snow blizzard in Labytnangi continues to blow . . .

DAY TWENTY

My overall condition has stabilized and, as a result, my sleep has become progressively more restful. I now get enough sleep, though it's still not very comfortable since I have to sleep in a jacket and socks. But at least I'm keeping warm. It's amazing how I feel better now than I did at the beginning of the hunger strike. It seems that my body has adapted, and the IV drips are finally yielding results. The only lingering issue, of course, is the feeling of weakness. But there's no way around it—I have nothing to draw physical strength from.

Once again, I experienced a cascade of diverse dreams, each of which could serve as the foundation for an entire movie franchise. These dreams offered a variety of plots ranging from science fiction and horror to action-packed adventures and heartwarming family melodramas. To recount them all would require a separate notebook, so I'll refrain from doing so.

It's difficult to make out what's going on outside my window—my view is almost completely obscured by frozen wet snow. But during clear intervals, I can observe the transformation of the barrack roof across from ours, changing from green to white once again. It's still too early for a swim in the Ob.

The duty officer came with a thermometer in the morning again, establishing a new ritual. At dinnertime, the duty officer was replaced by his deputy from another shift, the one whom I had had a falling out with at the beginning of my hunger strike when I handed him my statement. Back then, he looked very frightened and nearly dragged me by the collar to the duty unit because a hunger strike was an emergency for them, and nobody wanted that on their shift.

Now, he was unrecognizable, having undergone a clear moral transformation, and it seemed that he had also joined the local Good Cop flash mob. It was funny to hear the *balander* counseling him by the front door, pointing out all the intricacies of the no-eating ritual. The policeman, who had suddenly adopted a more polite demeanor, was participating in this charade for the first time and didn't want to spoil it, while the *balander* took part in it three times a day, thoroughly rehashing its every detail.

As soon as this new actor entered the scene, a minor embarrassment ensued. The primary iron door securing the cell not only has a lock but also a chain that prevents it from fully swinging open. Typically, the chief peeks his head through the gap, then extends a hand through to shake and verify the lock on the second latticed door. Only after that the chain is removed and the standard dialogue of greetings begins. I turn my face to the wall; after that the grate opens and the *balander* begins to flutter around with the plates.

But, today, the chain wasn't secured on its hook, and the iron door swung open immediately. The policeman initially fell into a stupor but quickly regained his composure and took a second look. He locked the door once again, added the chain for extra security, and proceeded with his routine, even though such actions seemed devoid of any common sense. Indeed, seeking any semblance of common sense within this system is always a futile endeavor. You just have to observe the provincial theatrical performance with a smile.

The Keeper of the Boiling Water, meanwhile, has aptly been renamed the Keeper of Silence. He regularly brings me hot water but doesn't engage in any conversation except for brief, practical exchanges, like when he hands me a razor to shave. I haven't glimpsed his face for a while. I'm content with merely his hands and voice—this suits me perfectly.

Meanwhile, my inner demons have grown dissatisfied with their recollections of nightly installments of restaurant menus and even the simplest homemade meals. Their cravings have evolved into a desire for something more tangible, like a hearty meal, and they no longer believe in my lofty promises. They are trying to unite and conspire with one another, to enter into collusion with my hands to snatch a couple of spoonfuls of porridge or soup while my back is turned to the camera. Demons lack moral principles. They fail to understand that you can deceive almost anyone, even video surveillance, but you can't deceive yourself. The key is that you must ultimately live with your choices, and as Solzhenitsyn instilled in all of us, a life worth living should be founded on truth, not lies.

Realizing that this plan has not yet succeeded, the demons sit in a hungry circle and dream of a diet, a reinforced ration that they will definitely enforce if I withdraw from the hunger strike. There's bread and butter—well, margarine—and rich portions of meat, along with half a mug of milk. But I do what I need to do to dispel these demonic gatherings because I'm not ready to change my principles for a reinforced ration or a stolen spoonful of porridge.

When I was ten or eleven years old, some of our relatives came to visit us in the summer. We had a lot of them, most of them from the Urals, while we were the only ones who lived in Crimea. They would visit us frequently and sometimes even stay with us for the entire summer. This was a common practice in the Soviet Union, not only among relatives and friends but also acquaintances. People were kinder and more open, and so was our family—we were always happy to have guests. As part of our vacation schedule, in addition to green countryside tourism and trips to the sea, mandatory excursions around Crimea were also included. We took our visitors to Bakhchysarai to see the palace where the Khan used to reside (it had since become a museum), along with other places of interest and attractions.

I had been to this museum before, and many times after, but one particular trip stayed with me. It wasn't just the trip itself, which lasted almost the entire day, but a guided tour through the Khan's palace. It wasn't making our way through the array of rooms, the couches where the Khan reclined on cushions, the courtyards with fountains, and so on. Truth be told, the palace doesn't leave a particularly strong impression, especially on adults—it's not as lavish as one might expect for a former ruler of Crimea. What struck me the most during that particular excursion was the scene depicted in a painting.

A man stood in the center of a room unmistakably in the palace. Judging by his attire, he was clearly of Slavic descent. The servants, close associates, and guards of the Khan were scattered around him in a state of fear and disarray. The Khan himself sat upon the throne, angrily stamping his foot and fixing his furious gaze upon the guest, who met the Khan's gaze with dignity and composure.

Our guide started to tell us about what was happening in the picture. I don't remember all the details, but the gist of the story was that an ambassador sent to the Khan didn't want to bow and generally didn't behave by local standards. The Khan was angry with him for this and threw him in prison for twenty years, where he died a sick old man. The story left a major impact on me at the time. It seemed terrifying and impossible to give up life itself, the warmth of summer, everything, in order not to bow once before some ruler. That ten-year-old boy couldn't emulate the ambassador's poise in the painting, so he just stood there, astonished. I'm glad that numerous experiences in that boy's life ultimately transformed him into a different person, and when the unexpected and unwelcome moment finally arrived, he made the right decision. Twenty years in a dungeon is preferable to bending the knee to a tyrant even once.

Meanwhile, the frost on the window has thawed out, as well as on the roofs and the path outside, but light snowfall is persisting, forming snowdrifts. Some of the prisoners have been tasked with removing them, and their shovels produce an unpleasant, grating sound against the concrete.

Today is a cleaning day. I tidied up my "small apartment," changed my bed linen and underwear, bathed, and shaved. It was a refreshing sensation, yet it also came with a feeling of weariness, like the exhaustion that follows unloading a truck full of coal. The phrase of the day went to the policeman on duty who escorted me: "It turns out that there are a great many interesting things about you on YouTube . . . "

DAY TWENTY-ONE

At night, I dreamed I was at Putin's inauguration, standing in the front rows near the stage. He sang a song with tears in his wide eyes, and the crowd sang along with him. I remained silent, even though a microphone was positioned in front of me and many others.

Then there was some sort of film screening about two indigenous girls from Central America who were building a hut for themselves in the forest. Only one of them lived there, while the other came on a bicycle to help her. Toward the end, I was standing in the reception area of an expensive hotel next to my prison bags. For some reason, the administrator was having issues with my registration, even though she said everything was fine, the room was reserved until the end of the film festival, and everyone was eagerly awaiting me. The pop singer Dmitry Malikov approached me with his wife or girlfriend. We greeted each other, he sat down next to the counter, and she hugged me from behind. They were so pleased to see me. But why were they even there?

Dreams have their own logic, or, rather, lack thereof. It's obviously not worth trying to find meaning in all of this.

In the morning, snow once again blanketed every inch of the exterior space, sparing only a few dark spots and stripes on the landscape. Then a tenacious battle resumed, with moisture regaining its territory, even conquering parts of the rooftops. The duty inmates were hard at work, diligently scraping the Main Alley with their shovels. They were hardly visible, but you could definitely hear them.

Yesterday's stand-in for the duty officer, a large man from Dagestan, came for the last time at the end of his shift today to oversee the distribution of food and measure the temperature indoors. The sizable street thermometer looked like a toy in his bear-like hands. He likely hadn't spoken the number of polite words he'd uttered in the past day in all his years of service. He was accustomed to using completely different language, and when that ran out, he quickly resorted to his fists. But now, he was completely different.

They brought me in yesterday and earlier today for my routine examination and check-up at the med point. This time, it was conducted by different medical professionals, not mine. It turned out that yesterday was the doctor's birthday. Despite his claims of not being a heavy drinker and not celebrating the occasion, especially considering the upcoming Festival of Bodun, a day of remembrance observed in June and July in some parts of Russia, his two-day absence strongly suggested otherwise.

The examination was conducted yesterday by a nurse. It wasn't even really an examination: blood pressure, pulse, temperature, weight, "How are you feeling?" But, being alone at the med point, she naturally transformed and played doctor for fifteen minutes, asking questions, making clarifications, and confirming banal circumstances that were already known to both of us. Everyone wants to seem important, especially in the absence of authority.

And today, the same actions were carried out by some young doctor as sleepy as a ferret woken up from hibernation. I'd seen him briefly a few times in the infirmary before. He always had the same look: swollen and disheveled. His nesting burrow must have been somewhere very close around here. He performed the same standard procedure but didn't put on any airs. A person with a medical degree doesn't have time for cheap show-offs when half asleep.

I weighed in at seventy-seven kilograms. The doctor called the young sleepyhead and said he would come closer to evening to give me an IV drip. Everyone that was gathered around expressed doubts about this. My veins have already begun to ache from the constant IV drips and drawing of blood, and my left arm has even become inflamed.

The doctor and I have an almost friendly relationship. In my four years within this system, I've never felt the desire to get close to anyone who dons epaulets or guards and commands me. But he is first and foremost a doctor, and the police officer's uniform he wears is just that—a uniform, not his essence.

At first, it seemed like quite the opposite. In the first half-year of my stay in this camp, we crossed paths only a couple of times, and always due to some reasons of conflict. He wanted to assert himself through verbal confrontations, but I've never been the type to bow down and silently listen to just anything directed at me. Our initial conversations were brief and conflict-ridden.

Our first exchange after I declared a hunger strike wasn't pleasant either. The doctor expressed his dislike for such things and accused me of playing games. Then he launched into solitary monologues on how he didn't see Ukraine as an independent state, that Ukrainians and Russians were one people, and we Ukrainians needed to get rid of our Nazis and repent to Mother Russia.

I had long been accustomed to such illogical constructs from Russian officers. But usually, they were also fervent fans of the Soviet Union and Putin, who gave them the illusion of a new incarnation of the USSR. The doctor genuinely loved Putin too, but he despised the USSR and communists because he was a monarchist who revered Nicholas II and was deeply Orthodox. It seemed that with such diametrically opposed positions, we had nothing in common to talk about. But we had to be together often and for long periods, and it turned out that we shared many common traits. We avoided politics—at least I did—and in other matters, the doctor certainly warmed up to me, so I responded in kind.

He has two children the same age as mine. He's also not from here, but from the south. He served in the army in Ukraine, and he only had good memories of the Ukrainian people. We have similar preferences in food, drinks, and lifestyle. Toward the end of one conversation, we discovered that we were also both fans of the Ukrainian computer game *S.T.A.L.K.E.R.* That was when the doctor's heart completely melted.

I'm an old-school gamer, and there's no doubt that it's one of the best games and a personal favorite of mine. But the doctor was a newbie, and this game was his first and only cyber-love. Later, he read about me on the internet because he began to doubt the truth of the verdict after getting to know me better. That was when everything fell into place for him. I warned him immediately that close interaction with me could negatively affect his career, to which the doctor responded, lighting up a cigarette, "I don't care. I can retire at any moment." And that settled it.

Against all expectations, the doctor showed up for work after lunch. He was full of life, looked fresh, and was in high spirits, just as you'd expect from someone celebrating their birthday. He hadn't celebrated yesterday, though. He planned to do so later today, surrounded by close family.

In this regard, we're similar. I also prefer quiet celebrations at home over noisy and crowded ones. He swiftly examined me, applied an iodine grid to the inflamed vein, and mentioned that it was all relatively minor until my kidneys started failing. But he assured me he'd monitor for any such signs and advised me to exercise caution, especially given my personal stake in the matter. The doctor then provided instructions to his young colleague regarding the IV drips before heading back to his familial haven. The younger doctor turned out to be a skilled physician and not as young as one might think—his child was starting school this year. He just had that perpetually sleepy student look. As the doctor remarked, "A small dog is a puppy until old age."

Meanwhile, the snow has stopped falling, and everything is melting. The summer in Labytnangi bears a striking resemblance to the winter in Crimea.

DAY TWENTY-TWO

In the morning, it looked like New Year's Day outside the window. Light snowflakes were falling, blanketing everything in white. The only thing missing was Santa Claus on his sleigh with bells. Instead, a paddy wagon arrived, and we were transported to the city hospital for a medical commission on the topic of Oleh Hennadiiovych Sentsov's health.

I had been taken there once before, six months ago, for a heart examination and an X-ray. During that previous visit, I was put in a paddy wagon with a cage and kept under guard while a second wagon carried an armed unit of *Spetsnaz* guys all dressed in black masks and armed with machine guns and a dog. As our group entered the hospital through the main entrance, people instinctively moved away along the walls as if a dangerous terrorist was being led through like a bear on a chain.

Today, I was expecting something similar, and I was already prepared for the unpleasant and almost forgotten feeling of iron shackles on my wrists. But everything turned out to be easier this time around. There were no *Spetsnaz* guys or machine gunners. They transported me in a mini paddy wagon, but they didn't even handcuff me. I suppose they made that concession because of my hunger strike. Or maybe they realized that, despite my red stripe, I wasn't going to run away.

I was accompanied mainly by the authorities' representatives, and I didn't notice anyone with a rank below major. The head of security, the commander of the security company, and even the head of the colony himself were already standing at the entrance to the hospital and were present until the end of all the examinations.

The police were more polite and courteous than ever before. The young security guard tried especially hard. He must have thought I'd forgotten the search and intake process from when I first arrived at the colony—when I was stripped naked and forced to squat to ensure I wasn't concealing any-thing in my rectum. He'd approached me from the side and, in his typical unrestrained manner, started shouting at me for not greeting him. He'd even filed a report against me for this but didn't manage to put me in solitary confinement as punish-ment because I was already kept in an isolation cell, so I got off with a penalty.

Today he was different. People can change when they want to. In his case, it's clear that this was not a result of inner self-improvement but an external act of mimicry.

It wasn't far to go, and the *chansons* of Mikhail Krug played quietly from the vehicle's speakers the entire way. It's not sur-prising that policemen would listen to the music of criminals. In their line of work, they immersed themselves so deeply in the spirit and life of crime that they could mimic it even better than criminals themselves. So, hearing Krug's songs in a police paddy wagon wasn't surprising.

Krug didn't lie to them, and that struck a chord with such listeners, regardless of whether you were wearing epaulets or a prison uniform. This time, our polite company entered from the back door of the hospital and ended up in the emergency room, where the entire council took place. I underwent tests; they measured everything imaginable and even brought in an EKG and ultrasound machines. It was a thorough examination. The room was quite large, but besides people in uniform and a couple of "comrades" in civilian clothes, it was also filled with a bunch of medical workers of various specialties donning different coats.

There were a dozen inspections and about the same number of measurements. All the doctors were polite and courteous, as was expected in their profession. Though there was one doctor who happened to be exceptionally rude and tactless, prodding me as if we had already shared a bottle of cognac and were old acquaintances. When he received a similarly sharp response from me, he seemed taken aback. Not everyone is prepared to confront their own reflection when it's held up to their face.

But then it turned out he was a resuscitator, and they were typically all big cynics, this one in particular. Because of that, the whole hospital didn't like him, and he, in return, hated the whole world.

My audience asked me why I was on a hunger strike, and none of them conveyed much belief in its success. I went through all the procedures as if strapped to a conveyor belt, and everything took over two hours to complete. The commission didn't manage to reach an official conclusion, but the gist of it was clear—nothing critical had happened yet.

On the way back, I glanced at my reflection in the polished

glass of the paddy wagon's windows. I definitely looked like a real convict—from my facial features to the prison coat and hat I was wearing. It's no wonder so many doctors rushed to see the enigmatic creature who'd arrived from the petting zoo.

Truth be told, my health has been better after three weeks of the hunger strike than it was at its beginning. They say that during this time, my body has transformed, purified, and rejuvenated itself. Now, along with weakness, a sense of lightness, brought about by curative starvation, has settled in. But this will only last for a maximum of one week, and then the harmful effects will start to manifest. My body will begin to eat itself; acetone levels will increase, as well as the protein levels in my kidneys. But what can you do? Let's wait and see. For the time being, I'm feeling pretty good and at peace.

The higher-ups summoned me to their office on the second floor for a meeting after we returned. There was a dilemma: two people had come to see me at the same time, and since I was supposed to have only one visitor, I had to choose. The first one was the Archbishop of Crimea, who apparently came on behalf of Filaret of Kyiv and my mother. The second was Askold, my pen pal, a colleague who was making a film about me. I declined the meeting with the priest and chose Askold instead. He was closer to me, and he could share some interesting news.

Besides, I don't have much affinity for priests, and the topic of their conversation is always predictable. I hope he wasn't upset, even though it took him two planes and one helicopter to get here. But I didn't ask him to come, or anyone else for that matter, including Askold. Regardless, the decision was made.

I looked forward to the visit. It was a chance to reach out to someone else, albeit through glass, from the free world. What was most interesting was that these acceptance and rejection procedures were carried out through official statements dictated by the authorities, all recorded on video. However, it turned out the camera's battery had died, so they requested another take, repeating all the actions and procedures. It felt like a free movie courtesy of the Federal Penitentiary Service of Russia. I even managed to say, "Action!"

My lawyer Dima came almost immediately after my meeting with Askold. We talked until eight in the evening. During those three hours of communication, I learned more than in the last six months. Protests in support of my release and other political prisoners have been taking place all over the world, from ordinary people to the leaders of the G7, who at their summit in the near future plan to discuss this very issue, among other things.

The wave is coming, and I didn't think it would be this big. Four more political prisoners have joined me on my hunger strike, including Sasha "Tundra" Kolchenko, my companion and colleague, a real revolutionary, with whom I was put on trial.

But a hunger strike is not for Tundra! He's already in poor health and has always looked like a man from the extras of a film about a concentration camp. On the other hand, his spirit is incredibly strong, and that's what truly matters. I didn't invite anyone on this journey, but welcome, guys! Together till the end!

Today turned out to be pretty eventful. It began with a trip to the hospital, followed by my little film for the Federal Penitentiary Service of Russia, a visit from Askold, a meeting with my lawyer, receiving fresh newspapers, swapping out library books, and obtaining various toiletries that I'd requested earlier. They also collected the newspapers I'd already read, given that there were other guys out there waiting for that delayed dose of truth. I spent only two hours in the cell during the day, and all the rest were related to this or that activity.

Tomorrow, my lawyer is expected to come again along with the priest. I was incorrectly informed by the authorities that I had to choose one visitor because it turns out that I have the right to meet with a clergyman at any time. The priest actually came along with the lawyer and Askold, not so much to dissuade me from the hunger strike or promote his religion, but to have a conversation and get acquainted.

He isn't involved in missionary work but assists Ukrainian political prisoners, functioning as a sort of Orthodox human rights advocate. I drafted a new statement, and maybe he'll be able to reach me tomorrow.

Meanwhile, spring has arrived. The sun has been shining since noon and nearly melted the snow. They say the ice on the river has started to break, and that the weather will get warmer. But today, I distinctly sensed that somewhere far away, much thicker ice has begun to crack. So loud, in fact, that the noise has even reached me here . . .

DAY TWENTY-THREE

There was sunshine and relatively warm weather in the morning, signaling a clear shift in the seasons. I'm currently feeling fine. The night passed peacefully, but I woke up pretty early considering my routine.

I dedicated the first two hours of the morning to trying to remember the name of the director who made *2001: A Space Odyssey*, *A Clockwork Orange*, *The Shining*, and other masterpieces. I really like his work—it's so diverse. I've read a lot about him, but his surname slipped my mind, and I couldn't recall it. Finally, the mental block dissolved, and enlightenment washed over me. Stanley Kubrick! Of course! It's amazing how such prominent names can sometimes slip your mind. I was thinking about him in relation to the fact that yesterday, at my request, they swapped books for me and brought me some science fiction novels by Stanisław Lem and Arthur C. Clarke.

I'm no longer escorted to the library because I'm in isolation, so I have to request books based on my memory of what was available. The camp's library is actually pretty good. I've already read almost all the classics they have. Lately, I've been drawn to something lighter.

It was a while since I'd read any science fiction. I really enjoyed it in my Soviet youth, along with historical novels, but that was pretty normal for any guy. I'd read the classic Bradbury, the adventurous Heinlein, the captivating Harrison, as well as many others, but those three were my favorites.

I would hate adults admiring the Strugatsky brothers back then, calling them "legendary." I read *Space Mowgli* and *Roadside Picnic*, but they didn't impress me much. And then, in my late thirties, a couple of years before my prison saga began, I rediscovered their work. I dove into it and devoured, in both paper and electronic formats, nearly everything they had written, whatever I could get my hands on. I was fully immersed in the world of the Strugatsky brothers for an entire year. I even went so far as to call them "remarkable" after that. I haven't read better science fiction, and I doubt that I ever will. Not everything, of course, sent me into rapture, but the majority of their works really moved me. Their style of minimalist science fiction, with their focus on the individual, their world, and relationships, with the invented environment just there to reveal it all in a new light—that's what drew me to their books. And judging by their reputation, I wasn't the only one.

So I decided to read Lem and Clarke. Previously, I'd only seen Tarkovsky and Kubrick's classic film adaptations of their works, and I knew that the directors diverged pretty heavily from their source material. I wanted to read both books and see what else they had going on.

Recently, I finished re-reading Ostap Bender's adventures. *The Antelope*, which I first read back in my late childhood, was certainly not as funny as *The Twelve Chairs*, but it was more dramatic. It had a very powerful ending that beautifully revealed the main character's true nature. Despite all his light-heartedness and carefreeness, he was still a very lonely and unhappy person. How he longed for his seemingly despised and poor companions! That orphan wanted a family with anyone. He understood that a life without love, family, friendship, and genuinely close people had no meaning, gave no pleasure, even if you had a suitcase full of money. I wonder why the authors didn't write a third installment of his adventures? Did they feel they couldn't sustain that level of intrigue anymore, or did they realize it was their hero's final chapter? Unfortunately, I had no one to ask.

Closer to lunchtime, the second installment of the film series about police and priests took place. The irate authorities, accompanied by their own priest, interrogated me at length about why I didn't believe in God yesterday, but suddenly believed today and insisted on meeting with a priest. Apart from attributing this to my sinful soul's enlightenment, I couldn't explain it to them. I also pointed out that yesterday they didn't clarify that I could meet with a church representative at any time outside of scheduled appointments. An animated administrative-spiritual discussion ensued. The priest, whom the police offered in exchange for the one who came from Crimea, was actively involved in the conversation, likely due to my newfound enthusiasm for seeking guidance from the church.

I told them that not all priests are the same, and I was the least interested in the one with epaulets under his cassock—so, I wanted to go with the one who'd come from Crimea. Then the conversation escalated and took a new turn.

One colonel, officially designated as the human rights ombudsman, exhibited the most fervor. He was supposed to advocate for me, but his behavior made him seem more like the administration rights ombudsman. I wrote an official statement rejecting the meeting with this priest, and the opposing sides of the denominational conflict dispersed. The priest grumbled, questioning what a priest from the Orthodox Church of Ukraine was doing on the territory of the Russian Orthodox Church. He claimed that the other priest had no authority to perform any actions here. This servant of God turned out to be first and foremost the servant of the state. And so, by chance,

I found myself at the center of a larger battle between the Moscow Patriarchate and its Ukrainian adversary. Judging by the fact that there was silence for the rest of the day—no one took me to the priest or my lawyer—the focal point of this confrontation had shifted to higher spheres of authority.

It wasn't until later in the evening that they finally brought me to my lawyer. He and the holy father had been engaged in a spiritual battle against the forces of darkness since early morning, trying to make contact with me. The authorities kept stalling them under various pretexts, presumably consulting even with the Metropolitan, and in the end, they didn't allow the Crimean priest to meet with me. They cited the absence of certain documents and permissions, but, in reality, it was because they simply wouldn't allow it. He was allowed to visit other inmates in other prisons across Russia, but, on this particular front, the Russian Orthodox Church vehemently opposed it. Well, never mind. I wrote a brief letter and passed it through my lawyer to the heroic Crimean father, apologizing to him for the situation, asking him to return home and help local Ukrainian political prisoners and others in need, advising him against spending the night outside the camp walls, since it was futile to seek entry at this moment. He'd come to support me, but I wrote that I didn't require special support—my moral strength is strong, and if needed, I can support myself under even worse conditions. I briefly discussed the case with my lawyer and wrote a few lines to those who needed them, and he hurried back to the plane along with Askold and the holy father, promising to return in two or three weeks.

He didn't bring good news today. In addition to the setbacks with the priest, my daughter couldn't go on her trip abroad, and there were other issues to contend with as well.

Outside, a continuous gentle autumn rain has been falling. It seems like today is one of those days.

In the evening, the most significant event of the day occurred: I was moved from isolation to the med point! The doctor had mentioned he would try to arrange this, but I didn't think it would actually happen. Yet I found myself gathering my belongings and following the attendant.

Things are unquestionably better here, but I'll provide more details tomorrow since it's now getting late.

DAY TWENTY-FOUR

To mark my move to a new place, I've started using a new pen. My IV drip began later than usual yesterday due to all the commotion surrounding sectarian conflicts and my relocation to the med point, so the procedure finished around midnight.

But that was fine. The rules here weren't as rigid, and the doctor wielded the influence of a king or a god. In the evening, I even had the chance to take a shower.

The shower facilities are located right here at the med point, so you can technically freshen up almost every day if you wish. It's like a slice of heaven on earth, nothing less.

I saw myself from the waist up in a large mirror of the shower room for the first time since the hunger strike began. Of course, it was quite frightening to take in, as I looked like a Buchenwald prisoner. But the die has been cast, the roulette wheel is still in motion, and it remains to be seen which number it will ultimately land on.

The hospital has two floors, and it's not that big. On the ground floor, there are examination and treatment rooms, including a dental office and X-ray facilities. Upstairs, you'll find administrative offices, including one where my doctor works, a small treatment area, and a med point. The med point has five patient rooms, a dining area, a TV room, and a washroom with a toilet and shower, all secured behind a locked gate.

A separate four-bed ward was assigned to me, positioned closer to the entrance. The other inmates were moved out of the room, and two video surveillance cameras were installed in their place upon my arrival. The room is spacious, with four beds with an equal number of bedside tables and stools. A single set is enough for me. There are also two large windows, unbarred, like the ones you might find in an ordinary home. The view remains unchanged from my previous room despite being on the second floor. It's the same main alley, but with a different barrack opposite. Half of the view is filled up by the sky, which is a pleasant sight.

Today, the sky has offered little excitement—just a continuous gray mass with intermittent light rain. Typical autumn weather but strange for early June. I know that it only feels that way to me and the locals are used to it. The radiators aren't emitting much heat, but the room isn't chilly.

For the first time in three weeks, I blissfully slept without socks at night. But I didn't sleep well in the new place, and by morning, I felt a bit cold. I asked for a second blanket, and they immediately brought it. Now, I'm lying under it, sipping my boiling water from a mug that sits next to me on the window-sill, and writing these lines. I have the feeling that I didn't move from a prison cell to a hospital but comfortably settled down in a five-star hotel room. My condition remains stable, though the doctor keeps cautioning me that this won't last long—maybe a week at most—after which a decline is inevitable with unpredictable consequences, possibly leading to a crisis. For now, I'll take it one day at a time and appreciate the moment.

There are three *kozly* and a couple of *obizhennyy*—untouchables—who work at the hospital. The *kozly* take on various roles, ranging from specialists—some can operate both EKG and X-ray machines—to nurses and orderlies. The *obizhennyy* are tasked with cleaning, maintaining toilets, and taking out the garbage. It's always been like this. All in all, they're normal guys because the doctor wouldn't keep bad guys around him. There are only around a dozen prisoners in the hospital, among them four *muzhiki*, the inmates who refuse to cooperate with prison authorities. One of them is bedridden, another is in a wheelchair, a third is on crutches due to a missing leg, and the fourth is simply limping. At least there'll be someone to talk to, unlike the Keeper of the Keys, who was maintaining a vow of silence.

There are also sick prisoners of various types here: *kozly*, former "activists," *obizhennyy*, and those who are no longer considered *muzhiks* due to serious misconduct.[*] Any interactions with them are limited to maintaining a distance of two outstretched arms. I have nothing to talk about with them.

---

[*] In the Russian criminal world, men who fall out of good standing with *muzhiki* are referred to as *sherst,* or "wool."

They were also all warned to stay away from me, to be honest, but that's understandable. I'm not looking for friends here either. In prison, that's generally the last thing on your mind. Relationships between people are slightly different in this environment. They eat their meals in the mess room, while mine, according to the ritual, is brought to the ward and put right on the bedside table in the presence of an attendant. The hospital's *balander* also wears a white coat, and, finally, a white cap has made its debut on the stage. Not quite yet a chef's hat, but the first step toward it.

The ritual for measuring the room's temperature has been simplified, as there's a thermometer displaying a comfortable twenty-one degrees Celsius hanging right in the ward. It's also recorded on video.

There's a TV in the TV room, but it's only turned on twice a day, once in the morning and once in the evening, according to the schedule. That suits me fine—I can catch up on the news, and the rest doesn't really interest me. The only exception is on Sundays when you shouldn't miss Putin's TV preacher Dmitry Kiselyov. I'd already missed out on the antics on his show for the past three weeks.

Everyone has been running around since early morning putting things in order. Some high-ranking colonel from Moscow is coming, most likely to visit me. She's supposed to be some kind of big cheese in the medical field. The doctor isn't anticipating anything positive from her visit. He believes that she has been instructed to take certain measures because, I quote: "Not every authority decides to cross the Ob in such weather . . . "

But the dreaded colonel didn't grace us with her presence today. Theories about a capsized canoe or an unopened parachute were being tossed around. Numerous other delegations did visit. First, all the top brass arrived with cameras, along with a gray-haired man sporting a dyed mustache. I'd encountered him a few times before—he's the regional head of human rights.

On previous visits, he tried to insist that he was just passing through and decided to stop by, even though he had rarely been seen at the colony before. This time, he didn't conceal the fact that he had come, or rather, that he had taken a newly launched ferry specifically to see me. We discussed my health, my condition, and the future. This man has never ceased to amaze me. Initially, he remarked that I hadn't changed much in these three months since our last meeting. Well, yes, I hadn't sprouted an extra pair of ears, and fifteen kilograms of weight loss wasn't that dramatic.

Then, he expressed his disapproval of my supposedly privileged conditions. I questioned what constituted those privileges. I hadn't requested a separate ward, and those two video cameras in the corners weren't for my exclusive use, so I wasn't any better off than other inmates in this hospital. Finally, he asserted that I wasn't a political prisoner, but an ordinary criminal since I was convicted under a criminal statute. He believed it was out of the question to discuss exchanging political prisoners for regular criminals.

In response, I asked whether there were specific political charges in Russia under which political prisoners were prosecuted. This line of inquiry left him dumbfounded, but he extricated himself by simply shaking his dark mustache. He's just another administration rights ombudsman, only this time without the uniform insignia. Though it seemed he had only recently removed them after wearing them for quite some time, leaving their indentation. Eventually, the conversation reached a more level footing. He confirmed my determination to continue the hunger strike at any stage and shook my hand before departing.

Just half an hour later, a different delegation arrived, this time under the leadership of two supervising prosecutors. Their tone was more formal and concise. They inquired about the conditions and whether my grievances and statements were being addressed. I replied that I had never submitted any complaints or statements, especially to their organization. These individuals, accustomed to adeptly sidestepping prisoners' appeals, seemed a bit taken aback, shrugged their shoulders, then took their cue to exit the stage.

Shortly thereafter, the lower-ranking bosses arrived, including the chief operating officer and the security officer. For some reason, they were curious about who had advised me to send a message through my lawyer to the leaders of the G7. They seemed to think it was my idea to shift the focus of the meeting from environmental issues to Ukrainian political prisoners. Well, at least they didn't accuse me of organizing the meeting itself. You never knew what to expect from such politically astute individuals.

Toward the end, they posed the question: "Who is Ukraine engaged in a hybrid war with?" I replied that I wasn't in a position to answer rhetorical or foolish questions. They couldn't suggest any new topics and began to say goodbye. When I inquired about letters, they informed me that the mail system, including email, was not functioning reliably, so I had to be patient. It wasn't clear whether to trust their words or their smiles more. The bosses departed, and I remained sitting on my bed. This time, during the conversation, I'd remained seated while they stood—a departure from the usual protocol—but today the rules seemed to have changed for the hunger-striking terrorist criminal.

The doctor requested that I measure and document the amount of my urine near the end of the day. I couldn't decline, especially if he thought it was necessary. He provided me with a clear measuring ladle and a diary for recording the fluid I pass. I'll begin keeping track of it starting tomorrow.

DAY TWENTY-FIVE

With the aid of two blankets, the night was warm and cozy, allowing me to enjoy a good night's sleep. Achieving restful sleep can be challenging due to the lighting; it's become increasingly difficult to differentiate night from day—during the latter, the overcast sky outside doesn't permit much sunlight to filter through.

My condition has been relatively stable in terms of how I feel these days, though weakness and a lack of physical strength are clearly noticeable. I don't get out of bed right away. When I do, my head starts to spin, so I need to muster energy for it, and my internal batteries are somewhat depleted. There's no desire to wander around my new spacious dwellings at all. I'm more inclined to sit and even more so to lie down. I only get up and walk when it's necessary to use the bathroom, get water, go for check-ups, tests, and procedures, or catch up on the TV news twice a day.

This morning I felt pretty bad. Rather abruptly and intensely. During the medical examination, they measured my blood pressure: the top number was seventy-three. Well, no wonder I felt so knocked out. Let's wait for the IV drip, it usually helps after that.

On a positive note, my bed is located right by the window, and I can lean against the windowsill and read while sitting in natural daylight. After so many years of reading under electric lighting, this is pure bliss. My eyes are thanking me. Though I can feel that my eyesight has still deteriorated over this time, which is not surprising.

The door to my room is made of semi-transparent glass and is located next to the entrance doors to the ward, the washroom, and the dining area, so all the local routes and movements pass by it. I'm not very interested in what's happening out there in the corridor, but the passing inmates are keenly interested in the life and circumstances of a so-called dangerous prisoner. I feel like the sole participant in a reality show called *Behind the Glass*. But it doesn't bother me, especially since I know this initial interest will soon fade, as it usually does.

In the clinic on the ground floor, there's a police officer on around-the-clock duty who monitors the visits of the inmates to the med point and the closed-off ward. He's the one who now conducts my daily checks and marks off the two-hour intervals. The deputy of the colony chief has finally been relieved of this minor task, but he still oversees the rituals of delivering meals back and forth and measuring room temperatures.

During my last trip to the shower, I was struck not only by the skeleton in the mirror but also by the cubicle standing there. Such a nickname hardly suits this plastic monstrosity, though. I hadn't encountered anything like it before in prison.

Typically, the "shower" in a place like this was just an iron spout without a funnel, two taps, and a hole in the floor. A rubber mat was a luxury. But here, despite being a bit beaten up from use, it was a quite modern, elaborate contraption. It was large enough for two people to shower comfortably, though inmates don't typically welcome such communal practices. There was an electronic control panel for various modes, multiple types of showers, a seating area for hydro massage, and so on, right down to a color-music lamp and a speaker.

I'm not one to sing in the shower, so I didn't bother with the karaoke settings, but this cubicle earned my respect, even though most of its functions weren't working. The secret of its appearance at the med point turned out to be simple. The doctor had brought it from his old apartment, where it practically took up the entire bathroom. It annoyed him greatly, but it was the cherished wish of his beloved wife to have it. Upon moving to their new place, it turned out that the bathroom there was even smaller, so they had to part ways with the behemoth. The doctor happily gifted it to the med point.

Some people bring things from work, and then there are those who bring things to work. It depends on whether you consider the work to be your own or someone else's. The doctor was one of those who brought things to work, to his little clinic.

Today in the news, on the scrolling news ticker, it was announced that the renowned director Kira Muratova had passed away in Odesa. A sad event. Though eighty-three is quite a lifespan, and during that time, she accomplished a lot. I wasn't personally acquainted with her, but I held great respect for her contributions to the arts, and for her unique cinematic language. She wasn't among my top filmmakers, but I enjoyed her early works, especially *Long Farewells*, from which I drew many insights for myself upon exploring the mother-son relationship in my first feature film. I never came close to Muratova's level, though. Glory to the departed master, and may a good person rest in peace.

The little demons, still residing somewhere deep within me, once again started their old tricks, whispering to anyone they can, urging them to sneak a piece of bread and eat it under the covers at night, so that the cameras wouldn't notice. I chased them away with my truncheon to their hideouts, and the rest scurried beneath the prison beds.

Finally, they brought me letters, printed-out emails, and one handwritten letter. Maybe there was indeed some glitch, or maybe something else—there's no trust to be had in anything here. It was nice to receive messages from familiar people, and I promised myself I would write responses to all of them later. One letter particularly pleased me; it was entirely devoted to a story about the recently concluded Cannes Film Festival. I've always loved letters with something specific and interesting addressed to me, rather than empty verbosity and sentimentality. Especially considering that when it came to cinema, I'd fallen out of the loop over the last four years, only managing to watch a couple of good new films. Everything else has been about prison and politics. So, it was really a breath of fresh air! Thank you.

The dreaded Moscow inspector, the chief, arrived. Instead of being a presumed disagreeable hag—it seems she hadn't managed to cross the river yesterday—she turned out to be a pleasant middle-aged blonde woman. She was responsive and intelligent, with a competent medical and humanistic approach. She made a show of briefly looking around the camp and the med point, but it was clear the main purpose of her visit was a certain inmate on hunger strike, not them. She carefully reviewed my medical records and analyses, doctors' conclusions, and the medication I've been administered.

In principle, she was satisfied with my doctor's work and agreed with plans for the future in case of further deterioration, which could occur quite soon, as the analyses had already begun to indicate negative trends. Then we had a private conversation, but it ended up being more about Crimea—which she'd been happy to visit last summer—rather than about me. After that, she went to the city hospital where I was examined earlier this week to check their facilities, including the intensive care unit, so she would know where I'd be taken if I started "fading." That's when we parted ways, leaving a seemingly positive impression on each other. Emotions from unexpectedly meeting a good person are always positive.

Meanwhile, the day is coming to an end, along with the second notebook. I continue to be amazed: every day something comes up that can be written about, even though it often seems like nothing particularly special is happening.

Tomorrow, I'll start a new notebook or maybe continue writing in one of the old ones that still have some space left. But for that, I need someone from my colony squad to bring my bag with my belongings, where my literary archive is stored.

DAY TWENTY-SIX

The crisis that the doctor had been warning me about arrived. It began yesterday, but it finally became obvious today. My deterioration came abruptly, immediately, and forcefully.

It felt like my motor was ready to give out. My legs and hands were ice-cold, almost blue. I had dyspnea. I felt nauseous, and everything was foggy. My body had depleted its reserves and was dependent on its existing resources. My systolic pressure in the morning was seventy, and my diastolic pressure was completely inaudible, the same with my pulse. I felt like crap. Being on an IV drip yesterday for almost five hours, including new drugs with amino acids and other additives, didn't level the situation yesterday. After the procedure, I hurried to the toilet and almost fainted there. I barely reached the bed. I drank a lot of water. It was already close to midnight.

During the night, I seemed to rest well enough, but I got very cold—they'd completely turned off the heating because of the season change. But outside the window, there were dark clouds and rain periodically turning into snow all day. It corresponded to my condition and mood, which was anxiously combative.

The results of my medical analyses also pointed to deterioration on all fronts. There was increased acetone in my urine, and it was the only taste I felt in my mouth for the second day in a row. My mouth was very dry despite drinking a lot of water. The water balance, even when factoring in the liquid administered through droppers, indicated that I was losing more fluids than I was gaining.

The effects of dehydration had begun, and my body was no longer retaining water. My kidneys were at risk. But most of all, the doctors were concerned about my heart. The EKG indicated nothing good—a slow heartbeat and irregular rhythms.

All three of them have been here almost since morning: my doctor, his boss from the department, and the inspector from Moscow. Three lieutenant colonels with medical diplomas are now occupied with only one problem: keeping me alive. At least they understand that it's useless to try to persuade me to end the hunger strike. The doctor's boss and the inspector, it seems, are not planning to return to their office and will be staying here until the situation stabilizes or clears up. The doctor himself is more worried than me. I have to comfort and support him.

His hands were shaking slightly today. It's evident that he takes my situation to heart. And not at all because of the fear of worsening the mortality statistics in the colony, but for other purely humane reasons.

The three of them decided to urgently gather a council of doctors at the city hospital again to hear opinions and recommendations. It was originally planned to take place tomorrow, but because of newly discovered circumstances it will be held today, right after lunch.

There'll be another trip through the city, a convoy to the

hospital, a series of examinations. This, of course, is a tedious procedure, especially in my current state, but I understand that it's necessary now and no longer an empty formality.

The city doctors may offer for me to stay with them, but I will refuse. So far, there's no need for this, and I trust them less than the local doctors at the prison. That might seem strange, but it's true. They'll want to start force-feeding me. And this is a very humiliating procedure before which you are injected with some drugs so that you relax and don't resist. I don't really want to lie like a vegetable receiving nutrients through a tube in my nose. My prison doctors are still trying to avoid it, and I agree with them on this matter. For now, we'll stick to the current plan and rely on IV drips. The only change is that they'll be administered daily and with some new additions.

The police are currently preparing everything for transfer, and the doctors are filling out paperwork on my latest tests, so I have time to write these lines while lying in bed. Prison may lack a lot of things from the outside world, but it does have one advantage: time. You have more than plenty of it. Some have ten years, and others twenty. You can think of many things during all that time, like how a segment of your life has passed, what happened, what you experienced, or your mistakes, failures, and losses.

I'm grateful to fate that I've had the opportunity to live such a difficult and interesting life, but I wouldn't want to repeat it again. I have no regrets and wouldn't change anything from my past. Not because it's impossible, no—it probably all had to happen. Nothing is by chance. When I thought of the concept for my film *Rhino,* I tried to put the main character's thoughts about his tough life into words. He first asks himself

"Why do I have to bear all this?" Near the end of the film, he has his answer: "Not *why*, but *for what*."

A few years later, and I've found myself in the same situation. And the end is near too. The expression "Victory or death!" has never been as relevant to me as it is now. Considering that Putin rejected my exchange again during his annual televised national Q&A event, victory remains distant, and the specter of death looms ever closer.

We went to the city hospital for a second medical council dedicated to the now critical condition of the sickly Sentsov. Yet again, there was a whole set of different police chiefs, all three chief doctors, and a variety of other doctors. Our communication was very brief and tense. At first, they kept me in a paddy wagon for about forty minutes while the meeting carried on and my latest medical tests and EKG were being reviewed. So many police officers were crowded inside the vehicle that two of them didn't have enough space and were traveling in an area meant for prisoners. When we finally went up to the emergency room, the doctors simply presented me with a fact and a choice: my condition had deteriorated dramatically to the point where my life was now seriously at risk. My heartbeat was only half the normal rate, and this limited reserve would likely last for a maximum of two days. I either had to end my hunger strike immediately or, due to my critical medical condition, be placed in intensive care. There, I would be secured to the bed, administered a sedative, and nourished through both front and back channels; otherwise, the little time I have left would be measured in hours.

I refused to end my hunger strike. There was a short and heated "one-on-several" dialogue with many spectators. A compromise was proposed: to administer this mixture orally, with my voluntary consent, meaning I would swallow it and not spit it out. The decision was left up to me. There was a moment of pause, and silence settled over the room, echoing like a plastic tennis ball bouncing on a tiled floor. I looked into the doctors' faces and realized they weren't joking around. Within the hour, I'd be strapped down and have two tubes inserted into my mouth and my ass. I told them that I would not resist mouth feeding, and everyone breathed a sigh of relief. The doctors began to gradually go about their business. I wrote a refusal to be hospitalized in the city hospital and consented to the intake of nutritional formula. As I signed the statement, a drop of blood from one of my fingers that had been pricked for analysis earlier dripped onto the paper. I practically sealed the deal with blood. Well, good that it wasn't a deal with the devil.

The colony's med point lacked the required special mixture, but the resuscitator, the very same doctor with the distinctive golden chain with whom I had had a heated altercation last time and another clash with this time around, proved surprisingly generous. He retrieved it from his reserves, even adding some additional drip mixtures. The tension between us gradually subsided, and we spoke to each other normally. As I was told, all resuscitators were like that—they were the smartest of doctors because they saw death more than others. So that's why human life was probably not something abstract for them, but a very concrete thing that they dealt with daily.

I didn't hold a grudge against him, especially since the conversation was straightforward. He pointed out that the mixture was not a solution, not a panacea; it would not replace food for me. It was only a delay, and how long I would last on it was unknown since my body was already very weak. He promised that next time he would definitely get me into his intensive care unit—it turned out he was the head of it—and would do everything his own way. A couple of the other doctors spoke in the same manner: why did you bring him to us if he doesn't want to live, you distract us from our work, leave him to us, we know how to deal with him.

That's why I didn't want to stay there with them: the doctors from the outside see me as a convict, whereas the prison doctors see me as a human being. That's why I went home with my doctors to my med point.

The psychologist came again, with her unhappy eyes and banal phrases. She already understood that any communication with me would be brief, so she only left me a brochure on the dangers of fasting with pictures of starving people in it and a "twenty plus" days picture showing a figure of a man with a skull in its center.

Death will not come today; it has retreated. Now they will hook me up to an IV drip again and, judging by the volume, it will once again last through the night.

The rain has stopped outside the window, but the clouds haven't yet dissipated.

DAY TWENTY-SEVEN

The morning started off with sunshine and a clear sky. My condition, compared to the previous two days, has been decent. The weather somehow has adjusted to my state, or maybe I've adjusted to it. Yesterday, the IV drip lasted again until midnight, around seven hours in total. They inserted a peripheral venous catheter to make this process easier and to avoid losing the veins that were already punctured and starting to disappear.

I'd seen how those old Soviet-era catheters work and was dreading this procedure. But the modern ones turned out to be different. They placed one in my forearm and it wasn't painful—it was hardly even noticeable when it wasn't in use. It's really convenient for receiving long infusions. The doctor who inserted the catheter and administered the drip was the one who resembled a sleepy ferret. It turned out he wasn't a doctor but a nurse, though he felt flattered when the inspector referred to him as a paramedic. Even without a medical degree, he performed everything skillfully and quickly, and it wasn't painful. He had a light touch.

Yesterday morning, when I was unknowingly starting to die, my vital signs were being measured by the ever-complaining nurse who couldn't find my pulse or diastolic blood pressure. She immediately began to talk about a pre-comatose state, how it could sometimes be hard to wake up such patients in the morning, "and then you touch them, and they're already cold . . . " Later, when she conducted my EKG, her hidden talent as a professional mourner was revealed. I couldn't take it anymore and suggested that she keep her emotions to herself, sparing me the extra horror. My mood then corresponded to my condition. Of course, she flared up and said she wouldn't tell me anything about the results of my EKG, even though it was really bad, like with those who were about to fall into a coma. People can't be changed, especially when each one believes they're in the right and entitled. It turned out she wasn't a nurse but a doctor.

There isn't that much staff here—a maximum of about ten people—but I still sometimes mix up their statuses because my interactions have been limited to their supervisor's office. But yesterday, he was busy there all day, discussing and reporting to higher-ups along with two other doctor-supervisors about my health and how it's being managed. So, I received my infusion in my room yesterday and got acquainted with the rest of the staff.

It's not that everything around me is whirling and spinning, but something akin to it. Soon, I'll forget that I'm still in prison. But the police periodically remind me of that fact. They've resumed their daily routine searches, even though they forgot about it for three weeks—looks like it's time to get back on track.

Thankfully, I managed to warn them about the catheter before the quick personal inspection started. They turned the bed and the bedside table upside down as well. What were they constantly looking for? A makeshift shiv? No sensible inmate would hide it in their belongings—that's just asking for trouble. There were plenty of hiding spots, or pigeon-holes, where it could be retrieved if needed. Or did they want to find a piece of bread hidden under the pillow or in the socks, which my demons, the ones I've written about, were supposed to steal? But the police, with their demons, didn't understand that in my current state, a crust of bread was not my salvation but destruction. Well, intelligent people didn't typically become guards.

Take this morning, when they brought me two fresh issues of *Novaya Gazeta*. Well, fresh is a relative term in these parts, as it arrived with the standard two-week delay. Several articles had been cut out of both issues. I suspected they were about me. And what was the point of that? Did they think they could somehow limit my access to information—thereby violating the law—by mutilating the sad newspaper I subscribed to? No one seemed to consider the consequences of this foolishness.

I still can't get used to their stupidity and shortsightedness, even after all these years. Not allowing the Ukrainian priest to visit, not giving me the letter brought by my lawyer, and now censoring an official publication. Where was the logic? In response, there was only silence and a faint rumble in their empty skulls.

The main thing is that I have genuinely felt better today. It's like driving out of a deep pit onto a small hill. My blood pressure was low—eighty over sixty—but not critically so, and even though my pulse was still weak, at least it was there. It would have been strange if it hadn't improved considering how many supplements they've pumped into me. The nutritional mixture began to do its job too. At first, I thought it was something like baby food or protein, since it looked very similar. After reading the label on the box, I realized that it contained minimal protein and calories, with approximately 80 percent of its contents consisting of vitamins, minerals, and other nutrients designed for weakened bodies. Well, fine. I was starting to think that by taking this nutrition orally, I had hit a new low in my hunger strike—but fine. It wasn't food, just support. I didn't go through the whole spectacle of being spoon-fed either and drank it myself.

The mixture was diluted in a few spoonfuls of water and brought to me every four hours. The portions were small, but that was to be expected. The warm liquid gently caressed my stomach, serving an additional function by safeguarding the mucous membrane, which was compromised during a hunger strike. The mixture tasted somewhat chemical and milky. I couldn't define it more precisely, as the taste receptors in my mouth have started to atrophy.

The doctor said that over time, my sense of taste may partially recover, but might not fully. My tongue has become the same light beige color as the walls in my room. There was also the persistent smell and the sensation of acetone in my mouth. There was nothing that could be done about it for as long as the hunger strike lasted because my body was still lacking nutrition, and it continued to consume itself. The presence of acetone was just another indication of this unfortunate process.

Over the past four weeks, I've picked up some knowledge about medicine in general and the human body in particular through firsthand experience. I'm used to observing and understanding things, and in this case, it's about what's going on inside me. My weight is now seventy-six kilograms, and it's decreasing gradually, which is typical in the later stages of a hunger strike. I didn't have much extra weight to start with, and muscles burn slower than fat.

The doctor examined me and said it was too early to celebrate; my heart was still weak and unstable, but the situation was better than yesterday. The inspector who checked on me last night, leaving a rather memorable impression, has already returned to Moscow to report her involvement in the operation to salvage my hunger strike.

They set up another long-lasting drip for me. This time, a new nurse, who might have been skilled at distributing painkillers to the inmates but struggled with the drip, took care of it. Though she did notice that my face looked a bit healthier after the six-hour drip, and I no longer had the pale complexion from the morning. Fortunately, she didn't see me yesterday . . .

I took a shower and shaved. Some skinny guy with bones sticking out in all directions was still residing in the mirror. He looked like he hadn't gotten any better in the past week—if anything, he'd gotten worse. His head seemed disproportionately large, and his face, you could say, was almost gone.

Hygiene wasn't much of a priority the past few days, so I needed to take advantage of this opportunity while I was feeling a bit better. Usually, this combined procedure takes me about twenty minutes. Today, though, I struggled for over an hour. I felt like an old geezer: no energy, everything I did was slow and difficult. My hand with the catheter wrapped in a plastic bag was getting in the way. But it was alright, I managed.

I changed the bed linens and rested to catch my breath. Today's relief didn't mean things were getting better. It was expected. The doctor said my condition was stable for now, but we couldn't predict when the next crisis would hit. It was inevitable, and the next one would likely be worse, with that relentless resuscitator getting involved.

But I hope my body can hold on for two more weeks—it seems that they'll be decisive. I hope I can hold on until then.

Lights out. Even though the lights are switched off, the room remains so bright that you can read and write without having to inch closer to the window. In the evening news, they reported that the Ukrainian and Russian presidents had spoken by phone. The topics were all the same: Donbas, ceasefire, POWs. They agreed to arrange mutual visits of the ombudswomen to prisons. If this sort of conversation had happened for the first time, I might have been pleased, but over the past four years, this has happened so many times that you believe in and hope only in yourself. Let's see. Two weeks.

DAY TWENTY-EIGHT

It turned chilly overnight. I woke up with a cold nose and ears, but I slept soundly. I even had dreams again, which hadn't happened during the tough preceding days. Outside, the weather has been rainy, windy, and damp, with temperatures near freezing, and the sky has been covered in a continuous gray haze.

Yesterday's brief taste of spring, when a few fluffy clouds floated by, is gone. But in this kind of weather, I always sleep well, much better than on quiet, bright polar nights.

They brought in a small heater to keep the room warm all the time, which is a great comfort. I have to lie back down for another IV drip.

Only now, as my condition has somewhat improved, am I starting to grasp the depth of the abyss I narrowly escaped and how the coldness of death seemed to linger close by. Occasionally, I still feel a shiver down my spine, but in my spirit and, most importantly, in my heart, which now beats steadily if not strongly, there is a greater sense of calm. I can finally relax and savor this moment.

The last day of this intense and eventful fourth week has turned out to be quite simple and unproductive. It's reminiscent of the Bible, where on the seventh day, God, tired from his work, rested and encouraged us to do the same. I spent the first half of the day hooked up to an IV. They replaced the catheter with a new one, and I received over two liters of various fluids, including what the resuscitator had administered the day before to avert a crisis. I've been drinking more than four liters of water, but it seems like I'm expelling more than five, leaving about a liter unaccounted for.

The doctor explained that it was being expelled through my breath and sweat. I've started to retain fluids a bit better than before and have even gained nearly a kilogram in weight, though I understand it's mostly water in my belly, making gurgling sounds like a merman.

At lunch, I had a brief conversation with the doctor who came to see how I was doing. Basically, not bad. I've been feeling fine since morning, but weakness now comes in the late afternoon. More analyses and an EKG are planned for tomorrow.

I watched a TV show about dragons and seven kingdoms with other guys in the TV room during the second half of the day. I didn't like the show at first, but it turned out to be pretty good. This is the third time I've started watching it during my imprisonment, and I still find it interesting. The plot is excellent and unpredictable, with good actors, artwork, and special effects. I'm not alone in this—the saga is really enjoyed by the whole world.

In the evening, between the last episodes of the season, during commercials, we switched to Kiselyov for a few minutes. There were two moments in the program when my situation was discussed. First, at some briefing, Putin commented on yesterday's conversation with Poroshenko about the release of detainees. And then, the walking TV guru himself was talking about Kyiv's offer to exchange me for Kirill Vyshinsk, the chief editor of the Russian propaganda media RIA Novosti-Ukraina, who was arrested by Ukraine's State Security Service on suspicion of treason in 2018.

They made it seem like it was pushing the envelope to swap an honest journalist with a bloody terrorist, and they even used my picture to illustrate their point. While neither the father of All Russia nor his faithful servant spoke out in a form that sharply rejected such a possibility—and this instilled some hope in me—it was still hard to believe. On the flip side, what were the odds of a segment featuring me not once, but twice? Maybe someone from on high wanted to send me a subtle signal—a green light, perhaps signaling an Exit? Either way, everything will become clear soon.

Here's the joke of the day: yesterday the almost-grandmother, who doubles as an almost-nurse and struggles with my IV and catheter, decided to handle the equipment in a peaceful nighttime setting. The result? She accidentally turned off the "head" of the new device. Surprisingly, the doctor didn't scold her for it in the morning. He just sighed and checked her personnel file to see how much time she had left before retirement, which prompted a second sigh.

DAY TWENTY-NINE

The fifth week of my hunger strike has begun. What it will be like—manageable, critical, or decisive—no one knows. We'll see based on the results.

I slept until almost nine in the morning, with minor disruptions to standard procedures and routines. I got a good rest again and currently feel quite well, which is certainly pleasing.

Once again, a bunch of different dreams came to me. I could vividly remember them in the morning, but by lunchtime, only tiny fragments were left, fading into fog.

One dream stood out: I was walking with a friend from Crimea along a well-trodden path in a snowy park, with his wife and mother-in-law just ahead of us. They didn't approve of me. But it seemed they didn't approve of their own close "relative" either, as they turned aside somewhere without saying goodbye or looking back. I pointed this out to him, but he just waved it off, indicating that their family had long been on the brink of collapse. And so, we continued walking side by side, without exchanging a word. He was a good friend, old and reliable. But over the past four years, he had never made himself known. He didn't actively participate in the events on the Maidan or Crimea, but he cared and supported them from a distance.

I find it easier to believe he disappeared in Donbas than to think he gave up his position due to terrorism accusations. Though it's quite doubtful—if he didn't have the courage to go to the Maidan, it's unlikely he would suddenly have had the courage to join the Anti-Terrorist Operation. But there's always a desire to see the best in people and not pass judgment.

Everyone has their own journey and makes their own decisions.

I've completed another round of medical tests. They're preparing the IV drip as I write, and this seemingly slow but tiring process will start soon. The catheter from yesterday got blocked, so they've decided to switch back to regular needles because my veins have improved a bit over the past three days. They gave me a keychain with an emergency call button to reach the nurse at her station because yesterday when I needed to change the bottle, I couldn't find her or the emergency orderlies for half an hour. They usually patrol the corridor. I've placed the button on the bedside table. If things get really bad, I can find it by touch, and the volunteer helpers now peek through the window every fifteen minutes to see if I need anything.

I don't know why I'm writing all these details here—there's not much to write about. I guess this diary is not only a record of events or a way to let off steam, but also a sort of barometer for my psychological state: is my handwriting distorted, and am I starting to write complete nonsense? Over extended periods of a hunger strike, the brain and consciousness can suffer as well. For now, everything seems to be OK. The only important organs taking a hit are my kidneys, liver, and heart. While my problems with the first two aren't that significant, my heart, due to a childhood health condition, has been hit the hardest. The fact that my body isn't retaining water—because my kidneys aren't working well—and the smell of acetone in my mouth—indicating my liver is breaking down—are also concerning signs, but my heart remains the most important and problematic issue.

But now, thankfully, the situation has stabilized in terms of my condition, my well-being, and the test results. They certainly weren't good, but they were no longer critical. Though the doctor still told me not to get my hopes up. Intensive therapy with the medications they gave us from the city hospital's intensive care unit helped.

But they're supposed to run out today, so we're going back to pre-crisis medical support, plus a nutritional mix a few times a day, about half a cup each time. According to my doctor, this wouldn't be enough. Intensive care pushed me back from the edge and somewhat stabilized me, but he repeated that he didn't know how long this state would last and when the next crisis would come. I told him I needed to hold on for two more weeks. The doctor wasn't even sure about one. We'll see.

But I don't want to take these rare and expensive medications from the intensive care unit, where they could really help those who need them more, like burn victims, comatose patients, and those recovering from severe accidents and surgeries. I no longer want that. They need them more. Those medications save lives. I'll manage because I'm doing this voluntarily to myself, and they aren't to blame for ending up in hospital beds, only to be transferred shortly to a gurney headed straight for the morgue.

Spring tried to break through the clouds several times during the day. The sun would start shining from the blue sky, warming everything, and even a couple of birds timidly sang. Maybe they were just sparrows, shedding their winter coats after what seemed like an endless season, but even that would be good. Warmth brushed against my soul. But then, everything would become obscured by dark and tattered clouds, the wind would blow, and raindrops would fall. An hour or two later, the sun would return. Autumn was battling with spring. The weather closely resembled my condition, well-being, and test results these days. But warmth, spring—and following that, summer—are inevitable!

Psychological hunger pangs stopped bothering me a while ago. There are no images of food floating around in my head; it's like they've been cut off. I don't even see any little demons— maybe they finally starved to death in their hideouts. When I see the *balanda* in the room—no one thought to cancel the ritual—or the other guys devouring it, I don't feel any emotions at all, let alone cravings. I know that in the future, this might lead to a problem—some people who have experienced deep hunger can later have difficulties with their appetite, even leading to anorexia. I don't think that's in the cards for me, but who knows? In any case, we'll solve these problems as they come. For now, it's not a problem, even the opposite. It's a bonus because it's not interfering.

The doctor suggested porridge once more, describing it as a chemical mixture with very little protein and calories. It wouldn't be considered real food, and it would only slightly delay, but not entirely halt, the negative processes. I refused again.

You can fool the police, you can fool surveillance cameras, you can fool anyone. But you can't fool yourself, and you have to live with such decisions for the rest of your life.

The doctor gave me a wooden medical spatula designed to remove the white coating on my tongue, which can be harmful, especially for those who are persistent and principled about their health. I spent a quarter of an hour on this activity in front of the mirror in the washroom. Now only half of my tongue is white; the other half is red. Too bad there's no one to show off this beauty to.

DAY THIRTY

Today marks a special milestone: thirty days. I woke up in the morning and saw a clear deep-blue sky through the window, without a single cloud blot. It was the first time I'd taken in such a view during my entire stay in the damp polar Labytnangi. The sun was not visible as it shone from somewhere on the side but conveyed a big hello to me in the form of corresponding light projections of the windows on the walls of the ward.

The overall state of my health and mood continues to be consistent with the weather.

Today isn't just a personal celebration for me. I heard on TV that it's Russia Day, one of the newer holidays celebrated here. As usual, most people don't pay much attention to it.

This holiday was introduced under Yeltsin after the collapse of the USSR. After that, all the former republics went their separate ways, like pieces detaching from a satellite, and started celebrating their own independence days. Some did it with genuine enthusiasm, while others did it more formally. Ukraine, for example, only recently fully understood the cost of its independence, and both the people there and I started to appreciate the significance and value of that word.

In Russia's case, there was no one to separate and declare

independence from, as it was the other republics that were moving away from it. Then this artificial holiday was created, though some supporters of the Soviet Union would observe it as a day of mourning, using names like "The Day When Everyone Left," "The Day of Dependence on Your Ambitions," or "The Day of Memory of the Ruined Empire," and so on.

The regular folks, at least those around me now, hardly noticed the holiday. They wouldn't have known about it if it hadn't been repeatedly mentioned on TV throughout the day.

Aggressive propaganda and mindless TV shows are slowly taking their toll on people in Russia. They are becoming increasingly uninformed and less knowledgeable, and that's scary. It's a dead-end situation. How—and more importantly when—they can break free from it is entirely unclear. It feels like when the current captain finally leaves this ship, dining orchestras, tears, and the cries of the crowd, then the state, and most importantly, the people will face significant challenges. They seem deeply and hopelessly entangled in all of this. Maybe, somewhere, there are glimmers of hope and different perspectives, but definitely not where I currently am. Let me share an example.

Our group of guys here was tuned into a news channel. In honor of Putin's visit to China—another attempt to strengthen relations—the entire broadcast was filled with stories and documentaries about the current state of China. The country was doing well, very well, and it seemed like it was going to keep improving, and most importantly, thriving. All of this was portrayed in a way that suggested it was thanks to the Russian president, or at the very least, with his approval. That was the underlying message, which of course was followed by its intended result: my neighbor on the right asked me a question, thinking of me as some sort of "political expert" because I was featured on TV the day before yesterday. "Do you think Russia and China will unite soon?" he asked.

I responded, "What do you mean?" He continued, "You know, become one country?" I was puzzled, but he persisted, "We have so much in common!"

I replied, "Maybe, but it could take a hundred years or so. Though, they may not unite, one might absorb the other, and it definitely won't be called Russia . . . "

Despite its vast territory, oil and gas resources, tanks, and nuclear missiles, Russia still appears somewhat artificial. Nothing personal, dear Russians, and Happy Holidays! Enjoy the celebrations for now. China is in no hurry, but it's not backing down either.

Ukraine was once again in the news. The foreign ministers of the Normandy Four met in Berlin a year and a half after their last meeting. Unfortunately, there hasn't been any progress since then. The same questions, words, and statements were repeated, and the result remained unchanged. The Russian leadership seems fine with allowing the conflict to linger without a real resolution while people in front-line trenches or in their homes continue to suffer and die.

Even though I've been feeling stable and less tired, especially in the mornings when I get enough sleep, today I experienced discomfort in my chest and got the chills. I was dressed warmly, even wearing a prisoner's sweater, lying under the blanket with the heater humming along cheerfully. It was a sunny day outside, but I was shivering. Could I be getting sick? Maybe

I'd caught something from one of the other patients? The doctor mentioned more than once that my immune system was much weaker, so it wouldn't be surprising. Let's see how I feel by evening after the next IV drip.

A couple of days ago, I informed the colony's head through a doctor about the foolishness of his subordinates who were cutting articles from *Novaya Gazeta*. I warned him that I would publicly address this issue, and he would have to deal with the consequences, which likely wouldn't be good. During dinner, one of the attendants, the video surveillance recording them, solemnly handed back both confiscated articles to me. I let him know that the matter was resolved. As expected, the articles were about my hunger strike, but there was nothing new in those two- and three-week-old newspapers. Maybe they thought that if I found out about the broad support through these articles, I would give up my protest. They don't understand that even if I'm completely isolated, I won't back down. Well, it's too late to try to understand the logic of the prison authorities; it's a futile effort.

I received some good news today—they allowed me to have a phone conversation. Usually, only Zoya Svetova, a well-known Moscow journalist and human rights activist, could reach me through the regular procedure, and this time it was her.

I briefly shared my concerns with her, and she updated me on the outside world's news. Overall, the current situation and the prospects regarding my fate seemed quite positive. At least that was how I saw it from here. She mentioned various forms of support, including letters and messages of solidarity, and even how she had had a friendly conversation with Macron in St. Petersburg when she was there as part of a voluntary delegation advocating for my release. She reassured me that my fear of the focus being solely on releasing one person was unfounded and that it aligned with my goals.

It would be devastating for me to be released alone, so I was glad to hear that they were talking about releasing a group of prisoners. Thank God! Of course, it wouldn't be possible to release everyone at once, but the more, the better.

I also learned that my colleague Sasha Kolchenko ended his hunger strike a week after he started it. This was excellent news. Given his weight and health, he shouldn't have embarked on a hunger strike in the first place. But he did a remarkable job by supporting me for as long as he could, even to the point of losing consciousness.

Overall, our conversation was productive and informative. I appreciate conversations that are short, to the point, interesting, and kind.

They took me from the med point to the duty room for the phone conversation, which was quite a stroll through the camp, about seventy meters in total.

The weather was lovely today—warm and sunny. Sparrows were chirping (haven't seen any other birds yet), and there was no wind—almost blissful. It once again seemed very much in line with the current state of affairs.

DAY THIRTY-ONE

By yesterday evening, the weather had worsened a bit—not too severely, just clouds, with no rain or wind this time. I wasn't feeling well either. My heart was causing me discomfort, so I didn't have the energy to do anything, including writing. I was feeling lethargic, lying under my blanket without the strength to move. But I did manage to get some rest during the night, and later, my heart felt better. I had a good night's sleep, and in the morning, as the sun rose, my strength returned.

There's still a chill in the air, like before, and my throat has started to ache—maybe it's tonsillitis or the beginning of a cold, but no fever so far. I have enough energy for about half the day, much like the good weather outside.

The doctor wasn't happy with my test results. Nothing critical, but nothing good either. He was especially concerned about my heart—the EKG still didn't look good. He explained that my heart muscles weren't getting enough oxygen to function properly. I asked, "Should I breathe more often?" He smiled and said, "No, oxygen comes in with nutrients, and there's a shortage of those for your heart and your entire body in general." He suggested increasing the amount of the nutritional mixture I consumed, but I declined—it was already the maximum compromise I could allow myself.

Yesterday, we went back to the "usual" three-hour IV drips because we'd run out of the extra support medications in the large two-liter bags. The intensive care unit doesn't have them anymore, but I'm categorically against using them anyway.

The doctor sometimes finds it a bit challenging to deal with my preferences, even though he has said I'm a cooperative patient overall. In any case, he's quite pessimistic about the next ten days I still need to endure, assuming my calculations are correct. So far, everything is going as planned, and even better than I expected, but no one knows the final outcome of this life-and-death race. The doctor is solely focused on my health, which is good because it allows me to think about other, more important things.

Today marks one month since the start of my hunger strike. Everyone understands that there won't be a reason to celebrate a second month of it—my body definitely won't hold out that long, and I can feel it. It's also my forty-second birthday today, my fifth birthday in prison, but I won't be celebrating it here. It's not because I never celebrated the previous ones—my cellmates had no idea about them. Even before prison, in my former life, this date had lost all importance for me.

Birthdays are primarily for children and young people, and I'd already transitioned to a more "mature" outlook on life. I only celebrated birthdays for my kids because they truly enjoyed it, and their happiness made me happy too. A celebration isn't just a date on the calendar; it's the state of one's soul. That's why I've been celebrating them according to my mood, and not out of obligation, for a long time.

My blood pressure is still low, but at least it's not dropping critically anymore. My weight has settled to around seventy-six to seventy-seven kilograms, but that's mainly because of water retention. As a hunger strike progresses, weight loss slows down—around one hundred grams per day or even less. At this stage, the body has used up the easily accessible reserves and starts tapping into the harder-to-reach ones, mainly its own organs, like the liver.

During lunch, a group of local officials, led by the chief, paid a visit. They were all smiles and shows of concern, making cautious suggestions to end my hunger strike as if to imply that

I'd achieved my goals. Naturally, I politely declined because this wasn't yet a victory. They also remarked that I looked noticeably better than last week, which was evident even without any medical analysis. After exchanging pleasantries, they left, wishing me a speedy recovery. All that was missing for them to be mistaken for my relatives was a bag of fruits and cookies.

My interactions with the authorities didn't end there. First, they brought a paper with an official explanation for denying my meeting with the Ukrainian priest, which echoed last week's events. The tone of the letter surprised me. It started with "Dear," followed by my first name and patronymic, and ended with "Yours sincerely, So-and-So."

In the free world, these are common expressions for official letters, but not in the prison system, where superiors usually write refusals to prisoners in a strictly business-like manner, using only surnames and initials. They might even include the word "convict" to remind you of your status. But not every convict is shown on television, and not everyone is mentioned twice a week by Putin.

Then, the head of the colony, often referred to as the "boss" here, appeared once more. He began by politely and cautiously asking about the upcoming visit from the Ukrainian ombudswoman. He mentioned that he didn't know the exact date of her arrival since he'd learned about it, just like me, from the television. Though it wasn't her visit that concerned him. It was the possibility of Ukrainian journalists accompanying her. He was worried about how to handle them if they attempted to see me.

I reassured him by saying that I'd taken the stance of not interacting with the press while I was in confinement, and

I didn't intend to make any exceptions for anyone. I added that my lawyer and my sister Natasha were the only ones I trusted. He was pleased to hear that I wasn't seeking contact with journalists or any publicity, but he looked disappointed when he heard my resolute sister's name. Apparently, he regularly read her Facebook page and there was a lot there he didn't like. I told him there was nothing I could do about that. Natasha would be pretty surprised to learn she has secret followers among the ranks of Russian Federal Penitentiary Service officials.

I also asked the boss for permission to watch soccer broadcasts on television outside the regular schedule. He agreed, mentioning that there was actually a directive to encourage watching matches from the World Cup, which started tomorrow. We discovered a shared passion for soccer, even though I wouldn't call myself a big fan, more of an enthusiast.

I've been following World Cups and European Championships, and, of course, the Champions League since I was fourteen. The smaller tournaments interest me only if there are exciting matches. I asked for this not just for myself but for all the sick inmates and those in the infirmary. The boss nodded again. Given the current situation and my circumstances, I suggested that a soccer ball with the autograph of a player like Artem Dzyuba would also be a nice idea. The ball would surely show up, but the question was what to do with it afterward and who would buy such a dubious relic?

Over the past four years, I've tried not to ask the authorities for anything to avoid being in their debt. But today, as we ended our negotiations, the boss hinted that maybe it was time for me to at least start eating porridge. It was honestly like being back in kindergarten.

Moments like this make you momentarily forget which prison you're in. But it's essential not to forget that friendliness isn't widespread here. They address you by your first name and patronymic and use words like "Yours sincerely." But for another inmate, today might have been a hellish all-day affair.

DAY THIRTY-TWO

I've been feeling unwell since this morning. I have a sore throat, runny nose, headache, and a slight temperature. But these symptoms aren't that noticeable because I constantly feel a slight chill. My hands and feet are cold and have trouble warming up. It's likely that my heart isn't functioning properly. No matter how many EKGs they do, my condition won't change for the better. My heart rate remains below normal, and there are clear signs of it weakening.

Last night, I visited the city hospital's endocrinologist, who delivered a discouraging prognosis. While my heart muscle had stabilized, it wasn't in good condition. It was unclear how long it would hold up, given the damage it suffered already in my childhood. I couldn't recover because I wasn't getting enough nutrition, and this path could only lead downhill. Oxygen deprivation might well lead to heart ischemia and, ultimately, a heart attack, and all this was happening naturally.

Despite all these alarming medical stories, I'm determined to continue. I realize that if I don't stop this hunger strike now, I may harm my heart even more, potentially shortening my life, but I see no other option. I need to hold on for another week and a half if my calculations are correct. At this point, I'm not thinking beyond that. It would be a shame to give up before achieving victory, even though it's uncertain if victory is near. I won't be able to feel disappointment if I lose, as I won't be able to feel anything at all in that moment.

To support my heart, I'm taking a medication called Meldonium, which is made in Russia but contains the same active ingredient as Mildronate. Based on the fact that the capsules often break when I try to remove them from the package, the quality doesn't seem to be very good, and the effect is still nonexistent.

Outside, the clouds have returned, and the weather has become chilly and damp. Lately, I've become so accustomed to the fact that my health matches the weather that I take it for granted. I've started to take it in stride, even though I used to be skeptical about such things.

Though I didn't mention this to the doctor to avoid sounding crazy. I also kept quiet about my frequent chest pains, otherwise his heart would hurt even more than mine.

With all the turbulent events of the past week, a TV in the background for a few hours, and a stack of outdated but still enjoyable magazines, I haven't had a chance to get back to Lem's *Solaris*. Yesterday, I finally picked up the book again, and I plan to finish it today. I've been enjoying it, but I can't help but think of scenes from Tarkovsky's film adaptation. In my opinion, the movie is definitely better. The director cut out the excessive technical details and focused on the more essential human aspects that drew him to the original material. As for my final conclusions, I'll reserve my judgment until I reach the last page. Either way, without Lem's book, there would be no film.

•

I finished reading *Solaris*. I'm not a critic, and I don't know how to describe other people's work in fancy terms. But I definitely preferred the movie over the book. Not because I like movies more than books or because Tarkovsky's filmography is beyond compare.

To me, the film adaptation was more precise. It only added what was needed, and the film's language captured Lem's idea better than his own writing. The ending was also different and, in my opinion, better. In the book, the main themes were about fatherhood, home, land, and Earth. The protagonist still held out hope for understanding the rainbow planet-ocean, seeing it as a flawed god in its infancy. Tarkovsky, on the other hand, took Lem's idea and developed it further. He emphasized that humans didn't need to conquer the Cosmos, they only needed each other. This aligned with the director's favorite and main theme in his work—love, but through a different divine perspective.

This is definitely closer to my own view. Lem categorically disliked Tarkovsky's film adaptation, and I understand why. The book and the film are very different. Tarkovsky adapted three literary works into films, including *Ivan* and *Roadside Picnic*, but he reworked them considerably with the help of the authors or screenwriters. He injected so much of his own creativity into them that it's hard to recognize the original source in his films. That's what made all his film adaptations great. He didn't just bring someone else's words to life with visuals, he showcased his own world and ideas on screen. This is the only way to approach film adaptations if you're an author.

For the past few days, I've been pestered by periodic itching on my abdominal skin. Sometimes, it gets so bad that it causes redness. It could be due to an allergy to the medication or the use of a detergent on my underwear that's irritating my skin. But honestly, that's the least of my worries right now. Even if I sometimes look like a homeless person scratching myself.

Another doctor came to visit me from the city hospital. She's the one who had been quite vocal during the previous council, shouting that I was basically a corpse when they brought me in. Today, she seemed friendlier and was satisfied with my test results and medical examination. Apparently, things have improved compared to the last time she saw me. She's also some sort of department chief at the hospital, and it's clear that she's a skilled specialist.

She emphasized that the main problem remained my heart, which was still holding on, but the future was uncertain. It's the same thing I've been hearing from all the doctors for the past few days, and something I'm feeling myself. She advised me to think about what lies ahead, to which I replied that I already had.

Today's notable event: the grandmother-nurse decided to retire early! This was a big deal for our med point, even more so than the opening of the World Cup. It seemed that the catheter situation had finally gotten to her. To mark this occasion, the doctor asked for a mixture of alcohol with glucose and drank a couple of beakers' worth. The grandmother must have had a sense of what was coming because it was just announced on TV that Russia would significantly increase the retirement age. The elections are over, so they can do it now, and they might also raise the VAT while they're at it.

They also mentioned on the news that Stanislav Govorukhin had passed away. Even if he were a Putin supporter three times over, I would still love his films and consider him a talented director. Another loss. May he rest in peace.

DAY THIRTY-THREE

I had a dream in which I was driving a large truck. I couldn't make a turn on the wet road, so I had to veer onto a dirt one through an old, overgrown garden or forest. It was getting dark, and the path was narrow. I couldn't turn the truck around, so I had to keep going, with low branches hitting the truck's roof and windshield. Eventually, I reached some locked gates, but I managed to maneuver the truck a bit. The guard wouldn't let me go any further, so I asked if he wanted to buy my cargo— all fruit. He didn't seem interested, and when we checked the cargo bed, we found that all the goods had rotted, and the guard didn't even want them for free to make moonshine. That's the kind of dream it was.

Some Freudians or other such enthusiasts would see bad omens in this dream, but I don't believe in that sort of thing. A dream is just a dream, not a glimpse into your future. Your future only depends on you and God. Do what you need to do, and let things unfold as they will.

In the morning, the sky appeared mostly clear, but it had a slightly dirty-blue hue. The sun briefly sparkled through a crack in the window glass and then disappeared. My condition has remained the same as yesterday—neither better nor worse, except for an unpleasant cough that suddenly worsened.

On TV, they aired Stanislav Govorukhin's film *Ten Little Negroes*, which is an adaptation of Agatha Christie's *And Then There Were None*. I caught the second part of it. It was a really good movie and yet another example where the movie surpassed the original source material. The book didn't provide even half the suspense found in the film. Moreover, Govorukhin completely changed the ending and elevated the entire story to a new level of psychological impact. I've enjoyed most of Govorukhin's works from the Soviet era, from the beloved Zheglov story that every policeman adored to *In Search of Captain Grant*. I've watched them all many times, and I have a deep appreciation for them. He was indeed a great master of film.

His films—even if you know every detail—never get boring, which speaks volumes about the quality of his work. For me, the mark of a good movie is one that you want to watch over and over again.

The film was even aired with a small black ribbon in the corner as a sign of mourning for the director. However, it wasn't the main national channel that aired it. They had different priorities, focusing on non-stop soccer celebrations, shifting from pompous openings to jubilation and hysteria over the 5–0 defeat of the Saudis. Russia will face tougher opponents ahead, and if their team can't progress from their weak group, yesterday's victory over Saudi Arabia won't be enough to save them. The excited fans of today might soon turn on them. Let's see how it goes. Anyway, I'm rooting for Germany since Ukraine didn't qualify for the tournament.

The opening ceremony unfolded with maximum pomp, most notably in the enthusiastic commentator's words. They rejoiced and claimed that such a grandiose ceremony would be remembered in sports history for the next one hundred years, which was a highly debatable assertion that didn't quite correspond to reality.

Robbie Williams performed, and he was a highlight of the program, still unaware that upon his return to his English homeland, the press would crucify him for entertaining people who, in the middle of the day, poisoned others in the parks of misty Albion. Putin also gave a speech, but there was nothing new in his remarks. The only interesting thing about his speech was the cottonwood fluff floating in the background. Some foreigners among the billions who, according to the commentator, were closely following this spectacle, might have thought it was Russian snow falling. What surprised me more was the head of FIFA who spoke next. His speech was brief and, to put it plainly, utterly idiotic. He said, "I believe that soccer will now conquer Russia, and then Russia, through soccer, will conquer the whole world . . . " Did he even understand what he was saying? Because even if Russians forgot the word "soccer," the desire to "conquer" would still remain.

The weather up here changes every half hour, with the sun appearing, then clouds racing across the sky, and sometimes it gets cloudy. Then there's a break before it starts all over again.

Despite the unpredictable weather, there's a sense of calm today. I'm lying under the IV drip and feeling relaxed. Maybe it's because the cold seems to have let up, or maybe because my heart didn't bother me this morning, or maybe someone had a positive thought about me. Or maybe things are just going well. Life can't be all hardships, right? Even life needs a break.

They brought five copies of *Novaya Gazeta* today! The boss joked that it was to celebrate yesterday's 5–0 victory. The most recent issue was ten days old, which was fresh by local standards. They've stopped censoring the newspaper before delivering it to me. Turns out even police are capable of having moments of enlightenment.

Novaya Gazeta has been actively supporting me, and they've been featuring my hunger strike in every issue. In the most recent one, my determined face took up the entire front page. That issue seemed to have come out after my lawyer's visit and Russia's nationwide protest in my support, which Ksenia Sobchak had mentioned to me earlier.

It's really a strange feeling to read about yourself, as if the person they're writing so much about, the one lying here on the bed with this newspaper in hand, has no connection to you at all. You even look different in the photograph. I wonder if I'll ever manage, like others, to reconcile this Sentsov, the real one, with the one portrayed in the media. It will probably be an intriguing challenge. Many may even feel disappointed, as often happens with fictional characters.

Meanwhile, in an earlier issue, there was a lengthy article about the Norilsk prisoner uprising in 1953 that caught my attention. It happened right after Stalin's death. The stories and materials were gripping, and the writing style was engaging. Once again, I realized and felt ashamed of my relatively "light" status as a prisoner compared to those people and what they had endured during that terrifying time. What a cursed country.

Ukrainians described the USSR as the "Land of Tears, Suffering, and Slavery." They were first captured by the Soviets in '39, then by the Germans in '41, and once more by the Red Army in '44. They experienced nothing good under those authorities. For resisting, offering aid, or merely sympathizing with national rebels, they were killed, tortured in prisons and camps, and exiled from their homeland. They were the foundation of the prisoners who revolted sixty-five years ago in the Stalin-era camps of the Norilsk division of the Gulag, as well as in others.

A great and accurate article. Its main idea resonated perfectly with our current times—the era of resistance by a new generation of Ukrainians: "The weak almost always bring down the strong. A handful of Christians brought down the unshakable Rome. The day comes when it is discovered that the world is not ruled by rockets, corporations, or tons of money, but by pure idealism and a handful of outcasts hidden somewhere in the mountains, simply strong in spirit. This is the only thing that always triumphs. The free spirit breathes wherever it wants."

Today, that grizzly bear–like Dagestani once again substituted for the duty officer. He rarely takes on this role, so he carried it out very seriously, especially the ritual with the *balanda*, which he recorded on video himself. But then he turned it off, along with his official tone, and switched on his seldom-used smile. He was interested in the state of my affairs and health, clicked his tongue and nodded when he learned about the duration of my hunger strike. He also mentioned the victory of the Russian national team yesterday.

It seems that many policemen are interested in just two questions—namely, whether their soccer team will advance from the group and how much longer Sentsov will hold out. Predictions, bets. Though neither takes the victory in these competitions seriously.

I just read in the newspaper that Aleksandr Askoldov, the director of *The Commissar,* passed away at the end of May. This film was banned in the Soviet Union and was only shown for the first time in 1987. What's happening? Another talented person gone in the same week! I know nobody lives forever, but why all of a sudden like this? The newspaper also included an old interview with him, where he talked about how the Soviet regime had impacted his health. It's sad to think about how the system impacted his life. Even before *The Commissar* and during its filming, and especially after the Soviet authorities slapped him with a "wolf ticket," a professional disqualification for life.

It makes you wonder how much beauty he could have created if it weren't for the Soviet system. Some people praise the Soviet Union for its cinema but don't realize that the best work came despite the system, not because of it. So much potential went unrealized, stifled by regulations. All of these were individual destinies, creative lives held back. May they rest in peace.

I was brought a stack of sixteen letters. Some were from people I already knew, and others were from those who only wrote their first names, without an address or last name. Acts of civil courage, with precautions taken.

DAY THIRTY-FOUR

After lights out, we enjoyed an exciting soccer match between Spain and Portugal. It was a game filled with skillful plays and goals, a full hour and a half of non-stop enjoyment. It's safe to say that it was the best match of the group stage. In fact, considering the level of play and the intense 3–3 draw, it could easily have been a final match.

Later, I dreamed of playing soccer with other inmates using a cardboard box as a ball. Only three of us were in the duty unit, and a small window in the lattice wall served as the goal. But then, I was informed that another term was being added to my sentence for some kind of theft, and I was being moved, possibly to another facility or barracks. The new place was enormous, with endless rows of double bunk beds. During my stay there, someone stole a large piece of lard from me, leaving only a small portion behind. Just as I was about to enjoy it with a ration of black bread, it was time to wake up, and they brought me the morning *balanda*.

Nighttime dreams often reflect the events of the day, distorting them. That's why I don't really put much stock in dreams.

For the first time this month, I dreamed about food, but it wasn't because I was hungry. Instead, I felt upset about something unpleasant. When I fully woke up, I realized that no one had stolen anything from me because I didn't have anything to begin with. I was still in the hospital, not in a new barracks facing more punishment. I breathed a sigh of relief.

Outside, the weather has been getting colder, with an overcast sky and occasional rain. The raindrops fall slowly from the roof, tapping gently on the window sill.

Physically, I'm OK, but I still feel weak in the mornings. It has been a struggle to move my legs. Most of the time, I lie in bed and only get up when necessary, without much enthusiasm. Even watching soccer from a bench becomes a small torment, but I can endure it for an hour and a half. Such events don't come around every day, or even every year. My chest bothers me constantly. Lying on my left side is uncomfortable—it feels like something's pressing down on me—so I've switched to lying on my right side or back. But these are minor issues, at least for now.

Two prisoners are shuffling around the hospital, a couple of nail-swallowers. One of them is a *kozel,* who worked as a supply manager and was doing well by local standards. But then he made a big mistake, so the police stripped him of his privileges and began to coerce him to start working in the operational unit. To get out of this situation, he swallowed a screw and landed at the med point. But the screw soon stood upright in his intestines, and he underwent surgery at the city hospital.

Now he walks around pressing his hand to his mended stomach and reflects on his future fate. The second prisoner is a *muzhik* and an Uzbek Muslim. He seems quiet and non-aggressive at first glance but has his own set of cockroaches in his head. When he arrived at the colony three years ago, he got an overly rough welcome at the "reception,"* so now he walks with a limp and he'll be crippled for the rest of his life. Deep down in his heart, he hates the police because he feels that they, along with the "activists," singled him out more than the others, though that wasn't the case. But he had his own perspective. He believed that he wasn't allowed to perform his religious rites correctly in the residential zone of the colony, so he thought of how to land himself "under the roof"—in a strict regime punishment unit for repeat offenders who disrupt the established order of serving time.

The repeat offenders, mostly his Muslim brothers, are kept there, and he thought that it would be easier for him. He was ready to stab one of the *kozly* at night or even attack a policeman, but he was repeatedly kept from doing it and dissuaded. He was ready for this because he was imprisoned for slaughtering a man on the outside. Silent waters run deep, as they say . . . Then he decided to take the path of self-mutilation and swallowed three nails at once. They wandered somewhere in the depths of his intestines and scratched at the walls, but so far, they have had no intention of coming out. He also refused to have them removed surgically, so he drags himself around the med point, not complaining, but suffering greatly. It was unclear what to do next. The doctor gave up on him a long time ago, considering him a lost cause.

But I get along with him fine. I just remind myself that trying to make sense of the darkness in someone else's soul is a

---

* A "reception" is when prison guards line up on both sides with batons and stun guns to "welcome" new inmates.

waste of time. People tend to do what they think is best, and they usually believe they're right. This is often what leads to conflicts between people.

I'm no exception. I also make decisions based on what I believe is right. Life has taught me that I'm not always right in my judgments. In recent years, I've tried to steer clear of conflicts, not because I'm afraid, but because they often serve no purpose. When I can't avoid a conflict, I always aim to take the side of truth.

Lying under the IV drip today, I saw my hand as if from the outside. It had dried up like an old man's, and the skin became very wrinkled and dry. The palm itself seemed to have decreased in size, and somehow all the bones, joints, and tendons were bulging out. It felt like it wasn't my hand, an impression that caught my attention.

Later in the evening, I plan to go to the shower to see the crazy-eyed old man who lives in the misty mirror there.

I spent some time rereading the letters from yesterday and responded to a few of them. Some of the letters were not meant to be replied to, simply containing words of encouragement mixed with subtle hints to stop my hunger strike. There were also more direct appeals not to harm myself. There were both handwritten letters and printed-out emails, and the sender could request a response to be written on a separate sheet and delivered within a couple of days. It's a convenient system, even though it takes longer than regular emails, which provide near-instant feedback. Still, it's much faster and more reliable than traditional letters, which can take months and often get lost.

This time, I replied to friends and acquaintances, including two from Crimea. They no longer supported my hunger strike and instead discouraged me, emphasizing the importance of my children. But they didn't support the Maidan either, even though they were undoubtedly on my side. I didn't appreciate them relying on the children as an argument. It made it look like I had a simple choice—either continue my hunger strike or return home to my children. From their perspective, I was stubborn and proud, so I'd chosen the hunger strike over being with my children. I tried to explain all this to them in my responses.

Receiving letters can be quite interesting, like corresponding with aliens or the spirit world. Everything is so different, considering how they live and where I am now. Some letters leave you unsure of how to respond. For instance, in one recent letter, I was told not to demand anything from Vladimir Vladimirovich Putin because he was God incarnate on Earth, and one should only make requests to God. Thankfully, the author didn't suggest praying. What's most important to note was that it wasn't meant as a joke. As I read the whole letter, I realized it was a form of insanity.

Today, me and the other guys watched two exciting matches that were quite similar. In both, the favorites of their groups faced off against the middle-of-the-road teams. The favorites had a tough time scoring despite their constant attacks, while the middle-of-the-road teams held their ground admirably, occasionally scoring as well. Australia had a bit less luck and ultimately lost to France with a score of 1–2. The heroic Iceland managed to hold its own against Argentina, led by the brilliant

Messi, to a 1–1 draw. Messi didn't perform well, to the point of missing a penalty.

In these matches, I found myself rooting for the weaker teams more, but overall, I'm a fan of good soccer. The official video replay and goal-line technology work well when the referees choose to use them. We're definitely in the twenty-first century.

The championship has been proceeding well, with beautiful and spectacular matches, but you can't shake the feeling of the 1937 Olympics in Nazi Germany. It's impossible to forget that unscrupulous individuals organized this event to conceal their crimes behind a colorful exterior, diverting the world's attention away from the fact that Crimea is occupied, there have been ten thousand casualties in Donbas, a downed Boeing, bombed-out Aleppo, and so much more. Watching the broadcasts evokes mixed emotions. If it's just about enjoying a match, it's more or less fine—it's soccer, after all. But when you tune into the news or hear the enthusiastic voices of sports commentators and paid announcers during breaks, you immediately feel sick. They all sound the same, delivering the false enthusiasm of Russian propaganda.

During the halftime break, we tuned into the news. They showed the Russian ombudswoman who was supposed to meet her Ukrainian counterpart and visit a Ukrainian inmate in the Omsk colony. But there was some misunderstanding, and they went their separate ways, much like friends parting ways in a park. The Ukrainian ombudswoman attempted to visit me, but she wasn't allowed in, while the Russian ombudswoman stood at the gates of the Omsk colony, expressing her bewilderment.

What stood out most was that she mentioned, without explicitly using the alarming word "exchange," that they planned to visit all Russian prisoners in Ukraine and Ukrainian prisoners in Russia, as per a list of thirty-two individuals. Regardless, this was a positive sign, and we'll see what happens next. One of these days, they'll probably come to see me, and maybe I'll learn more details.

Just before bedtime, it started raining, followed by a flash of lightning and distant thunder. Almost immediately, the lights went out at the med point. But that was alright because it was time to sleep anyway. It reminded me of a line from Yuri Shevchuk's song: "May thunder has struck . . . " Whether it's a month or even four years late, somewhere, the thunder is audible . . .

DAY THIRTY-FIVE

At night, I had two dreams. In one, I was at a funeral and placed a wreath into a large pile of flowers that had formed near the widow, who looked very much like the neighbor from my village street. Placing the wreath by the coffin seemed impossible, as there was already a whole mound of condolences—bouquets. The widow stood alone, quietly crying, and slightly hunched over. I pondered for a while whether it would be appropriate to give her money, and it seemed like I even took out a handful of small bills, but the dream ended there. Well, what inspired it was clear—there was a news story yesterday about saying farewell to Govorukhin.

The second dream was, as often happens, about prison. I was in a large cell with many people. The guard came in and ordered me to gather my belongings. I started getting ready quickly, not yet knowing if this was a transfer to another cell, a transfer to a different colony, or finally, my release. I didn't have many belongings—the longer you sit in prison, the less you need and the less you carry with you. My main burden was an archive of letters, books, and a stack of draft notebooks—the most valuable things I had. I could easily toss the second half-empty bag, containing the minimal necessities for an inmate, at any moment. But I didn't do that because the guards didn't inform me where they were taking me. Usually, they didn't even know; their task was to take me to the assembly box, and from there, other staff would take me further. I distributed some of my extra belongings among the other inmates. There's a tradition among convicts to be released without possessions, to give away everything, leaving things where they're needed since you're starting a new life. But since I didn't know where I was going, I didn't give everything away.

I woke up in my ward when the nurse brought the morning portion of the milky-chemical mixture. No one had the intention of releasing me or even giving the order to gather my belongings, of course—this dream came after yesterday's story about the lost ombudswomen. But I wasn't disappointed. I've been in prison for far too long, and this wasn't the first dream with such a plot; no need to take it to heart.

The nighttime rain stopped almost immediately, thunder and lightning were a one-time occurrence, and the electricity was restored.

The sun timidly peeked through the ragged clouds, and it even managed to dry the central pathway. They said it was fifteen degrees Celsius outside. I didn't believe those rumors, and I wouldn't have given it more than ten degrees judging by the inmates moving in their gray formation down the alley.

My condition has been more or less stable today. My cold is starting to pass, leaving only a lingering cough as a rearguard action. However, the itching has now spread almost all over my body, despite yesterday's wash, and it has been bothering me. It must be the medication. For the past four weeks, they've been continuously pumping various fluids into me. I know I wouldn't have lasted this long without them, though.

I didn't have much energy in the morning. I sat on the bed for a long time before gathering my things to get dressed and go to the washroom.

It seems to me that people often lack self-confidence in this life. That's why they seek it externally in religion, superstitions, horoscopes, divinations, prophetic dreams, advice from psychologists, or acquaintances. Why don't people want to turn inward and draw strength from themselves? A person can make themself strong, not only physically, but spiritually. These things can be "acquired" within oneself, just as you can build muscles or learn boxing techniques. I remember myself from childhood and adolescence, how weak and frail I was, both outwardly and inwardly. I can't recall exactly what motivated me and at what age it happened, but eventually, I understood that I needed to change myself and improve.

I read one of Dale Carnegie's self-help books when I was around twelve or thirteen years old. At that time, I felt I could never become like the people he talked about. One of the most influential forces during that period was Viktor Tsoi's music, especially his song "Mama, We've All Gone Nuts," where he sings: "What will thousands of words be worth when the strength of your arm is important? And there you stand on the shore and wonder, to swim or not to swim."

That song motivated me to make up my mind—I would swim. After a serious childhood illness, I was told not to engage in physical exercise. But I did anyway. I began with running, then moved on to push-ups, dumbbells, pull-ups, and more. I wasn't fond of my personal qualities either. In fact, I almost despised them. I felt weak, sensitive, and shy, among other things. So, I took a piece of paper and made two columns— one for what I needed to get rid of and the other for what I wanted to acquire. Nearly thirty years have passed since then, and I can't recall exactly what I wrote on that paper because there were more lists to follow in the years that came when my aspirations began to take shape.

I stopped taking notes since then, but I've always kept my goals in mind. I've never stopped working on myself, not even for a single day. Even now, there are moments I'd like to improve and things to add or learn. Perfection may be unattainable, but it's essential to keep striving for it. I can't quantify how much I've improved over the years, but I've realized one thing: if you can envision your goal and are willing to do whatever it takes, you will inevitably achieve it sooner or later.

I've been talking less with the doctor lately, but not because our relationship has soured. It's simply because I spend most of my time in my ward under the IV drip, and that's where I do most of my activities. The doctor stops by occasionally to check on me and have a brief chat. He's got a lot of work to do, especially with another big medical commission coming next week that he needs to prepare for. As for me, I only go to his office when there's a specific matter to discuss. I don't like to bother people unnecessarily, and I'm not a fan of idle conversations just for the sake of talking. I wonder if that's a good quality or a bad one?

My veins have started to tire and rupture under the strain of daily IV drips once again. Today, they let the medication flow twice via different arms, and it went under the skin, forming solid bumps. Now I need to monitor this process carefully. I might have to switch back to catheters again to give my veins a chance to recover.

Today, the man with the freshly dyed mustache came again, the one who pretends to be a human rights official. He brought along a small group of local and administrative leaders who acted as his entourage. He exchanged pleasantries with everyone and then eventually came to see me. I happened to be lying under an IV drip, so he didn't miss the chance to showcase his limited knowledge of medicine, revealing his ignorance. Toward the end of his—this time, much to everyone's delight—brief visit, he asked, perhaps out of formality, if I had changed my mind about the hunger strike or had any questions for him. I replied that my stance remained unchanged and I wouldn't abandon the hunger strike.

Though I did have one question: What rank had he retired with? After a moment of hesitation, he said he was a retired colonel from the Prosecutor's Office and a major general of justice in a similar capacity. As he finished speaking, it appeared he wanted to convey his pride in these achievements, but he also sensed some hidden motive. I informed him that I had no further questions for him in that case, and he left the room deep in thought. How could someone who spent their entire career sending people to prison suddenly retire and advocate for their rights? Who was he trying to fool?

It's not an isolated case, either. In Russia, most of the so-called human rights officials are like this, including a certain ombudswoman who looked bewildered standing near the fence of the Omsk detention center yesterday.

DAY THIRTY-SIX

The weather has finally warmed up. Yesterday, the sun provided some nice warmth all afternoon, continuing into the morning. The inmates, who usually lined up along the path for the morning check, were finally able to shed their winter coats. Not because they wanted to but because they were ordered to. Everything here happens according to orders.

In that sense, the med point is like an oasis of idleness in this regime-regulated place. Roll call lasts only a few minutes in the hallway, not an hour outside. The guards don't punish you for a button left unbuttoned somewhere on your sleeve. They often check on me or take care of things right by my bedside—either I'm on an IV drip, or they're performing some other medical procedure, or they simply don't disturb a hunger striker lying down. It's like a prison paradise.

Yesterday, instead of watching Kiselyov's regularly scheduled spectacle, we enjoyed some evening soccer. There were two fantastic and quite similar matches where the underdog teams put up a strong fight against the favorites. Switzerland managed to secure a draw against Brazil with a score of 1–1. Despite Brazil's star-studded team and their usual flair in attack, the five-time world champions couldn't break through the stubborn Swiss guards. The superstar Neymar spent much of the match on the ground and the rest hobbling around the field due to rough tackles that prevented him from showcasing his skills. The referees in this championship have been allowing a more physical style of play, resembling the English style, with fewer whistles, which makes the matches more interesting. Meanwhile, the reigning champions, Germany, struggled in the first half and even conceded a goal to Mexico, who played exceptionally well. In the second half, the Germans practically camped in the Mexican penalty area, but it wasn't enough as they lost 0–1, marking the first major upset in the tournament.

My overall condition is stable, and the test results seem somewhat promising, but I sense my strength diminishing with each passing day. Yesterday, I could barely stay awake until the end of the broadcast and had to crawl into bed. A persistent cough started right in bed and lingered for a while.

My mind is starting to become sluggish, I forget things, and I double-check tasks several times when my confidence wavers. I understand it's because my brain, like my heart, is slowly slowing down due to the lack of nutrients.

The doctor explained that these two vital organs didn't have their own nutrient supply, so they suffered the most during starvation. But that's OK—let them suffer for now.

I managed to sleep a bit longer today and felt more refreshed when I woke up. There was a slight energy boost in my veins for the first hour or two. It's still a blessing to have a decent night's sleep and feel a little invigorated at the start of the day. But after lunch, my energy level depleted rapidly, and all I wanted was to lie down. It was even challenging to write or muster the desire to read.

But I must endure and not fall apart—I don't have the luxury of giving up.

The past week, the fifth one, passed without any significant events. That's both good and bad. Good because nothing critical happened, but bad because I needed progress. Now, the sixth week has begun, and according to my calculations, it should be a crucial one. It doesn't seem like it will be decisive, though. This means I'll have to hold out beyond the fortieth day. I hope something changes out there, and the situation doesn't remain deadlocked. In that case, there will only be one option—I'll have to open the Kingston valves.

Outside the window, the clouds arrived from all directions, dispersing the timid beginnings of summer, much like a police rally.

Today, they inserted a catheter and administered a drip through it, but it hurt quite a bit, as all punctured veins tend to after this much time and under such stress.

I read an excellent article about Zinedine Zidane in *Novaya Gazeta*. I've never had idols I wanted to imitate or be like, except maybe in childhood, when it was to be expected. I've never envied anyone. I've only celebrated other people's successes and major victories, knowing how challenging they must have been, which motivates me. Zidane always left a deep impression on me—his game, achievements, conduct, and his genuine demeanor as a man. He's forty-one years old and has accomplished everything, including becoming a world champion and a millionaire.

He's the coach of the team that, under his guidance, won the Champions League three consecutive times. And now he's leaving the team at the height of their fame. Just like that time in his final match when he headbutted his Italian opponent, received a red card, and left his team to face defeat. Honor meant more to him than victory.

Now, life holds more value than staying at the pinnacle of success. That might be the only way to go—leave at the peak because from there it's only downward. You shouldn't cling to an elusive pedestal with your ski poles, waiting for new champions to force you into retirement, like the great Bjørndalen did. You must choose to leave yourself. And Zidane made his choice. He's not going anywhere in particular—just to live his life. He deserves esteem and respect.

We're the same age. I'm also forty-one. But I don't have anything—no achievements, no money, just a twenty-year prison sentence. By this age, he'd accomplished everything and was free to go. Cheers to you, Zidane! Shame on you, Sentsov! I haven't achieved anything, and I can't even go anywhere. There are bars, fences, and the threat of being shot if I attempt to escape. If I'm lucky, I still have accomplishments left in me, if I'm fortunate enough and have enough time, I mean. If I fail, this journey might end quickly here in Labytnangi, or it could be a long one, but if I give this hunger strike up, I'm still stuck here . . . While I've been marking time for forty years, Zidane has achieved everything and can now be free.

DAY THIRTY-SEVEN

I dreamed that I'd been transferred to Lefortovo Prison with a group of inmates, and there, in the assembly area, a small vestibule housed a snack bar with chocolate bars, packs of cookies, and other food items placed on a small table. The inmates had enough cash to buy these items, though strangely enough, only in hundred-hryvnia notes. But they ultimately couldn't make a purchase because the vendor had no change. Then, a familiar guy from the colony's prison block who had been taken away to a tuberculosis hospital approached me and asked if I'd brought the cargo for him: some trail mix. Surprised, I answered that no, I didn't know anything about it, and I had eaten the mix long ago. It was a typically illogical dream, as most dreams in prison settings tend to be (the majority of inmates' dreams take place there).

The weather has deteriorated completely—clouds, wind, rain. A typical northern autumnal summer. My well-being matches it.

Yesterday evening was particularly bad. I could hardly watch the soccer match, but lying down in this state was even worse. My cough has been bothering me pretty badly in the evenings now, especially when lying down. I tried to distract myself by watching evening matches, and then immediately went to bed as if sinking into a dark pit.

My morning vigor has also disappeared. Now, the first half of the day goes by in a "more or less" state, and the second half is between "so-so" and "poor," gradually worsening toward evening.

Nowadays, I mostly write in my diary during the first half of the day, but then I lack both the energy and the desire, so I sometimes describe events after a bit of a delay.

Yesterday, I struggled for a long time to fall asleep. My cough wouldn't let up, and my heart was pounding as if I had sprinted up to the ninth floor and struggled to catch my breath, despite the fact that my only physical exertion before bed was brushing my teeth. No matter how often I brushed them—like my tongue, which was still white as before—the unpleasant taste of acetone and some other foulness from my mouth didn't subside. Well, that was understandable, as its source wasn't the mouth. I looked at myself carefully in the mirror. I had conjunctivitis again, but it was affecting both eyes at once. I looked like a vampire: pale and gaunt, with red veins in the whites of my eyes and an unhealthy sheen to my pupils.

Today, during the IV drip, I didn't have the strength to call out loudly to the orderlies passing in the corridor to ask them to summon the nurse to change the solution bottles. A total weakness had set in, affecting even my voice. Movements and even conversations were difficult. This all crept in gradually and somewhat unnoticed over the past three days. The doctor confirmed my condition with the most recent test results. Everything was plummeting, especially the protein levels in my blood that should fuel energy and life.

But I understood this today, even without his input: the anticipated second crisis wave has finally arrived. Not abruptly this time, but gradually—unstoppably gaining momentum.

When the doctor went through the test results and EKG readings, his hands were shaking, just like last time. The EKG

didn't show anything promising—ischemia and oxygen deprivation to the heart had intensified. I was slowly but surely
crawling toward the edge again. The doctor wasn't very keen
on taking me back to the city hospital. I fully supported him in
this. They wouldn't tell me anything new with their perpetually
annoyed professional voices. All that awaited me there was the
intensive care unit, a bed with straps and tubes delivering the
mixture into every corner, not to mention their magical drips.
But the issue was that the mixture couldn't work its magic anymore, as they had warned. I had been on it for ten days, but now
it wasn't enough. Especially since, as the doctor said, the only
pharmacy that had it had run out, and nobody knew when the
next delivery from the mainland would arrive. The remaining
supply would only last until the end of this week.

But I had never believed that this week would be decisive.
In any case, I persuaded the doctor to wait it out. He wasn't sure
if I could endure it properly. He was no longer hinting but suggesting and even insisting that I incorporate some food into my
diet. I declined again because that wouldn't be a hunger strike
anymore; it would be deceit. The doctor was concerned that,
due to the medical commission that had come yesterday, which
would require him to run around the whole administration, he
wouldn't have time for me, and might lose me. I encouraged
him and told him I would try not to go toward the light in his
absence. I left the office. As I closed the door, I saw the doctor
lighting a cigarette.

Soccer is a welcome relief here. Watching the matches
helps pass the time and keeps my mind occupied. My days in
prison have been far from dull, but a little variety doesn't hurt.

Yesterday, there were three matches. I caught bits of the first two, but they weren't very exciting. Sweden and Belgium handled their weaker opponents with varying degrees of success. The last game was England vs. Tunisia. The north African team was decent, and it was interesting to see how the English performed.

They brought a strong squad for the first time in years and had high hopes for a top placement, if not winning the championship outright. Their players were genuinely talented, but their teamwork left room for improvement.

They had more missed scoring opportunities than anyone else in yesterday's matches. After numerous lackluster attacks and one goal, it seemed like they might have been in for a landslide victory. Tunisia held their own and responded with a penalty goal. The game seemed headed for a draw as England lost momentum in the second half. They only managed to score again in added time, ending with a 2–1 win. The Spanish team stood out the most at the end of the first round.

But the World Cup is a month-long marathon, and often, the initial frontrunners lose steam by the end, while the teams that might have seemed clumsy and inexperienced at first gradually improve from game to game and clinch medals. That's what makes the global championship so interesting. We'll see how the rest of it unfolds. I just hope I can continue watching it. I doubt there will be a TV in the intensive care unit. There certainly won't be one in the morgue.

Two

Two

DAY THIRTY-EIGHT

THE WEATHER IS GETTING WORSE. It's cold, and it looks like it's going to snow. But the inmates wandering down the alley haven't put their winter coats back on just yet.

My condition has somewhat stabilized, but I'll have to wait and see what the upcoming test results reveal.

Yesterday, after dinner, I found the strength to write a story. It was like settling an old debt. It was a story I'd started back in the Yakutsk camp for a collection about prison. Here in Labytnangi, two more ideas came to me. I wrote one almost immediately, but procrastinated with the second.

It wasn't fully developed yet, and I've always preferred writing about events with some time and distance once the initial emotions have cooled. This approach has helped sift out unnecessary, empty, and weak ideas over the months and years, leaving the strongest and most potent ones to mature and gain depth. It helped me choose the most important topics and let me write about them more objectively, especially when it was personal.

Memories tend to become polished and embellished over time, but this approach has always felt more authentic. I often let an idea roll around in my head for years, like a scarab pushing its ball, without making any writings or notes. Then, when the time was right, I'd write a script or something else over the course of a week or two.

Recently, I've become more efficient: I write a lot, fearing I might forget some details. I make rough notes for future use, and I've trained myself to work in the morning, not just relying on sporadic nighttime bursts of inspiration. The gap between an event or a new idea and the appearance of the first draft, which often remains close to the final version, has also shortened from years to months or weeks.

I always let the material settle in my mind, cool down, and germinate. I only picked up the pen when the seeds that had sunk into my soul began to sprout. My method could be summarized like this: think long, write fast, and edit little. I edited sparingly, not because I was lazy—hardly anyone could accuse me of that—but because I wanted to preserve the sincerity of my initial creative impulse and words. I would leave some roughness in the text, even some imperfections, so it all served one purpose—the truth. As my colleague Zhenya used to say, "The first thought comes from God."

But lately, even in captivity, where I've also done some writing, I've paid more attention to editing and improving a text while trying not to dilute that initial impulse. It's like carefully weeding a flower bed to remove weak shoots and weeds. I've been pleased with the results and intend to refine this approach further.

The collection of prison stories I've been working on follows my usual method. But the last story remains unfinished.

I procrastinated, waiting for the right inspiration. I believe it's better not to write than to do so half-heartedly. "If you don't feel the urge to write, then don't bother" has been one of my main principles in literature. But this unfinished story hung over me, so I forced myself to complete it yesterday. It turned out poorly—sometimes the first pancake comes out lumpy, and this was as lumpy as it got. I've already compromised the idea, as I never rewrite a text from scratch on a second attempt. It's better to set it aside for a long time or, as they say, "throw it behind the stove." I've never actually thrown any texts into the stove—I'm not one for dramatic gestures. But this time, I fired an empty bullet. Once again, I've seen the unfortunate consequences of straying from one's principles, both in life and in literature.

They took me to the laboratory on the first floor to conduct some tests. It happens every other day. The elderly laboratory assistant, who, according to the doctor, has been working here longer than we've been alive, was a kind woman with curly white hair. I just noticed today that the same radio is always playing in her office, spouting out *chansons*. The colony's atmosphere affects even such peaceful-looking grandmothers and their musical tastes.

There were two exciting soccer matches yesterday in a group without a clear favorite. These teams were of average skill level, promising a real competition, and that's precisely what we got. In both games, the so-called weaker teams triumphed over the stronger ones: Japan defeated Cameroon, and Senegal secured a victory against Poland. Both matches ended with the same score, 2–1.

The trend of weaker teams achieving victory or at least a hard-fought draw has remained a defining feature of this championship, making it particularly interesting. It's part of a broader trend where the talent level among national teams worldwide is becoming more balanced. While the gap between the top teams and the underdogs remains significant, it's no longer as stark as it once was. There's now a substantial group of mid-level teams that can challenge anyone, regardless of their reputation. This dynamic makes nearly every match more exciting.

Yesterday's match of the day featured the Russian and Egyptian national teams. The outcome of this game determined whether Russia would advance from the group stage. Many, including myself, wondered if their earlier 5–0 victory over the Saudi team had been a fluke. It hadn't. Despite some flaws, the Russian team put on another solid performance, winning 3–1. Egypt scored only through a penalty kick. So, for the first time in thirty-two years, Russia advanced to the championship playoffs.

The TV broadcasts have been buzzing about it. Suddenly, every pundit considers themselves a soccer expert. Where were these expert voices in the years when the Russian people were being inundated with narratives about Western conspiracies and Ukrainian "fascists"? It seems this country only recognizes the importance of sports, especially on the home turf or during Olympic events. But why doesn't this nation want to foster international friendships through sports instead of relying solely on tanks? Suppression, whether through gas, nuclear threats, or soccer, seems to be the hallmark of Russian policy, and it enjoys enthusiastic support from most of the population.

This happens even while the state claims to pursue a peaceful agenda. A quick look at the map reveals this is not true: bloodshed, land grabs, and the need to crush opponents are deeply ingrained in this country.

Once again, the colony authorities, headed by the mustached commissioner, paid a visit. He claimed to be here for other camp-related matters but avoided admitting that monitoring me was part of his assignment. He has constantly repeated this cover story that he was just passing by. Today, it hit me who he reminds me of—a retired sergeant from an over-the-top vaudeville act. The Mustache paraded through my room, inspected the solution I was being administered, and asked me four times how I felt. After hearing "I'm OK" for the fourth time, the Mustache tried to steer the conversation in a new direction. Upon spotting Lem's book on my bedside table, he eagerly inquired, "What are you reading?" He glanced at the book's title on the cover and triumphantly proclaimed: "*Solaris* . . . Philosophy . . . "

I corrected him, saying, "Actually, it's science fiction." The Mustache promptly abandoned the literary debate, realizing his strengths were in medicine and human rights, though I'd argue it's mostly marching in goosesteps. Then, the non-commissioned officer noticed the absence of a toilet bowl in my room and asked if I used the toilet. Some questions leave you utterly speechless. Did he think that because I'm not eating, I don't need to? I explained that I drink three to four liters of water daily, and there is a restroom in the hospital, just not in my room. The Mustache nodded approvingly. Next, the appointed official mentioned that the Ukrainian ombudswoman had requested my photo. He theatrically patted his pockets, indicating his mobile phone had been confiscated at the colony entrance. When I suggested asking the colony authorities to take a picture for him, he flinched, mimicking Pierrot the clown's gestures, and claimed he couldn't do that—it wasn't within his authority.

The officials lingered for a couple of minutes longer. They gathered around my bed on both sides and began to insist that I had already achieved my goal, and my case was resonating at the government level, so it was time to stop harming my health and start eating porridge. I said I wasn't a child who needed convincing to eat. They retorted that they were adults, too, and weren't trying to persuade anyone. After that, they left the room, departing in an orderly fashion, according to their ranks and positions.

Last night, as I was drifting off to sleep, I decided to count the number of days I'd been in prison. It added up to precisely fifteen hundred days. I couldn't help but smile at such a round number, yet at the same time, I felt a sense of dread—what a grim milestone.

Sometimes, I involuntarily shudder when I realize just how long I've been incarcerated.

DAY THIRTY-NINE

I had a dream last night that I'd joined the *kozly*. I don't remember the reasons or details, just the fact of changing sides. I woke up sweating but immediately breathed a sigh of relief—it was just a dream, and I remained in the decent crowd. The *muzhiki* wouldn't have approved of such an action on my part.

From the outside, it might seem that all inmates are the same, given that they wear the same uniform, but in reality their world is much more complex and highly differentiated. It's just that all of this is hidden, and an outsider can't pick up on it.

It's rainy and damp outside, though there's no wind or extreme cold.

This morning I felt normal—better than during the previous days. Probably because I'd had a good rest, and I stayed in bed until the 9:00 AM morning check, with breaks and interruptions for the required morning activities, of course. But then I fell asleep again. I really need more sleep—my body can't stay awake as much as when I'm starving. In a state of anabiosis, it's calmer. The itching has almost gone away just as suddenly as it appeared, leaving behind only a slight unpleasant sensation. Yesterday evening, my cough wouldn't let up again, making it difficult to watch soccer and fall asleep.

It was a dry, persistent cough. The doctor didn't like it. He was concerned that I might catch an illness because treating my weakened body for any virus or even strep throat would be problematic. I told him I'd try not to catch anything, but I couldn't promise. He asked me to drink less water: my protein levels were dropping significantly, my kidneys were clogging up and struggling, and he was worried that water might start accumulating in my body's internal cavities, which would be very bad. I gladly reduced my water intake from four/four and a half to three liters.

Maybe I'll stop feeling like a gurgling bubble and shed that water weight. Today, the scale showed seventy-seven point five kilograms, even though I didn't look heavier.

Yesterday, the doctor came to work after lunch, along with the Moscow inspector from the comprehensive medical commission. She's from the Federal Penitentiary Service's medical team at the Main Directorate. She'll be here until the end of the week. During our meeting, she seemed knowledgeable and rational despite the authoritative tone of her voice. At the request of her superiors, she naturally focused on communicating with me and reviewing my medical records.

Taking a fresh perspective on my situation, she seemed generally satisfied with how I appeared for such a period and how the doctor had managed to maintain my condition. But she was deeply concerned about my heart and kidneys, more so the latter.

This looming second crisis has spread like butter on bread, and I'm slowly sliding toward the edge. A sudden drop with the failure of one or the other organ, or perhaps all at once, is inevitable. Predicting when this unfortunate event will occur is impossible—one can only say that it's inevitable, along with its fatal consequences.

I'm not afraid of all these warnings because I've been hearing them for the past two months. Besides, it's the truth. I fully understand all of this. But I won't back down, as I told the colonel. She replied that she couldn't dissuade me, then embarked on a lengthy monologue, repeating, "We're all adults here" about ten times. I heard the same thing from other officials today, and that the nutrient mix didn't compensate for a lack of eating. She mentioned dried apricots with honey twice, claiming that eating it wouldn't violate my political hunger strike. It would just help preserve my heart or at least my kidneys because, as we all knew, dried apricots with honey were beyond politics. I politely declined her proposed menu, stating that my heart and kidneys were on the platter of revolutionary struggle and I wasn't entitled to remove them. With that, we bid each other farewell, wishing each other health and success.

Later, I ran into the doctor in our hospital washroom. He went there to smoke since he didn't dare do it in his office, which the inspector occupied. Despite being worn out by this medical commission, the doctor was in a good mood. I told him about the Mustache's visit, which amused him even more. Then I warned him that the ombudswoman planned to send an independent medical commission. I learned about this from today's operetta-style general. The latter bit of information disappointed the doctor. He found it entirely unnecessary, as did I. I've said so many times that I was under good medical supervision, but people from the outside often seem to think that they know better regarding what I need.

I'm already tired of fighting this battle, explaining that if I need something, I'll ask for it when the time comes. Unnecessary fuss and empty activities aren't needed—sometimes they can even be harmful. They don't understand how delicately things are arranged here. Well, never mind, I understand that they all worry about me a lot, sometimes too much. They want to demonstrate maximum attention and concern, but sometimes, it's just to show off to others. If my lawyer comes at the end of this week, as planned, I'll try to convey through him the uselessness of such a medical commission.

Meanwhile, my life in the prison hospital has gradually settled into a routine so that I spend the entire day on autopilot, and it's pretty convenient—wake up, breakfast ceremonially presented on a tray documented by the duty nurse with the video recorder, supplement mixture, medications, examination, data measurements, analyses, IV drips, reading, lunch ceremonially presented in the same manner, measurements, supplement mixture, journaling, rest, news, dinner ceremonially presented in the same manner, soccer, nutritional mixture, lights out. During breaks, I go to the toilet and the washbasin twice a week for a shower. That's all. Well, the highlight and variety of the day, of course, involve interaction with the doctor, but lately, less frequently and mostly only for specific matters. The least enjoyable part of the day has been visits from the prison supervisors.

Once again, a colonel from the administration paid a visit today, accompanied by a whole entourage. He seemed somehow new, as I didn't recognize him. Dealing with local authorities, even beyond this month, has felt like a never-ending parade of officials that just won't stop. Right off the bat, this one started scrutinizing my routine, asking why I wasn't clean-shaven, why I was wearing a sweater instead of the customary robe, and so on. He probably would have asked why I was lying down, but he saw the IV stand. Then he brightened up a bit, inquired about my pre-incarceration occupation, and mentioned to someone nearby that they needed to find a spot for me. It was as if he had stumbled upon a stray puppy in the street. The local boss chimed in, mentioning various opportunities for me to apply my directorial talents: in a club, on the colony's cable TV channel, or even in a computer class. Everyone seemed surprised I declined these seemingly alluring positions that any of the *kozly* would go for. I told them they shouldn't count on me to enhance the local amateur scene. The colonel gave a slight chuckle, referred to me as a "young man" twice, then discovered I was already forty-two, chuckled again, and departed. They all exited just as they entered, in formation and with a strict sense of hierarchy.

I'm surprised that despite my current thinness, deepened wrinkles, and growing gray hair, people still perceive me as much younger than I actually am. In this camp, they typically shave it down to a buzz cut every couple of weeks without considering your preference. Taking advantage of my current state, I haven't cut mine for a month and a half. It has grown a bit, but that hasn't made it better. The bald spot that began on my forehead may be out of sight, but now I've discovered that more than half of my hair is already gray. I started graying quite early. The first white hairs appeared around my twenties, and their number gradually increased as I progressed through life's interesting and not-so-interesting events.

Due to recent years' events, the gray hairs have chosen to launch a determined offensive and have almost gained control over the majority of my scalp. I saw the wretched old man in the mirror yesterday with his gray tufts, and he looked even worse than usual. Even the doctor noticed it, so they'll call in the local camp barber for my next bath to give me a camp-style haircut.

Seems like that style will stay with me even on the outside. But that's not a problem. I've always sported short hairstyles, and I'm ready to leave my old hairstyle as a memory of prison—as long as I can get out of here.

According to the rules of the colonies, female staff must

always be accompanied by a guard when in contact with the inmates. This applies to the medical personnel as well. This requirement isn't as strictly enforced here because it's something of an oasis, but since I'm in a ward under the watchful eye of two surveillance cameras, everything that happens around me follows a certain feng shui routine: there's the nurse with a syringe, and beside her, a staff member with a baton and an additional recorder, documenting every action.

The nurses come in different types as well. One rushes back and forth ten times to fetch everything needed for the IV drip. Even though it's always the same things required, she always manages to forget something. Another one pours so much alcohol onto the cotton ball that it could serve as an adequate hangover remedy. Then there's the perpetually sleepy male nurse who takes his time and moves so slowly that he often plugs the needle wound with a piece of dried-up cotton. But at least he's the only one among them who can insert a catheter professionally.

Today, the Dagestani bear was on duty again. After turning off the recorder following the official mealtime, he smiled at me as if he'd encountered a relative at a wedding. He inquired about how I was doing and bid me farewell with wishes for "strength, health, and luck." I suspect he has placed a bet on me at the bookmaker's and now awaits his winnings if I make it to the date he's counting on.

Yesterday, three interesting matches took place, but they all seemed almost identical. Uruguay, Portugal, and Spain defeated their weaker opponents in their respective groups with the same score of 1–0. Their less established adversaries were far from weak, though. They held their ground, launched danger-ous attacks, and came very close to securing the draws they needed. But they lacked the game-changing skill. Once again, I'm convinced of the gradual leveling of the playing field among teams and how intriguingly this championship is unfolding.

But the most important news of the day wasn't about that—more importantly, I received some letters. Not as many as before this time, but still quite a few. A couple of postcards from England, along with one from an acquaintance who seemed to be on vacation in Bulgaria, sharing the scent of the sea and the splashes of waves in her message. There were also a couple of printed-out emails from Ukraine and a letter from my mom.

I was hesitant to open her letter, afraid that she might judge me, reproach me, or plead with me to stop. I unfolded the small sheet; it seemed she didn't have enough paper for more. She wrote that everything was well with her and the kids. Though she didn't approve of what I was doing, she wrote that she sup-ported me and would always stand by my side because she believed in her son. A weight lifted off my chest. I'd been most worried about how my hunger strike would affect her health and well-being. But I have an amazing and incredibly strong mother. I wrote back to her, expressing my feelings and letting her know how much I loved her. It's a pity I didn't say these words to her earlier when I was still a free man—better late than never.

DAY FORTY

I woke up early today, at the usual wake-up time, and couldn't fall back asleep, so I was feeling a bit groggy this morning, but overall, doing fine. Outside, the sun was peeping through partially cloudy skies.

I've reached another benchmark—forty days. For some reason, I anticipated something significant to occur by this date; it felt like an important moment was on the horizon. This is probably how hope manages to live on, by setting the date of happiness and constantly, as it approaches, moving it to a later date.

However, "something like that" did happen yesterday. Toward evening, they called me to my lawyer, who arrived as promised. The censor had given him the letter for my mother after reading it, but I will find out about this later today when he comes to visit me again. He brought a lot of interesting news and letters, but he couldn't say anything specific about our situation because no official statements had been received from government officials, though there was a lot of behind-the-scenes movement about Ukrainian political prisoners and Ukraine as a whole. But still no results or announcements just yet.

I hope that all this stirring is not without reason and that such announcements will be made later on when everyone agrees with everyone about everything. I'm glad that even if I didn't initiate this new phase of change, then at least I contributed to it with my hunger strike.

The first letter was an official one from the president of Ukraine, written on a letterhead with the golden trident. He addressed me with beautiful words and heroic rhetoric, including a brief account of the efforts being made for my release, and wishes to see me soon. There wasn't any specific information, however. Either such information was truly unavailable or the situation hadn't progressed.

I didn't respond because I didn't have anything to say. Instead, I've been taking action. I hope he's doing the same, not just for me. Being selective and exclusive when it comes to releasing prisoners is a very unpleasant matter.

Then there were letters from friends. Some were from Kyiv and Crimea, from close individuals with whom I'd collaborated on my movie. The most unexpected, and therefore heartwarming, was a letter from Zhenya. She's my only friend and closest colleague, without whom my film wouldn't exist, or at least, it wouldn't be what it is today. We both have challenging personalities, and it was tough for us to connect at first. Once we did, we became inseparable.

She isn't involved in politics, so she hasn't written to me much these past few years, although she did attend my trial once in Moscow. Sometimes, when people are closest to each other, they find themselves in situations where words are hard to come by. The dearest people to me barely wrote during these past four years, but I understand and don't judge them at all. I'm deeply grateful for their silent support, as I feel that they haven't distanced themselves from me in the slightest. It's just that certain things are difficult to discuss, let alone put into writing, especially when they concern someone who holds a special place in your heart. Zhenya is one of those people.

The tone of her letter felt somewhat final as if it were a farewell. In response, I reassured her that I had no intentions of giving up yet. I simply intended to fight until the end, and that wasn't the same thing as dying. The risk of death loomed with the constant threat of kidney or heart failure, but that was the price of this endeavor, the ultimate goal of which was victory, no matter the cost.

Zhenya also wrote that she'd gotten married, had a daughter named Eva, and was happy. She resided in the Seychelles, where her husband, a doctor, had a two-year contract. I'm genuinely thrilled for her! I also know that if I manage to successfully escape from this place of voluntary sacrifice and return to filmmaking, she'll rush from the other side of the world to stand by my side. That's what true friends do.

I was surprised to learn from my lawyer that the money for his trips was being allocated not by the state of Ukraine but by Russian film directors—everyone chipped in. Shame on you, gentlemanly state officials! Thanks, fellow filmmakers!

Then my lawyer and I discussed other affairs—as always, in detail and to the point. I don't like empty talk and actions or making a fuss. My defender is the same and cheerful too. So I got very lucky with him. Thank you, Dima, for the work you do not only for me but the rest of the political prisoners you're trying to save from the jaws of this Moloch.

When returning from my meeting to the med point, I caught a glimpse of the *muzhiki* from my barrack, standing near our free-walking section. They were not afraid to greet me openly, which is always punished by the administration here. I greeted them back and saw on their faces not only support but also amazement—they hadn't seen me for a long time and felt uneasy at the sight of my very thin face.

Walking for a minute along the alley, accompanied by the on-duty officer, I realized that it was much warmer outside than it seemed to me from the ward window. I walked without a coat, and I was warm. "At home" I still shiver periodically—my body temperature has dropped during the hunger strike.

Yesterday they brought me several printed-out emails. I was especially pleased with one in which a woman said that she often photographed my portrait with the number of days of my hunger strike against the background of some monument to a famous Russian cultural figure, like Pushkin, Tolstoy, or Vysotsky . . . She believed all these people would support me if they were still alive. She even sent a photo of the seventeenth day against the background of the monument to Brodsky, I think. The quality of the image was poor. All this reminded me of the movie *Amélie*, where the main character's friend, who works as a flight attendant, flies around the world, photographs a garden gnome against the backdrop of various sights, and sends it to her.

The evening news reported yesterday that Poroshenko had called Putin again, after which he even convened his Security Council for a meeting. The theme was the same: Donbas, peacekeepers, the exchange of detainees. It's starting to look less and less like an empty bustle. Maybe this is what my intuition was waiting for. OK, let's try to live long enough to see. The key word here is "live."

Yesterday's matches were also good as expected, and they weren't even the main ones. But at this point in the tournament, each match is crucial. That's why each one has been such a struggle. Denmark drew with Australia 1–1, and the future of both teams is still uncertain. France narrowly defeated Peru 1–0, securing their spot in the playoffs, while the Peruvian team headed home. But the main event of the day was, of course, the

Argentina-Croatia game. Everyone knew that "the Croats were serious guys," but the Mighty God Messi played against them, and he was not alone. It was a very interesting match! Closer to the end, the more the Balkan guys pressed, the more Messi and his teammates looked helpless and were mostly playing defense. As a result, Croatia simply trampled them: 3–0. This was even more significant than Germany's loss in its first match. Germany still has opportunities to advance, unlike Argentina. Argentina's progression from the group stage is now uncertain, and it depends on factors beyond its control. Meanwhile, Croatia has rightfully secured its place in the playoffs.

Today, I finally finished reading Lem's science fiction collection. I liked his second novel, *Invincible*, even more, maybe because I knew the plot of *Solaris* beforehand and constantly compared it with Tarkovsky's film, to which the novel, in my opinion, was clearly inferior. Or maybe it's because there was more action than in the first novel, with four characters locked inside the station and their own inner struggles. The plot of *Invincible* also revolved around the idea of attempting to make contact with something alien, incomprehensible, and hostile. While *Solaris* explored contact with a living ocean, it was with evolved equipment on an abandoned planet that operated without thought, following its own aimless and reflexive set of laws. The central theme of the book was that "Not everything and not everywhere exists for us." All in all, it was a very engaging read.

I wonder if *Invincible* has been adapted into a film. If not, it seems ripe for a Hollywood treatment, and I'd love to see it on the big screen someday.

DAY FORTY-ONE

I woke up early again, but I felt rested. Probably because yesterday, after lunch, I was really tired and took a nap.

Throughout the night, I dreamed I was traveling somewhere in the *Stolypin* wagon, then in a train more resembling open railcars offering a good view of the passing forest, then the peacefully endless sea, distant skyscrapers glowing in the night, and finally, an airplane with its wings folded, taxiing on the airport runway. In one of the railcars, there was some girl with an unmemorable face in a checkered white shirt. All of this seemed more like a regular journey in a compartment with three fellow travelers. However, prison dreams are still prison dreams—even in them, you remember quite vividly that you're in captivity, and therefore, you don't feel entirely free. Unpleasant sensation, but I got used to it a long time ago.

The northern summer resembles a timid teenage spring. The sun shines and it's warm, but windy. It seems like the weather has reached a level of stability. It would have been that way if the wind hadn't suddenly intensified yesterday evening, rain clouds hadn't rolled in, and it hadn't cooled down to the point where they closed all the small windows in the room.

Despite the relative warmth, I still wear a sweater under my robe during the day, and I sleep in a warm jacket under two blankets. It doesn't seem as chilly, but it's not warm either. I've stopped using the heater.

My condition has also been "stable." In the morning, I didn't have a sudden surge of energy, but I felt decent, not too shaky. Weakness and fatigue have tended to pile up more toward the evening, but not as intensely as at the beginning of the week when I thought that a new crisis had begun. It turned out to be only a temporary dip. The visiting colonel, who looked at me for the second time yesterday, quickly pointed out that I shouldn't get too hopeful.

My body isn't adapting so much to negative changes as it's becoming accustomed to them and not reacting. I should be prepared for it to worsen at any moment. But the doctor and I are vigilant. Even without the colonel's reminder, I know that not everything is smooth sailing. The frequent heaviness in my heart and the slight but prickly sensation on my left side, along with the dull ache in my kidneys, prevent me from fully relaxing and convincing myself that everything is fine.

The colonel, along with the other members of the medical commission, is staying at the same hotel as my lawyer. He told me this yesterday when I visited him for a follow-up meeting, right before his departure. Both Dima and the officials "spotted" and identified each other, but they didn't engage in any contact. They only exchanged sidelong, unfriendly glances from across the hotel lobby. This encounter wasn't coincidental —Labytnangi's a small town.

This second conversation with my lawyer was also interesting and relevant to the case. I wrote a couple of business letters for acquaintances and friends, including an open letter to Russian directors who have supported me. He shared news, including everything he knew about our movement. It seemed that the movement was indeed significant, not subsiding, only gaining strength. It had even reached the head of the U.N., who made a statement about me and the other Ukrainian political prisoners and flew to Moscow yesterday—likely not specifically for our case, but hopefully it was related. The most important thing, the lawyer said, was that the recent month's surge in international pressure and attention on our prisoners happened thanks to my hunger strike, as interest in the topic had already started to fade before that.

I'm glad that my plan has been working so far, and that I calculated everything correctly, acting as a kind of catalyst for this process. The foundation for it was built up slowly, but there were no breakthroughs. Then I lit the match, and everything started happening. Now I just need to hold on a bit longer so that this dish gets fully cooked and try not to burn before it's done.

The letter to my mom was delivered to my lawyer by the police—that's the good news. The bad news was that my daughter couldn't go on her planned trip to Canada after doing well on her exams—no more precise information as to why. I was very disappointed because you shouldn't lie to your children or promise them something and not deliver. I've never acted like that, but it happened, and even though it wasn't my fault, I still blamed myself.

My lawyer and I agreed that he'd come back in a month, after his vacation, and my sister Natasha would come for a short visit in two weeks—if my heroic little sister would find the time for it, of course. She has already dedicated four years of her life to fighting for my release, and it has intensified sharply lately, entering the final stage. They're tearing her apart over it in Kyiv. She couldn't even find time to pass on the letter to my lawyer, only briefly summarizing the information from ten lines over the phone, adding that she didn't have time to write anything to Oleh at all because she was too busy with his matters, and hung up.

Poor little sister, I dragged her into this whirlwind! But it's OK, what matters to me more is the movement itself rather than the information about it. I'll find out everything later, although perhaps after victory, it won't matter anymore. The main thing is never to forget what this whole group of people has done for me, Natasha first and foremost.

Recently, an old man who has been in prison for so long that he went mad appeared. Ivanych. He was sentenced to twenty-five years, of which he'd already served eighteen.

You can see signs of a lobotomy on his bald head, and he walks with a shuffling gait, his lips making slurping sounds as he enjoys tea with bread. He's a frail but cheerful old man with a mind that's not entirely gone.

Yesterday, he pulled an interesting stunt. We were watching the evening soccer match. Nigeria was playing against Iceland. Ivanych watched, observed the African players running with the ball, and then asked: "And Nigeria—is that a capitalist country?"

"Ivanych, you old geezer, you're not in the '80s anymore, what's with the Soviet terminology?" I replied. "In Africa, they stopped pretending to be communists as soon as suitcases with money stopped coming from the Union."

"Well, maybe there are some persistent holdouts . . ."

But those "persistent" dark-skinned guys not only didn't know the term "socialist country" anymore—they'd also learned to play soccer, as they demonstrated in yesterday's match by defeating the Vikings 2–0 and practically dashing their hopes of getting into the playoffs, which had seemed so close.

Now Iceland needs to beat Croatia to have a chance, which is unlikely. Though Argentina's chances of advancing from the group have suddenly improved if, of course, they don't lose to Nigeria, that would be too much.

Switzerland, in turn, fought hard but secured their place in the championship's final stage by narrowly defeating Serbia 2–1 in a tense match. They conceded an early goal in the sixth minute and then endured what seemed like endless pressure from the Serbs. Toward the end of the second half, they managed to turn the game around, scoring two goals and rightfully claiming victory. This demonstrated the importance of giving your all until the end.

Even more dramatic was the match between Brazil and Costa Rica. Brazil was the clear favorite and Costa Rica seemed to be the doomed underdog, but the score remained 0–0 after ninety minutes. The Brazilians' nerves were fraying, they were receiving yellow cards left and right, and even the most well-paid player in soccer history, Neymar, resorted to deception. He dramatically fell in the opposing penalty area when a Costa Rican defender simply brushed against him.

Neymar collapsed, waving his hands as if he'd been shot, and the referee immediately awarded a penalty. Everyone started running and shouting; a scandal and a brawl started brewing rapidly. The referee, using video replays, radioed the main referee to inform him that things weren't as they seemed and rushed to the justice booth to personally review the fall.

Afterward, he returned to the field and reversed his initial decision to award a penalty. The game continued, the video replay system worked, and Neymar would be shamed for years to come. The referee didn't even give him a yellow card for it.

The Brazilian superstar received it a bit later, after slamming the ball to the ground with his hands in frustration at the sound of the whistle. It seemed like another scandal was about to happen. But in the additional six minutes of injury time, a miracle occurred. Or rather, even in the last four, which were worth watching this match for, and were perhaps even a reason to live for some people. The Brazilian team scored a beautiful goal and breathed a sigh of relief, along with millions of their fans, after which, relaxing, they demonstrated that high-class, flowing style of soccer that everyone loved them for. When the long-awaited ball hit the net, the entire substitute bench, led by the coach, rushed onto the field to embrace the team. The coach stumbled on the grass and rolled along seemingly endlessly. And no one doubted the sincerity of this fall. In the final seconds of this dramatic—in every sense—match Neymar managed to score a goal even more beautiful than the first and somewhat restore his reputation. When the final whistle blew, he sat in the center of the field, crying, covering his face with his hands, as if he had just simultaneously lost and won the final.

I'm very glad that such an exciting championship coincided with the difficult second half of my hunger strike—it was a great distraction. And I'm still able to separate pure sports from the dirty politics surrounding it.

DAY FORTY-TWO

Yesterday, after lunch, I started feeling pretty bad, and with each passing hour, it got worse. I experienced nausea, dizziness, and an overwhelming sense of weakness. By evening, they measured my blood pressure, and it was alarming. The upper reading was almost seventy, and the lower one was extremely low. They also conducted an EKG, which showed a heart rate of around forty beats per minute. It became evident why I felt so drained, but it didn't ease my discomfort. Things started to improve this morning, though I still had some lingering chest pain.

It's likely that my health has become sensitive to the weather after spending over two years in northern penal colonies. It's not so much due to the harsh climate itself, but its rapid and drastic changes. People with hypertension and heart conditions don't fare well here.

So, yesterday, as my health took a sudden downturn, summer also made an abrupt entrance in Labytnangi—a surprise attack similar to Germany's invasion of the Soviet Union. There was hardly any wind, and the sky was clear blue, with only a hint of white clouds. The sun was shining brightly, and the temperature soared to well over twenty degrees Celsius. I finally mustered the courage to take off my sweater and even slept with the window open, foregoing a warm jacket but still lying under two blankets. It was a real pleasure to sleep without extra layers, without shivering, and still get a good night's rest! Before drifting off, I felt a bit breathless, but I understood why—my heart wasn't in the best condition yesterday. Well, keep hanging in there, buddy.

The fear of getting cold and removing the sweater was mostly in my head. It reminded me of my time on the Maidan. When I returned to work at the headquarters after three intense days of clashes on the direct contact line, I wore a bulletproof vest for an entire week, taking it off only when I had a rare chance to sleep. It gave me a sense of security. It felt like we had won by then, and the danger of being shot at had diminished, but the constant feeling of peril still lingered. Eventually, it faded away, just like my hesitation to remove the sweater yesterday.

The doctor diagnosed me with conjunctivitis due to my persistently red eyes and prescribed eye drops. Another medical commission also visited me yesterday. This time, it was a public one, led by a timid and apprehensive young chairman, who was accompanied by camp authorities. He had visited me once before, right at the beginning, a fact he kept reminding me of. But I recognized him even without his reminder. He also proudly mentioned that he had received a new mandate, probably expecting some congratulations from me.

All I wanted to ask was, "Was this mandate issued in Smolny?" But I didn't say anything. This representative from the Public Monitoring Commission authorized to investigate confinement conditions with his new mandate seemed very anxious and kept walking somewhat sideways, as if he feared that the accompanying policemen would suddenly turn into guards, put him in a prisoner's uniform, and assign him a bunk in one of the barracks. He repeatedly asked if I had any questions for him, receiving none in response. With a sigh of relief and frequent glances back at his surroundings, as if he had just committed a theft, he left. Who could he protect or assist here? He looked like he needed some form of guardianship for himself, preferably armed protection. Another pointless formal visit.

Yesterday, it was haircut day at the med point, and a convict armed with clippers went about giving everyone a standard buzz cut without paying heed to personal preferences. Unlike the local bosses who had long stopped insisting that I should either trim my hair—which had grown back over the past month and a half—or at least shave, we political prisoners on hunger strikes were entitled to exceptions. I still couldn't get used to looking unkempt, so I sacrificed my gray curls to the clippers. I managed to shave myself, though.

It didn't do much to make the old man in the shower room mirror look any more attractive or younger—he appeared even more like a skeleton. He may have still been a walking skeleton, but at least he wasn't completely bedridden.

My condition is still far from stable today, but better than yesterday.

I didn't catch most of the matches and spent the day in bed. I later learned that Belgium and Mexico effortlessly defeated their opponents, securing their places in the playoffs. I only managed to watch the main game of the day, which could have been called "Germany trying to beat Sweden." The Germans dominated possession of the ball and controlled the game but struggled to score for the second consecutive match. After conceding a goal in the first half, they risked repeating their previous failure, as with the game against Mexico, and exiting the tournament in disgrace. The coach of the reigning champions seemed to age before our eyes as he watched his team's impotence. In the middle of the second half, after finally converting their tenth scoring opportunity, Germany equalized. But a draw wouldn't have been enough for them, as they needed a win to have any chance of advancing from the group. They stubbornly pressed forward, not giving up even after one of their midfielders received a second yellow card and was sent off. In response, the Bundesteam coach substituted another defender for a forward, signaling they were going all-in on the attack. The last ten minutes were filled with drama. While the Swedes clearly played for time, content with a draw, the ball stubbornly refused to find the back of the net, either hitting the post or getting caught by the goalkeeper's barely extended glove. It was only in the final fifth minute of added time that the soccer gods, having thoroughly tested the nerves of the German team and its fans, allowed their striker to score a decisive and beautiful goal from a last-minute free kick, seconds before the whistle. It was an incredible match, much like the entire championship. Just when you think you've already witnessed the best fight, the next day brings an even more impressive one.

At midnight, I went to the toilet. The window looked out onto the opposite side, where you could see the city, the forest, the distant mountains, and the sunset. I saw the midnight sun for the first time. It didn't quickly disappear behind the trees—it only hid for a short while, leaving the area in a soft twilight. Two hours later, it reappeared on the opposite side of the forest, marking the start of a long new day of the northern summer, which officially began yesterday.

DAY FORTY-THREE

I had a good night's sleep, and now I feel fine. By yesterday evening, I was really exhausted, but that has become routine. It's concerning when I can't even get up properly in the morning. The weather outside is warm and sunny, a beautiful day.

The sixth week of the hunger strike has ended, which, contrary to all expectations, hasn't brought any new or significant developments. Now, it's time to establish a new set of expectations. It's easier that way. When faced with a huge task that seems impossible to conquer, you break it down into small assignments, tackle them gradually and sequentially, and eventually achieve the desired outcome. A massive, seemingly immovable stone on the road is broken down into smaller pieces and moved one by one. You climb a tall mountain step by step to that little hill, that tree, that rock, until you find yourself at the summit. This method works for long prison sentences too, when you set yourself a nearest date to survive, to endure. Even if you understand that, most likely, by that date, nothing significant—let alone the main thing, release—will happen, you still set a little flag in front of you, in your immediate perspective. It's easier to exist in these small time intervals. You reach the end and set a new milestone . . . that's how it's been for the past four years.

My previous one was forty days—June twenty-third, the summer solstice, and all that. Nothing has changed, but it's not a big deal. We keep moving forward. Let's mark July thirteenth, my birthday, sixty days of fasting, the end of the World Cup, as a reassuring carabiner for climbers—we'll crawl toward that date over the abyss. Beyond that, it'll be difficult to predict anything both in terms of health and the entire situation surrounding Ukrainian political prisoners.

All of this increasingly reminds me of the old merry-go-rounds we used to ride on with the kids when we went to the city park. This whole process of waiting tosses you up and down in terms of how you feel. No children around now, though—they're far away and growing up without me. I alone am being tossed around in circles, and there's no end in sight to this exhausting ride. It seems like I've acquired a season pass for it. But there are plenty of spectators, even sympathizers and those who worry. Will I be thrown off by the front carriage running me over, or will I finally ask for mercy and let the attendant switch off the power?

Everyone around, even those who see me often, has said that I lost a lot of weight recently. It's hard for me to judge myself—I don't look at myself in the mirror every day—but it seems like the weight is coming off very slowly, around one hundred grams a day and no more. I've started drinking exactly three liters of water daily to balance out my body's hydration and spare my kidneys from excessive strain, avoiding fluid buildup in my internal cavities.

The scales showed seventy-six point five kilograms earlier today. The robe, under which I stopped wearing a sweater and underwear due to the sudden heat, now hangs on me as if I had put it on after some fat guy.

Yesterday, on Sunday, we enthusiastically watched another season of that American TV series about the Seven Kingdoms and the struggle for the Iron Throne. The old tortoise, Ivanytch, once again made his appearance around the sixth episode. "And what century is this, I wonder?" he posed another question that plunged everyone into silence, including the on-screen characters, only to answer himself, displaying the facets of his knowledge and eccentricity: "Sixteenth, probably."

"Of course, Ivanytch! The sixteenth, what else! Right after Bartholomew's Night. Though, for some reason, they've dubbed it the Red Wedding! The dragons will have grown by then..."

"Dragons?" the old man, hunched at the waist, expressed surprise. "There weren't any dragons left then. So, even earlier..." Ivanytch might not have the best hearing, vision, or comprehension, but he tries not to fall behind the collective, even in mass entertainment.

Yesterday's soccer matches weren't as interesting as the previous ones. England played against Panama and won 6–1, setting a record for the highest score in this championship and securing their spot in the playoffs. Japan and Senegal couldn't determine a clear winner, playing to a draw with a score of 2–2. Colombia joined their dispute in the last group stage match, eliminating Poland with a score of 3–0. Today, Uruguay and Russia will compete for the crucial first place in the group. Deep down, I've always dreamed of supporting some Latin American national team, and the opportunity has finally presented itself.

My inner demons, which hadn't been heard from for a week, gathered in force during the broadcast yesterday when they saw a McDonald's advertisement. They flocked to it as a group and started contemplating every item on the menu. When they reached the ice cream and desserts, I dispersed this hungry assembly that retreated gloomily to their respective corners, no longer putting up the same fierce resistance as before.

The best view from my two windows is the sky above—it's beautiful. I rarely glance at the neighboring long barracks and the rows of inmates marching in formation below. The spectacle has become rather tiresome for me over the past few months in this camp. But I constantly hear the sounds of commands and synchronized footsteps through the open window. The police officer casually walking by isn't the one issuing orders to the inmates; it's the *kozel* "herder" who is responsible for leading the formation—that's his role. He ensures everyone stands straight, turns in unison, and cheerfully greets any passing staff member.

And there are plenty of those. The formation is halted, faces turn toward the approaching police officer, and the *kozel* herder shouts, "Hello, Citizen Chief!" The doomed choir of inmates obediently repeats the phrase, which has already become rather grating, after him. The officer passing by gives a quick nod, even if he's just a junior sergeant, and the inmates continue to be led, say, to the mess hall. Though it's not a long walk—everything is quite close here, maybe even too close—because there's only one road into the camp, and everyone walks along it. Inmates on one side, police on the other, and these brief greetings happen pretty frequently. Without these stops, you'll hardly get anywhere.

Here in this place, the rule that says an inmate must greet an administrator, even if they've seen them six times in a day, is interpreted in a rather unique way. It's particularly strenuous in the barracks when some nitpicky officer is making his rounds, forcing everyone to greet him incessantly, like a bunch of parrots. In the beginning, when the police are still breaking in the newcomers—so that they fully understand where they've ended up—they make them ask for permission to pass by each police officer. And during this tough time, when the incoming group is being marched up and down the corridor, just to spite them, the officers stand on every corner—and not alone, either. These sorts of refinements are mainly experienced in the local detention center or in quarantine. In the camp, they have their own set of techniques.

In the same prison rules, it's written that inmates must move with their hands strictly behind their backs but without using a marching step. They carefully and almost secretly adhere to this rule in this zone, but only in the first part. That's why, before they start moving, the *kozel* herder who's in charge gives the command, "Step off with the left foot, forward march! One... One... One, two, three" to make sure everyone marches together. If the squad doesn't follow this command properly—intentionally marching unevenly or making some other mistake in the eyes of the herder or the police—they're not taken to the barracks after the mess hall. Instead, they're led to conduct drills. They march back and forth for an hour along an alley, where there are always many chiefs of various ranks who must be greeted. This happens quite frequently, but the goal is always the same: to wear a person down to a semi-living state, to turn them into a zombie who obeys without question, both individually and as part of a group, never daring to challenge the system.

Back in my childhood, when I watched movies set during wartime, I used to wonder how a handful of convoy guards could manage to lead a compliant crowd of thousands of prisoners, and those prisoners wouldn't dare to attack them. After all, there wouldn't be enough bullets or chances to shoot them all. As I got older, I came to realize that people in these situations were bound together by one common factor: fear. Along with fear, there wasn't so much physical exhaustion and tiredness as there was a sense of oppression and a herd mentality. I had only known this in theory, and I had witnessed it, at most, on a television screen. It wasn't until I ended up here that I truly understood how it operated in reality. I've been to various places, some quite bleak, but this one exceeded them all.

Once the initial wave of pressure due to my status as a newly arrived Ukrainian terrorist deemed a threat to Russia for not celebrating the "return of Crimea" began to subside, I collected my thoughts and assessed my surroundings. I stopped doing things that weren't prescribed by the prison rules, but that the inmates were made to do by the local police. The most noticeable divergence was my refusal to march in step with everyone else. Standing at the front of the formation, in the first row, like a red-striped runaway, I wanted to be visible. And when it came time for everyone to step off with their left foot, I stepped off with my right. It might have seemed like a minor detail, but only at first glance. It was like not saluting Hitler at a fascist rally or refusing to stand up during the performance of the Soviet anthem. Because of me, the formation started to march unevenly, awkwardly—the well-oiled mechanism had faltered.

The herder was the first to react: he stopped everyone and personally told me that we started the movement with the left foot. I loudly responded that marching steps violated standard prison rules, and they wouldn't make me do it. He swallowed that, and we continued marching. Then the police officer noticed, and the story repeated itself. I was dragged to the duty section. After keeping me in the glass box to punish inmates for about four hours and saying a lot of unpleasant things about me, the police officers still didn't dare lay a hand on me. Eventually, they sent me back to the barracks. That's how our small war began.

I added to my refusal to step off with my left foot by refusing to provide explanations for any reason, invoking Article 51 of the Constitution of the Russian Federation. I also declined to greet the staff in a circle for the second time and resisted various other demands that the police, contrary to official rules, imposed to transform the camp's inmates into a docile, zombie-like crowd. In response, the police, with active involvement from the *kozly* in the barracks, initiated a series of retaliatory measures, including constant searches, overturning my bed, and nitpicking over any triviality, along with threats and intimidation. They also attempted to influence me indirectly by targeting those who associated with me, swiftly transferring them to other barracks if they drank *chifir* with me more than once, creating a kind of isolation zone around me. These were just a few examples of the harsh treatment that could be inflicted upon anyone in this grim environment, particularly those who openly defied the rules.

The *kozly* and the other caretakers, however, didn't march in formation—they moved in smaller groups or even individually, as some held keys to the enclosed walking section of the colony. This entire system was designed to suppress

individuality and worked against those who refused to collaborate with the administration, like the *muzhiki*, and others
unfortunate enough to be entangled in the system's web.

I was brought to the duty section twice a day. This happened early in the morning, right after the morning exercises.
I attended the exercises along with everyone else, even though
I didn't actively participate, unlike most who gave them their
best. Standing in the glass box after that, I explained to the
angry supervisors that I hadn't broken their rules, I'd attended
the exercises as required, and since standard prison rules didn't
specify how they should be done, I'd performed them according to the best of my modest physical abilities. The police officers frequently lost their temper with me, but mostly verbally.
They still didn't dare to hit me or lock me in solitary confinement, and even stopped writing reports about me because that
would have required me to write an explanatory note, and since
I wasn't writing them either, it only multiplied their problems.
Later, right before their eventual surrender, some staff members stopped taking me to the duty section, where a conversation with the colony chief's assistant duty officer would prove
pointless as well. So, they would lock me in a small area right in
the open air to cool off a bit. Several of those long polar winter
dawns would prove hard to forget. In the end, the police gave
up. We didn't declare a truce or sign a peace treaty. The pressure suddenly faded after a couple of months of struggle, and
they didn't bother me much anymore, but I'd held my ground.
I was the only one who'd demonstratively stepped off with my
right foot while everyone else pretended that it was the right
thing to do.

When the *muzhiki* saw that I'd succeeded, we drank *chifir* together, and I said that it wasn't actually difficult. They respected my courage, but they remarked that I had immunity. They would first be hauled up during the duty shift, then dragged to the operational unit, where more seasoned operators would take care of them. After that, they would either be rolled up in a mattress for three days or stuffed into an iron cabinet, which no one had managed to endure for more than a day, drenched in their own urine, on half-bent knees that couldn't be straightened due to the tight space. After going through that, you wouldn't just march in step, but you'd even start singing that song about Marusya* without being given the command. Though newcomers only sang it in quarantine by then. They said the cabinets had been removed as a form of punishment, but it wouldn't take much effort to put them back, and the memory and word of mouth about them lived strongly among the inmates ... We finished our tea and dispersed. I continued marching with my right foot alone.

Nowadays, I only recall those events that seem recent but are already distant when I pay attention to the constant chant outside my window: "Step ... Step ... Step, two, three. Step ... Step ... Step, two, three ... " But when I see the faces of the police officers smiling at me tirelessly now, I still remember the iron cabinets very vividly and those crumpled up inside of them.

---

* Sentsov is referring to a song from the film *Ivan Vasilyevich Changes His Profession*, a science fiction comedy based on a play by Mikhail Bulgakov. The story is about an engineer-inventor who creates a time machine that accidentally transports him to the times of Ivan the Terrible in the sixteenth century.

DAY FORTY-FOUR

In my dream, I went to the library—colony one, of course. It seemed that, at first, I was choosing books for myself, then, for some reason, I suddenly began to organize rehearsals of the local prison drama club right against the backdrop of bookshelves. Even in the dream, the administration didn't stop trying to repaint me and win me over to their side. Then, turning over this dream, I bought a new car for myself. But for some reason, I was sitting in the back seat, letting two friends sitting in front try driving it. When we got stuck in a traffic jam near some gigantic quarry, I asked them to give me the steering wheel. They reluctantly got out of the car, and right there, in my hands, while I was adjusting the settings for myself, it began to transform into a bicycle.

I woke up late, just before the morning check, almost on autopilot. I slept well, and I feel fine.

I no longer experience that deceptive liveliness that the doctor calls pseudo-euphoria. The main thing is that I don't feel unwell in the morning anymore, and it usually hits me only in the evening. I've grown used to it. There are moments when I feel nauseous and dizzy upon waking up or getting out of bed. But that's just how it is, and I need to be careful. The constant weakness doesn't bother me as much either. People adapt to everything, even when they feel like an amoeba. Fortunately, the cough is no longer tormenting me, although it occasionally returns briefly. The itching problem has also disappeared as suddenly as it appeared earlier. All in all, things are fine.

Summer has ended, making way for autumn with its clouds, rain, and gusty winds. The warmth is still lingering, but it won't stick around if this weather continues. It's currently about twenty degrees Celsius, both inside and outside my ship. It's comfortable for now, but in this polar climate, stability isn't guaranteed. It reminds me of a joke: "Do you have summer up there in the north?" "Well, of course, but I usually work on that day."

Yesterday marked the start of the final round of group games in the World Cup. The matches in each group are now being held simultaneously to prevent any manipulation of results for playoff advantages. All four games yesterday were unpredictable, giving bookmakers quite the stir. In the first match, despite high expectations, Russia lost to Uruguay with a score of 0–3. The match revealed the true level of the Russian team when facing a formidable opponent. Although they tried their best, Russia couldn't match the strength of the Uruguayans, even after they'd lost a defender to two yellow cards. By contrast, the match between Russia's previous opponents showed their true quality, as Saudi Arabia defeated Egypt in the last seconds of the game with a score of 2–1.

There was no funereal atmosphere on Russian TV, everyone was rallying like doomed infantrymen near Verdun because Russia would have to face either Portugal or Spain in the next round, both formidable opponents. It was a choice between two evils.

Spain had a dramatic match against Morocco, managing a 2–2 draw, while Portugal, who led throughout the game, unexpectedly conceded a goal to Iran in the last moments, ending with a 1–1 draw. The ranking for first place in their respective groups, based on points and goal difference, came down to the number of yellow cards received. As a result, Spain secured first place and will play against Russia, while Portugal took second place and will face Uruguay. The real excitement is about to begin.

Prison provides ample time for deep reflection, leading to various conclusions. One realization is that there are four fundamental words and concepts in this world: life, freedom, love, and happiness. These concepts drive all human actions and serve as the driving force behind all goals and dreams, even if individuals are not consciously aware of them. It's crucial not to distort or reverse these pure concepts. For instance, valuing your life shouldn't involve sacrificing the lives of others to save your own. Likewise, speaking of inner freedom while living in an unjust, oppressive country requires meaningful action rather than hiding or fleeing. The number of romantic partners should not measure love, and marriage should not feel like a hostage situation. The pursuit of happiness often becomes an unending race for wealth, akin to a dog chasing a sausage tied to its nose. Some opt for a life of constant indulgence and questionable pleasures—from overindulgence to substance abuse. Navigating this path correctly is challenging, and I make an effort, though I don't always succeed. In truth, what could be simpler than living freely, loving, and finding happiness? To ensure you're on the right path and haven't veered into murky waters, a reliable moral compass is always a valuable tool.

After each step, pause and ask yourself: Do I have a clear conscience? Do I feel good after this—clean, light, and calm? If the answer is "yes," then you've taken a step in the right direction. If it's "no," you've ventured into the wrong territory, and from now on, you must proceed with greater caution. The path is narrow and hardly discernible, while the swamps are extensive, marshy, and enticing. These swamps may feel warm and inviting, making it easy to settle in them. But once you're smeared with their sticky mud, you'll find it impossible to progress, let alone reach the light.

DAY FORTY-FIVE

I haven't reread this diary, but judging by its volume, it seems to have become quite substantial—more than I initially anticipated. Most likely, I will even manage to preserve it. I often feel like I'm writing a bunch of nonsense in here. But as usual, I'm writing it primarily for myself, just like everything I wrote before. I don't perceive the diary as a literary work or, indeed, a historical document. It's more like an anchor, a pillar, a handrail that allows me to hold on and stand straighter without bending.

To keep track of the weather outside, I would need to maintain a separate notebook since the weather changes three times a day. It looks like summer has prevailed again, bringing sunshine and a clear blue sky, creating a pleasantly warm atmosphere. Strangely, I haven't had any supervisors visit me for the past three days. Not that I've been particularly missing them, but it's possible that everyone who wanted to or could visit has already done so. Alternatively, it might just be a quiet period before their next round of visits. Yesterday, a detachment chief officer came by and took photographs of my room from all angles, though he asked me to step into the corridor before doing so.

The doctor was finally able to escort his medical commission, which had been quietly bothering him for a week, to take blood samples. He had grown tired of dragging them around, and only yesterday, after eagerly welcoming the Moscow visitors he had been waiting for, he came to the base. He paid me a visit, and now he could finally head home with a clear conscience to enjoy some alcohol in peace. We had a brief chat, something we hadn't done in a while amid all this chaos.

I'm continually amazed, as is the doctor himself, by how different we are in character, political views, and, of course, our current roles as lieutenant colonel and convict. Yet, we share many similar life perspectives and habits, coinciding even in mundane details. Yesterday, for instance, we learned that he and I liked to marinate and grill kebabs the exact same way. Truly, there are remarkable similarities, though I'm convinced they're not mere coincidences. It had to be this way. I had to meet a person without whom my hunger strike could have had a much less fortunate outcome. Thank you, Doctor!

The eye drops I've been using for conjunctivitis are potent and sting pretty badly. Their healing effect only goes so far— the red veins and inflammation persist. This is likely due to my weakened immune system, as this condition tends to cling to individuals like me. Well, I'll have to wait for the final verdict at the bottom of the vial. The most challenging aspect, of course, has been dealing with my veins. They've become somewhat rigid and brittle, covered in adhesions and poorly healing marks from all the injections. The medical staff now thoroughly inspects my hands before attempting an IV, searching for a suitable spot to insert the needle or catheter.

Yesterday's matches in Group C were rather disappointing. Denmark and France were content with a draw to secure their progression from the group. They timidly and passively passed the ball around the field, wasting an excruciating hour and a half of my time, resulting in the first 0–0 score of this championship. Peru had nothing left to hope for, but they managed to win a matter of pride with a 2–0 victory over Australia, who also had little hope, and after such a score, their only task was to pack their bags.

In the other group, whose winners will face these teams in the playoffs, things were far from straightforward, meaning they were much more entertaining. Croatia, having already secured their spot in the next stage, claimed their third consecutive victory with a 2–1 win over Iceland, which still had some hope. And the Argentina-Nigeria match was truly the highlight of the day. The Argentinians, who had a dreadful start to this tournament, were in dire need of a victory, while Nigeria would have been content with a draw to make it to the playoffs, so the battle was fierce. The Argentine players, having practically distanced themselves from their coach, blaming him, as usual, for everything, relentlessly attacked the entire way, but the Nigerians put up a formidable resistance. In the end, the much-needed 2–1 score for the South Americans lit up on the scoreboard just a few minutes before the final whistle, which signaled that Argentina's national team had indeed crawled into the final part of the competition.

Yesterday I finished reading another novel by Arthur C. Clarke. He's also a classic science fiction writer, but after Lem, not as impressive, of course. He focused more on technical and scientific factors rather than drama and relationships. The issues Clarke raised were quite interesting, but still carried the sense of being more like a report or a prediction, which made his literature come across as somewhat flat and lifeless. The first novel I read about two isolated mini-civilizations on Earth that had retreated into themselves and abandoned space exploration turned out to be quite weak. The title was fitting: *The City and the Stars*.

I've long noticed that powerful works always have strong names and titles, and the less toothy and less memorable the title, the more amorphous the content tends to be. This also applies here. Despite the novel being set millions of years in the future and featuring advanced technologies, including near immortality for humans, it failed to captivate the reader.

Rendezvous with Rama, on the other hand, drew me in from the title and the first lines. This book echoed some of Lem's previous novels about contact between humans and aliens. In Clarke's case, it wasn't about intelligent life but rather its by-product, a massive cosmic ship that arrived seemingly out of nowhere, like an empty ark, and departed to an unknown destination. People landed on it, didn't understand much, and left on their own as the rendezvous time expired.

I personally prefer reading this kind of minimalist science fiction, where future achievements naturally stem from presently available data but serve as a backdrop and plot for more important matters in life, with humanity and relationships at the center. Clarke did a great job there, but he sadly didn't quite reach Lem's level.

I won't even mention the quantity and quality of the themes that the literature of the Great Strugatsky brothers provides. Because in this genre, they are the undisputed kings—all other science fiction is secondary to their presence.

I sent a messenger to the library to exchange these books for others "to my taste." They apparently decided that I preferred science fiction over classic literature and sent back Bradbury, Zelazny, and some other author. Well, I'll take a look. I respect those two authors as well, but right now, I've taken a pause to immerse myself in Ancient Rome of the fifth century by diving into Robert Graves' *I, Claudius*, a book that seems to have floated its way here.

The book-swapping errands in the library were handled by Smiley, a guy who lives up to his nickname, based on the perpetual look on his face. He's the one performing the duties of the med point *balander*, participating in the food ritual in his white coat, and also delivering tea to the doctor's office. Despite being one of the *kozly*, Smiley turned out to be a decent guy, having nothing in common with the others from the residential zone of the camp. Actually, the same goes for all three of the "activists" who work and live in the infirmary. The atmosphere here is completely different—no one snitches or creates trouble. They're devoted to the doctor, seeing him as their leader, and don't collaborate with the rest of the administration. Though it's not impossible that there might be a rat among them, someone working for the authorities. In this camp, nothing would surprise me—but I doubt it. The doctor has managed to create a small independent world within his domain, where, in his own words, "even the walls heal," and where even I have somewhat relaxed my soul and don't feel too imprisoned.

They brought a small stack of letters, mostly printed-out emails. But there were also regular, handwritten ones, including beautiful postcards. All of them were from abroad. I'll be responding to them now.

But that's not what has made this day important. Today is my son's birthday. He's turning fourteen, his fifth birthday without me. He's already been living a third of his life—the most conscious part of it—without his dad. It's been almost a year since the last time I spoke to him on the phone, and there were a couple of short letters from him. The thread is getting thinner. And not just because of his health condition or the fact that his grandma and sister are now closer and dearer to him. It's because his father should be there beside him. Forgive me for this, my son, and happy birthday to you! Grow up healthy!

DAY FORTY-SIX

Last night, the doctor conducted a routine examination and asked me to undress but to leave my underwear on in order to assess the condition of my muscle mass. "Yeah . . . pretty Buchenwald," was his brief verdict. I've started to feel like I'm getting smaller, even though my weight hasn't changed much. At the same time, my well-being has been normal for the third day in a row, which can be seen from the medical analyses— the deterioration of my organs has stalled and a certain feeling of stabilization of my health has appeared again.

But I know that this is all extremely shaky; the doctor knows it too, and he's especially aware of it. The next time, if, God forbid, I have to go on hunger strike again, I will do the opposite: I will try to gain maximum weight and internal reserves beforehand. Though it would be difficult to do this because I have never been overweight and it's almost impossible for me to retain at least some fat because of my constitution and increased metabolism. I hope that such a situation will not happen again in my lifetime, neither in prison nor on the outside. This hunger strike seems to have no end in sight. The shore is behind me, no longer visible, and there's no turning back. The other shore, where I'm heading, is still not in sight—just fog and uncertainty.

I couldn't fall asleep at night. In the silence, the barking of the guard dogs was clearly audible. German shepherds. You often meet them in this system, and they always bark, rush at you, pull at their leashes.

I've had three dogs in my life: a mongrel, a half-breed, and a Labrador. The first was shot dead, the second died of old age, and the third from illness. The last one, Grina, a girl loved by the whole family, considered only me as her true owner and saw me off on the night of my arrest. I was sitting handcuffed in my apartment while FSB officers were frantically looking for at least something forbidden in all the rooms. They couldn't find anything, and my Labrador came up to my chair and stuck her muzzle through my handcuffed arms. We were looking into each other's eyes for a long time. We were bidding each other farewell but didn't yet know that we wouldn't ever see each other again. Though I think she seemed to know. Dogs don't understand a lot, but they're good at picking up on feelings, especially when it comes to their master. Sooner or later, I will get myself a dog again. It will probably be the last one—we don't have many true friends in this world, even among animals. But I know for sure that it won't be a shepherd. It's a very good breed—smart and loyal. I used to want one. But I understand that I can no longer live with one. From now on, shepherd dogs will forever be associated with prisons, transfers, and convoys.

Yesterday's soccer delivered the first real drama-packed sensation. Germany, which had a poor start in this tournament, was expected to win against South Korea and secure a spot in the next round. Much to everyone's surprise, including their own, Germany lost 0–2, conceding two goals in the final minutes of the match. This unexpected turn of events was complicated even further by Sweden's equally unexpected 3–0 victory over Mexico. Germany ended up in last place in the group and left the tournament in disgrace. The curse, where the previous World Cup champion failed to advance to the playoffs in the next tournament, has now affected Germany, making it the fourth time it has happened. Mexico and Sweden advanced to the next round, while in South Korea, a national holiday was declared despite their team's elimination from the championship. In the other group, there were no major surprises. Brazil, despite some difficulties, defeated Serbia 2–0 and secured their spot in the playoffs. Switzerland, after a 2–2 draw with Costa Rica, also advanced to the finals from second place. Today marked the last day of group qualifiers.

I mentioned yesterday that it had been a while since the bosses dropped by, and immediately after dinner, a whole group of them, led by the Magnificent Mustache, paid me a visit. As usual, the Mustache claimed he was just passing by and engaged in some small talk. I gathered a few things from our fragmented conversation: First, he used the ferry like everyone else and didn't swim to see me like a walrus. Second, he was going on vacation in two days, which was good news for all of us. Third, the Russian ombudswoman, a retired major general of the police who's been on TV lately and sometimes mentioned in connection with my case, will be visiting me tomorrow.

And as a bonus, he shared some nonsense he'd read on the internet this morning. "You must have heard?" he asked. "I've been reading this morning on the internet . . . "

"No, I haven't had a chance to check the internet today," I replied, injecting a touch of cynicism.

The Mustache didn't seem to notice and continued, "There was a press conference yesterday in Kyiv, the OSCE . . . A military colonel claimed he'd personally provided you with explosives, but not for explosions . . . "

"You mean for blast fishing?" I inquired.

"I don't know," the Mustache said, "he didn't specify."

With that, Mustache and his entourage sailed away, and I couldn't help but wonder if they had some explosive news waiting for them in the morning. Perhaps it was another attempt to compromise someone or divert attention, and it had conveniently landed on my doorstep. I decided to wait for more reliable sources before jumping to conclusions.

Meanwhile, the med point was buzzing with preparations for the visit of a distinguished guest from another planet. Everyone was rushing around, even the doctor, who had swapped his usual Airborne Forces retiree T-shirt for semi-formal attire. I joined in the "Let's make our world more beautiful" initiative by removing my conspicuously drying socks and underwear from their prominent display.

The Russian ombudswoman arrived closer to lunchtime, accompanied by several important figures, including the mustachioed walrus. She immediately requested that they step out into the corridor, wanting to have a private conversation with me. They left one supervisor behind, presumably for her safety, and conveniently kept the door to the ward open to monitor everything happening inside. Despite these standard police precautions, the ombudswoman paid them no mind.

I was somewhat surprised when I first saw her—she was shorter in height than I had expected based on her TV appearances. What struck me most was that she didn't come across as a retired police officer with a tough demeanor. Instead, she seemed to be a kind, intelligent, and somewhat decent person in certain respects. She had a long history of working in the Ministry of Internal Affairs, primarily dealing with issues related to pardons rather than imprisonment. Afterward, she spent ten years in the State Duma before taking on her current role as an ombudswoman. It felt like the right position for her, even though I preferred her predecessor. Maybe it was just me.

We spoke for about an hour, and overall, both of us seemed satisfied with the conversation. I usually try not to drag out unpleasant discussions. Initially, she tried to persuade me to resume eating by discussing alternative methods, but I promptly interrupted that irritating and, more importantly, pointless discussion, and we shifted to other topics.

She made it clear that she wasn't involved in prisoner exchanges but that she was aware discussions about it were ongoing. That was fine with me. She and her Ukrainian counterpart, with whom she had little understanding and cooperation, had separately attempted to visit prisoners in both countries. However, they mostly encountered refusals, turning the monitoring process into a political quagmire. It seemed likely that exchange negotiations would follow a similar pattern. In the end, she remarked that I appeared to be in good health, even better than in my pre-prison photographs. I responded that I had been feeling reasonably well in recent days but had not entirely recovered. People tend to see what they want to see.

We bid farewell and shook hands, and she left, pretending to inspect the med point but likely seeking information from witnesses about whether I had fainted or not. Inside the doctor's office, she spent a considerable amount of time leafing through my plump medical record, demonstrating no more expertise than her mustachioed subordinate. Once she was satisfied that I was being well-monitored, this imperial cruiser set sail from our pier.

During the IV treatment, two of my veins burst again, which aggravated the already significant drug-addict-like problem I was experiencing—there were hardly any unspoiled spots left for injections.

Outside the window, the bright sun shone despite the howling wind—a summer blizzard.

DAY FORTY-SEVEN

In my dreams, I was pushing a cart filled with some large frozen fish, like sturgeon, through some market. On the way out, they frisked both me and the fish. These are the kind of dreams you have when you're in prison, always with a hint of jailhouse flavor.

Yesterday, after the IV drip, they called me for a meeting with a lawyer. Not mine, but with a new local one. As expected, he came on the consul's orders once again. This was the third time. For the third time, they sent a lawyer to me, and I sent him back in response because I have no faith in local defenders. They all work in coordination with the police. In the past, I verbally conveyed my refusals and requests not to come again since I already had a lawyer who suited me just fine. But it seemed this information was not relayed. This time, I wrote a letter to the consul about the same issue. If the local lawyer passed it along, then maybe this nuisance would disappear.

Why do people on the outside not want to listen to my words and requests? Why, when I say "no" or "no need," do they not want to accept it? I understand they're all concerned, and anxious to demonstrate their care. But why send lawyers to me at state expense when I promptly turn away and the person who actually defends and helps me has not been paid for his travel even once in four years?

The poor guy in a neat suit with the "law" badge and the face of a snitch briefly informed me that the Ukrainian ombudswoman, along with journalists, was standing at the gate. Then he started talking provocatively about phones that couldn't be brought in or given to inmates, though, in some colonies, inmates had their own. This was all in the presence of an officer, who, for some reason, stubbornly did not want to leave us alone, suggesting that we all pretend he wasn't there. I immediately got up, apologized, asked to convey greetings to everyone gathered at the gate for me, and announced that the meeting was over. The chief and I left, while another one of Sentsov's saviors remained in bewilderment, squeezing his eyes shut and holding my letter to the consul in his hands.

All this empty commotion irritates me! The Ukrainian ombudswoman was not allowed in last week, and she asked through my lawyer, Dima, how I was doing. I asked him to convey that everything was fine and that she shouldn't push through those closed doors. Instead, she should focus on the other thirty-four people on her list and monitor them. But no, she came again, this time with the support of journalists' cameras. Her Russian colleague from yesterday was no better—she hadn't helped her get into the camp or said a word about it. Just smiles. All of this reminded me of the bickering of divorced parents at the bedside of a sick child. The only phrase that pleased me was one I overheard on the radio from the duty officer when they were leading me past: "One film crew with a camera headed toward the eastern wall." The police had a sweaty day today running around and stopping brave Ukrainian cameramen who had started hunting for good shots from the colony.

More positive news from yesterday's eventful day: they brought newspapers. Just two of them, with the standard two-week-old freshness. But it was better than nothing. *Novaya Gazeta* has continued to advocate for me in every issue, trying to uplift me with the phrase: "The case of the release of the Ukrainian political prisoner has progressed beyond a standstill . . ." I would add: " . . . and drifted slowly into the distant fog." Otherwise, the topics remained the same—theft, everything was bad and falling apart, but there were still good people somewhere, Putin communicated with his virtual Russian people directly but with evasive answers. Nevertheless, it was interesting to read, as always.

Yesterday's matches on the final day of the group stage were not as spectacular as the previous ones because most teams had already settled their fates. Despite Japan's 0–1 loss to Poland, they've secured a spot in the next round and will be a formidable opponent in Round 16. Meanwhile, Colombia's 1–0 victory, which also secured their place in the playoffs, prevented Senegal from advancing. Colombia won't be an easy opponent for anyone to beat. In a match that didn't affect the standings for both eliminated teams, Tunisia defeated Panama 2–1. Belgium and England, using their second-string teams, determined the group winner, with the Belgians prevailing 1–0. No one wanted to exert themselves, saving their energy for the knockout stage, which begins tomorrow. Today was a break.

There's no wind today, and the sun was scorching—summer had returned, but for some reason, I didn't feel like going outside.

In addition to the physical apathy and weakness I've long grown accustomed to, a certain psychological fatigue has been creeping in. It's not that I'm ready to give up, not at all—it's more like feeling tired on a journey where you have to keep walking uphill with a heavy backpack. It's difficult, it's tiring, but you don't slow down more than just a bit. All of this reminds me of the Maidan that February when there was yet another ceasefire.

We had been standing there for three months, uncertain about what came next and whether it made sense to keep doing so or to move somewhere else. Many had dispersed back then, the protest had lost some of its momentum, and our make-shift revolutionary town had partially emptied out. I remember how they started handing out one sandwich at a time at the Ukrainian House where we were based, and that was with a badge—even with food, tensions had started to rise. I didn't leave back then. I continued to stand on the Maidan, and later, I started working at the headquarters. I'd also stood on the barricades in December. It was bitterly cold, we all suffered from a constant lack of sleep and chronic colds, but despite these difficulties, there was no sense of hopelessness or the futility of our cause. Even during those freezing December nights, the famous Ukrainian pop singer Ruslana performed the national anthem a capella every hour to keep us warm. But in February, I even occasionally felt that sense of emptiness like the one that's creeping in now. Back then, no one knew that just a week later, we would face three days of the bloodiest battles, although we would emerge victorious. I still had no doubt that we would win—the only question was when and at what cost. It took three months back then.

Here, I'm pretty sure I can hold on for two more. As for what comes after, I don't want to speculate: we'll see when we get there.

DAY FORTY-EIGHT

I've been feeling emotionally troubled for two days now. I'd rather have physical pain in my leg than this hard-to-define and intangible sense of foreboding.

I've been thinking about the Maidan. It was a turning point not just in my life, but for many others as well. It felt like a dividing line between two eras, like going from before Christ to after. I remember that I could only make it there in early December after the initial clashes had subsided. Earlier, I had been hit by a sudden illness, some kind of virus. While I was recovering and following the events online, I finally gathered the strength to take a train and rush to Kyiv.

Upon arriving at the Maidan, my first impression was that I was too late and that all the important and exciting things had already happened. I soon realized that the most critical and terrifying moments were yet to unfold. I wandered through the protest area with a sense that nobody really needed me there. Newcomers weren't warmly received, especially those on their own, and you had to fend for yourself. I quickly understood that this wasn't a protest orchestrated from the top, but a grassroots movement with remarkable self-organization, driven by the collective cry of "We've had enough!"

I managed to secure a place to spend the night in a tent where a bunch of western Ukrainians were staying. They didn't welcome Crimeans, but at the entrance to the tent, in addition to their signatures and identification marks, there was a sheet of paper with the word "Crimea" on it. And I said that I would sleep here, even if I were the first and last Crimean on the Maidan, I could fight with everyone who was against me doing so, one by one. The guys eventually made room, but not without grumbling. Then they offered me *salo* and *horilka*. I ate the *salo* but refused the alcohol knowing it was forbidden and, more importantly, that this was not the time to relax.

There was not a single thing I didn't do that month before the New Year—I volunteered, carried water and firewood, and was on guard duty at the barricades at night. Once, we were even instructed to guard the delivered Christmas tree so that it wouldn't be broken into branches for souvenirs, then, of course, our large crowd installed it. You constantly wanted to sleep, eat, and get warm. There was a whirlwind of people everywhere, and the atmosphere was rich and interesting, but I understood that this was not a holiday and our enemies would not give up so easily. The smell of war was already in the air.

During the New Year's holidays, I went home on a visit, and when I came back, I immediately joined the first battles on Hrushevskyi Street near Dynamo Stadium. Everything by that point was already serious. Cocktails, stones, and sticks on one side, gas grenades, rubber bullets, and clubs on the other. Burnt buses in the middle. There were not so many people on our front line; the bulk of them stood behind the buffer zone where grenades and bullets didn't reach and where, in case of a police attack, it was easy to retreat. The position of the viewer was always comfortable. I was not a bystander for long.

After a Berkut special police officer beat the guy on the roof of the archway with the end of his club, threw him down to the side of the police, and flipped off the indignant crowd, I stopped being a peaceful protestor. I stepped over my fear and those fifty meters that separated the auditorium from the confrontation arena. I returned to the tent only in the morning, once the battle had begun to subside. The next day, it all happened again. But the intensity of the first week of confrontation on Hrushevskyi Street also began to gradually subside, the energy that had splashed out on both sides fading away, and an armistice was declared. Then it turned out that my Crimean comrade was present there, on the Maidan—I learned about this by chance from our other friend. The fact that neither of us talked about our intention to go to the revolution was not surprising. It was necessary to keep quiet about this in Crimea since the identification system of "friend or foe" had already gone into force. It was better than in combat aviation, but there weren't enough of our people. My comrade and I immediately got together, and he pulled me into the Automaidan,* one of the cavalries of the revolution.

Life there was quite different, revolving mostly around wheels—actions, car rides, roadblocks, and encounters with *titushky*, who were undercover agitators during Yanukovych's administration. They often pretended to be troublemakers on the streets, provoking violence at pro-European and anti-Yanukovych political rallies to have protestors arrested. We also had our share of run-ins with traffic cops.

During the day, we moved around the city, but in the evening, we always returned to the Maidan. It was safer there, and we anticipated nightly attacks where every fighter would be needed. Though the real trouble came from elsewhere. The police gained access to our communication channels, leading several teams into ambushes simultaneously at three different city locations.

---

* The Automaidan was a sub-movement of the Euromaidan Revolution that used cars and trucks as part of the protest efforts against pro-Russian president Viktor Yanukovych.

When we realized what had happened, we rushed to those spots. My comrade and I and several other cars arrived at a chaotic scene near a hospital. There were three abandoned cars with open doors and keys in the ignition, and one car burned from the inside. No people were around, just signs of a struggle in the dirty snow. We stood there bewildered, unsure of our next move. Then we received information from one of the patrolling cars in the city that our captured guys were being transported by the Berkut* in a bus. We immediately gave chase. It turned into a twenty-minute race through the city at night, and we finally caught up with the old PAZ bus at the end of the Dnipro River bridge. Our car was at the forefront, with the others trailing behind in a long but not too extensive column.

There were fewer people willing to rescue our comrades from the ruthless and cruel Berkut officers than those who believed that simply roaming the city was how revolutions were made. The slow bus, noticing the pursuit, stopped at the side of the road, and a bunch of officers clad in protection gear and helmets poured out of it, carefully beginning to monitor the approaching cavalcade of lights. In the lead car, besides me and my comrade who was driving, there was another person in the back seat—he came to us because he was eager for a real fight and, according to him, had to die on the Maidan.

---

* The Berkut was a special police unit within Ukraine's Ministry of Internal Affairs that was formed in 1992. Berkut officers attacked protestors during both the Orange Revolution (2004–2005) and the Euromaidan Revolution (2013–2014), though they were infamous even before then. The unit was dissolved in 2014, shortly after the triumph of the revolution.

We stopped right in front of the bus, blocking its way, and were already preparing to get out to start negotiations on the extradition of our guys. It was good that we didn't have time to do this and open the doors. The Berkut were not in the mood to talk but immediately began to beat our car. A hail of blows rained down, and the rear and side windows were immediately smashed. The Berkut officers gathered around the car like armored beetles on a caterpillar. My friend didn't lose his composure and hit the gas pedal. The car didn't move forward; instead, it slid along the snowdrift sideways, tilting on punctured right-side tires.

"We've got flat tires," the driver said curtly. He barely steered the car straight, raking it along the snow-covered roadside at walking speed. The Berkut kept up with us and continued to mutilate our transport, trying to open the doors and get inside. My comrade and I were in bulletproof vests and helmets; wearing the badges of Maidan organizers and falling into the hands of enraged Berkut officers dressed like that was tantamount to death—our guys were sometimes beaten to death for a simple blue-and-yellow ribbon.

Finally, we managed to break away a little, the blows raining down on the car stopped, and they fell behind. But it was useless to try to ride off at a snail's pace only for the Berkut to catch up with us again. About a hundred meters later, we turned into a nearby alcove beside a house. We hopped out of the car, me with my wooden club and my comrade with his stick. We positioned ourselves in the narrow space between the car and the corner of the building. It would be challenging for anyone to approach us here, even if they had more people. As the bus drew nearer, our grip on our weapons tightened. It turned out to be a garbage truck. It didn't stop but just honked at us, and we heard laughter from inside as it sped away. Both of us let out a sigh of relief.

Then we realized there were only two of us; the third person had disappeared. Initially, I thought the police might have pulled him out of the car. We were running out of time. After regaining our composure a bit, we started changing one of the flat tires and wondered where we could find another spare. Suddenly, a car stopped on the opposite side of the road. Our missing comrade popped out from the back seat and called to me, suggesting we leave because the Berkut might return. I was surprised at how he'd ended up there, but it all made sense. I told him to go on without me and that I would stay. He didn't call me to save me but because it wouldn't look as bad if we ran away together in a cowardly fashion. He'd left because the police could return at any moment, and I stayed for the same reason. Everyone makes their own choice, and it seemed this man wanted to stand his ground on the Maidan, in front of the cameras and the sound of drums, rather than on some obscure street he probably didn't even know. Some of our people eventually returned and drove away, but a couple of crews, those who didn't dare to block the police bus but were still unafraid, pulled up to us. We managed to replace one of our tires with a spare, checked the battered car, then headed back to the Maidan.

So, between being "afraid" and "unafraid," only ten minutes could pass, sometimes even less. Those who didn't immediately retreat weren't cowards.

During that month and the next, there were many ups and downs, both good and bad, along with plenty of challenges and burdens. I'll never forget the Okean Elzy concert on the Maidan. The sound wasn't great, but the band's performance and the incredible energy, not to mention the thousands of lit-up mobile phones, made it unforgettable. I also managed to make a brief second visit home to hug my children and reassure my mother. During that time, I drove my comrade's car from Crimea to Kyiv because he couldn't return home anymore. He had been identified and was a wanted man, so his new home was there in the capital. It was an exhausting drive on a wintry highway. In the car with me were four Crimean supporters of the Maidan, eager to witness the revolution for themselves. Later, during the trial, I recalled that one of them was Sasha "Tundra," my brave companion.

Then came the capture of the Ukrainian House. I walked around the familiar building, its entrance shattered during the storm, reminiscing about the days when I used to bring Crimean teams here for the all-Ukrainian qualifiers for the world e-sports championship. Those times were long gone, replaced by a different era. Inside the room where the press center used to be, they decided to establish the headquarters of the Automaidan.

I volunteered to take charge of this task. It didn't happen immediately, and there was some skepticism, but eventually, they entrusted it to me. I found myself back in my element, managing and organizing people and processes. Once everyone saw that I could handle it, they started to respect me more, even inviting me to leadership meetings. But since these meetings were often filled with vague discussions and little concrete action, I usually ignored them.

I preferred the actual work of sorting out timely issues, which often extended into the late hours of the night, not talking shop or bouncing around universal ideas in order to overthrow the regime. In every tent, there was a meeting of Napoleons, and at every table in the cafes on our territory there was a club of Jacobins, but someone had to sort out the timely issues.

I arranged sleeping spaces for myself and a few others on cardboard laid out on the fire escape landing, but sleep was hard to come by. It was no easier than being on the front lines, perhaps even more challenging because there, where so much attention was focused on you, taking a brief break or having a meal unnoticed was nearly impossible. On the bright side, I could call my mother with a clear conscience and reassure her that I was working at the headquarters: "No, Mom, I'm not a clerk . . . " I still managed to find half an hour here and there to walk around the Maidan, even when there weren't any pressing tasks. I needed that time to soak up the atmosphere, absorb the energy, and observe the faces of the people who called the Maidan home. Those individuals were easy to spot in the crowd. They moved with the calm, confident stride of someone walking through their vast garden. They were always warmly dressed, moderately dirty, and wearing sturdy shoes that were essential for surviving the cold weather.

The Maidan wasn't just about locals—it welcomed people from beyond Kyiv who'd come for a day or two to observe and show their support. The sense of unity among these individuals, the shared spirit, was indescribable and could only be fully grasped by those who were there. To those who weren't, words wouldn't be able to capture it. But I really wanted to see this atmosphere and honest, free spirit extend throughout the entire country. That was the kind of country I wanted to live in, and I was far from alone in such a desire. In the days leading up to the decisive battles, nobody could predict what lay ahead. Everyone just smiled and believed in victory.

DAY FORTY-NINE

For the third day in a row, a nasty toad has been living in my chest and refuses to crawl out. I'm still reminiscing about the Maidan. Specifically, from February eighteenth to the twentieth. The last three days were impossible to forget. Especially the eighteenth, which became the longest and most challenging day of my life, and an even more arduous night when it seemed like we wouldn't survive until morning! Everyone understood that the so-called peaceful march, which had been planned well in advance, would not be peaceful at all.

I don't know who came up with the strategy of encircling the government district from all sides and what they ultimately wanted to achieve with such a dispersion of our forces, but it didn't go as planned. I had delegated responsibilities at the headquarters, put on my body armor and helmet, grabbed a baton, and joined the main column heading up Institutska Street, realizing that the most significant events of the day would occur there, closer to the Verkhovna Rada, the Ukrainian parliament.

But the passage to it at the corner of Shelkovychna Street had long been blocked by KamAZ trucks, and events at this intersection started unfolding rapidly.

I barely had a chance to check out the burning office of Yanukovych's Party of Regions nearby when the confrontation with the police at the main intersection escalated into a melee. Our side threw cobblestones from the dismantled pavement, and their side responded with gas grenades and rubber bullets. We managed to break through a row of trucks, but the police didn't allow us to turn around, so we had to retreat back to the intersection. Molotov cocktails flew, KamAZ trucks were set ablaze, shop windows were shattered, and several cars parked nearby were damaged. A few injuries were reported from rubber bullets and air rifles, but their guns didn't deter us. Several police officers climbed onto the roof of one of the buildings, threw flash-bang grenades into the crowd of protestors, and shot at people with their pump-action rubber bullet shotguns as if they were shooting insects. Some of our guys also managed to get onto that roof, via a different attic, and like a ninja squad, began sneaking up on the Berkut, who had relaxed due to their unchecked firing. The thousand-strong crowd below froze, waiting for the outcome. But at the last moment, the police noticed the attack and hastily retreated through some openings, not daring to engage in a rooftop battle.

I met a couple of familiar faces in the crowd. They suggested going to Mariinskyi Park, saying it was even more lively there. I told them that I wasn't bored here, and it would be very difficult to retreat from the other side, where one of our columns had initiated the attack, back behind the protective barricades of

Maidan. They left, and I never saw them again. As I later found out, things got very rough for our people over there.

Meanwhile, the standoff on Shelkovychna Street became a strategic matter. We started constructing a flimsy barricade, but since we lacked proper materials, it mainly consisted of burning tires and anything else that we could get our hands on. New police units were approaching from different directions. Small clashes occurred in alleys and passages. Their numbers grew, and we began losing ground and initiative. If in the morning we'd controlled the entire adjacent territory, and the Berkut had hidden behind a line of trucks, trying to hold that line, by the afternoon, we had only a portion of Institutska Street remaining, which led down to the Maidan. It was crowded with people, including our fighters and those who had come as demonstrators or just spectators. I remember how, through the rows of police officers, an old Zhiguli car broke through, and some desperate guy from the Automaidan had a trunk full of much-needed Molotov cocktails. The car didn't survive that jolt well, but the owner didn't seem upset at all—his gaze burned. An incoming grenade was always like a lottery ticket: it either exploded at your feet or farther away, it either doubled the image from the blast or struck again at your already ringing ears. You never knew if it would hit you or your neighbor. If someone nearby lost consciousness from a blast or just collapsed from a shrapnel wound to the leg or eye, you'd grab them and drag them fifty meters into the courtyard of a nearby building, where medics had set up a station. Then you'd return to the front line. I was well-equipped: in addition to my helmet and body armor, I had a respirator and protective goggles, so I could stand in the front row without being too concerned about gas.

When there were too many police officers, they began storming our defensive line. First in formation and then in a wave, but we repelled them time and time again. After a few hours, they started using water cannons. One at first, then another, and things started improving for the enemy. They gradually extinguished our fiery defense and launched a frontal assault, simultaneously striking from the side through an alley. We flinched and began to withdraw slowly, then retreated, and eventually just ran away. Some red-bearded Viking-looking guy and I were the last ones. He kept trying to charge into battle, going berserk and wanting to single-handedly defeat all the police officers. He clanged his bag full of Molotov cocktails, and I kept pulling him back by his collar, shouting something in his ear. He couldn't accept that there was nothing more for us to do there.

On that day, I understood the clear difference between retreating and fleeing. When you retreat, you walk backward with your face toward the enemy, but when you flee, you show them your back. Initially, the Viking-looking guy and I were retreating, throwing incendiary ammunition from his bulky bag under the feet of the closest police formation. But when the panic flight began, I lost sight of my momentary comrade—this was chaos and carnage now. Some fell, and some were caught and immediately beaten by the Berkut. Others tried to seek refuge in the entrances, barricading themselves or simply breaking into locked doors. I ran along with everyone else. I couldn't do it quickly due to the dense crowd and constant obstacles on the sidewalks. I didn't look back because I already knew what was happening there, and it was terrifying even without seeing it. I realized I was running in the last ranks, but just how close the enemy was became evident when I saw a Berkut officer right next to me, striking someone with his baton, then another one, and another. Everything blurred together—the last rows of those fleeing and the first rows of those pursuing. For many, this encounter ended very sadly and tragically. But I was fortunate.

I made it to the intersection near the upper barricade of the Maidan unharmed; realizing that it was better not to rush through its narrow gates, I turned aside and downward with a large part of the crowd. However, our speed had dropped to a walking pace, and the Berkut continued to strike from behind with their batons. Along the way, I grabbed a hesitant young girl by her collar. She had clearly just come to watch what was happening but didn't realize the gravity of the situation, and, still lagging behind, apparently thought it was just a crowd at the subway entrance. She protested, "Young man, don't push!" Having seen those who crumbled like beans onto the asphalt and whom I had to leap over like a saiga during my sprint, I wasn't in the mood for pleasantries but decided to rescue her. I said, "I'm holding onto you so you don't get trampled, you idiot." "Then hold me tighter," she said, finally understanding that the situation was indeed serious.

We descended about a hundred meters downhill. The Berkut didn't pursue us—they started regrouping to capture the upper barricades of the Maidan. In the dispersing crowd, there were wounded, mostly those with head injuries. We began to flag down cars to transport them to the hospital. I remember one businessman in a fancy Mercedes with his security in a Jeep. He picked up three of them. When the first calm moment arrived, I was surprised to see not only cars going about their business and pedestrians in a hurry, but also people peacefully chatting in cafés. It was astonishing: most of the population didn't care about this revolution or the fact that just a block away, there were intense street battles all day with casualties. But this revelation didn't last long. I had to return to the Maidan, where there were still those who cared about what kind of a country they would live in.

I entered the camp through the side gates and headed to the Ukrainian House, the headquarters of the Automaidan. Along the way, I saw the far barricades falling almost without resistance. There were very few people on the Maidan itself, and the spirit was nearing panic. I arrived just in time: the police were minutes away from seizing our base, and Hrushevskyi Street was already packed with police, descending through the empty barricade lines. Our team evacuated the headquarters, and there was a spot for me in the last car. Turning around, I saw a guy holding a wooden club in each hand, engaging in a duel with two police officers who were hiding behind shields. But it looked like that fighter was doomed. Just like all of Maidan.

The limping cavalry of the revolution gathered in a semi-abandoned bar that had become our makeshift headquarters after the evacuation. Everyone was in a subdued mood. There were about thirty to forty people, nearly half of them women. Some sandwiches appeared, and I took a bite. Everyone looked at my face, blackened with soot, and my jacket, charred and muddy. Someone remarked that I was covered in blood. I replied that it was someone else's—I'd gotten splattered by a guy with a skull injury, his blood spraying like a fountain. I wasn't even injured, aside from a few scratches and bruises.

The meeting dragged on until evening, with everyone offering their solutions for saving the country and the situation based on their level of radicalism, from writing an angry official Facebook post about being betrayed by everyone to seizing the Prosecutor General's mansion. One of my comrades whispered in my ear that if we ventured there, they'd probably kill all of us. I was the last to speak, stating that I had no intention of sitting here and that I was returning to the Maidan.

They tried to convince me not to go, claiming that the Maidan had already fallen, the subway wasn't working, the city was blocked, and troops were converging on it. I told them I believed my own eyes, not rumors, so I was going to check, and if the Maidan was still holding, then that was where I belonged. Four of us ended up agreeing to go: the driver, a curly-haired guy, and two pensioners. Among them, I knew only Misha, a retired military man who worked at our headquarters registering newcomers. He was memorable for once confessing to me that he had never had such a strict and diplomatic guy before.

We set out in one car, while the others stayed with their anxieties, predictions, and discussions. Upon arrival, Curly realized that these games weren't for him and "logged off." The rest of us armed ourselves with whatever we could find and headed toward the Maidan.

It was nine in the evening. The Maidan was still holding. Miraculously. All the barricades had fallen, including the two largest and most fortified ones. Part of the camp had already been seized. The blazing defense line was about fifty meters from the main stage. On the way to the front line, I saw people dismantling cobblestones and passing them along the chain toward the front. Women, pensioners, ladies with manicured nails and high heels, teenagers, a bespectacled nerd who looked like a professor—everyone was getting involved. Some girls were distributing Molotov cocktails. I reached the front and realized that I wouldn't leave today, if only for the sake of those who would now be behind me. I didn't call anyone or pick up my phone—the noise and roar were so intense that I wouldn't be able to hear anything anyway. Besides, who should I have called at that moment when everyone was supposed to be in the place where the fate of the entire revolution was being decided? The second pensioner who was with us got wounded in the leg by shrapnel almost immediately. The driver took him to the hospital, and many others during that night, as I later found out.

Misha and I stood there until morning, along with hundreds of other guys. I could write about this endless night—it felt like it could fill an entire book. But none of it could ever be fully conveyed to those who weren't there. Like the moment when, in one of the police attacks, the riot squad managed to break through our defenses in formation—we flinched, but seconds later, regrouped and, with wild cries, rushed at them, causing them to retreat in disarray, having lost a few of their fighters.

I managed to set fire to an armored water cannon twice with Molotov cocktails, but it stubbornly did not want to flare up, extinguishing itself with its own water before crawling back toward our ranks. During my third attempt, in semi-darkness, I came helmet to helmet with a policeman hiding behind a parapet—he emptied his shotgun at me, aiming directly at my chest, unaware of my bulletproof vest, but luckily, they were rubber bullets, so I came away unharmed. The Trade Unions Building was on fire, and a fire truck arrived an entire lifetime too late, taking down survivors from the upper floors.

Zhenya, the voice of Maidan,* had to single-handedly command our defense from the stage past nightfall because the entire leadership had gone off somewhere, as usually happens when things get too hot. He encouraged us every half hour, saying that buses with reinforcements from western Ukraine were on their way and that we only needed to hold out for a few more hours. I desperately needed a bathroom and ended up urinating behind the Independence Monument, in the buffer zone because there was no time, and because this was a one-time event—especially since life had shrunk to the dimensions of that night. Upon returning to the Maidan, I saw that we had a gap in our defenses, with no barricades or a line of fire, and a sea of Berkut black helmets swaying close by. I began organizing people to build a barrier there. A veteran of the Afghan war who had decided that he was in charge of this sector of defense stopped us, saying that it was too narrow for the police to advance from that side for now. They eventually formed a

---

* Yevhen Nyshchuk, "the voice of the Maidan," is a famous actor and the former Minister of Culture. He took part in both the Orange and Euromaidan Revolutions.

column and managed to enter the narrow space during the next mass attack, "occupying" the Independence Monument and threatening to come at us from behind. We had to set our own tents on fire to prevent that from happening, and then ignite a defensive line of fire, basically constructing a new line of defense, throwing anything and everything into the flames, including clothing and bottles of grease—we were critically short of tires that night.

The formation and its support group tried to break through along the wall of the Philharmonic building, searching for new holes in our defense, and we repelled them by throwing pieces of cobblestones from above, like mountain tribes against a Roman cohort. Both sides were exhausted by morning. The police had become weary of their attacks, but we were still holding on, though it was unclear how. Dawn came as a relief— the battle subsided, both sides remained in their positions, and they only occasionally exchanged fire. We sat down on some steps, and a girl handed us each a sandwich and a cup. We had no strength left to eat it all, but then Zhenya announced that the Berkut were regrouping uphill, near St. Sophia's Cathedral, preparing to encircle us from the rear. He asked anyone who could to go there to stop them. I realized that I couldn't make it up there, but a minute later, I saw new columns forming, and from their dialect, I understood that fresh reinforcements from Lviv had finally arrived, and there were people to take over this watch.

After getting some sleep, I spent the entire following day, February nineteenth, there again. We constructed barricades along the new front line, which ran through the middle of the

Maidan. Supplies, food, tires, and gasoline with oil for Molotov cocktails were brought in. The crowd had grown significantly, and we were much better prepared for an assault. But it never came, neither during the day nor, which would have been more likely, at night. By morning, I realized that I was exhausted again and went to my friends to rest and clean up.

I returned just a few hours later, still before noon on the twentieth. But by that time, everyone had been killed.

Living with the feeling that you missed the main and decisive battle of this revolution is unbearable. Knowing that you peacefully slept, took a shower, and had scrambled eggs for breakfast, while someone was crawling under wooden shields through sniper fire, is doubly unbearable. Back then, no one knew it was the end. I saw the wounded and the dead and heard the cracking sounds of a sniper rifle. But the idea of going to check how accurately a sniper could shoot didn't cross my mind, especially since by then the battle had ended and our forces had withdrawn back to the Maidan, fortifying their previously held positions. I also joined in constructing barricades near the Ukrainian House, our place. The much anticipated and feared assault never took place that night.

On the contrary, we initiated the attack—the Automaidan began organizing checkpoints at the airports. I was summoned to Zhuliany Airport, where I spent the next day taking control of the situation there. When I had more or less arranged everything, I handed over the responsibilities to other Automaidan activists and returned to the Maidan. The guy who drove me asked, "What do you do for a living? We don't want such skills to go to waste." "Don't worry, they won't go to waste," I replied.

I remember that evening of the twenty-first very well, when I returned from the airport to the camp. The Maidan was busier than ever before: crowds of people, cars, piles of tires, food, Molotov cocktails, stones, and more that were much needed three days prior. Everyone was running around, and I stood silently on the steps of the Ukrainian House, realizing that it was all over. Because we had already won. The Berkut had locked themselves in their bases, unwilling to fight for Yanukovych any longer, as he seemed to have fled, and the *sotnyas*—the hundreds—of Andriy Parubiy already controlled the Rada. I felt the relief of a long-awaited victory right there on those steps and would remember it forever.

Then came a very difficult week at the headquarters, which had been restored after being destroyed. It turned out there was even more work after the victory than before, including transporting medicines and food, arranging transport for the rotation of the security forces at Yanukovych's former estate, Mezhyhirya, and other important sites that had been abandoned, and more. There was even less time to sleep. Then, when it seemed like things had settled down, the "little green men" took over Crimea, and, after wrapping up my affairs, I went off to the new war, which was an underground one.

But all of that would happen later. At that moment, I stood there on those steps, entirely happy, smiling, and eating a banana while waiting for a friend to go to his place, have a proper meal, and get some sleep. On the way, we stopped at a street kiosk, and I got out of the car to buy some mineral water and something to eat with tea. Two men were standing in front of me by the window, both in cool NATO-style camouflage,

with Ukrainian flag armbands and other military gear. I immediately realized that they were our guys.

Before, it had been risky to walk around the city dressed
like that, but now, after the victory, it was not only acceptable,
but fashionable. I was so happy to see my fellow countrymen
proudly wearing national symbols that I shouted, "Glory to
Ukraine!" Both guys turned around and looked at me strangely,
then they took their purchases and walked away in silence. I
was a bit surprised. I didn't understand what had gone wrong.
After all, I was just like them! Approaching the window to make
my purchase, I saw my reflection in the glass and realized why
those guys were taken aback. In their eyes, I must have looked
like a dirty homeless person in a tattered and scorched suit that
had been nicked by someone else, with a sooty face and no distinctive marks. My blue-yellow ribbon had turned black long
ago, and I'd left my helmet and baton in the car. They must have
been wary of the sight of a young alcoholic who lived in a heat
duct. Maybe they were afraid that after greeting them, I would
ask them for money.

I took a bottle of mineral water and some cookies, paid
for them, and still somewhat perplexed by the minor misunderstanding, walked back to the car. As I walked, it struck me:
these two hadn't been where I'd been during those days! It was
simply impossible to stay as clean and tidy as they looked back
then. I didn't consider them cowards or judge them. Everyone
has their own path and choices to make. After all, I didn't know
what my life would look like later. But I was glad that during
those days, I'd been where I needed to be.

DAY FIFTY

Another milestone. There's no cause for celebration, but also no reason to be sad. The blues that troubled me for three days vanished as suddenly as they had come. While I was reminiscing about the Maidan, nothing special had happened in real life. The northern weather, like a capricious woman, remained fickle—it either got warm or cooled down, coquettishly covering the smiling sun with a lace of clouds, letting angry black clouds fall onto its brow, or even sprinkling with tears of rain. I've never liked coy chicks.

Mosquitoes have launched an attack on the med point, or you could say, conducted a raid. We fight them with gauze on the windows and folded newspapers, decorating the walls with black and red corpses, the mummies of small victories. But these quietly buzzing creatures still seep into our territory.

I accidentally broke my thermometer over the weekend. The chief entered the room while I was checking my temperature, and as I stood up, it slipped from my hand. We gathered the broken pieces from the floor using a piece of paper and later cleaned them up with a vacuum cleaner. Fortunately, we're not children anymore and didn't think of playing with those intriguing liquid mercury balls.

My condition has been relatively stable. Occasionally, my heart rhythm flutters, but everything else seems to be fine: weight, test results, well-being, and mood.

The most important thing was to see some progress in our case. However, over the past week—and could anyone believe we've already reached the seventh week?—there hasn't been any significant news. There was one provocative fake news story about a supposed Ukrainian soldier confessing to carrying explosives for me. It was a diversion, an attempt to shift the focus from my hunger strike to labeling me as a real terrorist. It was reminiscent of the infamous "crucified boy" story in Donbas that Russian propagandists fabricated in the nonexistent Lenin Square in Sloviansk. Eventually, it was exposed as fake, but it had a short-term impact at the right moment, leaving a lasting negative impression. These are the times we're living in; it's the era of post-truth and hybrid wars.

Less than two weeks remain until the next "flag of hope," but I don't anticipate anything extraordinary. It's just easier to cope and endure when you break time into intervals. It's fine. If necessary, we'll extend it by another two weeks, then another after that . . .

We've had two days of playoff games. The first match was great, with France defeating Argentina 4–3, also showcasing a strong performance and making a clear bid for possible victory in the entire tournament. Uruguay also deservedly beat Portugal 2–1. These two winning teams will now face each other in the quarterfinals. Yesterday also featured two less exciting matches that ended 1–1, even after extra time. A penalty shootout determined the outcome of these matches. In a surprising turn of events, Russia eliminated the world-famous Spain in a penalty shootout, even though neither team was exceptional—at most, the Spaniards demonstrated their passing skills.

Croatia and Denmark set a world record by both scoring in the first four minutes, but the rest of the two hours featured such unexciting soccer that I even nodded off during their attacks.

But at least justice prevailed and Croatia advanced further after the decisive penalty shootout at the end of the match. As we reach the middle of the championship, half of the top teams have already been eliminated, including Germany, Argentina, Portugal, and Spain, which collectively hold more titles than all the remaining teams combined.

That's what makes this tournament so intriguing. Following Russia's victory, the media has been celebrating for twenty-four hours straight, and it seems this excitement will continue until the next World Cup, if not longer. Nobody is willing to acknowledge that sometimes weaker teams get lucky while stronger ones don't, as was the case with Germany, who'd dominated the game but couldn't score.

But Russian reality seems to operate by its own rules, lacking an objective perspective, especially when it comes to themselves. There's a lot of pride, boasting, and aggressiveness directed at those who aren't on their side, but during soccer festivities, they hide their true nature behind false smiles.

I have mixed feelings about this tournament. On the one hand, I watch the games, trying to focus solely on the sport, but on the other hand, it bothers me that I'm passively supporting a regime that oppresses not only my country but also many others. But I know that sooner or later, this regime will fall and be held accountable, either through direct confrontation or in the court of history, the latter of which is even more important. Soccer will always endure, but dictators hiding behind soccer must go!

I received several newspapers and letters. The two letters from abroad made me smile. One was from France and the other from the Netherlands, from some film companies. Both have the same computer-translated text written in Russian with the signatures of the owners, apparently as part of some regular action to support filmmakers. But something else amused me: they wrote that they were following my fate very carefully, but the letter was sent to the Yakut colony and had then been forwarded here, to Labytnangi. This means you weren't as attentive to my fate as you thought, colleagues! But I'm still grateful for any support, especially this one.

One of the sick prisoners came up to me and cautiously said that he went to the duty unit today and saw other prisoners: "The zone is interested in you . . . They're asking if you're fine and how you are . . . " "Next time, tell the zone that I'm very flattered . . . "

There's a clock hanging on the two-story building of the duty unit. It always shows ten minutes to two. They say that it stopped about eight years ago but no one has been in any hurry to fix it. It hangs as a symbol of the frozen time in this camp. The situation has improved slightly here, but the current regime is based on the memories of the previous bloody orders that were carried out to maintain "order."

Back then, there was a red Soviet flag waving on a flagpole next to the duty unit and traffic lights hung in the center of the alley. And when the detachment formed up in order to go somewhere, it was necessary to wait for the green signal, which was turned on by whoever was on duty, and only after it did the *kozel* herder begin to command his usual: "Left step . . . March . . . One . . . One . . . One, two, three . . . " It happened that the traffic lights were not turned on for quite a long time, and people, like a trained herd, stood on an empty road waiting for a green light. The traffic lights were removed eventually, the Soviet flag as well, but now the new inmates transferred to this camp were disciplined in quarantine for two weeks so that they proved how glad they were to have come to serve their sentence here.

At the same time, no one has canceled the "at attention" formation. The Soviet marches sound out at wake-up calls as well as during physical exercises and formations for checks. The Soviet Union is still very deeply embedded in the minds of many leaders of this country, and in recent years its influence has even begun to grow again, just like a brain tumor. The worst thing is that this disease is contagious and affects even young people who didn't live through the times of that dead monster.

DAY FIFTY-ONE

Summer has once more come to an end. It's cold outside—wind and clouds. The inmates in the alley are once again wearing their overcoats. Inside the ward, it's seventeen degrees Celsius.

I slept in warm underwear under two blankets again, and during the day, I wore a sweater under my prison uniform. Due to the cold weather, they returned a small heater to me. It was useful because it started to freeze last night, just as it did tonight.

My feet and hands still feel icy. But not just from the cold—I can feel that my engine is not running smoothly again. I can barely shuffle around my cell, and shortness of breath has returned, even when I'm just sitting. There's increased pressure on my heart, both from hunger and this wildly fluctuating weather outside. My weight is also fluctuating due to excess water, but overall, it continues to decrease slowly. Earlier today, the scales showed less than seventy-six kilograms.

My lawyer told me that human rights representatives claimed a couple of weeks ago that either I had stopped my hunger strike or gained two kilograms. Where do they get all this information? Rumors are everywhere, and people's heads even more so. Or did I gain two kilograms from those fake explosives they accused me of having? Well, then it smells like suicide belts . . .

Yesterday, on the news ticker, it read: "Kyiv listed the names of Russians it proposes to exchange for Ukrainian detainees." Strange. They never used to utter "exchange," especially between Russia and Ukraine. Now, they're cautiously mentioning such a possibility. Either they're preparing the ground and testing the public's reaction to such an action, or it means nothing at all, just another distraction and delaying tactic on this issue. We'll wait for further developments—if, of course, they're to follow.

Meanwhile, during the World Cup, which, unfortunately, took place in this country, Brazil beat the Mexican national team in a hard-fought and beautiful match. Japan nearly pulled off a miracle by defeating one of the tournament favorites, Belgium, with a score of 2–0 and dominating the game for most of the time. But the descendants of the Flemings were able to rally and break the Children of the Samurai. In the last twenty minutes, they scored three goals against them—the last one in the last minute, which we have seen more than once during this World Cup—and deservedly, albeit with difficulty, advanced to the quarterfinals. Japan's going home, but they'll return as heroes after such a battle.

They brought me a bunch of letters again. I'll sit down to answer them now. There's some stuff from acquaintances, but mostly stuff from strangers. Though after such letters, it's no longer possible to call them strangers. More like distant, unknown relatives.

I remember receiving a letter from the Czech Republic informing me that they had reserved a spot for me at a table in a great tavern called Kit, where I would be in good company. Offer accepted. If I'm passing through, I'll definitely stop by for a couple of glasses of beer with boar's hoof and potatoes.

People often ask me in letters not to die. I'm already tired of explaining that I'm not suicidal, that suicide is a sin, the fate of cowards and weaklings. I'm not starving myself in order to die, but in order to win. And dissuading me from using any methods or arguments is completely useless. It's like trying to persuade a fighter running to attack not to die. He's in no hurry to die! He runs toward the enemy trench to defeat his enemies. Yes, he understands that he can be killed, but what can he do? That's life, and he loves it very much, but he cannot do otherwise because there are more important things. I look exactly like such a person with a rifle at hand. Only I don't run, I lie down. I don't shoot, I starve. Everyone has their own war, their own trench, their own enemy.

DAY FIFTY-TWO

Summer has returned. I removed my sweater and turned off the heater. Despite the nice weather, my health hasn't been great. Even those around me have noticed it, and I feel another wave of discomfort settling in. Counting these ups and downs, along with the changing weather, has become exhausting. This time, they don't seem to align, but I don't care anymore. I'm overwhelmed by a sense of fatigue, both physically and mentally, leading to apathy and indifference toward everything. Despite this low point, I'm not giving up.

My sister Natasha is coming tomorrow. I knew about her planned arrival, I just wasn't sure of the exact date. But yesterday, I was finally granted the long-promised telephone conversation with her. It got postponed due to local bureaucratic issues, and yesterday was also frustrating, with problems like my application and phone number not being endorsed correctly by the authorities, among other delays.

Beyond the fence, when people hear the unhurried rattle of the penitentiary machine and see the illogical results of its work, it seems that this is all done on purpose. But only after being inside, between its millstones and gears, do you understand how slow and dumb-headed a monster it is. This is how things are always done here, and it doesn't matter who's in charge. In general, it's the usual situation: there are more people who are easily fooled than those fools who believe in conspiracy theories. I'm one of the simple ones.

Natasha didn't pick up the phone three times yesterday, but I persuaded the head of the detachment to try to get through once more in the evening. We tried again and got through. But I'd rather not have done it. Apart from the fact that Natasha is arriving in two days, there has been no more good news. Nothing new has been heard about the exchanges.

And most importantly, there was no good news about the

children. The people who promised to organize a trip for my daughter to Canada for a month of summer holidays disappeared at the last moment. The FSB officers warned relatives that if she came to Odesa, to the film festival, then they would all have problems. What's it to them? Were they afraid that an unfortunate child whose father is starving in a Russian prison would be presented to the world? We'd wanted to avoid that very outcome: she would have been there under a fictitious surname, and no one would have disturbed her. She would have just watched good movies and had fun.

But the blockheaded security forces officers have their own logic. And on top of that, my ex-wife rebelled. She didn't want to give her daughter the go-ahead to leave for Kyiv, even though she hadn't lived with her mom for the third year in a row and had generally renounced her mother a long time ago. In general, nothing good.

To make things even worse—and this was the news that really struck me—they forgot to buy a birthday gift for my son, a new laptop to replace the already ancient ten-year-old one that he'd inherited from me. It really killed me. I started asking for it three months in advance and wrote yard-long letters about how it was important! With exclamation marks! In advance! A computer for my son and a trip for my daughter.

I personally haven't needed packages, transfers, or money. Those things for my children were my main needs. I'll always be patient as long as my kids are OK. This was the only thing I could do for them, far away. I was assured that everything would be done, that these were trifles, and that I shouldn't worry. But I was still worried, and I continued to write in my letters the word IMPORTANT in all capital letters, putting exclamation marks after it. I was once again assured that everything would be fine and asked what could be done for me personally. I replied that, apart from this, I didn't need anything, and again wrote IMPORTANT, this time not only with exclamation marks but underscores. And here was the result. This shocked me so much yesterday that I still haven't been able to get back to normal today.

I don't know what to say about it to Natasha tomorrow. She tries very hard—like thousands of others—to help me, but why can't they just read what I write? For them, these are "little things that we will do anyway," but they don't do them! And again, there will be empty conversations and appeals, and questions about how to help me, yet another vicious circle. It's like the situation with the woolen socks: I've been asking them to give them to me for five years now, but they never reach me. They send whatever comes into their heads, except for this simple and necessary item in any prison, especially in the north.

Ten simple pairs instead of one woolen pair, a juniper coaster for a tea mug, steel spoons and vessels, and a set of stationery. Most of this, of course, is not allowed through because it's sent without consulting. I understand the sincere desire to help, but why don't they read what I write to them again? Do people on the outside really think they know better what exactly I need? It's the noise of a crowd of enthusiastic readers in which the voice of my small request drowns. As a result, I still walk around without woolen socks. I put on three pairs of simple ones. But these are minor complaints in the greater scheme of my poor health and other issues.

The other day, a couple of *muzhiki* from the barracks came with a fever and a cold to the med point. One of them, Lysy, I know somewhat, and the other, Horvat, came to the camp recently. He's a Croat who's been living in Russia for five years, and he speaks Russian quite well. He got ten years for murder, but he's a soccer fan, just like Lysy. So, our group of fans is growing.

He mentioned that in the prison, with all these medical commissions endlessly visiting me, it's become a bit easier to breathe over the past month. The police aren't so frivolous, they behave quietly and politely, and they don't even try to "strengthen" the quarantine that much, trying at any cost to turn the inmates newly arrived from transfer into "activists." Well, I'm glad I could help someone at least a little bit.

Yesterday there were two matches in the playoffs. The duel between Sweden and Switzerland, as expected, took place without much heat. The score was as expected, with Sweden winning 1–0. But the surprise was that Sweden won. The second match, Colombia vs. England, was anticipated to be an exciting game, but it turned out to be dirty, rough, and unpleasant. Almost every attack or play ended in a foul. It was the match with the most yellow cards in the tournament. Two English players received cards, as did half of the Colombian team, and their behavior resembled a group of *gopniki.** England had the upper hand both in the game and on the scoreboard, but Colombia managed to equalize toward the end, resulting in a 1–1 tie. Once again, the outcome was determined by a penalty

---

* A delinquent subculture in Russia and elsewhere in eastern Europe.

shootout, and England performed better, advancing to the quarterfinals.

The quarterfinals will begin the day after tomorrow, but for now, we have two days of rest.

DAY FIFTY-THREE

I felt pretty awful yesterday evening. Maybe it was because of the weather, or maybe some other reason. I had a splitting headache, so I asked the perpetually drowsy nurse for two dro-taverine before going to bed.

I got a good night's sleep, and I'm feeling fine now—my reflection in the mirror is also more or less normal. This is good because Natasha, who is supposed to come for a short visit today, shouldn't be too alarmed when she sees me.

Last night, I dreamed about our country house again. First, I carefully led my father inside, his injured arm was bandaged, then, once we were there, I embraced my mother for a long time. Lately, my dreams have often featured my parents, which wasn't the case before.

It's still warm outside, but my feet are cold. Winter is approaching. Autumn begins here in August.

The scales showed seventy-five kilograms and change. During my hunger strike, I've lost ten kilograms, plus an additional five before that during my preparation, totaling fifteen kilograms.

It doesn't seem like a lot, considering it's been nearly two months. But there's not much more to lose for someone who was already quite thin, even during a hunger strike. On the other hand, overweight individuals lose weight faster, theoretically, and should be able to sustain themselves longer with their accumulated reserves. In practice, that doesn't happen—overweight individuals are too dependent on food, both physically and psychologically. There seems to be something broken inside them, so they don't handle hunger strikes and various dietary restrictions well, as if these emergency situations "didn't agree with them." People with the physique of greyhounds, on the other hand, endure for much longer and with less difficulty. Maybe in such lean bodies, there's a similar spirit, very different from the soft and flabby?

I had a visit from my sister Natasha. I walked along the alley as usual, accompanied by the duty officer, and it was as quiet as a kindergarten during nap time inside the camp. Natasha wasn't alarmed by my appearance—she was prepared to see the worst, especially since, in some Ukrainian media outlets, I've been reported as "dead" a couple of times, with claims that "Russia is hiding the body until the end of the championship." I was also very glad to see her, even though we were speaking through a telephone and a glass wall. Over the course of two hours, we discussed seemingly everything. But she did most of the talking because, apart from saying that I was feeling fine and had no intention of stopping, there wasn't much else to say.

My sister told me about various actions in support of me in Ukraine, the world, and Russia, but she didn't have the full picture. It has been very difficult to keep up with everything: it's growing exponentially, like a snowball. Some people burn out, get tired, and leave, but for everyone who falls, two rise up to take their place, so the public pressure doesn't diminish.

European politicians are also getting more involved because they can't ignore it anymore.

Next week, Natasha's flying to the United States, where the International PEN center, actively involved in this matter, will connect her with American congressmen. In general, things are moving forward, to the point that even Russia is making statements about a possible prisoner exchange, and such things don't happen in this country without orders from the top. Initiative always comes from one person here, and everyone watches his mouth, his body language, trying to anticipate and discern his thoughts and desires.

Natasha also talked about how she has limited herself to five interviews a day in the media, as she couldn't handle more, though it used to reach up to seventeen at its peak. She gets hundreds of calls and thousands of messages each day. People write and show their support, everyone from Stephen King to some wizards who ask for my old handkerchief for rituals to bring about my release. There are a lot of unstable individuals involved in all this. But, most likely, they are simply more noticeable—I believe the statistics suggest we have more healthy people than sick ones in this world.

There are exceptions. For example, that case with the ATO veteran who managed to grab the microphone at a conference and *allegedly* defend me, but then talked about explosives being delivered to me. He turned out to be a twice-concussed, mentally unstable person registered with the authorities, not a paid provocateur. However, the Russian propaganda machine has milked this situation for a week and now, when necessary, it can refer to this outbreak of a sick imagination as an indisputable, proven fact. The logic is simple and common to both propaganda and ordinary *vatniks*—if it was shown on TV, then it must be true. This applies to everything, from weather news to Igor Prokopenko's insanely ridiculous, pseudoscientific, anti-western, and anti-Ukrainian programs.

But, in any case, the meeting with my sister was pleasant and useful for both of us. After passing on my latest instructions regarding my family and the kids, we said our goodbyes, pressing our palms against the glass, each on their own side. It was really great to be reminded that I wasn't alone in this struggle.

DAY FIFTY-FOUR

The weather is unstable again, much like how I feel. Both my condition and health are not great. It's unclear whether it's due to the new fluids in the IVs prescribed by the doctor or something else, but it sucks.

Fortunately, when my sister visited yesterday, she didn't see me in this state. Otherwise, she would have been worried and raised her concern with others. No matter how unwell I am, in any situation, I always say that I'm doing fine and put on a smile. I can't afford to show weakness, especially in public.

The whole week feels kind of empty, reflecting the lack of news and inner feelings, or rather, the absence of them. I have no motivation to read, write, or do anything at all. Sometimes, even lying down is hard . . .

The medical commissions and chiefs haven't been very visible lately either. The head of the colony went on vacation, and his deputies did not even think of checking in on me. But this is for the best—I've grown tired of these endless monotonous visits, a series of military star rankings, and feigned smiles on police faces. Let's take a break from each other.

I've only had brief encounters with the doctor lately. He has mostly been occupied with paperwork, reports, and his own travels, returning to the routine he had set aside when he was devoting more time to me. Now that there's some relative stability, he has been catching up on his duties, still aiming for a promotion, a pension, or at the very least, a vacation.

I received two letters today: a handwritten one and a printed-out email. Both were from Kyiv. The handwritten letter was from a schoolboy, who, judging by the handwriting, appeared to be in middle school, but pretty clever. He'd read my stories and watched my film *Gamer*. He liked it, and he was monitoring my situation, also sending me the results of the Cannes Film Festival in a letter. This was very sweet and touching—thank you!

The second letter was from the father of another boy, a younger one who was ten years old. His son didn't like to read, but had read my stories too. He said that he liked them, especially the one about the dog, even though it was sad. There was a photograph of the reading boy, enclosed as proof. If this was sincere and not forced, then I'm also very happy and grateful! Then I immediately recalled how a year or two ago, I'd received a whole bunch of letters from schoolchildren of the same class. They wrote letters to "any political prisoner" in class. The text was identical and contrived. I felt pity for the children who, during such political information or class hours, were forced to engage in written carbon-copy patriotism. But for some reason, we try to make a boogeyman out of everything.

There's a bell in our corridor, just like at a school, and it rings periodically. If it rings one time, it's a call for a *kozel* who works here to go down to a nurse or a police officer on duty; two times—another one; three—a third one; four—the fourth *kozel* comes.

The fifth one, the caretaker, is a more serious figure—they don't use a bell to call him. In the detachments, it's the same story with calls, but they're given by the orderly who stands under the clock near the entrance to the barracks. He signals by pressing a button and then loudly announces the upcoming event. It can be a wake-up call, lights out, marching to the dining room, to the bathhouse, to the club for a boringly ostentatious lecture, check-ins, and so on. Always at the same time, always with the same doomed intonation. Inmates, like zombies awakened by Pavlov's whistle, start emerging from the barracks to form a line, as you can only go to the toilet with others. This whole situation feels like a school for challenged, grown-up guys. The only difference is that you can't go home afterward.

DAY FIFTY-FIVE

Today was easier than yesterday. The only thing was that in the evening I started to really feel bad, so much so that even those around me noticed it, and the doctor began to worry, canceling the new IV drip with amino acids. Maybe it had made me feel bad, or maybe it was because of another change in the weather: the short Labytnangi summer was heating up outside. It became stuffy at the med point, even though the windows were open. They were covered with mosquito netting, and those that had gotten in before quarantine measures were either exterminated or they themselves, having drunk enough of our blood, died of happiness.

Even though I wasn't feeling great, I kept an eye on the soccer matches yesterday. There are only a few matches left, and they've all been quite interesting. France confidently defeated Uruguay 2–0, even though Uruguay put up a strong fight. But the French managed to outperform them, bringing them two steps closer to claiming the top spot on the podium. In the second match, Belgium secured a 2–1 victory against Brazil, despite Brazil's impressive track record. It was a highly engaging and intense game from the very beginning to the end. After scoring an unfortunate own goal and then a simple but beautiful one, the Brazilian team spent most of their time launching dangerous attacks but only managed to score once. It must have been disappointing for them, but in sports, it's always the strongest team that prevails, and yesterday that team was Belgium.

Everyone here is looking forward to the game between Russia and Croatia; it's the focus of all the local TV channels and the population. Horvat and I are probably the only ones here who'll be cheering against the Russians, but two voices are better than one. Interestingly, this Balkan guy turned out to be a very pleasant person, always cheerful and positive.

During one of my clear-headed moments, I even played chess with him. He was a good player, but his choleric nature made him rush, which led to his defeat. But he took it in stride without any hard feelings.

How a person handles failures and defeats, even small ones, says a lot about their character. In this regard, Horvat isn't a bitter or vengeful person, despite serving a ten-year prison sentence for a conflict that ended in him stabbing a Serbian colleague from their construction site days. Horvat was a small boss there, and the other guy was just a driver, but that wasn't what led them to quarrel. It also wasn't fueled by national or wartime tensions, but rather the simple influence of Russian vodka.

This poison has claimed the lives and fates of many Slavic souls, including these two Balkan men. But in prison, nobody judges you for such matters, unless, of course, you're a rapist or someone who has harmed women and children. Otherwise, they're indifferent to matters of life and death, especially when it involves disputes between men. There's no tragedy made out of such incidents, and perhaps that's how it should be. That's the code of men here.

The veins in my arms have started to swell in some places, and for some reason, they've also decided to ache. I've been smearing restorative ointment on my hands, about as ineffective as the eye drops for my stubborn conjunctivitis. I'm not giving up. I'll continue to apply the ointment and the drops, even if I don't expect miraculous results. It's a bit like my hunger strike—I'm exhausted by all of this, but I'm not giving in. I won't surrender, because I refuse to betray myself or those beyond the prison walls who believe in me.

DAY FIFTY-SIX

My condition improved a little. I stopped being short of breath, although my chest is now constantly aching. The weather worsened, but at the same time brought relief from stuffiness. The sky grew overcast with clouds and started dripping with tears of rain—almost like the fans of the Russian team.

Yesterday, the Russian team lost to Croatia in a tense but one-sided match. The Croatians maintained control over the ball and dominated the game, but they struggled to score many goals. Russia couldn't take charge of the game or retain possession, revealing its true skill level. However, Russia managed some occasional and successful counterattacks. The result was a 2–2 draw—even with extra time—and a penalty shootout. Both teams have already gone through this before, literally in the last round, but this time the truly strongest one was lucky. Croatia is heading onward in the tournament with 4–3 on penalties.

But we'll remember this game more than others because probably the most rotten policeman of this colony tried to ruin our watching it. His name is Kalmyk, and he's known for constantly creating problems for prisoners, exerting his power over us at every opportunity. Despite the unofficial permission given by the authorities to watch soccer at the med point after lights out, he had already dispersed us twice during his shifts, and yesterday he did it again. But this time we decided not to give up. Not all of us, though. Lysy and another inmate, hearing the barking of this watchdog, immediately rolled into bed. Even with such little things, the spirit of a person can be tested.

What's there to fear—camouflage uniforms and insignia? They won't shoot you, and it's unlikely they'll even use physical force, but many prisoners in this camp are afraid of them. When Kalmyk, with his imposing stride, left the building, slamming the door loudly, we posted a lookout by the window in case he returned, and we continued to watch the match, which was reaching its decisive moments. As the penalty shootout approached, Horvat's nerves couldn't take it anymore, and he changed the channel to something else—he couldn't bear to watch and experience the potential loss of his team. But to his delight and the disappointment of almost everyone else, the Croatians didn't disappoint us, unlike the Russian team. Nevertheless, there's jubilation on TV today, celebrating the national team's success, with Putin even extending an invitation for them to have tea together.

In the second match, England beat Sweden without any problems and will now face Croatia in the semi-final, which is set to start in two days.

They delivered the latest newspapers to us. Lately, for some reason, they've started giving them on weekends. There was a very interesting article about the Gulag. It seemed like there was nothing more to add to the description of this dreadful phenomenon after Solzhenitsyn's *Gulag Archipelago*, but no—there will always be something little-known and new to discover. The scale of this horror was simply too vast. Fifty million sentences during the years of Stalin's repressions! That included those who were executed, imprisoned, dispossessed, and exiled. Some of them were run over by the roller of repression two or three times, but all the same, the numbers were shocking.

What's truly frightening, though, is that back then, people supported all this madness, genuinely believed their leader, and didn't want to know the truth until this death machine crushed them beneath its wheels. What a cursed country. And what do we have now?

The second shocking number was forty. Forty percent of the population in modern Russia said that they believed these sacrifices were justified for some great goals by the sick mustachioed executioner. Nothing has changed. It seems like the curse is still in effect and impacts the people too. There was also a quote from the poet Naum Korzhavin, who recently passed away in exile but managed to live through the cult of personality and suffered because of it: "Russia can only survive if it rejects Stalin with shame."

DAY FIFTY-SEVEN

In the morning, the sun was shining through the window, but I had another bad EKG. My heart rate was fading again. I could feel it without any tests. It has been a prolonged process: fading, fading, not fading away.

Another busy week has passed, full of events, content, and feelings. The next one is approaching, it seems like the ninth. But for some reason, I'm not expecting anything special from it. This is actually a very sensible attitude: not expecting anything from life, dancing by the stove, starting from scratch, where everything that happens to you is a plus, a pleasure, and a joy.

There's a well-known formula, where the end result - your expectations = happiness. The less you wait and expect to receive, the happier you are with what you get. I've been trying to live by this simple and correct system for a long time, but it doesn't always work out. Maybe this time it will go more smoothly. The same applies to people—don't allow yourself to be charmed by them, so you won't be disappointed later.

I read a good article in the newspaper about Soviet dissidents. I knew about many of them, the cases were already well-known, but it was still interesting. The "post-thaw" era, from 1968 until *perestroika*, was, of course, not as brutal as during Stalin's time, but it still shattered human lives. Those who spoke out against the regime or simply did things differently were imprisoned, and every ventilation hole for fresh air was sealed, preserving a country that had filled up with the smell of stagnation. The article also mentioned Anatoly Marchenko. To my shame, I'd known nothing about him, even though I was compared to him because he too went on hunger strike, demanding the release of all political prisoners. He was on hunger strike for 117 days, and artificial feeding was administered to him from the second week onward. He died in the hospital just a few days after ending his hunger strike. Did he have an impact on anything? Possibly. But those were different times: Gorbachev and the beginning of *perestroika*.

Now, with Putin, there's not even a scent of it—there's stagnation mixed with the smell of blood and gunpowder at best. Will my hunger strike and its possible sad end have an impact on anything? I don't know. Will I hold on for as long as Marchenko did? I don't have an answer to that either. One hundred seventeen days is, of course, a very long time. But my current fifty-seven days seemed like a big number to me back when I started. We'll see. In any case, I have no other choice but to crawl to the end through this pipe.

The duty officer and Smiley the *balander* came by, and they presented me with lunch, along with another psychologist. Not the young redhead in uniform, but someone else, in civilian clothes, with an even sadder look. Once again, I politely declined the offer of urgent psychological help, along with the food. She wasn't surprised, but still tried to smile and bid farewell, wishing me a pleasant meal. Her wish, coming from her, didn't seem like rudeness or mockery toward the person on hunger strike, but foolishness. She probably wanted to appear polite but ended up looking quite the opposite. In any case, once again, I had no regrets about refusing to interact with these unprompted specialists.

DAY FIFTY-EIGHT

In my dream, I went on a tourist trip to what seemed to be Thailand. For some reason, I was alone. At first, I sailed in a pleasure boat along the clogged Asian canals, then went on a minibus to the Maritime Museum for an excursion. But there, for some reason, I acted silly at the entrance for a long time and couldn't really understand how to buy a ticket and then squeeze through the turnstile. At the same time, I had little money left, and eventually, my time for sleeping had expired.

In the morning I stepped on one leg awkwardly, and something quietly crunched and shifted, maybe the meniscus. As a result, I've been limping all day like an old horse. In general, knees are a sore point for all inmates who have spent a long time in prison conditions where there's little mobility—the body ossifies. That's why many do physical exercises in their cells. I also did this all the time before the hunger strike, but now I have no time for it.

The results of my latest medical tests have arrived. It was

the worst yet, as the doctor said. But I felt that without all those rows of numbers and letters. Even in a state of feeling constantly unwell, it turned out that this was something I could get used to.

One of the reasons for feeling unwell and the worsening test results was that the infirmary had run out of one of the most powerful drugs that they used for my daily IV drip, a solution with a mixture of amino acids. Replacing it with a new one didn't work—that made me feel even worse. For the fourth day in a row, we've continued with the same glucose and vitamins, but at this stage of my hunger strike, they no longer make much of a difference.

Today, more entertainment was added by a nurse with the eyes of a sheep, and the same temperament, who was coming back to work after vacation. She replaced her colleague who constantly forgot everything and the one who loved cotton wool with so much alcohol in it that you could wring it out.

This one was new to me; I'd seen her only a couple of times, at the very beginning, when I was still in the isolation ward and they took me every other day to the med point for IV drips. The nurse showed off her sense of logic: "Oh, I haven't seen you for a long time . . . "

"Hmm, well, you were on vacation for a month, so you probably haven't seen everyone here for a long time."

"Well, in the sense that you haven't been here for a long time . . . "

"Actually, I've been lying here for a month, so it turns out it is really you who hasn't been with us for a long time."

All in all, the conversation went nowhere, and she continued with the medical procedure.

But it would have been better if she hadn't. In two minutes, she unsuccessfully pierced two veins in both arms, which immediately burst, then began to pump the solution under the skin. "Oh, what veins you have," said the nurse, damaging the first one. "Looks like I'll be suffering with you a lot." But when, after damaging the second one, she began to prepare for the third, the last vein still alive, I said that she had exhausted her attempts for the day. The nurse snorted and went to complain about me. A limber young paramedic was invited to replace her, but he was even less skilled than she was. In the end, I trusted only the supply manager.

He doesn't have a diploma, but he's been working in this med point for almost ten years. The supply manager deftly and quickly pierced the last, more problematic vein. By the way, he's a very good guy; he also loves soccer. He's serving a sixteen-year term—robbery with one casualty—but this morning there was a court hearing regarding his parole, with a positive outcome. If the prosecutor's office doesn't file a protest, then he'll be a free man in ten days, tossing away the more than five years left in his term.

I read an article in the newspaper about Moscow human rights activists visiting the infamous IK-7 in Omsk, the cruelest zone in Russia. Well done guys for seriously dealing with that bunch of sadists and scumbags. And well done, those spirited prisoners who were not afraid, in the presence of the camp authorities—their torturers and so-called local commissioners for administration rights—to spill the whole truth about that terrible place.

Torture, violence, beatings, and humiliation are a part of

daily life in that colony. In the prison world, everyone knows about it. When they transferred me, I crossed paths with several people who had escaped from that hell on earth. They were broken, morally and physically crippled, but even sitting in the *Stolypin* train car, they felt like people who had already been liberated, for prisons vary a great deal.

There are still many such sad places in Russia, and the only good news is that judging by the stories of the prisoners, their numbers are slowly becoming fewer and fewer—thank God. The Labytnangi camp used to be like that too. But now here, as with many former bloody places, instead of unpunished cruelty, there's only a regime that suppresses free will and a suffocating atmosphere of fear and denunciation. Yes, there are press huts, where authorities put pressure on inmates, but there are also press zones.

IK-7 is one of the holdouts. There, for the slightest offense or at least a hint of disobedience, they not only beat, strangle, and suspend you from the ceiling for several days in handcuffs but also torture you with electric shock, applying current to your testicles. As for the *obizhennyy*, their bodies are wrapped into a mattress while they get penises waved around by their faces. I hope that such places will sooner or later disappear from the Russian penitentiary system and it will turn into a system of assistance to those who made a mistake.

Though I may be too idealistic, as one operative once told me. To this, I replied that it is better to be a romantic than a scoundrel.

DAY FIFTY-NINE

Yesterday, after lunch, the civilian doctor with glasses came by again. She said that in the two weeks since she'd last seen me, I had lost weight and looked worse. Strange, what did she expect to see? I've been on a hunger strike, after all. She listened to my heartbeat and shook her head even more grimly. She started her mournful song again about fading heart rhythms, oxygen starvation, ischemia, and other pre-heart-attack and pre-death conditions. But I had long stopped reacting to these lamentations and told her once again that I wouldn't stop, despite all their warnings and negative forecasts.

Yesterday was generally an unlucky day. The always-smiling boss came by and gently got under my skin, revealing something about an acquaintance with whom I had been communicating by email in the process. Turned out she had been posting them on the internet. Why do people do such things as expose private correspondence? I was writing to her, not to the world. There was nothing special, let alone intimate, in those messages. We weren't particularly close, and now we definitely won't be. But why? Was she so hungry for attention that she needed to show off? Living life in the open, for everyone to see. Unpleasant, as if you were caught in your underwear in a crowded place.

In the evening, the unpleasantness continued. The annoying Kalmyk was on duty again, and, flaunting his petty position as the assistant on duty, he once again stirred up the whole section with soccer even before the start of the broadcast: "Only Sentsov can watch, they gave him permission!" A provocation!

He had already been told a hundred times that everyone was allowed to watch, but taking advantage of the fact that there was no one from the higher-ups around so late, he started to make a fuss again.

But Kalmyk clearly didn't know me well—I refused to watch it alone. The phrase "inmate unity" is not meaningless to me.

In the morning, we checked the report on yesterday's match in the morning news. We hadn't missed much; the game was so-so. The French took the lead at the beginning of the second half with a score of 1–0, then focused on maintaining that lead, which they successfully did, even though it didn't make for exciting soccer. They played similarly against Denmark. But in the end, the most important thing is victory, and the French are now just one step away from their second championship.

I finally finished reading the book about Ancient Rome, Claudius, Augustus, Tiberius, and the other Caligulas. It was well written, and the topic was interesting and familiar, but it was somewhat hard to get through. Though everything seems difficult for me now, life itself has become bland recently, without seasoning and vivid impressions. Today, I started reading a collection of three science fiction novels by Roger Zelazny. It's also been slow going, but at least I've been filling the voids with this so that negative thoughts don't creep in.

For several days now, there has been consistently good summer weather, almost hard to believe. It's been warm but not hot, sunny, and the sky has been calm, with no wind. From the bathroom window, you can see the distant greenery, giving the feeling of a Crimean May. But I'm not in Crimea, and I doubt I'll ever make it there again.

My medication arrived, and the long IV drips have started again. They're draining, of course, but maybe things will get a bit easier with them. The doctor came to see me today when the drips had already begun, looked critically at me, and said that all that's left of me now are my ears on the pillow. I didn't doubt it—I saw myself in the mirror yesterday and realized that I had started to resemble my companion Sasha "Tundra," suffering naturally from unhealthy thinness. Now, we've become allies not only in spirit, but also in appearance.

Today, the psychologist in civilian clothes visited again, the third time in a row. And each time, she has had an expression on her face as if a close relative were dying. She didn't listen to my refusals and drummed forward with her speech like a robot. Today, it involved a picture that, according to her, should bring me into a calm, stress-resistant state. The picture was some intricate pattern in the style of Indian Vedic culture, with the yin-yang symbol at its center. The psychologist referred to all this as a brief session of visual therapy, which firmly convinced me that she was deeply mentally ill.

I could only protest against this surrealism by closing my eyes. Fortunately, the session turned out to be very brief and ineffective. After that, the psychologist left, wishing me, with a sidelong glance, all the best and, most importantly, recovery, her voice like the one used on a train to announce the next station. I didn't respond by wishing for her recovery in return—it could have prolonged the already unpleasant procedure. The psychiatric ward on wheels with deflated tires stopped right in front of our window . . .

DAY SIXTY

Another meaningless milestone. It's getting harder and harder to write about anything, getting harder just to write. But I need to continue to hold on to this diary like a handrail. There are only a couple of matches left until the end of the World Cup.

Yesterday was the second semi-final: Croatia vs. England. Almost the entire med point supported Horvat and his native team, with rare exceptions. The English scored a goal almost immediately and, despite the opponent's subsequent pressure, repeatedly counterattacked. The Croatians increased the pressure throughout the second half and at the end were able to level the score by moving the game into overtime for the third time in a row at this stage of the playoffs. Here, too, things almost came to a series of post-match penalties, but ten minutes before the end of the time, Croatia snatched a victory from England 2–1 and, for the first time in its history, went to the final. In three days, they'll be facing the strong French team, but as they say, anything's possible. That evening, our Horvat walked along the length of the hallway for a long time, shouting fan chants in his native language.

I barely made it to the end of the match, and it was even difficult for me to speak if someone addressed me. It became quite difficult to walk, and not at all because of my knee, which no longer hurt. It was like there was no strength to carry my body on its unruly legs. Twenty steps to the washbasin and back was already a long trek, and the TV room was a little closer—fifteen. Yeah . . . I realized I wouldn't be able to run cross country again any time soon. It was good that the doctor didn't see me in the evening. But looking at me in the morning, lying under an IV drip, he stated that I was on my way out.

If this story ends well, I can clearly see how journalists in softly lit studios would ask with sympathetic and admiring voices, looking into my eyes: How did you manage to hold on like that? I'll have no answer, not then and certainly not now. These are all words, but I have always preferred actions. And if the stars don't align and my heart doesn't make it through, then I know that it'll happen late in the evening or at night. In the past few days, I've felt how precarious this time is, how my body has weakened when it doesn't get enough air, and I become acutely aware of life or, more accurately, its darker aspect.

They brought a dozen letters from Ukraine and abroad and a lot of printed-out emails. There were very good ones. I will answer, albeit briefly. But most of all, I simply liked the photographs of Labytnangi and its environs, the ferry, the river and nature. Judging by the date on the local postmark, Natasha did it when she arrived last week, or someone who was with her.

It turns out that life is going on very beautifully somewhere very close by, behind the fence. It flows like a river in a photograph.

DAY SIXTY-ONE

July thirteenth. Forty-two years old. Two months of hunger strike. None of these numbers hold any importance to me. I'm only interested in the date of our release, if it even exists and is recorded in the Book of Fate. But it seems that this tome is gathering dust somewhere on a distant shelf.

For two weeks now, there have been no developments or news. But nobody intends to back down—I don't, at least. I never thought I'd make it to this point and this date. But nothing particularly special, let alone magical, has happened. All the magic happens on birthdays and New Year's; they're reserved for childhood. It's about time to grow up. But so far, I'm only getting older.

Alright, let's set a new milestone: August first, the eightieth day. That's another two and a half weeks from now. They might well be the most challenging ones, and it's not certain they'll be decisive. But one must set the nearest goal and move toward it. Now, it's there.

I felt a bit better today. Maybe the newly prescribed medication was starting to work, or maybe it was something else. The doctor noticed today how I wobbled when I moved around the section. I've no longer noticed it, but the doctor's observation didn't bring him any joy.

After a break, the bosses started coming around again. First, the prosecutor visited. He asked about my condition and whether I could still move independently. He was young and very energetic. Next time, if I continue to answer quietly and lie under the IV drip, he'll likely touch me with his finger to make sure I haven't gone cold yet, just so he won't forget to note it down in his report.

Then he left. After that, the local chief came and asked if I would communicate via video link with the ombudswoman, the one who had come with great pomp two weeks ago. I said I would—maybe she'd have something new to say, although that was unlikely. It seemed more like a formality related to my birthday. Then the head investigator came, cheerful and empathetic, playing the role of a *kum** in line with his official duties. He congratulated me on the holiday, inquired about my affairs and health, and politely began to suggest that maybe I shouldn't communicate with the ombudswoman. They were so jittery here that they feared any unnecessary contact, even with Russian government officials, especially those from Moscow. Given this, I was especially anxious not to refuse the conversation with her. When I asked what they were afraid of, the investigator smiled again, fidgeted a bit more, and left.

They brought another batch of letters. I think there will be even more next week. A surge of activity from the lead-up to my birthday. People wrote from everywhere, and there were interesting messages and funny postcards. Today, in Odesa, another film festival was opening, actually, the main one in Ukraine and one of my favorites overall. There were many good films and people there, summer, sun, the sea, and a cool atmosphere that you'd want to preserve even after its conclusion. It's doubtful that this has changed in the five years I've been forced to miss it.

They asked me to write some kind of message to the participants, as well as my directorial vision for the film adaptation of my play, a project that will be presented at Odesa Film Pitching. I have no thoughts or words for either occasion, but I'll try to

---

* The term "kum" applied to a police officer in a penal colony should not be confused with the literal translation "godfather," which could in this context be inferred as a leader of a mafia family/criminal organization. Here, a "kum" is a colony chief or operations police officer who tries to influence inmates.

write something by evening. As usual, it will be spontaneous, but I hope it works out. That's how it always used to be.

The most interesting thing is that I write all of this by placing a large notebook with a thick cardboard cover underneath as a stand. And that notebook was given to me in the same Odesa, at some e-sports tournament, many years ago. Inside the notebook, among other notes, is the draft of the play. They confiscated this notebook, along with many other things, during their initial search of my apartment, but then, a year later, they returned it here in prison because there was nothing about my so-called terrorist activities in it—just like with everything else they'd taken at the time. And now, on my birthday, I'm going to write a letter to the very same Odesa on top of this Odesa notebook for the presentation of the planned film adaptation of my play, the source of which is in this notebook. Such is the dramatic circle, one of those things that life throws at us so interestingly and unexpectedly—if, of course, you can notice them. Or it might well be God using these coincidences to maintain His incognito. It all depends on what you believe in. I don't believe in coincidences.

DAY SIXTY-TWO

My condition seems to have stabilized again. I'm getting tired of these ups and downs.

The doctor insisted that this apparent improvement in my well-being was just temporary, and he foresaw an inevitable decline, hoping it wouldn't be sudden—not in just one day.

I've grown tired of listening to this and thinking about it.

The doctor also hasn't received any sense of satisfaction from the endless operations to save me since I'm not completely sick, and I don't want to recover, which is to say, to withdraw from the hunger strike. Everyone has become slowly mentally and physically exhausted by this endless marathon. But the end is not yet in sight.

Recently, the *kozly* brought a DVD player and a collection of movie discs that circulated the camp. The "activists" here have many opportunities to improve their lives, but we, mere mortals, also sometimes get some, and in this case, it is cinematic culture, albeit with very dubious content. The list included mostly Hollywood consumer stuff, but I didn't expect to see auteur movies.

I watched two recently made Russian films: *Coach* and *Sobibor*. In both, good actors played the main roles—Kozlovsky and Khabensky, respectively. And both were the directors of these debut films. *Coach*, clearly a sports drama, was very poorly and flatly done. You could see that Kozlovsky was trying both in the frame and behind the scenes, but unlike the success of an insignificant team according to the plot, there was no artistic result in the end. I've seen an infinite number of moments and scenes copied from Oliver Stone's great American sports movie, *Any Given Sunday*. It's one of my favorite Hollywood productions; I've watched it at least twenty times and know it by heart. You cannot build happiness on stolen money, love, or ideas, as in this case.

Sobibor, of course, was several levels higher in terms of art, camera work, acting, and, of course, in terms of its theme. Everything was alright with it, with no glaring issues, but it didn't move me. Even though it was about war and a concentration camp, and it was based on real events—it's a well-known story. Even the long continuous shot of the prisoners escaping to freedom, led by the main character, didn't stir my emotions. Why? I have no answer.

By contrast, even after the fifth viewing of the final part of Marlen Khutsiev's 1970 film, *It Was in May,* your heart aches and your eyes water. It's just a chronicle of modern Germany with rare photographs from concentration camps. Why did one film work brilliantly, while the other didn't?

That's the riddle of cinema to which it is not I alone who would like to know the answer. For there is no answer. I don't know it, but at least I can distinguish a real movie from a well-made project.

DAY SIXTY-THREE

Yesterday, toward evening, the weather started to change, affecting me as well. I experienced shortness of breath and a fluttering heartbeat. Because of this, I had trouble sleeping at night, and in the morning, this suffocating feeling didn't go away. My blood pressure was low, and my heart was pumping blood poorly, which meant there was insufficient oxygen. Maybe after the IV drip, I'll feel better later.

There was a consolation match for third place: Belgium vs. England. The Belgians scored an early goal, and then, for the rest of the game, the English attacked relentlessly to equalize. In the first half, their efforts were in vain, and in the second half, they posed a much greater threat but still couldn't reach the net. Ultimately, the Belgian national team countered and scored another goal, sealing a 2–0 victory and securing a spot on the world podium for the first time in their history, earning a bronze medal. The final is later today, with France as the favorite, but Croatia is expected to put up a strong fight as they've unexpectedly reached the final for the first time.

While watching yesterday's soccer match, a Romani grabbed my ear. He recently showed up at the infirmary, although he doesn't look like a patient. He was imprisoned when he was still a minor, then he worked his way up to adult camp for some big crime, and as a result, he has been in prison for thirteen years. A real hardened convict—cunning, talkative, and shameless, like most of his compatriots. He had tattoos everywhere, even on his forehead, as well as numerous cuts and scars, which he'd mostly inflicted upon himself, cutting himself open with and without violent adventures in the prisons and camps of the country. He'd even spent time in a prison mental hospital, which was also striking, and he himself did not deny that he had mental problems.

Yesterday, he tired me out with a story about how, already in prison, he'd asked his mother-in-law to take out a loan to place bets in an online bookmaker's office. He, like many Romani, had gotten married early, even before he came of age.

In the black zone—a colony in which life was ruled by thieves and inmates' mores and traditions—he had a phone with the internet, so he could play his luck and try to earn money. His mother-in-law took out a loan and sent him the money, and he sent it to Fortune, but she deceived him: the bet wasn't in his favor.

Then the Romani, in order to return the money and, perhaps, take revenge on the entire female race, began to make a profit by scamming women for money on dating sites, which was very popular among prisoners with access to the internet. Hiding behind other people's names and photographs, the prisoners made acquaintances, then pressed pity on unsuspecting young ladies on the same dating sites or simply on social networks, telling them stories of amazing sincerity and tragedy with only one goal: to pump money out of them. After that, they immediately cut off contact and went in search of a new simpleton. The Romani was pressed for time and a large amount of money, so he found one for himself, persuaded her with passionate speeches to have virtual sex, and then, having received several very candid photographs of his partner, said that he would post them for everyone to see because he already knew her profession and where she worked. The "wild female," who turned out to be a school principal in real life, paid the required amount for dropping the evidence of her passionate nature. The gypsy liked this way of earning money and continued hunting.

But I was no longer able to listen to the story of his next victory. I felt unwell, had a desire to watch soccer, and, most importantly, this way of life didn't suit me. I expressed this directly to the Romani. He was shocked by this, especially since he tried his best to communicate with me, as with everyone here at the med point, either on his own initiative or by "carrying out an assignment from the center." Then I knew that he was the police informant.

They'd found something to hook him for, which came to

light under the "roof," where he was serving time, or rather "working" before that, and then the police hid their agent, first close to them in the cell of a safe place, and now transferred to the med point.

This camp was full of such double and triple prisoners, who hid under various guises but in fact, snitched to the *kum*, the main operative. The second of the *kum*'s snitches, who has been planted in our hospital for two months, is a young guy originally from Ukraine, near Vinnytsia, who goes by the nickname Khokhol.* He's not even twenty yet, grew up in an orphanage, and is physically strong and athletic, but his intellectual development is at the level of a teenager.

He'd come to Russia to sell drugs, but he was caught during the very first run—this was a standard scheme for luring and imprisoning foolish Ukrainian boys. He was strong in body, but not in spirit: he couldn't stand the Labytnangi "reception" and joined the *kozly*. In his earlier youth, he used to hang out with Nazis, in memory of which he had tattoos in the form of portraits of Hitler, a fascist cross, and the number eighty-eight.

Khokhol also tried to find a kindred spirit in me, since we were both from the same country. He shared an intriguing story—in his view—about how he and his friends had fabricated fake documents to make him appear as a soldier and a participant in the war in Donbas. They then used these documents to secure a loan from a bank, swindling them for one hundred thousand hryvnias, which they promptly drank away. In response, I had to explain to the boy that he was dishonest

---

* This is an extremely offensive slur Russians use for Ukrainians.

three times over by prison standards: a Nazi, a drug dealer, and a *kozel*. Not to mention he was a traitor to his motherland, based on my own personal perspective.

You encounter a lot of characters here that make you want to smash a chair over their heads, but you can't. The hospital is a holy place for all prisoners, and it's not OK to raise your hand here. And you can't get rid of every troublemaker because there's a whole brood of them in this zone.

In the afternoon, after the IV drip, my condition really did get better. The heaviness in my chest still hasn't subsided, but it became easier to breathe. The state of affairs could be accurately described in prisoner's terms: "From foot to foot."*

DAY SIXTY-FOUR

Yesterday evening, I felt unsteady, like after a knockout or right before passing out, with shimmering circles and dots in my vision. However, I'd had a good night's sleep, woke up refreshed, and felt better. It might have been because they started my IV drip early this morning. They were expecting a call from a neighboring universe today, from the ombuds-woman, and they wanted me to be available during the day. My soul felt light and at ease.

The sun roasted in earnest, and the Labytnangi summer was in full swing.

Yesterday's final was very interesting. Usually, the decisive match of the World Cup is not very spectacular—the teams

---

* Neither good nor bad—something indeterminate.

don't risk it until the very end because there's too much at stake. But yesterday, the stakes were no less high than they've been every four years, and the game turned out to be very open-ended and tense. Six goals were scored in total, which was a rarity for the final. The Croatians went on the offensive for almost the entire match. France, even though it was an evident favorite, defended positionally, while also counterattacking frequently and very dangerously, and scored two "cheap goals": first an own goal and the other from a penalty kick.

The Croatians concentrated even more, and by the end of the first half they won back the ball, with the score being 2–1. In the second half the French scored twice, but the Croatians didn't give up and continued, albeit looking more doomed, to go forward. They scored only one more goal, also "for free"—a gross mistake of the opponent's goalkeeper. The final result was 4–2. France deservedly took the championship title for the second time; Croatia earned silver. Everyone was happy.

Russian TV propaganda was especially happy, tirelessly trumpeting on about the fantastic championship, joyful fans, and a new image of Russia that all foreigners have finally discerned, understood, and loved. A monster under a carnival mask. But the holiday is finally over, so what will happen next? I don't think anything will change drastically. Putin met with Macron yesterday and is going to have a meeting with Trump today. This month he has received a whole bunch of secondary world leaders, but he's unlikely to become a different person. The crocodile will not be moved by the ball game; he prefers a different one—a game of fate, one that includes Ukrainian prisoners.

Feeling fine today. I finished reading the collection of Zelazny's works. It wasn't bad, but not entirely meant for me, not catchy. Reading it was meant to kill free time and distract myself from unnecessary thoughts. There has been a slow decline in literary talent regarding my reading, from the Strugatskys to Lem, then on to Clarke, and now to Zelazny. I could keep sliding this way down to some Lukyanenko. But no, tomorrow I'll have a conversation with an old man named Bradbury, and I hope he won't disappoint me.

In the meantime, they brought a newspaper, the last of this season. The subscription for the first half of the year has ended, and I didn't renew it for the second. It was already somewhere beyond the horizon of grandiose events. But here I am, paddling toward that date, a milestone I never thought I could reach.

There's no other way—we're moving on, albeit without *Novaya Gazeta*. I'm thankful to them for having been with me in such a difficult time.

DAY SIXTY-FIVE

I've already started the fourth notebook for this diary. I couldn't have imagined that it would be so extensive, and this story so lengthy. But the most important thing should be that the ending is a happy one, or at least that there be an ending, as right now there seems to be no end or resolution in sight.

Yesterday was the hottest day yet, which led to a stuffy, sticky night, complete with mosquitoes. I began covering myself with just a thin blanket and leaving the window slightly open at night, but I still slept very poorly. In the morning, the sky had a mix of clouds and patches of blue, and there was a light drizzle, bringing some relief from the heat. By noon, the sun was scorching again.

I just can't get used to the climate here. There's no such thing as comfortable weather—it's a constant cycle of extremes that sharply transition from one to the next. In other words, it's the north.

Putin met with Trump yesterday, and for the second day in a row, the TV has been trumpeting this "historic" and "turning point" event. Russia is once again starting to make friends and share the world with America.

No matter what image you show to schizophrenics, they see naked women everywhere. It's George Orwell's legacy in action: Oceania is no longer at war with Eastasia. In a few years, it'll be the other way around. Sometimes, Turkey is a friend, sometimes an enemy, then a friend again. Sometimes America is hindering Europe from making friends with Mordor, and sometimes Europe is hindering America. Sometimes Soros is to blame for everything. Some terrible American elite is holding its president's hand and preventing him from falling into the embrace of his Kremlin friend. Everyone is an enemy and guilty, except for the local goblins and orcs, who naturally don't consider themselves to be ugly.

The two leaders talked for a long time about everything under the sun, then went out together, happy, to the press. Brief, streamlined results from both, but, of course, it's too early to talk about specifics—it's good that they at least met and started talking. Then, for half the briefing, both of them fought off accusations of collusion and Russian interference in the American elections. A journalist from the official Kremlin pool asked a prepared question about the Syrian issue. It was more like a pass—Putin immediately gave the ball to Trump with the words that he was now on his side. Standardly prepared cheap improvisations. American journalists did not engage in the game of giveaway but asked point-blank questions, in particular about the presidents' opinions on the status of Crimea.

Here, Putin made a mistake, saying that Trump still considered the annexation of the peninsula to the Russian Federation illegal, but "we held the referendum legally." Interesting Freudian slip. The Crimean referendum, despite all its caricature and external controllability, was officially carried out by the leadership of the republic, not by Russia. Putin subconsciously let that slip, admitting that the referendum was carried out by the Russian state, which he leads, and not by the people of Crimea. I wonder if anyone else noticed this line and its double meaning? I think they probably did—the meeting definitely took place under the closest attention of the whole world. Well, all the better that the thief's hat was on fire, and his tongue blurted everything out.

The expected call from the ombudswoman didn't come through yesterday for some unclear reason. Instead, they delivered a package sent by some unfamiliar woman from Odesa. They opened the package in my presence, carefully recorded the contents in an official document and had me sign it, then sealed it back up for further inspection. It was just like in the 1980 cartoon about Prostokvashino and Uncle Fedor: "You've received a parcel, but I won't give it to you." Judging by the contents I saw, there was nothing to regret about not receiving it: Ukrainian-language newspapers with Yanukovych's portrait and handwritten comments in the margins, some printouts, drawings, announcements, and other trash from the closet of a lunatic. I've received such strange letters before, ones that typically go straight into the trash, but someone here went as far as sending a whole package of nonsense.

Later in the evening, they brought the regular, normal mail, mostly printed-out emails and telegrams with standard greetings. Some of the telegrams were pasted onto identical postcards—apparently, the Russian Federal Penitentiary Service provided this additional service. However, one thing certainly made my day: a musical greeting card. I opened it, and an electronic melody started playing. An invaluable thing in prison— you could open it a couple of hundred times until the battery died or until you went crazy and started writing comments in the margins of newspapers.

But, in any case, I'm grateful to everyone for their attention and kind words! Thank you all, good people!

DAY SIXTY-SIX

Chest pain really can be worse than a toothache. A knife in the chest would be the only way to put it. Because of that, the night was both agonizing and scary. Then, in the morning, as if nothing had happened, I felt good, probably for the first time in a long time. I thought these were just personal feelings in contrast to yesterday's crisis . . . But the doctor, who came to see me in the morning, also noted that today I looked normal. This was good.

Tomorrow, my lawyer is supposed to visit, and he'll find me in a stable condition—which means he won't freak out, and, more importantly, he won't alarm my family.

My veins continue their daily struggle with needles. They swell, burst, and twist, but they don't give up. Almost like their owner. The makeup of the med point has changed. The gypsy was driven back to the camp after they transferred him to a new labor front, so to speak, no matter what he said about it. Horvat, Lysy, and a couple of other guys were discharged, and three new ones came in their place. All of them are *muzhiki*, all with a spirit that this system hasn't broken through suppression, both psychological and physical. One is Russian, from the locals, and he can hardly walk because of a blood clot in his leg. Two are Muslims, Caucasians—an Azerbaijani and a Circassian. Both are *krytniki*, meaning they spent most of their time "under the roof" in punishment cells meant to break prisoners. They lost their health in prisons, but not their conscience and spirit.

Now, I'll have good, decent prisoners to talk to—those who go smoothly through this life. One of them arrived here recently, and the second is already finishing his thirteen-year term, half of which he spent "under the roof" for participating in a small uprising in the same zone seven years ago, when some of the *muzhiki* rebelled, murdered the presumptuous *kozly*, and set fire to the barracks. As a matter of fact, this camp is noted for its interesting statistics. Nearly all the guys from the Caucasus, as well as those from Central Asia, have refused to cooperate with the prison authorities. But the Slavs—Russians and Ukrainians—tended to give up after the very first "roasting,"* and almost all of them served the administration. This mainly concerned young people, of course, but has the Slavic youth really become so weak in spirit? Everyone arrived frail, as if they'd just been taken from underneath their mother's skirt the day before, then were caught with a joint, then these little ones were in a hurry to cleave to the uniform pants of the citizen chief. It's disgusting to watch.

I finished reading Ray Bradbury's novel *Something Wicked This Way Comes*. The old man did not disappoint, as expected. It wasn't science fiction, it leaned more toward the mystical, falling somewhere on the spectrum between Edgar Allan Poe and Stephen King. Regardless, it was a piece of literature. Mysticism was part of the plot, but there was also philosophy in the novel, and life itself—mainly through the eyes of two teenage children. It was very well written and evoked that aching feeling from my own childhood in the depths of my soul.

A child is always ashamed of being little and wants to grow up quickly to become an adult, then, having become an adult, yearns for childhood all his life. And at the same time, I recalled that, with my actions, I stole part of my children's childhood, but didn't become any happier, and neither did they.

A long time ago, I formed a system for matching a person's age, not only to the time of year, but also to the month, and even to a specific date. If the first of March is taken as the beginning, then the first eighteen years of life (childhood) is spring, which lasts from this date until May thirty-first. The next

---

* Slang which refers to the process of psychological and physical humiliation for new inmates.

period—from eighteen to thirty-six years—is youth, summer, from June to the end of August. Maturity—from thirty-six to fifty-four years—is autumn, from September first to November thirtieth. Then, the end of life—from fifty-four to seventy-two years—old age corresponds to winter, from December to February. Periodically, I check my time against this vital annual dial, considering five days of such a calendar as one year. I just turned forty-two, so it's the first of October. There's still time to do at least something in life before the New Year holidays, after which it will be necessary to rest.

DAY SIXTY-SEVEN

The sun and clouds drift across the sky, changing almost every half hour. So, the weather is spinning again, but at least the exhausting heat has subsided.

There's heaviness in my chest again and darkness in my soul. The first one is a sign of progressing ischemia, and the second has its own explanation—I got an unpleasant letter yesterday.

Yesterday's mail consisted mostly of handwritten letters and postcards from abroad. One was from a friend in the world of cinema, and the other was from my ex-wife. I stopped communicating with her a long time ago, but she still periodically sends me messages in which everyone around was to blame, mostly me.

She bathed in her own sorrow and brought up topics from eight years ago. I didn't understand why she continued to do this, tormenting herself and trying to get under my skin somehow, after so many years and even with such a distance between us. I stopped playing this endless mind game a long time ago, but she couldn't seem to get over it and move on. Well, let it be. But in this envelope, there were scribbles in the form of a letter from my son and recent photos of him and my daughter. This both softened the feeling of negativity and brought joy, while also saddening me. The children have basically grown up without me. But you shouldn't dwell on the past, tormenting yourself and others. Life, no matter what it brings, goes on, and you have to move forward. Though there's nowhere special to go here.

My lawyer came to visit, and I walked through the camp along the central alley. Of course, it was cleared of people for this occasion, but the inmates still peered out from behind windows, bars, fences, and cracks. They saw who was being led around, and some cautiously greeted me with gestures or nods, but most just watched with an interested gaze. This was probably how a crowd watches someone sentenced to execution.

The meeting with my lawyer was short this time. He had a plane to catch in the evening, and there wasn't much to discuss. I wrote an encouraging letter to my mom and kids, once again telling them how much I loved them. Now, I will never tire of saying it to compensate for all those times I stayed silent before. Additionally, my lawyer brought a letter from my sister Natasha with brief updates, including the news that I'd died on my birthday for the third time now and rumors that something might happen regarding exchanges after the twenty-fifth of this month.

It's hard to rely on this unofficial information, especially since such encouraging news has come in more than once in past years, and the issue of Ukrainian political prisoners hasn't yet shifted. More precise information suggests that the president of France has actively engaged on this issue and is discussing it with Putin. The French press attaché called my lawyer, Dima, and inquired about my health and how they could further assist, even offering medical treatment in France after my release. A tempting offer, but I'd need to be discharged from the Labytnangi hospital to go to the French sanatorium, and the Kremlin's chief doctor hasn't signed the corresponding order yet.

There's also information that the leaders of the Crimean Tatars are actively lobbying for Turkey's president to get involved in our release. In October of last year, Putin pardoned two Tatar political prisoners in Crimea at his request.

I doubt this will happen twice. Well, we'll see, especially since there's only a week left, and this deadline is even closer to the date—August first—which I've clung to and crawled toward like a wild cat scaling rocks. But overall, our situation continues to be pushed forward, mainly driven by Europe and Ukraine. Protests come in waves, but people are, of course, starting to get tired of all this. And not just them. As I feared, the game is becoming deadlocked.

DAY SIXTY-EIGHT

It's quickly getting colder. At night I took out a warm jacket and a second blanket because I was very cold. Now that I'm emaciated, I've become even more thin-blooded.

My condition has been stable for the past day, which is rather strange. Even though my lawyer said that I looked even more haggard and aged yesterday. Well, it's easier to notice for people from the outside. That's normal, though. It would have been weirder if I'd looked younger.

The doctor finally received his colonel's epaulets and left earlier today, as he's throwing a party to celebrate his new rank. He wasn't looking forward to the upcoming celebration, explaining that it was a tradition to drop the stars into a vodka glass and drink to the bottom. The doctor wasn't a fan of such things. The last time, when they "washed down" the lieutenant colonel, he swallowed the five-pointed piece of metal as he was finishing the prescribed dose. The most interesting thing was that the order to award him another rank was given on my birthday. These were the loops twisted by fate, weaving our destinies together in some unknown way.

Yesterday, I watched a TV program about the Soviet film director Stanislav Rostotsky, his fate and films. I learned a lot about him as a person and an author, and also—in my opinion—his best film, *The Dawns Here Are Quiet*, shot in 1972. It was a very touching film about the war, real, without lies or pathos, based on a story by a good writer and staged by an excellent director, who both went through the war and understood what they were writing and filming. Rostotsky worked in an unexpected way on the set, aiming for authenticity. For instance, during scenes depicting the death of a girl or the reactions of her friends, he didn't reveal the made-up "dead woman" to the actresses beforehand. They saw her for the first time during the initial take, and this approach captured natural reactions and emotions.

I also aspire to achieve the desired effect on the first take, rather than after the forty-first one. But there is only one way— to study and shoot.

In the evening there were again dramaturgical developments from a screenwriter named Life: they showed us a modern version of *The Dawns*, filmed a couple of years ago by director Renat Davletyarov. I saw this man only once. He had always been known as a producer, then he started making films, which, actually, he did quite well, as in this case. The new film adaptation of the book was almost a complete remake of the old film. Absolutely everything matched, from the locations and types of characters to dialogues, scenes, and even frames. Whether such complete copying was spurred by respect for the original film, or by the lack of one's own vision, was not entirely clear. Despite the extended backstories of the characters, everything else was the same, including the famously long bathhouse episode with nudity that was a rarity for Soviet cinematography. They all played well, filmed thoroughly. The set designers did their best, and the directing was on the right level, especially the fight staging, but all this was somehow scratching the surface. You could repeatedly compare the new production with Rostotsky's film and understand that everywhere, at every moment, in every line, the remake loses to the original.

It's like holding a Chinese counterfeit of a well-known brand in your hands. Rostotsky was more precise, more sensuous, and stronger. He knew exactly what he was making films about. And in the new film, one senses a degree of calculation. The first shot with heart, the second with wallet. But such remakes are still, it seems to me, necessary—to attract a new, young viewer, so that you can compare two films and talk about them. And most importantly, no one should ever forget about that war. Though constantly being reminded of the war doesn't seem to prevent Russians from supporting new ones. Maybe it's because they're now told about it by people unlike Rostotsky?

Today, I finished reading Bradbury's book. After the novel came the stories, which were also very good. There was little fantasy in them, but a lot of human elements. Maybe that's why I liked him so much: in the foreground, there was still a person, his thoughts and relationships, and not thoughtless pieces of iron.

Today, I'll ask Smiley to go to the library and exchange the books I've read for Nabokov—I once saw they had his complete works. I haven't read all of them, so I'll fill in the blanks. I also really like him.

DAY SIXTY-NINE

Waking up with chest pain was not the best morning sensation, but it gradually subsided and let me go. I got up for inspection slightly abruptly, so I had to squint my eyes and lean against the wall—the world began to sway and darken, but it passed without me fainting.

The weather played at being summer for half the day, and by evening, autumn arrived with clouds and the sense of impending rain. It has gotten colder, but the true cold weather hasn't started, despite the obvious portents. The next morning, all of this will repeat itself; it's been the same thing for three days in a row.

Are these fluctuations exhausting me, or am I simply tired? Physically, it's been a while, but recently—mentally too. Perhaps I'm entering a period of some internal burnout. But I still have no thoughts of giving up, and that's good. My lawyer likes to say I'm stronger mentally than physically. I don't know, maybe it's more visible from the outside.

Yesterday, the long-awaited phone call with the ombudswoman finally took place. They opened a laptop for me right here, in the infirmary, in one of the offices, and she was speaking from her Moscow office. We communicated via video call, but the sound quality was poor, and the connection was even worse—with lagging pixelated images. But we talked. She inquired about everything with persistent concern. I didn't ask for anything or complain. She lamented that there was more chatter on the internet about my deteriorating health, although she saw and felt that I was fine. She was sitting, to be fair, about five meters away from her laptop, in the background, but it seems that Russian officials are very good at diagnosing hunger strikers from a distance.

According to my lawyer, I'm almost dead, or at the very least, I've already started experiencing problematic states, since I asked him twice to clarify a date. More chatter speculating about my condition started on the internet, predicting my final demise or, at the very least, insanity. Well, the latter part was only according to the ombudswoman. You can't trust anyone to say, write, or explain anything correctly. I said that two teeth fell out, and people immediately concluded that I had scurvy. I wrote about thinning hair, and they all thought I'd been poisoned with Novichok. I asked about the date—Sentsov had lapsed into amnesia!

What's wrong with you, people? Where is your reason and common sense? Nobody wants to perceive information straightforwardly and realistically. Everyone goes for sensation, and the hotter, the better! Toward the end of the conversation, before bidding a long and polite farewell, I discussed my creative work with the ombudswoman, specifically the screenplay I've been working on. Those present nearby—in the office, not in the frame—nodded in agreement. They were aware of it, and probably even approved of this craft, as it testified to the fact that I still had strength. If only they knew that there was no new screenplay, that it was just a "legend" covering up the fact that I've been writing these diaries, which they wouldn't like if they ever got published. But what can you do? As Sun Tzu said, "All warfare is based on deception." That's why during childhood, in two completely different groups of friends, I was twice given the nickname Stierlitz.

They brought me everything by Nabokov, or more precisely, the books I haven't read yet. The rest—what I've already read—turned out to be in other hands. I'm very lucky, now I have four books on my nightstand. It should last for a few weeks, and in one volume, his works are both in the original English, and in translation, so I'll also practice my foreign language skills.

Today, I finished his first novel, *Mary*. What a wonderful writer. Such precise descriptions. Each sentence was like a piece of candy, a pastry with icing on a wrinkled napkin. I don't write like that, I can't, it's not my style, but I read it with a great appetite.

DAY SEVENTY

Another milestone without fanfare or festivities. Another empty week without events and news. There's another one ahead, and, most likely, it won't be the last.

Outside, summer had returned with a blast, cranking the temperature up to the maximum. The room grew hot and stifling once more. These constant weather changes could wear anyone out, not just those with heart problems. Fortunately, I wasn't feeling too bad. I took advantage of the sunny weather to read more. I've been enjoying Nabokov's work; it's a great way to pass the time.

My inner demons, which had been silent for a long time, resurfaced yesterday when I saw a variety of sweets on the table that the guys were enjoying with their tea. The demons growled with hunger. I already thought that those bastards had died, but no, they seemed to be immortal. On the other hand, I dealt with them; they could not force me either openly or secretly to take at least one crispy bundle. It was satisfying to know that I was stronger than my basic instincts and could manage them along with my life, not yielding to their influence. In prison, people often develop a strong craving for sweets. I'd experienced it myself. On the outside, there was a more varied diet and availability of groceries, so I never really liked sweets. But here, especially after a couple of years living off *balanda*, after getting into the camps, where food parcels were less frequent than at the central prisons, the craving for sweets became almost an obsession. Later, I realized that I was not the only one, and that it was a common predicament among prisoners.

The main thing is that after release when eating habits return to normal, this craving ought to disappear. So be strong, my dear demons; you won't get anything here, but on the outside, you will definitely be able to let loose. Though I know from my own experience that the expectation is always sweeter than the outcome, no matter what it concerns, be it a cake or a new car.

Today is my sister Halya's birthday. She is ten years older than me, and this significant age gap has kept us from being very close. Though we've always had a good relationship. That is, until recently when it became apparent that she supported Putin, the one responsible for the annexation, more than her terrorist brother. As a result, for the past four years, we've had almost no communication. Nonetheless, I'm immensely grateful to her because, during my time behind bars, she took care of my children as well as, if not better than, their own mother has. Thank you for this, sister, and happy birthday to you! All the very best to you!

DAY SEVENTY-ONE

I slept very poorly, didn't get enough rest, and woke up feeling beaten up. It has been scorching outside, above forty degrees Celsius, and in the ward, it's hot and sticky.

The doctor didn't show up over the weekend—he was recovering from celebrating his promotion and spending time with his daughter, who had returned from a trip abroad. He saw me today and said that I looked very bad, and my speech was slow. He was probably right—I felt somewhat the same way.

My blood pressure was very low, and my pulse was around forty. That was very low. My heart was barely running at low RPMs. Later, the results of my medical tests and an EKG will be available. The doctor left for his other duties, looking worried because of me. I promised to hold on until the evening and his return.

Life becomes remarkably clear and simple when you have a feeling that it might end any day. Oddly, my chest doesn't ache, but my hands feel a bit numb—likely due to poor blood circulation in my limbs. There's some noise in my head too. By the way, the doctor left to accompany his chief orderly from the infirmary, who got parole two weeks ago, and today they were seeing him off. A good guy who'd killed a taxi driver with his friends twelve years ago for no good reason. One of the few for whom prison turned out to be beneficial. He worked as a *kozel* for the doctor for almost ten years, and many positive changes in his life could be attributed to that. The orderly came to say goodbye before leaving—I was lying under the daytime IV drip—and he brought me a whole bag of toiletries: shampoo, toothpaste, and various pieces of soap for the last time.

Well, now my cleanliness is covered until the New Year. Though I understand that at the rate my health is deteriorating, my body won't make it to autumn. I wouldn't want that. Twenty-two years ago on this day, my father passed away. It feels like just yesterday. A year before that, he had a heart attack, then thrombosis. Cigarettes and alcohol. He was only fifty-six. Though he'd already walked with a limp and looked older. I don't want to end up like that. Not today.

DAY SEVENTY-TWO

The same heat mixed with stuffiness. The chill in my chest and the numbness in my hands from yesterday have subsided, so I'm feeling slightly better today. "Balancing out," as the doctor says.

Yesterday a guy from my former barracks came to the hospital. He got bronchitis in the summer. He told me some news, but there wasn't anything special, everything seemed somehow boring and insignificant there. But they were following the latest updates on my fate. The guy said that I was a celebrity. What was the point? The only useful piece of information I learned was that one of my close acquaintances, also from Ukraine, but living here for a long time, had been extradited back to our homeland. He'd been waiting for it for half a year, and finally set sail in the hope of serving the rest of his thirteen-year term there. Besides, he had already served half of it.

God, let everyone be released early—a human being has nothing to do in prison.

Once again, the soulless woman posing as a psychologist came. She has begun to appear every day in my life, like an obsession. When she rattled off her text with a robotic intonation, I suggested to her that she never come again, but she replied that it was her job and it was not for me to tell her what to do. The psychologist left, turning around on the spot and ignoring the other prisoners, who really wanted to talk to her and were waiting for her at the exit in the corridor. But she retreated in silence, accompanied by the officer on duty.

In general, it seems to me that this whole thing has been a

social experiment by the Russian Federal Penitentiary Service. While their psychologist was on vacation, they took a patient from a madhouse. I wonder how she would react if the next time she appeared I started rolling my eyes and pointing my finger, shouting: "Get out, witch!" This trick probably wouldn't even break her.

I continue to read Nabokov, mostly during the day, when my head brightens after an IV drip. Got to his stories. He certainly writes very well! All objects under his gaze come to life, and the world becomes dense and saturated. I will never succeed at this—I bow my head before the Master.

I noticed that the small, precise form of the story is closer to me than the ponderous narrative of the novel, which spreads out like dough. A story is like a life that needs to be lived in one day. There's no more space, and time is running out. In such moments, you capture in your writing something seemingly small and simple, but in reality, it's the essence of everything. It's what truly matters. It's life, after all. I wish I could learn how to write simply and honestly, avoiding slobbering falsehoods, writing down life, and not composing it, so that the text could be both interesting and penetrate into the very soul, if not for everyone, at least for someone . . .

DAY SEVENTY-THREE

The same exhausting heat again. It's been difficult for me to determine my condition, but they said that I still stagger when I walk. I speak slowly, as I also think and do everything else.

My heart is bothering me. The test results are consistently bad. Now, there are also very few red blood cells and other new cells in my blood.

The doctor said that the depression of spinal cord functions has started, this being responsible for the regeneration of those cells. He always has a couple of medical horror stories in reserve for me, but I'm not easily frightened.

Yesterday, during their shift, one of the security guards was in charge instead of the duty assistant to the head of the colony. He decided to play the boss. At first, he didn't like how the column of inmates lined up on the alley greeted him in unison. He made the inmates shout "Hello, Citizen Chief!" three times. Then he came to me for an unplanned search. The planned one had been earlier, during the day. He rummaged around my bedside table for a long time and even used a flashlight to inspect something. Then he took this diary in his hands and started reading it attentively, shining his little flashlight on it for added seriousness.

The duty officer tried to decipher something from it for a long time, and meanwhile, my palms were slowly getting sweaty. But since my handwriting was not very legible, and I wrote continuously without paragraphs or divisions—there was nothing to catch someone's eye—he couldn't really read much. He just asked, "What is this?" to which I calmly replied, "I'm writing a script." The notebook returned to the bedside table. The search, which was a typical way of creating disorder, ended. Thankfully, the guards here are generally not very bright.

Yesterday, I received letters. Some were belated birthday wishes with the standard hopes that these prison birthdays would be the last. I've been receiving such wishes for five years now. But the main thing was that I received a letter from home, from my mother. She wrote that everything was fine, no one was ill, they'd finally bought a laptop for my son, and my daughter had gone to summer camp. Well, that was good, albeit a bit late, but some wishes do come true. I won't reply for now; my lawyer will arrive at the end of next week, and it's better to pass on the message through him, faster and more reliable.

It seems I haven't received all of my mother's letters. But each one is like a holiday, like a real birthday.

DAY SEVENTY-FOUR

As bad as it's been these last few days, I haven't experienced anything like this throughout the entire hunger strike. Yesterday I lay in bed all day, it was even hard to sit. I started to get worse and feel dizzy. At night, my chest pain flared up again. When I stood today at the morning check, I began to feel so unstable that I almost lost consciousness. I didn't stand till the end, went to my room, and lay down so as not to fall. Immediately, a full ward of medical staff, led by a doctor, came running. They began to listen, measure my vitals, and set up the EKG machine, followed by the IV drip.

The EKG results were very bad: distortions, dystrophy of the heart muscle. There was not enough nutrition and oxygen for the heart, a pre-infarction state. The doctor was worried. Everyone said that I looked especially bad today—no longer white, but a sickly shade of green. I wanted to assure them that I felt even worse, but I only managed to smile. If I didn't, the lamentations about a future coma or, at least, dysfunction of some glands, in particular the testes, would begin again.

But at this point, as they say, count your blessings.

It was still hot outside, but I was freezing and shaking. The head of the colony came, just from his Crimean vacation, looking tanned. He talked about the new bridge, about how good everything was there, what was being built, when it would be completed, how it would be even better. When he saw me, he said that I'd begun to look worse, turned even more pale, and lost weight. What did he expect to see? He also carefully began to push me to stop.

I was told they would take me to the city hospital again if I got sick at the same pace, and such a prospect meant one thing—forced resuscitation while being strapped down to a bed. I didn't want this, but let them do what they want—they'll take me anyway, and they won't ask for my opinion.

Fatigue, weakness, and apathy. If I quit now, I'll regret it for the rest of my life, no matter what happens next. Though maybe there isn't much time left. I can sense it; those ominous portents are there. So, the end might be near, just not as happy as I'd hoped. It could be more like a finish line marked in black instead of red ribbon.

DAY SEVENTY-FIVE

I woke up in the middle of the night. It could have been because I needed to use the restroom, or perhaps I was thirsty, or it might have been due to the whining flight of a nearby mosquito or the distant whistle of a train. Then, I couldn't fall asleep again for a long time, struggling to breathe in the stuffy night air.

The morning was somewhat easier than yesterday. I had chest pain, of course, but there was no feeling that I was on my way out and needed to write a will. The doctor was quite nervous yesterday because of me, but after he got home, he drank a good amount of alcohol, and today he was in a good mood, especially when he found out that I hadn't died overnight.

He can already recognize my "bright" and "dark" periods of well-being with the naked eye—these can change during a single day. Yesterday, besides my critical condition, we had another problem with the European Court of Human Rights. This charitable organization, concerned about Mr. Sentsov's condition, had issued a resolution calling on him to end his hunger strike and for the Russian Federation to urgently begin his treatment in a medical facility outside the prison. For some reason, the Russian Federal Penitentiary Service decided to play their hand on the same day and planned to transfer me to the local hospital. I understood why they wanted to do this, but they couldn't comprehend from afar that the local civilian hospital would put me in the intensive care unit, where I'd be lying naked on a bed, restrained with handcuffs, and they'd be pumping whatever they wanted into me, forcibly ending my hunger strike, with reluctant nurses occasionally changing my bedpan. And the only entertainment there would be a sadistic resuscitation specialist and police guards.

No, thank you, I'll be just fine here. So, yesterday evening, the doctor had phone conversations about this matter, trying to keep me in his facility. Ultimately, I wrote another refusal of hospitalization at the local civilian hospital, and a compromise was seemingly reached. They even decided to hold the medical commission right here, at the med point, though in a truncated format.

In general, yesterday was a challenging day. A little bonus at the end was a batch of printed-out emails, mostly from Ukraine. A wave of persuasion to end the hunger strike has begun. Various arguments and beautiful words, petitions with a long list of names of people I don't know. I didn't even bother replying to such messages. But I was very pleased to hear that the adaptation of my play for the big screen was progressing well, and there was a good chance that filming would take place before the end of the year. The question whether it would be done with my involvement or not remained.

Today, the weather was scorching again. Only in the middle of the day was there a brief respite from the heat when some clouds gathered and quickly organized a little rain. The resulting coolness brought relief to the earth and its inhabitants. But half an hour later, this interesting attraction ended. The clouds dispersed in different directions as if they had never been, and the sun started to blaze again.

The robotic woman disguised as a psychologist came again today. But this time, in her usual script, a new phrase appeared: "I'd like to conduct some psychological tests to assist you in adapting to the conditions of captivity." Hello again, I guess. If she keeps coming to see me so persistently, she should have at least looked at my personal file. I've been serving time for the fifth year now, and I've been moved to a dozen different prisons and camps. I've long since adapted to everything. But madmen have their own logic. No one wants to admit to themselves that they're insane.

Taking advantage of a "bright" interval, I continued reading Nabokov, or rather, I finished the first volume and moved on to the second. It was both joyful and bitter. I was happy to be reading such a gem, but saddened by realizing the insignificance of my own literary abilities.

Today, the doctor said that I was a devil because I didn't wear a cross, and my pride would be my downfall. And if I went into politics, I'd definitely be blown up. He said that yesterday, after having a drink at home, he went out to smoke on the balcony and was thinking about me, or rather, considering all the possible scenarios were I to die during the hunger strike. Well, at worst, he'd get a reprimand. He'd already received a colonel's rank, and he could retire any day now, but it would be difficult for him to live with this much longer. He'd lost patients during his career and had occasionally gotten attached to them. So, it was both customary and sad. In written form, all his statements seemed somewhat cynical and melancholy, but when he was recounting them to me, they became somewhat funny.

DAY SEVENTY-SIX

It rained again last night, heavier than the late-afternoon rain, but brief. Thanks to it, the night was fresher and I slept well. I'm not as broken today as in previous days, and for the first time in a while, my heart doesn't groan.

The medical commission didn't convene yesterday, not even in truncated form, which was probably for the better—the verdict wouldn't have been a cheerful one. Only two doctors came, one by one. As for the rest—some were on vacation, others couldn't make it. The first one, who was a general practitioner, had already examined me several times before, a stern but competent woman with glasses. Yesterday, she again declared, after examining me and my test results, that it would all end soon and badly.

But she'd said so a month and a half ago when we met for the first time. This time, in addition to her usual coma-cardiac threats, she also added anemia, which I had begun to develop because of a prolonged refusal to eat. She again urged me to think and, even better, change my mind. Then she left, shaking her head.

The second one was some kind of psychiatrist. I hadn't seen her before, and it would be better if I never saw her again. She was a plump young doctor with an unnatural smile glued on her face who looked past me at the wall during the whole conversation. Jumping from topic to topic, not listening to any logic or arguments, she stubbornly babbled about my mental breakdown due to the refusal to eat. It seemed that she was the patient who needed help, and I was the doctor. Then, without even looking at me, she left, stating at the end that, by a court decision, I should be hospitalized in a psychiatric hospital for forced treatment and feeding.

I could imagine what an uproar would have risen on the outside if I had told them that they wanted to put me in a madhouse for forced therapy, how the head of the Russian Federal Penitentiary Service would have started smoldering, and everyone involved would have scattered and squealed. And this woman would sit somewhere on the sidelines, looking at the wall, smiling at her thoughts, having previously swallowed something like Valium. But I wasn't going to create provocations or a circus—there were already enough of those around me who did so, and I wasn't about to hold a grudge against an unhealthy woman.

Yesterday, two new convicts were brought to the med point, both from under the "roof." They had cut their veins one after the other, though without discussing it in advance, since at that time, one of them was already in the cell of the operational unit, the so-called Petrovka. (I myself happened to land there twice, including at the beginning of the hunger strike.)

Ryzhy was the first to arrive straight from Petrovka, an experienced prisoner. Though still a young guy, he has already served half of his twenty-three-year sentence. He is an ideological fighter against the regime of the administration in particular, and this country in general. He constantly writes complaints, "falls out" with authorities, tells everything as it is, and "explodes," cutting his veins.

The doctor mended his wound, and while we were all talking and getting to know each other, they brought in another "exploder," Andriukha. But this one turned out to be a "whistle," a man with a shattered psyche. He cut his veins because he hadn't been given a new robe, an empty excuse for this extreme measure that every prisoner had at his disposal. With broken glass, he opened up the veins at the bends of his arms so severely that the doctor could barely sew them together, working until lights out. He lost a lot of blood, but today, after an IV drip, he already felt better, scuffing along the corridor. In general, you don't get bored in our house of fools.

Ryzhy is a cheerful, active guy. He also loves movies and follows political news. But I still have neither the desire nor the special strength to communicate a lot. I lie down more, resting from my most recent crisis, and, using this respite in the battles for my health, I try to read Nabokov.

I finished reading his *Invitation to a Beheading* today. It was an interesting novel, in the spirit of Kafka. It was, in my opinion, a weaker novel than the previous one I'd read. But the hero's agonizing expectations of his fate in the dungeon, the character's thoughts and the bifurcated worlds around him, the diary that he kept to escape from reality, or, on the contrary, try to hold on to it—all this was all too reminiscent of my situation. In the end, he nevertheless escaped execution. He left, splitting from his scaffold.

But the book about me hasn't been finished yet, its hero is still waiting . . .

DAY SEVENTY-SEVEN

The heat finally subsided completely, and it even became cooler. The sun hid behind light clouds, giving way to wind interspersed with rain.

The patient's condition is lousy but stable. In the morning, my pulse was still around forty beats per minute. My heart has been working at a low speed since then. It's not much of a concern, as long as it doesn't start getting rapidly worse.

The toughest week in terms of well-being and technical matters has come to an end. No news at all. Ahead lies emptiness; it has already set in internally. There are no thoughts or desires. I'm writing in this diary automatically, as a habit. I read in a similar manner. I grasp the meaning of Nabokov's sentences, but I no longer see the point of reading anything at all, including his work. But I don't give up on reading or writing.

Yesterday, I even watched a movie on TV, *Interstellar*, by director Christopher Nolan. I had heard a lot about this film, and, unlike in most cases, my expectations were not disappointed. It was a very good movie, solid minimalist science fiction set in our near future, dealing with the issues of black holes and relativity. Nolan has a penchant for playing with time in his films. I didn't like his previous works, but this one really captivated me. And, of course, not because of space travel and special effects, but because of what should be the main focus of a movie, the one thing that can truly captivate a viewer—human relationships. In this case, it was the relationship between the main character and his daughter, whom he was forced to leave on Earth at the age of ten while he went into space in search of a planet to save all of civilization. She held a lifelong grudge against her father for leaving her and her brother behind. This resonated deeply with me and hurt, which was probably why the movie touched my heart.

I sincerely hope that my own daughter doesn't hold a grudge against me. And if she does, I hope we can meet, understand, and embrace each other sooner than the family in the movie, which was destined to meet only after one hundred light-years.

DAY SEVENTY-EIGHT

The autumn installation continues outside the window. Preparations for it are in full swing: clouds and wind, rare rain, and an even rarer sun, which now only shines but doesn't warm. It's grown even colder, sharply and unpleasantly so. But at least the exhausting heat that shook my health last week has ended. At night, it's still light outside but not as bright as before. Summer is gathering its belongings.

Every duty officer who comes here six times a day during their shift to participate in and lead the already sacred ritual of delivering and retrieving my meals has, for some reason, started to inquire about my well-being. This wasn't something they used to do before. Had I really begun to look that bad?

At the end of the week my lawyer is expected to arrive; he'll say it more precisely because he sees me less often. I've somehow stopped noticing myself in the mirror. Perhaps it's indifference. In general, I have two standard answers to the standard question "How are you?": "Good" if I'm doing really well, and "Normal" in all other cases. I typically answer the duty officers that I'm doing fine, but even from their perpetually indifferent faces, I can see that they don't really believe me.

Lately, I've come to realize that almost every person on Earth, barring rare medical cases, has the potential to perform miracles. And this has nothing to do with magic, whether black or white, esotericism, religion, or tricks.

Every person has the ability to perform a miracle by bringing new life into the world. With the help of another person, you create a new life seemingly from nowhere, from nothing more than liquid droplets. As this new life matures from a fetus, it is eventually born into the world, and you take on the role of caring for it. Initially, it's about physical care, like changing diapers and providing clothing. Then it becomes more challenging: education, communication, dealing with potential conflicts, and watching them grow. Whether this new life resembles you or not, to some extent, depends on your influence, but not entirely. Regardless, what truly matters is that from nothingness, a human being has emerged—the greatest miracle in our world. And you created it, you wizard.

If you seriously think about it, you understand that all other activities, issues, actions, and deeds are nothing compared to this, the main thing in life. Maybe, and more likely even for sure, this is the real meaning of life. In its continuation, in its infinity, in your immortality through your descendants. Women understand this. For them, nothing else holds greater importance. Well, not for all of them, but for most. As time has passed, I've come to understand them better. To be precise, it's not just about understanding why they lead their lives this way, but also about embracing and endorsing a worldview where children take center stage.

Yes, a man's life is different from a woman's, and a man can't focus on children alone—after all, someone else has to hunt mammoths and pay the mortgage. And my life is no exception. But children are still the center of my world—where the heart is.

With the arrival of your own children, you start to understand your parents better because you step into the role of a parent as well, realizing that they went through the same experience. And in all likelihood, it was even more challenging for them without automatic washing machines and disposable diapers, with shorter maternity leaves and childbirth often taking place in less favorable conditions. One truly matures into adulthood only after becoming a parent and performing this miracle, often without fully grasping its significance.

Three

DAY SEVENTY-NINE

I FELT AWFUL AGAIN LAST NIGHT—whether it was my heart or something else remains unclear. But I didn't crawl, I preferred to lie down.

Today, in the morning, my normal condition returned with the sun. Neither the sun nor my condition warmed me that much. I understood it was all temporary, but I've perceived any day of respite as a blessing.

I got fresh mail today. The last birthday greetings arrived, including some from abroad, along with more invitations to visit places, especially to go to London. At the first opportunity! I must ask the wardens later today when the next train to the English capital is.

Overall, I've accumulated so many invitations during my time in prison that if things don't go well for me when I regain my freedom, I'll just start traveling—not at my expense but relying on these invitations. I'll arrive and present these letters to sleepy people because I'll appear, as always, at an inconvenient time and without warning so as not to scare them off. Then, before the new hosts come to their senses and, rubbing their foreheads in confusion, try to remember when they'd managed to write such a letter, I'll quickly settle into the best room and start demanding food, beer, entertainment, and so on.

I don't think I'll ever get to that point, but it's worth keeping such an option in reserve. Who knows how life will turn out in sixteen years, especially if I have to spend them behind bars? I wouldn't want that either, but it's also not wise to rule out the possibility of such a sad turn of events.

DAY EIGHTY

August first. I finally reached this date, but not without difficulty.

I haven't received an amino acid drip for the second day in a row, and to a large extent, I've been sustained by that medication. When it will be available again is uncertain; even the doctor doesn't know.

Yesterday I felt terrible, especially in the evening. Not only did my hands begin to go numb, but also the rest of my body, including my torso and my head. The doctor said that this was caused by insufficient blood circulation. A low pulse and anemia were to blame for such an unpleasant side effect. He also said that my complexion has become earthy. It seemed possible, considering that it has been difficult for me to see myself through the circles and dots in my vision.

Lately, my head is spinning whenever I get up, sometimes even when I just sit. A persistent pre-fainting state. My nails are blue again. I've been freezing, and my temperature is consistently around thirty-five point five degrees Celsius. My legs, even under two blankets, can't warm up during the night. It looks like this week will be even worse than the previous one.

Last night, I couldn't shake the feeling that, if I fell asleep, I wouldn't wake up. But this time, everything worked out. The morning brought a slight calm and a little relief. Taking advantage of this bright pause, I read Nabokov, but I couldn't do it for long. I didn't have enough strength or desire. I just wanted to lie under the covers with my eyes closed.

I've been reading his book of memoirs, *Speak, Memory*. Even in his memoirs, he had an excellent style, not like in this monotonous diary, hungry for events and good phrases. I caught myself thinking, while reading about his childhood, that there were parallels with mine. The same things were written to me by people who read my childhood stories.

Probably, this is how it should be, this is real literature: when the author writes about his own life, and the reader reads about himself.

I need to put the next point for myself, a mark on the rock, a flag. Let it be August tenth, ten days from now. It's unlikely that anything will change, and it's apparent that things are only getting worse in terms of my health, but I need to have a clear goal in front of me. Then, there will be a clear result. My goal is to hang on. Now, there's a date—August tenth.

DAY EIGHTY-ONE

Outside the window, it's the beginning of August—the start of Labytnangi's autumn. The overcast sky has completely swallowed the sun. It's getting colder with each passing day. Slowly, but inevitably. I turned on the heater again and started wearing

warmer underwear. Though I still have a chill, a sense of coldness. My condition is poor but stable. It's like riding a stormy
wave: you take a breath now and then, catch a glimpse of a
bright light, then something dark overtakes you from behind,
pulling you down, tossing you around, then you come briefly
back to the surface. It doesn't drown you or hold you down—
it spins you around. My body is fighting hunger as best it can,
while I can only observe.

Yesterday, the news reported that three Russian journalists
died in Central Africa. They had gone to cover the ongoing and
brutal war and were ambushed on the road, shot dead right in
their vehicle with automatic weapons.

I once crossed paths with one of the deceased, Orkhan
Dzhemal, in Crimea. He was a good guy with a salt-and-pepper
beard. He was a war correspondent who had covered many wars
and hotspots, and at that time, he'd come to write about the peninsula's annexation. I didn't know the cameraman, but I'd heard
a lot about the third person, the director Alexander Rastorguev.
He'd made very impressive documentaries and films with
non-professionals, and while the genre of his work was hard to
define, it was very interesting and unconventional cinema.

And now they're gone. They died due to recklessness in
someone else's war. In such wars, people often die like this. Rest
in peace, guys.

But the most disgusting part of the whole thing was the
reaction of Russian state media to this tragedy. They reported it
in the middle of a broadcast, almost in passing, with an under-
tone of, "What were they doing there? What were they trying
to achieve? Why didn't they inform the Ministry of Foreign

Affairs?" and other sneering remarks, as if they weren't discussing people who had died—their colleagues and compatriots. It immediately became clear that these were the "wrong" kind of journalists, the ones who hadn't toed the Kremlin's line. The ones who hadn't consulted with their "big brothers" on where to go and what to write.

Russian propaganda responds very disdainfully to the lives, and even the deaths, of such individuals, showing more sympathy for the stolen figurine of Behemoth the cat from the Bulgakov Museum. When will all this darkness end?

DAY EIGHTY-TWO

Nothing new, and nothing good either. I experienced a certain physical sensation regarding my body's need for nutrition. Not a hunger associated with appetite, which I don't have and haven't had from the very beginning of the hunger strike. It wasn't the frail psychological desire to eat something that my demons, who have long since retreated, would have usually shown me either. It was some new feeling as if my body was signaling it could no longer go on. Which, in principle, was not surprising after such a long time. They hadn't administered the nutritional mixture for a while, but it didn't manage to stabilize me.

My condition has been creeping lower and lower, though it constantly seems that there's nowhere left to go. My body has clearly been trying to say: it's over, your reserves are exhausted. It keeps reminding and warning me, like a fuel gauge arrow dropping below zero, under the persistently glowing red light. When it drops like this and stops trembling, it signifies just one thing—soon, the car will come to a halt. I'm hoping to make it a few more kilometers.

My lawyer hasn't shown up yet, and it's unlikely he'll show up this Friday evening. Most likely, he should be expected on Monday. Maybe he'll bring some news, maybe he won't. I'm waiting for them—out of habit, that is—because I'm already tired of all this.

On TV, they briefly shared a few details about the death of those three Russian opposition journalists in the Central African Republic. It turned out they'd gone on behalf of some Khodorkovsky-funded investigative center to shoot a documentary about Russian private military companies operating in that country. Naturally, PMCs operated there illegally since there was no law on PMCs in Russia, but they worked there with the approval and under the guidance of Russian Special Services, of course. I read about it in *Novaya Gazeta*.

But the newspaper no longer comes, and I can't expect the truth from the zombie box. So, I'll have to wait, as with everything related to this story. Maybe it wasn't an accidental ambush but a planned liquidation of so-called objectionable people.

How many people have perished since I've been in prison? I'm thinking not only about my acquaintances but public figures who were frequently or infrequently discussed and featured on TV... So many! And during the same time, many of my friends and acquaintances have also had children. The balance of life carries on out there, while I, though physically intact, feel I'm suspended like the butterfly under glass in Nabokov's memoirs. I can only observe life and reminisce about my past, but I can no longer take flight.

DAY EIGHTY-THREE

Outside, there are gray clouds, and my mood is about the same. I have dreams every day, but they're not always coherent. They fall apart and are forgotten almost immediately upon waking.

I had a whole slew of dreams last night, but only one still sticks with me. I'd never dreamed of my release from prison so vividly. It was as if they were taking me in a police paddy wagon straight to the airplane, reading out the pardon, and letting me go. I was alone. There was no one else, no exchange, and no other released prisoners. Then, I was sitting at some large intersection, covered either with a blanket or a towel because I was wearing sports shorts, and my bag was nearby. The intersection looked like Simferopol, but I understood it was in Kyiv—freedom. But I didn't get up or do anything, I didn't even feel joyful. A crowd started gathering at the intersection. They were clearly looking and waiting for me, but I didn't go to them. Maybe I was embarrassed about my appearance, or perhaps the attention.

Eventually, the people lined up in columns and left somewhere. Only after that, I got up and started walking down the street. Then I was walking through my village for some reason, turning onto the adjacent street, and the tractor driver who passed away long ago, after I greeted him, said he regretted that I'd called him. I woke up sweaty despite the cold air in the ward.

I know that seeing oneself undressed or naked is a sign of illness, and talking to the deceased is even worse. But I don't believe in omens or prophetic dreams. A dream is merely a reflection of our daily experiences and inner expectations. Moreover, right now, I feel freedom as distant from myself as ever.

A young, nimble prosecutor came by and took a written statement from me about refusing hospitalization in the city hospital. He left, seemingly satisfied with his mission. Then, the bosses came, bringing another priest. I told them I didn't want to confess, that it was too early for me to receive communion, so they had to wait a bit. I asked the bosses if they would allow me to call my mother next week. They seemed to promise they would.

Throughout the hunger strike, I haven't really wanted to talk to her on the phone because I was afraid she would cry and try to dissuade me from it. But based on her letters, she has been holding up, even supporting me in some ways.

So, I'll try to call, especially since I can catch up with my kids, and I really want to hear my mom's voice and say something nice to her—maybe for the last time.

My test results were once again very bad, with indicators not improving and steadily declining in almost all categories. The doctor was so worried that he seemed to be getting sick himself. He said this would all end very badly and most likely soon. Well, it wasn't the first time I'd heard that, and I had no doubt things were bad.

I've at least guaranteed myself anemia, and next up is a heart attack, and beyond that, I won't have time to understand anything anymore.

DAY EIGHTY-FOUR

A new nurse arrived: mature and seemingly experienced, but at the same time professionally careless and hurried. On her first shift, she found my vein right away, but she only did it on her third try today. I've chosen to no longer pay attention to such trifles.

During the IV drip, I could hear some strange sounds from the side of the street, or rather, the outer wall of the hospital—a shuffling, interrupted by a blow against the wall as if someone was sawing it and periodically breaking off pieces from it. The sounds didn't stop but continued to get closer to my window. Soon, a couple of prisoners appeared, and the answer followed. They had been scraping old paint from the wall with iron brushes and rearranged their heavy ladder with a loud thud. Having peeled off everything that the wall could give under their efforts, they began to renew it with a fresh coat of paint of the same red color. The prisoners worked professionally, calmly, and habitually, as if not looking into my window but noticing everything behind it.

I noticed a long time ago that all the Russian prisons I've been in are very fond of carrying out various repairs. It's profitable because the labor force is cheap, and you can write off any amount for this work, limited only by your imagination and budget. In this case, the conscience of the authorities as a natural limiter is turned off—more precisely, it's completely atrophied.

Yesterday at my doctor's appointment, I talked about the priest's visit and confused the day of the visit. I was sure he hadn't come on the same day but the day before. When it turned out that I was wrong, we had a laugh at my expense, but this may not have been a joke, and the doctor also understood this. I could start losing my marbles without noticing it myself.

I need to look at myself more carefully and try to pinpoint the moment when I start to go crazy. But not a single insane person could probably understand or feel this in advance. I don't want to end up in a prison psychiatric hospital or, even worse, end my sad days there. But, as they say, it's not for us to choose our path in life—it only seems like we can choose or change something. We are only passengers on this train, on which everyone has his own car, fellow travelers, and destination. We can only stare out the window at the passing landscapes and shorten this boring trip with empty conversations with neighbors or, at the very least, arrange a drunken brawl out of boredom.

Yesterday was bath day, and I got a haircut. I wonder if the next time they'll cut my hair here, or by then, it'll already be in a mental hospital.

DAY EIGHTY-FIVE

The weather is grim and endless, much like the past week, which has also been unproductive. This emptiness has been draining.

The White Nights have finally receded, and it's getting darker at night, with the zone's lights being turned back on. One of them shines directly onto my bed through the window. Though my poor sleep has little to do with that. Today was the first day in two weeks when I felt good.

It often happens for some reason when my lawyer visits, then consistently takes a downturn when he leaves. It's unclear why that is, but it's unlikely to be psychological because I'm waiting for news from his visit—not salvation. I won't worry about it too much.

Taking advantage of the additional daylight, I finished reading Nabokov's third book, his stories originally written in English during his time in America. It was a thin book, and I finished it quickly. Maybe he had somewhat dwindled in talent by that time, or maybe it was because of the translation not being his own, but these stories didn't captivate and enchant me as much as his earlier works in Russian. There were a couple of outstanding ones, but the rest were passable at best. The Nabokovian charm and intricate imagery seemed to have vanished in the translation.

Well, writing at a consistently high level is always challenging. Tomorrow, I'll try reading him in the original English if, of course, I'm not again sprawled out on the bed.

The bosses have been searching for my official request for a phone call to my mother since this morning—it seems to have disappeared. If necessary, I'll file another request. Then, apparently, they should approve it.

The doctor no longer hints, suffers, or persuades. He directly says it's time to end the hunger strike while there's still a chance not to inflict irreversible damage on my heart and vascular system. I nod understandingly as if agreeing with him, but I start playing the game of postponements to make him feel reassured, not press on me, and not give up on dealing with me altogether. Otherwise, they'll take me to the city's intensive care unit. But I somehow stopped fearing that already, like everything else—including the Grim Reaper.

DAY EIGHTY-SIX

My decent health lasted just half a day yesterday before I felt awful again, particularly my head. It must have been a reaction to yet another change in the weather.

It's been raining since morning, a gentle and somewhat autumnal rain. All I could do was lie down earlier and listen to it.

Such rain is typically very cozy if you're met by it at home and don't have to go outside. And if I don't open my eyes, I can imagine that I'm at home, it's my day off, and I don't have to go to work. And my relatives are somewhere around, nearby—I'll see them soon, I just have to open my eyes.

But I don't do this in order to prolong this illusion of warmth and happiness, at least for a while.

My long-awaited lawyer didn't come yesterday. He arrived only today, but he didn't bring any life-changing news. There has been a lull on the political front on our issue, as well as on many others. But he poured out a whole heap of letters from acquaintances and friends, not only concerning smaller issues. For most of the two-hour meeting, I wrote the answers right there, in front of him. But the main thing was that I conveyed a message to my mother and children so that they wouldn't worry about me, told them about my life and state of health, but embellished it a little so they would be less worried.

Another priest wanted to see me, once again bringing a petition asking me to end the hunger strike. They were proposing various options through the European Court to secure a transfer to a facility nearer to my home in Crimea or, even better, to their hospital.

I refused everything: I don't need priests, I won't stop starving myself, and I'm trying not to be transferred to another place, so this is a total waste of time.

The film adaptation of my play has been moving forward. I suggested that they put my colleague and second director, Zhenya, in charge of the production. Though I don't know if she can leave her tropical islands with a little child. She is the only person to whom I can entrust the shooting of my work with a calm heart. The others will definitely do it all wrong, and I probably won't be able to manage the process remotely from here.

In general, life somewhere out there goes on and is in full swing, and today, I was able to join it a little, basking in someone else's warmth.

DAY EIGHTY-SEVEN

I've become so accustomed to the taste of boiling water—the only available drink—that I've started to like it. Gradually, the taste of tea is fading from my memory, not to mention the previously forgotten coffee, juice, soda, and beer.

At the med point, there's a continuous, gradual rotation of people: some are discharged, others are brought in for treatment. Among the long-term residents, it's only me and the two disabled men, and no matter how long they keep them in the hospital, new limbs won't grow for them. Among the newcomers, there are some familiar faces with whom I used to cross paths in the barracks. They're interested in chatting, but I have no desire at all to talk. All voices from the outside seem to penetrate me as if through cotton and get lost in the buzzing of my head. Lying down is the best way to spend the day during a hunger strike.

I've been trying to read Nabokov in English—a bit of a struggle, especially when he starts weaving his laces of phrases and creating images that elude my language skills.

Yesterday, the doctor was very upset with my reluctance to end the hunger strike. He believed I'd crossed the point of no return a long time ago and that continuing further served no purpose and ultimately hindered the resolution of the issue. I didn't try to convince him otherwise and simply said that I had no intention of stopping. We parted coolly.

I haven't received any letters for over a week. The censor has either been on vacation or sick leave. It's been boring without them, even with Nabokov's exquisite writing.

DAY EIGHTY-EIGHT

The weather constantly changes. It rains at night, in the morning, the sun is like a searchlight, and by lunchtime, the clouds gather again and contemplate precipitation.

I also feel lighter in the morning, and in the evening, I'm wrecked, as usual. But it's better this way than when you're unstable and feeling horrible all day long. Maybe these moments of clarity are caused by the fact that they've started administering the IV drip with amino acids again, or maybe there's a different reason. I don't know anything anymore.

When I felt well this morning, I managed to write the above lines and read more Nabokov. An English dictionary came to my aid from the library, so heavy that one could easily knock over a couple of policemen. The dictionary, judging by the level of dust on the cover, had missed a human touch, so it was happy to help me make Nabokov more understandable.

The authorities from Moscow called the doctor and cursed him out, asking why I was still on hunger strike. According to their calculations, I should've either died already or withdrawn from it. I disappointed them.

But the doctor no longer scolds me as much—his sore back has gotten worse, and since then, he has begun to look at the world more kindly.

Yesterday, another prosecutor came and took one more explanation from me regarding something. After him, some other supervisors followed, local and of lower rank. Everyone was so polite and helpful, it was sickening. One of them turned out to be a secret admirer of my work and quietly asked me in private what else he could see or read. I said that I had nothing to please him, especially new stuff. They said there were no letters because the prison system's email system didn't work well, but then it seemed to have started working, and I could wait for some news.

My mood has been peacefully comatose, despite the negative forecasts and news on all fronts. Monotony, of course, could be deadly—I no longer experience Groundhog Day, but Groundhog Life.

But one thing has been encouraging, and that's the fact that nothing is forever, neither good nor bad. Since I haven't seen anything good in my current situation, any changes would bring me joy. All that's left is to wait.

DAY EIGHTY-NINE

Since early this morning, there's been a commotion in our mad-house. Someone important is coming to see me again, some kind of commission, but they haven't even informed the doctor about who it is. The *kozly* and the *obizhennyy* have been busy cleaning the med point. They've already cleaned my ward twice and wiped down the door at least five times. The chief came with a video recorder and took a picture of my ID without explaining the reasons or the future audience of this photo session. But they should show up soon enough. Judging by their level of preparation, they'll be no lower than the director of the Federal Penitentiary Service or a deputy minister. They've brought a dozen chairs into my ward, turning it into something resembling a small TV studio or a lecture hall.

The doctor came, saw these rows, and told everyone not to go crazy. They removed half of the chairs, then another two. Then another chief came, and they took away the last three.

Everyone was waiting for some terrifying visitors, but it turned out to be just a modest girl from the Public Monitoring Commission, along with the priest who came last time, but today he was dressed casually. Damn! Everyone let out a disappointed sigh. A mountain of fear gave birth to a mouse of human rights. They were accompanied by the cream of the colony's leadership. They'd deliberately brought those three chairs. They sat me opposite the inspectors. Another empty and pointless conversation ensued: How do you feel? How long do you plan to continue the hunger strike? How do your relatives feel about this? And so on. The girl mainly conducted the interrogation, though the young priest also tried to shine, but only made a fool of himself: "How's the food here, are you satisfied?"

"I'm refusing food altogether."

"Oh, right, I mean, is the medical service good?"

It quickly became clear that I didn't need anything from them, and they, in turn, couldn't help me.

Once everyone had left, one of the chiefs returned and informed me that they had indeed lost my request to call my mother. I immediately wrote a new one and handed it to him. Let's see what happens. Still no letters.

We've reached the next control point. I'm scheduling another for two weeks from today, which happens to be Ukraine's Independence Day. I've been feeling normal for the second day in a row, so I'm confident I'll be able to make it. But making predictions is very difficult here—the black wave can engulf you at any moment, and the white light can dim until you forget not only what your name is, but even what day it is. I'm hoping for the best despite the endless black tunnel that's faintly visible ahead.

DAY NINETY

Another non-celebratory milestone. Ninety.

During a police search, my doctor saw me from a distance in my underwear and later commented that my body resembled that of a ninety-year-old. I couldn't argue with that because I felt just about the same age.

It's been rainy and cloudy outside the window, and my condition mirrors the weather.

Yesterday's council of doctors, equipped with test results, said things weren't too bad. I wouldn't die tomorrow, but there were no positive forecasts for the future. The heart muscle dystrophy and ongoing blood anemia were still persistent.

The only long-awaited joy of today was the call from my mother, which finally took place. Mom didn't expect such happiness. Tomorrow is her birthday, and this was the best present for her. We talked about what we had time for in an eternally short fifteen minutes. The main thing was that they were all doing well, waiting for me and hoping for the best, and they hadn't lost heart. To put it briefly: my family.

I also had a short talk with my son. His voice has started to deepen and his foot has already grown to a size forty-three. A little more and we'll carry one pair of skis for two. I didn't catch my daughter. She'd returned from the camp, seemingly pleased, and went to her friends for a walk in the city. Everything seemed fine with them, only her move to Kyiv and a trip to Europe were under threat. My ex-wife wouldn't give her permission to leave.

Why put up these barriers if neither I nor my daughter have been living with her for several years—when we don't even communicate? I'm afraid that without me, they won't be able to resolve this issue, and it'll be the same outcome as it was with Canada.

DAY NINETY-ONE

Lately, the same image has been stuck in my mind: a scene from a movie and real life. It happened around ten years ago when I watched *Blow*, starring Johnny Depp. The film was about a drug dealer who quickly made it big but then just as quickly spiraled downhill. He lost his criminal empire, all his money, and his wife along the way, leaving him with only a young daughter of around ten, who was forced to live in foster care. After all his adventures, the main character spent several years in prison. When he got out, he decided to start a new life—there was no other choice. He also wanted to reconnect with his daughter, realizing that she was the most precious thing in his life, something he hadn't understood before.

He met his daughter and made arrangements to pick her up the next day. But he needed money quick and decided to make some fast by getting involved in a drug deal, just not on the same scale as before. He got arrested during the deal and was given a huge sentence for being a repeat offender. Meanwhile, his daughter sat waiting on a bench with her suitcase the whole day. At the end of the film, they showed a picture of an older man in prison attire and a woman in her thirties. They were the real father and daughter, on whose lives the film was based. He continued serving his sentence. But the image of the girl waiting on the bench has stayed with me for life.

I know that people have intuition and premonitions. In the week leading up to my arrest, the image of the girl waiting for her father on the bench from *Blow* kept coming to my mind. I had a feeling that something bad was going to happen and that my daughter and I might well end up in a similar situation. We were supposed to go on a hiking trip, and we'd even bought a new backpack and sleeping bags, but it didn't work out due to bad weather. We never went on that trip.

The day before my arrest, my children and I were visiting my mother in the countryside. My daughter sat next to her grandmother on a bench, looking at me. I had just received a phone call, and I understood that I was being sought out, but I didn't know why, so I decided to find out.

I only learned the truth after my arrest. Since then, I've served five years out of my twenty-year sentence. My daughter is now fifteen years old. I don't know when we'll see each other again, but I'm sure it won't be here.

And for several days now, I've kept returning to those two moments with the girl waiting on the bench, one from the movie and the other from real life. I don't know what to say or do. How can I explain myself when there's no way to make amends? A simple "I'm sorry" won't be enough. I really don't want to end up in a photo like that, an old ex-convict next to his grown-up daughter. It's hard to write about this, but it's even harder to live with it.

Today is my mother's birthday. Happy birthday to my beloved mom.

DAY NINETY-TWO

I had nightmares at night that alien robots had taken over Earth. I was hiding with some people in a large garage where we were trying to make weapons for the resistance. We were all found there, and I was hiding under a car. But I woke up not because of this. I was very cold, especially my leg—for some reason, one of them was colder than the other—and I had an aching pain in my chest.

For a long time after I couldn't fall back asleep; I warmed myself up, then listened to the heaviness in my chest. When I finally fell asleep in the morning, I dreamed that I was living with my grown-up children in some house, old but my own, and the neighbors, the bastards, had fenced off part of our site for themselves, so I argued with them.

It was really cold outside in the morning. The inmates down in the alley were again walking around in coats and winter boots, typical for the middle of Labytnangi's August.

Another week has passed, mostly calm in terms of health, except for today's mini crisis. It was even weird to not feel like a wreck. This meant that the body still had some reserves left, but they, of course, were not going to last forever. I thought that they all had already been used up a long time ago, but apparently, my body was smarter than me. Both the doctor and I understood it was just a respite, a pause in my state.

I've already gotten used to the fact that there is no news and progress in our case, so I move on as if by inertia until I fall.

Yesterday, another inmate was brought to the med point who'd cut open his veins. A spirited Caucasian from the *muzhiki* who'd quarreled and hit the supply manager a couple of times in his barracks. He said he did it for a cause, meaning he'd been provoked. Without waiting for the police to take their revenge, he almost immediately cut open his veins. They sewed him up and brought him back to life and to our hospital. Hello, welcome!

Here, everyone has their own little war, their own life, and their own little tragedies.

DAY NINETY-THREE

Since early in the morning, the sun has been shining outside, and it has warmed up noticeably. The onset of autumn has been temporarily delayed. As usual, it'll come suddenly and unexpectedly.

There was a lot of hustle and bustle in the infirmary this morning. They were cleaning and tidying everything up again, and it looked like some commission was expected today, probably related to my situation.

The main event from yesterday was the letters! They brought a whole stack that had accumulated over the past two weeks. I didn't even have time to read them all last night, so I continued to go through them this morning. I won't respond to all of them. There were some that were not quite rational, and some that were just not interesting: someone you don't know who writes you just two lines and expects a detailed response to nothing.

But, this time, in the pile of letters, there was a lot of good and interesting stuff. There were letters from my mother and sister, from old acquaintances and close friends, and from some interesting people—you could tell from the letter—who made me want to reply right away.

Two duplicate telegrams also arrived from some bishop who was already in Labytnangi and seeking a meeting with me, asking me to help him from the inside. But he didn't ask if I needed this. Why were these priests coming here, treating it as a sacred place? Had I invited them? Did I want to see them? Why didn't they ask these questions and instead "foresee" whether or not I was expecting them?

Someone else sent some poems. I'm not particularly into poetry, but these were by Zhadan and Polozkova, and they were actually quite good. There was also a printed-out tweet thread about an operation to rescue a Russian mountaineer stuck in the mountains of Pakistan. His climbing partner fell off, or "flew away," as the survivor described him. On TV, they reported a week ago that he had been rescued, but in this printout, he was still there, on a snow-covered ledge. It was very interesting and captivating to read these seemingly brief lines about bravery.

There were many letters urging me to end the hunger strike. I didn't respond to those. There was also a printout of part of Voinovich's interview, the last one he'd given on my birthday, talking about me two weeks before his death. I wasn't a big fan of his work, but I had great respect for him as a person, a fighter, and a dissident who'd lived a long, challenging, and honorable life. A shining example for many, including me.

Today is the fourteenth of August. Exactly three months into my hunger strike. The main goal remains unattained—no one has been released, and the prospect of this remains unclear. But judging by what people wrote to me in the letters, I've at least managed to achieve a certain intermediate result: Ukrainian political prisoners are being discussed at many levels. It's still not enough, so my journey continues until something more significant happens.

DAY NINETY-FOUR

At night, they called me to the head of the colony, who read out the decision that my twenty-year term had been reduced to nine. A strange deduction, I thought at that moment, and even more strange that the paper he read didn't look like it was written officially but more like in children's scribbles. When I woke up, I understood everything.

Outside, the sun keeps shining, and it's getting warmer, but now and then, clouds appear out of nowhere, like school kids at a snack break, bringing brief showers and then moving on in different directions, as if following a script.

My peaceful phase has passed, and in the evenings, I feel a storm brewing inside me. It's like someone's shaking my world, and at times, everything turns dark, just like those old black-and-white TVs.

Yesterday's eagerly awaited special guest turned out to be Zoya Svetova, the journalist and human rights activist from Moscow. She was the first to visit me as a member of the Public Monitoring Commission when I was in Lefortovo. She also attended the courts in Rostov and has been a constant source of support throughout. Somehow, she'd managed to gain access to my current location through a public council. She came alone, but local authorities were present during our conversation. As usual, she shared a mix of news, some helpful, others not so much.

The big news was that Macron had recently called Putin. Among other things, he inquired about my situation, expressing concern that my health was deteriorating and that I should receive help, ideally in the form of a pardon and release. Putin made a solemn promise to provide his French counterpart with a comprehensive health report on me. This was typical of the Russian president's style: when asked about one thing, he often responded with something entirely different. In this case, a request for a pardon led to the promise of a medical certificate. The Jesuits of the world must have given a standing ovation.

Zoya stayed for about three hours, and during this time, she managed to tire out the bosses first, then the doctor, then me with her questions. Finally, she departed, and I needed a rest, as if after unloading coal.

Yesterday, late in the evening, they called me to the prison lawyer, who was sent by the bishop, who had been besieging the camp for a week already with the aim of breaking through to me for some reason. Apparently, it was to inform me about something very important that I didn't know.

The lawyer turned out to be a well-fed man with a fat mug and the habits of a former policeman. He immediately showed me a sheet with the text of the priest's telegram: "Did you receive one like this?"

"Yes."

"Do you want to meet him?"

"No."

"So, that's that."

I left without even having settled into a chair. I hadn't intended to drag out the conversation anyway, just to politely refuse the lawyer and church services. It turned out that he was the one doing the talking, and it felt like he hadn't come to visit me but that I had come to him for an interrogation. To complete the scene, all that was missing was a nod from his head to the duty officer who had brought me, indicating, "You can take him away."

As they say: once a cop, always a cop.

DAY NINETY-FIVE

Today, the nurse set a personal record, managing to insert the IV only on the fourth attempt, even taking a break for her own hysteria. It was a good thing that my veins couldn't speak. Otherwise, I would have heard many unpleasant things about myself and people in general from them.

At the med point, there has been another change of characters. All the previous patients were discharged, and a whole new group of *kozly* have arrived. Among the old-timers, only the disabled men and I remain, and those four who work here. There's also a young Khanty man in the isolation box—a small isolated room with its own toilet, a door that locks, a window, and bars. He has chickenpox, and now his entire face is adorned with green spots. He sits on a stool all day, swaying slightly, and quietly sings something to the wall across from him. It's both unpleasant and tempting to look at as if he's a zoo animal on display.

I finally managed to finish reading Nabokov's novel about Professor Pnin in English. Overall, it was interesting, but a bit of a struggle. I understood the dialogues and actions without a dictionary, but when it came to descriptions, even a dictionary didn't always help me catch the subtle and fleeting thoughts and images, which were like snowflakes on my fingertips.

Now, there's only one unread novel left ahead. That will have to wait until tomorrow. I'm tired today.

I just found out that Putin denied my mother's plea for my clemency, the request she wrote several months ago that we all had so much hope for, even me. Today was undoubtedly bleak.

DAY NINETY-SIX

I got myself another notebook. More precisely, I sewed together some more A4 sheets folded in half. This is already the fifth one. Every time I start such a notebook as a diary, I hope that it'll be the last one. And every time there's something else to write into it, and it eventually ends, unlike this already endless hunger strike.

The situation, as I feared, has reached a stalemate: they can't let me or anyone else go, and I can't afford to give up. But this time I have a strong feeling that I won't last long enough to finish this notebook.

Last night, I dreamed of a sea with heavy waves, and I was on board an old wooden ship. In the morning, the sky was filled with autumnal clouds. Later in the afternoon, under my window, a group of quarantine arrivals* took a walk along the alley. There were about fifteen of them, led by the *kozel* herder under the watchful eye of a policeman, the burly Dagestani officer. They marched in unison, stopping at the end of the alley, turning around, reaching the middle, stopping again, and then repeating the process. They greeted the chief loudly and in unison, said their goodbyes, and then marched back and forth dozens of times. As the parade's organizer grew a bit bored, he gave

---

* The word "quarantine" in the Russian prison system has a double connotation—it's not only about checking new inmates for diseases and maintaining hygiene standards. It also refers to the period where new prisoners must adapt to the rules of the colony, and in some cases, when they are beaten down by officers and the "activists" who serve them.

the command, and from that point on, the whole procedure took place with the inmates singing "Katyusha"* in unharmonious but earnest voices. It was a scene that made me think of a factory churning out obedient zombies.

DAY NINETY-SEVEN

It's foggy outside, and it feels like there's fog in my head too. My body is numb, and I'm constantly dizzy.

Today, my pulse was alarmingly low again: just forty beats per minute. I'm slowly losing weight, and earlier, the scale showed seventy-three kilograms. I'm not well.

During the visit of some troublemakers to the med point, the head orderly also arrived, and he had a brawl with a Caucasian guy. They patched him up quickly and discharged him in just a few days, but this well-groomed troublemaker still wanders around the hospital, keeping a close watch on things.

I don't think he's here on official business. The police are keeping him under wraps, not sure where to place him after that incident. It seems he's just snooping around out of habit,

---

* "Katyusha" is a famous Soviet song from World War II about a girl longing for her love, a soldier, to return home safely. It is also the name of a rocket launcher built by the Soviets and used during World War II, infamous for its high-pitched wailing sound when fired. The cult of World War II in Russia—where it is called the Great Patriotic War—has only grown under Vladimir Putin's rule, and it has corrupted the legacy of those who fought against the Nazis in an effort to "justify" Russia's war against Ukraine, which they falsely claim to be run by Nazis.

especially when it comes to me, keeping his ears warm by eaves-dropping when I engage in the occasional conversation.

I've been reading Nabokov's novel *The Gift*. Progress is slow, about twenty to thirty pages a day, that's all I can manage. Still, it has been very interesting. I've found that I have a lot in common with the main character, who feels like he was mod-eled after me: he was born on July twelfth and lived a life of creativity and solitude. He often recalled his childhood as the happiest time, a period when everything seemed to be laid out and shaped for a lifetime.

The news said that Putin will meet with Merkel for exten-sive negotiations, including discussions about Ukraine. I have no doubt that the topic of Ukrainian hostages will come up, and I also have no doubt that it won't change anything. Just like numerous previous meetings haven't changed anything. In the worst-case scenario, if Russia is put under severe pressure, they'll release a medical report about my health.

The doctor came and solemnly announced that I'd died once again according to the internet. This time, it wasn't so far from the truth.

DAY NINETY-EIGHT

The sun shines through the window, but inside, there's only darkness and emptiness. It feels like the world is closing in, causing dizziness and numbness.

I didn't feel well while hooked up to the IV, and they had to stop the procedure because my vein burst again.

I lack the energy and motivation to do anything—to write

or even think. The meeting between Merkel and Putin yesterday ended as expected, with the usual vague statements.

I have to endure for another five days until the next scheduled date. Thankfully, I don't need to go anywhere. I can just rest. Exhaustion has taken a toll on my soul, and I'm just going through the motions.

DAY NINETY-NINE

They say that it's getting warmer outside with each passing day. I don't particularly feel it—I'm constantly shivering and running a fever. The morning light is getting shorter and less bright. Yesterday evening, while walking to the bathroom in the corridor, I nearly fainted. I stumbled into the dining room and collapsed onto a nearby bench and table. I quickly came to and just as quickly recovered, but it startled the guys who were sitting there. I hope the doctor doesn't find out. Otherwise, he'll start nagging me again, but lately, he seems tired of doing that.

There is talk again of a possible meeting of the Normandy Four, but there's no date set yet. Another illusory hope for yet another round of empty negotiations. It's like in a movie about attempting contact with extraterrestrials that I recently watched on TV: you don't understand what they're saying and what they ultimately want, and everyone is just stuck. It's similar to negotiations with Russia, the only difference being that the extraterrestrials are peaceful, unlike these unfriendly neighbors.

I've noticed that I'm speaking vaguely again and my handwriting has become even more distorted. Forming thoughts is difficult too, as if there's fog and noise in my head. Sometimes it takes time to remember what day of the week it is or the date. But I still try to read and write in the mornings.

In the evenings, I don't have strength. Sometimes the most difficult moments occur in the evenings, which is what I'm afraid of—I start feeling unwell even while lying down. But I still try to live and be happy even in this situation because if I become a happy person now, it will be much easier to remain one later too. The doctor, who often sees me smiling even when in a very bad condition, keeps saying that I'll be smiling even in the coffin. I don't know, we'll see when the time comes, but preferably as late as possible.

DAY ONE HUNDRED

I reached the biggest milestone without any hint of celebration or corresponding mood. In the morning, the doctor came with a bright smile to congratulate me on this occasion, even offering to bake me a cake. The head of the colony arrived in his wake, equally pleased, as if he had received a high rank, and also spoke about celebrating the occasion, though limited his offer to freshly brewed *kissel.* I didn't want anything. I felt so exhausted that it seemed even if they were to release me today, I wouldn't have been very happy, and I wouldn't have known what to do next.

I felt a bit lighter, not struggling to breathe as much. I sensed the warmth from outside through the open window and even turned on the fan to mark the occasion.

Yesterday, a visiting commission of doctors, in a reduced lineup, took place here again. The cardiologist mentioned that my heart wasn't better or worse, the tests and EKG didn't seem to have changed much, so why was I feeling so unwell? The therapist provided the answer, explaining that I had progressive hypoxia—a shortage of oxygen supply to the brain.

In the future, I should expect more fainting spells and then irreversible changes to my mind; I would start going completely crazy.

But lately, it feels like I'm already at the beginning of that journey. Ending life in a psychiatric institution wouldn't be the best fate, but whatever will be, will be. No, this isn't resignation to my fate; it's merely part of accepting any of its decisions, even the harshest ones.

There haven't been any letters for over a week again. It was only when I reminded the chief about it in the morning that they finally delivered them in the afternoon. Not many letters, and all of them had arrived a week ago. This time, they didn't bring much good news—only problems. The bishop remained persistent and continued to try to reach me about important matters. Does the word "no" have different interpretations? After all, we're not in China . . .

As for the theatrical production and the film adaptation of my play, things weren't going smoothly either. But they were determined and unyielding; Anya, the producer, was trying to break down barriers and expected me to be fully involved in the process.

I reassured her that I would help in any way I could, but she shouldn't think of me as just working in a remote office. The speed and volume of communication were different now, and so was my performance. I suggested she take some time to google what dystrophy, anemia, and hypoxia meant so that she could better understand my condition.

Later in the evening, there should be another phone call from the persistent Zoya Svetova. Yes, theoretically, anyone could request a phone conversation with me. Many have tried, but in the time—almost a year—that I've been in this camp, they've only arranged them regularly for Zoya. What kind of serious influence does she exert in the Russian Federal Penitentiary Service? Of course, I'll participate in the conversation, but I don't expect much from yet another empty exchange. Though, lately, I haven't had any other conversations of note.

DAY ONE HUNDRED ONE

Despite a night of bad sleep and restlessness, I felt good in the morning. It seemed like the sudden darkness that had enveloped me was finally easing up. I noticed that summer had returned to Labytnangi. There was a clear blue sky outside my window and bright sunshine, and it even felt a bit hot. I still kept my warm underwear on—either these past days left me chilled or it was a psychological defense, I'm not sure.

In any case, I'm currently no longer trembling or shivering. I never thought my body would adapt so well to increasingly harsh conditions.

The numbers related to the hunger strike have become somewhat surreal, and I never intended to rely on them. The way forward remains unclear. It's a dead-end situation, so all I can do is keep going as long as my body allows.

During the morning check, I was surprised to find that our hospital was already full, with seventeen people occupying all the beds, except for my single ward. It's been this way for three days, they say, but somehow, I didn't notice—there hasn't been much time.

Yesterday's phone conversation with Zoya Svetova didn't happen due to a lack of connection. It wasn't the work of enemies, as she might have thought—it genuinely was a technical issue, and as a result, another person from the med point also couldn't take a call.

I replied to yesterday's letters. I provided my further instructions and suggestions for the film adaptation of the play, along with comments on the scenery sketches sent by the artist.

I'm tired, that's true, but I've gained a bit of energy. Work, especially creative work, has lifted my spirits, as if I were right there with them, preparing for filming in the next room. In general, creativity has been a significant source of support for me throughout my years in captivity, mainly psychologically and spiritually, and not only during my hunger strike. It has also had physical benefits. After all, I write everything in notebooks; there were about a dozen of them back then, and now, with the hunger strike ones, there are fifteen.

They saved me during the stages when I was isolated in a cell which was almost like a punishment: an iron bed with narrow and cold welded-on iron strips, and on top of them, a mattress so thin that I had to lie almost directly on the iron with just a sheet covering it. I'd spread out my notebooks, placing these scattered pieces of cotton wool sewn into a mattress pad on top, and carefully lay down, rarely turning from side to side at night to avoid disturbing this fragile structure.

My creativity, in the most literal sense, preserved my body during those times. Those notebooks are now among the most valuable possessions I have. If, for some reason, I'm told tomorrow to get ready and take only my most valuable items, I'll undoubtedly take them, leaving behind without hesitation my prison clothes, meager belongings, books, letters, and even the few souvenirs I collected as humble gifts for my friends and loved ones. For now, though, no one is calling me to go anywhere.

DAY ONE HUNDRED TWO

I had a dream last night that I was flying. Not on a plane or with any devices, just levitating high and fast, but it wasn't scary at all.

They say dreaming of flying means you're growing, which is why kids often have such dreams. Oddly, I don't remember having had these dreams as a child, but as an adult, I have had them occasionally, though not too often. Maybe it's because I haven't really grown up yet?

My decent state of well-being from yesterday only lasted until the evening, then I felt cloudy and weak again. In the morning, I experienced a prickling sensation in my heart, and my head felt numb, like cotton. This time, I almost fainted when I got up, which was a first for me. Fortunately, after receiving an IV drip, I started to feel better.

Sometimes, I can't help but think that this diary, in which I observe my own condition, sounds like the complaints of a loser. Today, when they removed the IV stand, I accidentally bent my arm in a way that made me see it for the first time—there was loose, hanging skin resembling the paw of an elderly turtle. What an abomination. Is my skin really sagging like this everywhere?

The chief operations officer came yesterday and circled around me for an hour and a half, like a shark around Robinson after landing on a tiny atoll. Smiling and chuckling, he played counterintelligence with me, asking questions to sniff out everything. In the end, he suggested I give up and withdraw from the hunger strike. He began to pile up ridiculous arguments, like the crocodile that put out a burning sea with mushrooms and pies in Chukovsky's surrealistic verse. He did this, however, without much hope of success, and, naturally, did not achieve it. We parted politely.

Today, after my usual medical procedures, it brightened up a little again—both the sky, which was frowning at someone in the morning, and my mind. Taking advantage of the respite, I finished reading Nabokov, finally parting with his work.

The Gift was certainly not his best, but still very good. As always, it was very personal and autobiographical. In many ways, it was a study of the life of Russian prose writers and poets, and of creativity in general. It was very interesting, especially the part devoted entirely to Chernyshevsky. I knew very little about him before that, just some general information. And here, with the help of Nabokov's peculiar approach—somewhat similar to the way the Soviet-era writer and literary critic Yury Tynyanov, whom I also respect, wrote about poets and writers—I was able to look and get to know this person deeper, from an unusual angle. And most importantly, I discovered a lot of coincidences between mine and Chernyshevsky's fates. He was born a day before me on July twelfth, similar to the main character in the novel who writes his book about him. He started off in economics, then turned to literary pursuits, and eventually got involved in revolutionary ideas. At the age of thirty-six—just one year earlier than me—he was unjustly imprisoned based on fabricated charges and false testimonies because of his beliefs rather than any actual actions.

He served twenty years, most of it in Yakutia—another coincidence in regards to both the term and the place where he served it. He was pardoned and allowed to return to Central Russia at the age when they planned to release me, according to my sentence. He died six years after that, sick, poor, and alone. He remained in history as one of the people who gave rise to revolutionary ideas in Russia. He left behind a small and highly controversial artistic legacy, which would hardly have been noticed if not for the story of his imprisonment.

Up to this point, everything is very, very similar. I don't know to what extent I'll have to repeat his difficult fate in the future, but if it turns out to be the same, I won't grumble. Each is given his own cross to bear according to his strength.

DAY ONE HUNDRED THREE

At night, I dreamed about freedom again—about Simferopol. I was walking down the street with someone I barely knew, heading to his sister's wedding, or rather, her marriage registration. On the way, I stopped at a small shop and bought some yogurt and a bread roll. I paid with some old and worn-out money. It wasn't enough, so I had to give back the crumbs that had fallen off the roll for the final payment.

The cloudy morning gradually turned into a sunny day. I basked by the window like a cat.

I'm feeling OK for now. Of course, I had a rough evening yesterday, but that has become routine. Today is Ukraine's Independence Day. I won't write any colorful words about it. I'll just pause in memory of those who gave their lives for it. They gave the most precious thing they had for something even more valuable: freedom.

I can't figure out which week this odyssey is coming to an end. I've been keeping count for months already. Today is another milestone. I'm setting the next one for September first. Another week in this piggy bank where I'm saving something unclear for an unknown purpose. A week isn't long, though. I'll definitely hold out for another week, then we'll see.

Every day follows such a well-established routine that you can't distinguish them anymore. Every action, even gestures when you stand up or lie down, dress or undress, take medicine, hold a cup, hold a thermometer, extend your hand for the IV drip, go to the bathroom, wash your face, take a toothbrush, hang a towel in its place, and so on and so forth, is so rehearsed, monotonous, and boring that you involuntarily start to feel like a robot, a machine operating according to its program. One that doesn't live, but only functions, not knowing or understanding its goals. Emotional emptiness.

I found out that the Russian Federal Penitentiary Service has complained, with clear displeasure, that over a hundred and forty thousand rubles have already been spent on medicine for me.

Well, at least I inflicted some economic damage on the enemy.

DAY ONE HUNDRED FOUR

I've been feeling unwell since this morning, and not even the IV drip helped. The weather has worsened, with clouds and growing darkness. Hypertensive patients at the med point are suffering, and I'm suffering along with them.

The new inmates were taken out to the yard to march and sing the same old "Katyusha," and she went out to the riverbank for what must be the twentieth time already.*

All day yesterday, I tried to retrieve my letters from the prison bosses, and in the evening, I finally received them. A whole stack had accumulated over the past week. Lately, the mail system hasn't been working smoothly, causing delays. There was a letter from my mother, written even before our last phone call, assuring me that everything was fine with them. But her handwriting suggested that her eyesight was deteriorating. She lives solely for her children and the desire to see and hug me, just as I do.

There were postcards from abroad, including one from America that made me smile, with early Christmas greetings almost six months in advance. There were business and creative

---

* Sentsov is joking about the song's line: "Katyusha went out onto the riverbank."

letters regarding the production of my play adaptation. The preparations were in full swing, and my active involvement, albeit from afar, was necessary. However, correspondence had been slowed down by the Russian Federal Penitentiary Service.

I'll respond to all of them tomorrow because today, I have no strength and my mind is foggy.

Sasha Kolchenko and I were sentenced exactly three years ago, and in response we sang a hymn. At that time, it seemed like everything would end well—would end soon.

Today, I don't have that same feeling, but I won't give up, even if I end up being alone. Though I often have the feeling that I'm alone, and all these people in my letters, offering support from around the world, beyond the prison walls and the security barrier, seem almost unreal. My reality is this ward, where there is no one but me.

DAY ONE HUNDRED FIVE

Last night I felt extremely cold. My hands and feet went numb beneath the blanket, and even my ears and nose felt icy. I woke up shivering, and it took a long time for me to warm up.

In the morning, some sunlight came through the window, providing a bit of warmth. I still felt like I was freezing from the inside, and my legs were even cramping up. I moved around like an old person using crutches. My condition hasn't improved since.

They released a couple of *kozly* from the med point and brought in two guys who were previously "under the roof," having served seven out of their nine- and ten-year sentences.

They'll be released soon. One is Georgian, and the other is Chechen. They got their reputation as "roofmen" being part of a small group that caused a riot in the camp seven years ago, beating up *kozly* and setting fire to the barracks. It was a famous story of one of the resistance attempts at this camp. Three of them have been released since then, one passed away here, and only this duo remained.

They have quite the spirit about them, unlike the newbies who arrived yesterday and were so enthusiastic, endlessly marching and singing "Katyusha." Today's inmates appear sheltered as if they were taken from their mothers' aprons and immediately placed in prison. I'm not sure how much of a beating it would take to make me march down the alley like they do. But for them, a couple of kicks or a slap during the intake— and sometimes just a stern word from the police—seem to be enough.

The doctor visited the infirmary over the weekend and scolded me once more when he saw my condition. He didn't understand why I was still waiting when it seemed like I couldn't achieve anything. I didn't explain it to him. He informed me that in a week he was going on vacation, leaving me in the care of another doctor, a Korean who will eventually take over when he returns.

The new doctor probably won't spend much time with me and will swiftly transfer me to the local intensive care unit the first chance he gets. It's sad to part ways with my current doctor, and it seems like he feels the same way, but there's nothing I can do. The resolution of this situation will come to pass without him.

DAY ONE HUNDRED SIX

The nights are getting colder, but the sun shines during the day, and it's generally warm. I'm not getting better, but at least I'm not getting worse. I try to read every day to keep my mind occupied; otherwise, you can really start feeling unwell in this place.

I recently started reading short stories by John Galsworthy, but after three of them, I decided to stop. It just wasn't my style. They felt too old-fashioned, simple, and repetitive. It was my second attempt with this author. The first one, with *The Forsyte Saga*, didn't go well either. As they say: different strokes for different folks.

But I stumbled upon a novel by Remarque that I hadn't read before. I've always been a big fan of his, and I thought I had read all of his works.

Remarque's writing can be very powerful, though some of his later works are rather average rehashings of his earlier works. His themes are always the same: war, wandering, death, love, friendship, and life—eternal themes that are always relevant. They say anyone can write at least one good and honest book about themselves, but only a true writer can write more than one. The essence of talent lies in the ability to care about others.

This particular book was about World War II. It told the story of a German soldier returning home from the eastern front, hoping for a break from the horrors of war, only to find that there was no home left, both literally and figuratively.

Remarque didn't fight in World War II—the first one was enough for him. He went into exile to escape the fascist nightmare in his own country. But his experiences, sensitivity, and talent allowed him to vividly describe World War II, its aftermath, and probably any other conflict.

But what struck me most was how the German wartime hysteria and propaganda reminded me of modern Russia. If Putin were to openly attack Ukraine tomorrow, the fervent crowd would likely support him in that and more. People don't want to learn from the mistakes of other nations or even their own.

DAY ONE HUNDRED SEVEN

Neither the weather nor my condition has changed. I've got the chills, and the ringing in my ears has returned, making my head spin and forcing me to close my eyes for relief.

This week, my lawyer is supposed to visit and bring some news, but he hasn't arrived yet. I did, however, receive a letter yesterday, an official one. A small delegation came to deliver it—a notice from the regional clemency commission, stating that only I could request clemency, not my mother or anyone else. I've known this for a while, but the official document arrived just yesterday. What caught my attention wasn't the content but the dates. It took exactly two weeks for the envelope to travel from Salekhard to Labytnangi, which is a neighboring town about ten kilometers away.

You can see it from the central alley across the river. It's as if they're using actual snails for postal deliveries to have covered such short distances in such a long time.

I'm still reading Remarque's book, in which the main character, on leave in his hometown, can't find his parents there, only their bombed-out house. Eventually, he receives a package at the post office. His mother sent it to him at the front, but since he had already left, the package was returned to the starting point. It took three weeks for it to go there and back, from the German rear to the Russian front and back again in 1943—during wartime, no less.

In modern Russia, it's one and a half times slower, even for just ten kilometers. I don't think a war would significantly increase this speed; it's probably something else.

DAY ONE HUNDRED EIGHT

Insomnia at night. In the morning it rained, and my chest hurt.

Yesterday was an unusual day. The first half of it passed, or rather dragged along, as usual. After lunch, I was invited to the doctor for an appointment. He noticed that I had become very weak lately, but my usual positive and energetic attitude turned out to be more to his liking. I replied that he couldn't demand much from a dead battery. Still, the conversation gradually went down a political cul-de-sac, and the doctor again began to prescribe his Great Russian interests, ambitions, and approaches to me. I wound up and also went on the attack, without noticing how this cheered me up.

Then, they brought the mail in two acts. The first involved removing a handkerchief from some envelope and forwarding it to the warehouse with my civilian items. The second involved the destruction of two tea bags and an instant coffee packet that had arrived together in the same envelope as contraband. I didn't know what to laugh at more, the bureaucratic rules of this system or the person who thought to send me such things. What do such people have in their heads? Did they want me to drink *chifir* one last time and wipe away my tears?

The letters were good, though. They were from French citizens who supported me, from Ukraine with explanations that everything was not so bad in our country in my absence, along with requests to hold on because I was about to be released. There were also requests to stop the hunger strike because I had achieved my goal and should take care of my health, adding, "We'll still save you."

But the main thing was a letter from my cinematic comrades in arms Zhenya and Nastya, who were ready to join the team for the film adaptation of my play. That's why I spent the whole evening yesterday writing responses, first and foremost to them, distributing organizational and creative instructions.

At the same time at the med point, there were all sorts of things going on, everyone suddenly needed something from me, so I was much in demand. I got tired, but it was a good kind of fatigue, a work-related one that didn't exhaust me. On the contrary, it somehow inspired and even over-excited me, so much so that I couldn't really fall asleep later. I had already lost the habit of living at such a fast pace, but found that I still liked living life to the fullest with the gas pedal pressed all the way down more than lying down and decomposing in the bed.

Today, I had an IV drip on a reduced program because the amino acids had run out again. In a few days, it will become very difficult for me without them. In the meantime, my mood remains normal, and my well-being too.

The clouds have dispersed, and again the sun is playing by the window. I am basking in it, like an alley cat in March. For now, life seems to go on. Let it continue to be the same.

DAY ONE HUNDRED NINE

Autumn has descended upon the camp, bringing rain, wind, and clouds. It seems like warmth won't be returning anytime soon. August surprised us with decent weather for this region, but now the days are getting shorter, rushing by like a train.

Along with the amino acids, the hospital ran out of the other strong solutions they used to give me every day, which helped me survive. All that was left were glucose and salt. They promised to send more soon, but until then, things might be tough.

Strangely, I don't really care anymore. I'm exhausted from waiting and worrying about things. The doctor has some fancy medical term for this state, but I can't remember it. There's a decline somewhere in there, but I couldn't care less about that either.

Yesterday, more letters arrived. Not a lot, but at least they were written recently.

It seems like letters are coming in more frequently now— better than receiving a stack every two weeks.

Other prisoners continue to open up their veins. Yesterday, one was brought to the med point. He'd already slit his wrists a month and a half ago and now he'd gone for a second round. Apparently, it was his tenth time. His arms were covered in poorly healed wounds. The cause? He'd had a conflict with a policeman under strict regime confinement: "I'll open 'em!" "Open 'em!" He opened up. Straight to the med point. The doctor helped him, and now there were new marks under the white bandages on his forearms.

I finished reading Remarque's novel about World War II. It wasn't his best work, but I still enjoyed it. The book was filled with a lot of passion and the author's strong anti-fascist and anti-war beliefs. This might be because he wrote it from the safety and quiet of emigration, but some of the emotions and plot twists feel a bit forced. In his earlier works about World War I and peace, everything felt more genuine, profound, and subtle. He didn't spell out the important things directly. Instead, they lingered between the lines, leaving an impression after reading and staying in your memory forever. Maybe it was because he was writing about his own experiences and observations in those, or maybe he was just more passionate and inspired back then. Hard to say.

The secret of creating a good book, like a good film, is—in my opinion—something that can't be fully understood. You can write a book or make a movie that's very well-received and liked by people, but comprehending exactly how it happened—for you or for others—is often beyond explanation.

DAY ONE HUNDRED TEN

Last night, I had a dream about our old red car. It was parked near our village house. Peering through the side window, I saw my intoxicated father behind the wheel. I offered to drive instead, but he declined. Mom was in the backseat, but it wasn't clear if she looked ill or upset. She mentioned that Dad would drive her to the doctor, and I should prepare an IV drip for her. So, I went into my old room in the house and started working with a plastic tube and some fluids . . . Then, I woke up. I've never dreamed about my parents as frequently as I have in these past three months of the hunger strike.

Today the weather outside is dry, but the sun struggles to rise above the horizon and break through the endless clouds. It's getting colder.

The nurses keep poking at my veins. My weight is seventy-two point five kilograms. I seem to be improving, but I often feel on the verge of fainting. When I get up, everything goes dark, and I feel the blood noisily rushing from my head. I squint and grab onto something. After a few seconds, warmth flows back into my brain, like water. It eases off, I open my eyes, and I can slowly move to where I need to be. The world settles back into place, but with a slight wobble.

In the morning, the cat proudly paraded through all the wards with a small mouse it had caught, showing off its still-trembling prey. After its triumphant tour of the med point, the cat settled down in the corridor to play its favorite game: "Last Chance." The mouse finally gave up in the third round.

Some prisoners who aren't exactly sick are housed in our hospital for unknown reasons. Meanwhile, those who can barely walk or have self-inflicted injuries, like the one from yesterday, are quickly released. These are maneuvers orchestrated by the operational unit, playing a constant game of counterintelligence, weaving its own intrigues and schemes. Many prisoners are involved in this, either willingly or unwillingly.

Ryzhy has been at the med point for a month now, but for different reasons: he refuses to play these games with the administration and challenges the system by bombarding various authorities with complaints about the prison, most of which never leave its walls.

On the outside, Ryzhy used to associate with skinheads and was known for killing Tajik migrant workers, which landed him behind bars at the age of nineteen with a twenty-three-year sentence. He's already served half of it.

It's unlikely he suddenly developed sympathy for migrants during this time, but maybe he's realized there are other ways to find purpose in life. He's an intelligent and well-read guy who has seen a lot of films, plus he has a keen intellect and a grasp of politics and economics. He's an oppositionist and an extremist, making for interesting conversations. There's always something to talk about with him. Such individuals are rare in this system.

Due to his brief interactions with me, he's faced new problems: the authorities are trying to create a sort of exclusion zone around me, even though I don't actively seek out interactions with other prisoners. I understand how dangerous and complicated such associations can be for them, and frankly, I don't have many people to connect with here.

DAY ONE HUNDRED ELEVEN

I've reached the next milestone in my hunger strike, lasting for three and a half months. I've been feeling OK today, so I decided to set the next checkpoint for two weeks from now, on September fourteenth, which will have marked four months. It feels like there's no end in sight to this ordeal. None of us imagined I would endure such a prolonged hunger strike.

The Russian *chanson* singer Iosif Kobzon and the head of occupied Donetsk, Aleksandr Zakharchenko, have died. Kobzon from cancer and old age, Zakharchenko from an explosive device—possibly because he possessed sensitive information too.

I don't believe it was divine punishment or the existence of mythical saboteurs responsible for the explosion in Separ* Cafe where Zakharchenko was. It's worth noting the comment from a correspondent on the scene: "This cafe, with its significant name, was first opened by members of the militia . . . " Their time seems to have come to an end as the FSB systematically began removing its associates.

This will serve a dual purpose, installing more agreeable and manageable figures while simultaneously blaming Ukraine for disrupting the peace process. I doubt it will fail. After some noise and outrage, things will likely continue, especially now that one more obstacle has been removed. Putin appears weary of the war in Donbas, given its ongoing drawbacks, and he seems to prefer to focus on the Syrian conflict, which offers him more advantages. In any case, Putin expressed condolences for both deaths. I don't feel sorrow for either collaborators or for those who support them.

---

* Short for "separatist," a term that Russian propaganda pushed to further the narrative that people in Donetsk and Luhansk oblasts wanted independence from Ukraine. In reality, Russian soldiers with the aid of collaborators have fought and carried out occupation in parts of both regions.

First of September. The Day of Knowledge. My kids went to school. Very far from me. My lawyer never showed up this week, and there have been no letters from my sister for a month, so I don't even know if they were able to transport my daughter to Kyiv as planned, or if she went back to her already boring Simferopol gymnasium.

In the new school year, many prisoners also go to study. A third of them here never completed their secondary education. The Russian Federal Penitentiary Service strictly monitors this, so starting in September, strings of overgrown students, some of whom are already in their thirties, will be brought to the local prison school, where the teacher is fenced off from the class by bars. Buratinos go to school with ABC books and onions ...*

DAY ONE HUNDRED TWELVE

I had a dream about fishing at the lake, or more like feeding the fish breadcrumbs. One of them was white, almost albino, with big bulging eyes. It swam up to the surface and started pinching pieces of soaked bread. I tried using some of the same bread on the hook as bait, but it scared the fish away, and they darted into the depths.

It's morning as I write, and rain has been falling from the gray, leaky sky for the second day in a row. I'm feeling OK, except for this strange pressure and prickling sensation in my chest, making it hard to breathe.

---

* Buratino is the Russian equivalent of Pinocchio. Papa Karlo—the equivalent of Geppetto—feeds him onions.

Not long ago, at the doctor's office, I overheard him reporting to someone higher up about my health. While he was examining me, his landline phone rang. He glanced at the caller ID, answered with a single word, "relatively," then returned to work.

It turns out they call him from headquarters every morning to ask about my health. To avoid unnecessary small talk, he came up with this vague and uninformative answer: "Relatively." I imagine it has confused the higher-ups on the other end of the line, but the doctor doesn't seem to care.

His vacation begins tomorrow. It's a shame because things will be much duller without him.

One of the biggest problems in prison, for me and many others, is the lack of privacy, the inability to be alone. The constant police surveillance isn't the issue, however—it's being around people 24/7, day in and day out, for all these years in the same cell or barracks. Not all of them are pleasant. You eat, sleep, wash, and even use the restroom together. You talk. But the only thing you have in common with most of them is the prison itself, so it dominates your conversations, just like it does for many here. But you adapt. You get used to both the physical and emotional closeness.

Then, there are those rare moments when you break free from this routine, like in solitary confinement, an isolation cell, or in a separate hospital room, as I am right now. That's when you realize the joy of having personal space and being alone, with your only company being an annoying and elusive fly that refuses to die. You quickly get used to this newfound comfort. I shudder at the thought that if I ever give up my current struggle,

I'll have to return to the overcrowded barracks. It's one of my strongest motivations to stay put.

DAY ONE HUNDRED THIRTEEN

In my dream, I found myself sitting at a restaurant table with an unknown couple. Initially, I was alone, but they later took the empty seats. I ordered several dishes, mainly fried fish, which turned out to be pretentious and tasteless, and surprisingly expensive, leaving me struggling to pay for it later, even though the establishment wasn't luxurious.

In the morning, there was some rare sunshine mixed with frequent clouds. While there was no rain yet, the persistently gray sky suggested it would rain soon.

During these past few days of respite, I managed to read another novel by Remarque, this one about German emigrants, a recurring theme he often explored. It was reminiscent of his famous work, *Arc de Triomphe*.

They say every true author continually writes about the same subject, but in different ways, creating their own unique world. Remarque undoubtedly had such a world, and I found comfort in dwelling within it for a while, even though his characters faced challenging circumstances. It was interesting to compare his depiction of emigration with Nabokov's, as they wrote about the same era and countries. Aside from the stylistic differences between these talented authors, there was a stronger sense of poverty in Nabokov's work, but also reflection on the loss of a comfortable homeland. In Remarque's, poverty and hardship were more prevalent, leaving no room for nostalgia, as many characters were already struggling before emigrating. Their sole focus was survival while also preserving their human dignity. I found Remarque's perspective closer to my own.

Tomorrow, I'll begin reading the last of his novels that I haven't yet explored, *Night in Lisbon*, which also seems to revolve around emigrant experiences.

But my bright period seems to be coming to an end. Without the strong medication, my pain has started to intensify again, and my body and limbs feel numb, as if they've been lying still for too long. My heart is pounding, and it feels like a thresher is at work inside my head.

The new nurse, who was administering my IV, accidentally knocked my slipper into the middle of the room. Over the course of two hours, she returned multiple times to replace the IV bags, but carefully avoided acknowledging the footwear item in the middle of the room, as if pretending it wasn't there, not even bothering to nudge it back to its place. This was pretty indicative of the disdain we prisoners often face—even our belongings aren't treated with respect. You get used to it, though.

In the coming days, I'm eagerly anticipating a visit from my lawyer, letters, and, hopefully, some news.

DAY ONE HUNDRED FOURTEEN

For the third consecutive night, I've been dreaming about fish, but this time it was salted and dried. I walked through rows of fish at a marketplace, closely examining the displayed goods.

Then, there were other parts of the dream, but those details have already faded from memory.

In the morning, the sun shone through the window, appearing warm, but I still felt cold. It was as if a storm was brewing, and a dark wave was washing over me. Though, when I closed my eyes, I could see distinct white circles and rings, similar to the afterimage you get from staring at a light bulb for too long. I continued to slowly read Remarque.

Once again, I was struck by the speed of European mail: a letter took ten days to travel from Nazi Germany to Austria, then to France, with three of those days spent wandering around Paris in search of a German emigrant without an address. This was happening in the mid-thirties. Eighty years later, it takes two weeks in Russia for a letter to cross a river—as if it were swimming.

I was also struck by the similarity between the propaganda of the Third Reich and that of the modern Russian Federation: "The leading newspapers were terrible—deceitful, bloodthirsty, arrogant. The whole world outside of Germany was portrayed as degenerate, stupid, treacherous. Everyone around was thinking only of how to harm Germany, so she had to defend her interests . . . "

The noise surrounding the assassination of Aleksandr Zakharchenko has predictably died down. Once again, they've started discussing the Minsk agreements on TV, emphasizing that there were no alternatives and blaming Kyiv for not complying. But it's clear who's really pulling the strings. Putin is keeping the situation in Donbas in a state of "no war, no peace," basically serving his own interests. With this tactic, he aims to exert some influence over Ukraine and, more importantly, to undermine Poroshenko in the upcoming presidential elections in six months. I feel like a small piece in this larger game. I don't like to think of myself as a mere pawn, and I don't accept that label or its implications. It's either everything or nothing. Either I'm the primary player, or I'm not involved at all.

DAY ONE HUNDRED FIFTEEN

It's been an unexpectedly fine and sunny day for the beginning of September in these parts. I've been warming myself by the window, feeling more or less normal, and my soul is at peace. I'm enjoying reading Remarque. I'm not sure how long this wonderful state will last, but I'm grateful to Fate for these occasional breaks. Without them, it would be quite challenging.

The local human rights ombudsman paid a visit, once again accompanied by a whole entourage of police chiefs. He never comes alone: at least seven people seem to be required according to their status.

I hadn't seen his dyed mustache for two months since he'd been on vacation. Even if he saw me in a coffin, he'd probably say that I looked good. Once again, he rambled on about vague topics like martyrs, heroes, the declining media interest in Ukrainian prisoners, the "unworldly" nature of this issue, and the stalled discussions about a prisoner exchange. He asked questions but didn't really listen to the answers, often continuing to talk over them. He shared stories about his wife, a homeopathic gynecologist, and his fifteen-year-old grandson, whom he'd accompanied to Crimea for a youth soccer training camp. These camps were held at a soccer facility just a few kilometers from my village—I used to pass by it when I went to Simferopol. It's strange how life can present these coincidences. I listened to his story about the trip, and it felt as if I'd revisited those cherished places. I was relieved when, after many drawn-out goodbyes, he finally left.

The Korean who's taken over during my doctor's vacation hasn't shown much interest in establishing contact or communication with me, but that suits me just fine. It's better if he stays away from me. Only today did he briefly glance at me for the first time to check how many days into my hunger strike I was, and then he returned as part of an official commission.

My lawyer, who was supposed to arrive last week, is still missing, as are my letters. I don't believe it's intentional. It's just a coincidence. It happens often—sometimes it's quiet, and sometimes everything piles up in one day, an endless stream of events and news.

DAY ONE HUNDRED SIXTEEN

The weather outside has been foggy, drizzling, and damp since yesterday evening. My chest has been feeling heavy since around the same time too. I had trouble falling asleep last night, likely because I was anxious about the letters that were delivered to me late yesterday evening.

Most of the messages I received were short, sometimes just a few words, obviously written with the help of an online translator. But they all shared the same message and goal: to support me.

There were also a couple of messages from unstable individuals, along with some bizarre essays or fairy tales attached to their main letters. It's the downside of popularity when you start receiving letters from nutjobs.

Additionally, there were a couple of messages from friends that felt like greetings from a completely different world, almost like receiving a letter from Cinderella after she'd moved to the palace.

What upset me were the updates about the play adaptation's production—it seemed to be headed in the wrong direction. I'll try to guide and correct their work when I write my response later today, and I'll send it through my lawyer, who will be here tomorrow. The deputy head of the colony delivered the news. Due to these developments, he spent an hour and a half trying to persuade me to end the hunger strike. They were facing difficulties because of me, you see.

But what about the problems my country has been facing because of your president? People are dying on the front lines every day; doesn't that matter to you? He tried all sorts of conversations and persuasion tactics, and even resorted to pressure, mentioning my mother and claiming that pranksters called her at night with false news of my release. But in the end, he left with nothing. I have no patience, not even for the whole of the Russian police force!

This morning, Vano, a Georgian refugee from Abkhazia, was released from the med point and into freedom. He'd served his full eleven-year sentence, most of it in strict regime confinement. He was a composed and rational individual. Like many Caucasians who moved to Russia as adults, he never fully mastered the Russian language. He'd never held a job in his life and was imprisoned for robbery. He didn't plan to work in the future, but he was also determined to avoid returning to prison. He hugged each of us in turn and then walked out past the fence. It wasn't the first time I'd bade farewell to a newly freed convict. Every time it has happened, others always celebrate, as if it's their own sentence that has ended. But it's undoubtedly a peculiar feeling to embrace someone who will be free in just an hour.

There was something amusing in yesterday's mail as well: Lech Wałęsa, the famous Polish revolutionary and former president, offered to nominate me for the Nobel Peace Prize. It all seems a bit excessive. Who am I, and what is the Nobel Prize? What have I done to deserve such an honor? Refusing to eat prison gruel isn't exactly a remarkable feat.

DAY ONE HUNDRED SEVENTEEN

Cold and cloudy, both outside and inside. It's freezing and unsettling. Today marks the same number of days as Anatoly Marchenko's hunger strike. He went on a hunger strike for the release of political prisoners during the Soviet era. He was force-fed for most of his hunger strike. Sadly, no one was released back then, even though it happened later during Gorbachev's *perestroika* era. On the hundred and seventeenth day, Marchenko ended his hunger strike due to critical health conditions, and a few days later, he died in the hospital. It increasingly seems like a similar fate awaits me. It'll be interesting to see how many more days I can endure, though I may never know if I set a record.

They keep trying to scare me with stories about physical decay involving irreversible organ damage that could lead to death or disability. But I don't care. They also share local stories with unhappy endings. A few years ago, at the notorious Polar Owl prison in the nearby urban-type settlement of Kharp, a guy sentenced to life imprisonment went on a hunger strike. It wasn't entirely clear what he'd hoped to achieve, but after three months, during which he was also artificially fed, like me, he gave up. A week later, he died from a heart attack.

When I'm told such stories I listen to them in silence, and after many hours of discussion, I reiterate that I have no intention of giving up. It's a dead end, and nobody knows what to do next. But nothing lasts forever, especially not lives or hunger strikes.

DAY ONE HUNDRED EIGHTEEN

It's been raining non-stop today, and it feels like it will never end. It's really getting to me. This morning, I almost fainted, but I managed to avoid it by leaning against the wall. It's started again.

My lawyer finally arrived yesterday. He'd been gone for a month and finally arrived a bit late, letting me know that he was staying for just one day. The police couldn't resist using this opportunity to stress me out a bit.

Early in the morning, when he was already in the colony, they'd called from the headquarters and said that I would be meeting with my lawyer and shouldn't be on an IV drip. But I knew they wouldn't take me there before lunch. They only came to get me closer to four in the afternoon, making both me and my lawyer wait all day. They also constantly tried to push him to convince me to end the hunger strike, threatening to take certain measures otherwise. In the end, we had only two hours to talk. We discussed the most important matters, and I hurriedly wrote crucial letters to the outside world that wouldn't have passed through censorship, and I couldn't have written in advance because they would have been confiscated during a search. I also managed to respond to some letters he brought with him, but I couldn't get to many of them.

Most importantly, there wasn't enough time to review the preparatory materials for the play adaptation, like costumes and locations. An employee from the prison abruptly ended our meeting, claiming that the workday was over. Bastards! They play cheap tricks!

My lawyer will attempt to pass the materials through the prison administration, but I know they won't let anything through, as they've never done so in the past. Instead, they might try to use it against me or twist it to their advantage. Lately, they seem to be particularly upset and under pressure about my hunger strike.

So, I returned to the med point, angry as a demon. It was frustrating that I couldn't accomplish much, and my lawyer hadn't brought good news either: my ex-wife had prevented our daughter from going to Kyiv, and negotiations for a prisoner exchange had completely stalled. My sister wrote to me that the whole world supported me, but apparently, that wasn't enough for Putin. The only person who hasn't made any effort for my release is Trump, despite contact attempts. There's little hope there.

All that's left are the aliens. I can picture it: an alien space-ship lands in Red Square, met by a delegation of women wearing traditional headdresses and offering bread and salt. The humanoids hold up signs in their five-fingered paws: "Freedom for Sentsov!" There's confusion. Putin dismisses it. Dmitry Peskov, Putin's press secretary, makes vague, ambiguous statements. The aliens leave without accomplishing anything.

During my absence, several more people were discharged from the med point, making it quieter and more spacious. Ryzhy received a disc in his package and organized a musical evening while I was hooked up to the IV, which was scheduled for later in the day. The door to our room was open, and I heard the song "Warriors of Light" coming from the TV room, performed by the incredible Siarhei Mikhalok and the band Brutto. This lifted my spirits—an unexpected and delightful surprise that brightened up such a long and dreary day.

DAY ONE HUNDRED NINETEEN

It's been a week without the IV drip with amino acids, and it has definitely been tougher without them, though they might not make a difference anymore. I've ceased understanding my condition and what affects it. My head has been spinning and feels foggy, and I often experience waves of either cold or pain throughout my body, but I haven't started getting frequent cramps yet. Getting up is a slow and cautious process, as there's always the risk of fainting. I've noticed that my thinking has slowed down, and remembering things has become more challenging. Scatterbrained.

Despite all this, I'm committed to maintaining this diary and reading books, even if it's just a few phrases written here and a few pages from a book every day.

I finally finished reading Remarque and started reading John Steinbeck. The library here has a good selection. Before this, I'd read his well-known work, *The Grapes of Wrath*, and a couple of shorter novels. The one I'm currently reading is called *East of Eden*. It's pretty long, but I'm already enjoying it. I've come to realize that my favorite foreign authors are mainly American writers from the first half of the twentieth century: Hemingway, Salinger, Faulkner, Wilder, Fitzgerald, and now Steinbeck. I'm not sure why, but the older world classics don't resonate with me as much, though I've read many of them too.

Today, I formulated four fundamental rules for myself to live by: do what you want, don't be afraid of anything, never give up, and rely solely on yourself. Something along those lines.

DAY ONE HUNDRED TWENTY

It's getting colder during the day and at night, sometimes dropping to zero degrees Celsius outside. I now typically wear a sweater, sleep in a warm jacket and socks, and keep the heater on, but I still feel chilly, especially at night.

Last night, I woke up feeling cold under two thin blankets, and there was a strange sense of darkness inside me, which was quite unsettling. It was hard to comprehend. Eventually, I fell asleep again, and the feeling went away. I even had a dream, but I can no longer recall the details.

The morning sun, though not very warm, helped dispel any lingering fears. I couldn't quite figure out if it was related to my heart, the cold, or something else. The most important thing was to ensure that this chronicle of my hunger strike didn't turn into a tale of madness, like something out of Gogol.

My health condition remains similar to how it was before. My weight has dropped below seventy-two kilograms, and I continue to lose more.

Yesterday, I watched *Forrest Gump* on TV, a film I've seen many times and love dearly. Despite knowing it by heart, I still enjoyed it. It's an all-around great movie, in my opinion, and I've yet to meet someone who didn't like it. It's the kind of film-making I aspire to learn.

Interestingly, the penultimate scene, in which the main character stands at his beloved's grave, talks to her, and cries, doesn't move me at all. But every time I watch the scene when he discovers he has a son, I can't help but cry. It's an example of how planned sentimental scenes don't always work, while the seemingly incidental ones touch you deeply. It's the magic of filmmaking that can be felt but is challenging to create or plan. Yet, this film achieved that effect multiple times. I truly hope to learn to create at least one such genuinely brilliant scene myself someday.

DAY ONE HUNDRED TWENTY-ONE

Last night, I had a strange dream. I was helping a zookeeper wash a giraffe's neck with brushes, and suddenly, the giraffe tried to bite me, but could only grip the sleeve of my denim jacket. I'm not sure how it ended because the dream took a bizarre turn where Crimea was annexed to Iran, and I woke up as I reached the end of a sunflower field.

Outside my window, the weather has been alternating between rain, sunshine, and clouds. My heart has been aching since morning, like an old, whining dog.

Finally, they delivered strong medications, and the IV treatments have become lengthy and tedious again. But maybe I'll start to feel better. The nurses take turns between vacations, and they keep struggling with my veins, but I've somehow disconnected from the process, becoming more of an observer. The Korean, who now supervises my medical care, doesn't seem overly concerned about me. I've only seen him briefly twice, and he didn't inquire about my condition on either occasion. Maybe it's for the best, since there are already too many people interested in it.

The weather is still chilly. I heard that the heating has been turned on in city houses for a week now, but it looks like there's no rush to get the camp's boiler room up and running. Which makes sense; they can save money on us prisoners.

I'm still reading Steinbeck.

DAY ONE HUNDRED TWENTY-TWO

Whether it was due to new medications or some other reason, I felt pretty good today, like a break between clouds. I still haven't completely shaken off the fatigue, but the fact that I wasn't feeling too bad was a welcome change. I've grown accustomed to the slowness in my speech, actions, and thoughts, along with many other things, like the dulling of my once-sharp mind.

The main event yesterday was a phone call with my mother. Surprisingly, they processed my request fairly quickly this time. Normally, it can take up to a month, and sometimes they conveniently "lose" the applications for operational reasons. But this time, I got to speak with her soon after applying. The good news was that everything was well at home. Everyone was alive and healthy, which was the most important thing. Despite the resistance from various quarters, my daughter was still determined to move to Kyiv, and there was still hope for that. My mom also shared that she'd bought a new washing machine, and a delegation of Finns had paid her a visit.

My son had gone to a seaside sanatorium and came back reasonably satisfied, though he'd lost some weight. But grandmothers tend to assess their grandchildren's well-being and happiness based on how chubby they are. I couldn't talk to the kids themselves since they were at school.

Upon returning to the med point, I received some letters. Not too many, but one of them was from my mother, so it felt like we had double communication in a single day. Unfortunately, they didn't give me the materials regarding the film adaptation of the play, as I expected.

The police seem to be searching for any angle to use against me or at least cause some trouble. But they won't succeed!

It has been three days without news because the TV broke down. This is no big loss. However, Ryzhy received printouts of three August issues of *Novaya Gazeta* in the mail. I read several interesting articles, including some about myself. The world and I aren't giving up. In a letter to one of my friends, I asked them to start sending me printouts of *Novaya Gazeta* in their delayed letters, along with those besieged materials related to the film adaptation of my play.

Yesterday, the Korean came along with an unfamiliar doctor from the outside, whose specialization and orientation were unclear. While the doctor examined me, I had a brief conversation with the Korean. He seemed like a good and competent person who preferred minimal interaction with patients.

It works for both of us, though, of course, I'd grown quite attached to my old doctor. But, as they say, nothing lasts forever.

DAY ONE HUNDRED TWENTY-THREE

Last night, I dreamed that I was in a car with some classmates I didn't recognize, and I was sitting in the driver's seat. We were parked near the institute where I used to study, waiting for someone to give me the keys to my apartment. Then I went to the mountains and played soccer like a boy on a homemade uneven field. I even managed to score a goal.

I woke up to the sound of rain and the dim light outside the window, even though it was already late morning. The autumn rain can create a cozy feeling, especially if you plan to spend the day at home. It reminded me of the good old days, back before my involvement in cinema, when everything was going well. My family was together, my business was thriving, there was plenty of money, and I even had a new car. But I don't regret anything because, in any case, it was a dead end. Being stagnant is a form of moral death, at least for me.

Now, I find joy in life itself, appreciating first and foremost that I have it and that it's diverse, challenging, and interesting.

There's a sense of forward momentum somewhere, and I hope that this direction only leads to more positive experiences in the future.

Yesterday's brief improvement in my well-being didn't last long. After lunch, I suddenly felt unwell, and it hit me quite swiftly, likely due to the changing weather. The discomfort in my chest subsided only this morning.

A local medical commission once again examined me. Three civilian doctors took turns. The general practitioner confirmed that my heart was still functioning, the psychiatrist determined that I hadn't lost my sanity, and the endocrinologist noted that fluids were still circulating in my body. I caught a glimpse of the Korean, and it seemed like my old doctor was there as well, but he didn't approach me for a conversation, so it might have been my imagination. That wouldn't be surprising, considering that the world, especially in the evening yesterday, felt incredibly small and confined.

I received about a dozen letters. None of them were particularly important, including those related to the play. Maybe the police were trying to exert pressure by holding back correspondence about it. Police logic and cynicism have remained consistent in their unpleasantness. Among the letters, as usual, were ones from abroad, from Ukraine, and from some eccentric individuals. There were also a couple of messages from old acquaintances I barely remembered meeting once or twice. Their refrain remained consistent: "We didn't have the courage to write to you for a long time (four years ago), and when we last saw you, we couldn't recognize who you had become. Now we think about you every day."

I still don't know what to think, let alone write, in response to such things. "The human soul is darkness," as one of my former comrades used to say. Though he changed sides during the annexation to the "self-defense" of Crimea and reported me to the occupation authorities.

I wonder if these correspondents truly believe they understand me now?

They've finally turned on the heating. The radiators are still only slightly warm, but it did add a touch of comfort to this cloudy day.

DAY ONE HUNDRED TWENTY-FOUR

Today, there was another medical commission. They heard I might be dying again so they came to see for themselves. They examined me, checking various parts of my body. Some areas felt hard and cold, but thankfully not dangerously so. While they were there, a vein burst as I received an IV drip of amino acids. It caused some swelling and discomfort, but the real problem was that it took a long time for the vein to heal, and I started feeling very unwell because the medicine wasn't going where it was supposed to. The medical commission noticed that I wasn't in great shape and quietly offered to intervene before it was too late. I declined their offer with a shake of my head. They responded by a collective wave of their hands, then left.

I realized that another important anniversary had passed a few days ago, marking the ten-year anniversary of the start of my journey into the world of filmmaking. I remember uttering "Action" for the first time on my debut short film set during that scorching September in Crimea. We were all new to it, filled with enthusiasm and camaraderie. The process turned out to be more enjoyable and intriguing than the actual result. Back then, I couldn't quite grasp the quality of what I was filming, but I was convinced everything was going splendidly.

The hardest things to film are animals, children, or the sea because they're unpredictable. In my case, I was dealing with a child and the sea, though that wasn't the sole reason it didn't work out. Nothing ever goes perfectly at the beginning, especially in something as complex as filmmaking. None of us had any prior experience. Someone who observed our work from the sidelines on the first day noted that I seemed lost for the first two hours, only to later act as if I had been making films all my life.

It's not that I'm a fast learner—when you're involved in every aspect of filmmaking from start to finish, and you're in control, you acquire the skills rapidly. My background in business, working with people, and e-sports greatly aided us in terms of organization and planning. As for creative achievements, I had to wait until we started working on *Gamer* before seeing some progress. Yes, a lot more could have been accomplished in the subsequent ten years, but it's important to consider that I've spent four and a half of those in prison. The rest was dedicated to learning and establishing myself in the world of cinema, which took a considerable amount of time during the initial stages.

I may have encountered a setback right at the beginning, but I know I still have the potential to catch up and achieve much more, as long as I don't grow too old here. If only I make it out . . . if only . . .

DAY ONE HUNDRED TWENTY-FIVE

In my dream, I found myself in a forest, taking part in a shoot-out. It was like a scene from World War II or some kind of computer game. After that, I was at a seaside resort, walking with two girls and holding a one-year-old child. Our relationship was a bit unclear, but there seemed to be some connection. We eventually went into a cafe and sat down, then they left, leaving me behind to clean up. As I was leaving the cafe, I bumped into them again. They were cheerful and a bit tipsy, but they had lost track of the child because it had gotten dark.

In prison, dreams are often more vivid and captivating than reality. They can feel more real, blurring the lines between what's real and what's not. It's hard to tell where nightmares end and moments of relief begin.

Outside, it's gray and damp. The room isn't exactly warm, but it's not cold either. At least I haven't been shivering for the past two days.

It's been four months since I started my hunger strike. It feels like I'm lost in a dark forest. I have no clear sense of where I've come from, where I'm going, or where the path lies ahead. I navigate by touch, moving forward almost blindly. The goal and the path to reach it are obscured by the tall trees surrounding me. But I can't just stay still; it's even more futile. I'm extending my target date once again, this time to October first. I don't expect much to change before then. I've stopped dwelling on it altogether.

I felt pretty good today. On days like this, I can even think about holding on until the new year! On tough days, it feels like

I might not make it that far, but I'll continue moving forward, one step at a time, from one pine tree to the next.

DAY ONE HUNDRED TWENTY-SIX

Yesterday, I suddenly started feeling really unwell. It happened all at once. I was in the TV room with some guys in the evening, just chatting. Then, out of nowhere, I started feeling sick, and it felt like the room was spinning, even though I was sitting down. I managed to make my way to the bed and collapsed onto it. I stayed there until it was time for lights out.

I still have this nauseous feeling that has persisted throughout the day, and my head keeps spinning. Before, this worsening felt like a heavy burden slowly piling up. But it hit me suddenly yesterday, like everything collapsed at once. On days like this, it's not just the new year that seems unreachable—it feels like October first is a date I can't reach either.

I'm back to mostly lying down again.

DAY ONE HUNDRED TWENTY-SEVEN

Monday. Another quiet day. It's autumn, and the room is dim. There's slush, and the weather is gloomy outside the window. But the radiators have started to warm up a bit, and the room is slowly becoming cozier.

Today, a cheerful young prosecutor and the camp's head came by for a checkup along with the Korean doctor. They wanted to make sure I was still alive and relatively healthy. The prosecutor's main question was whether I could move on my own. Judging by his look, he must have been hoping for my legs to be paralyzed.

I just finished reading Steinbeck's novel. I liked it, but I wasn't completely moved by it. It was a retelling of the classic biblical story of Cain and Abel, set in the context of two generations of an American family in the California valley. There were many characters, most of them interesting, but I couldn't really relate to any of them. That made it hard to empathize and connect with the story. Almost all of them did things I wouldn't have done. Maybe if I were in their shoes, I wouldn't have repeated their mistakes, but I'd make my own. After all, your own mistakes always feel closer to home.

I plan to borrow the other Steinbeck books I haven't read yet from the library, maybe today or tomorrow. He's still a very good writer in my eyes.

DAY ONE HUNDRED TWENTY-EIGHT

The weather outside has been pretty rough. Rain and wind have really been putting the window glass and the wires on the electrical pole to the test. Our hospital is in an old wooden building, but it's actually much warmer here than in the newer stone barracks. Even though it's built on permafrost, this little house has a bit of a personality, as if it moved and breathed. The rafters constantly make creaking sounds, kind of like a person with rheumatic joints. You notice it most in the quiet of the night.

The first time I heard it, I thought someone must be walking around in the attic, but then I got used to those little wooden crackles. Maybe that's why, or maybe it was something else, but the roof in the building had started leaking, and water was dripping from the ceiling. The new inspector who took over the shift saw the dripping puddle and jokingly declared, "Your roof is leaking," which was his way of asking if I was losing it. I replied that my roof was holding up fine and that it wasn't my responsibility to fix the hospital's property. He seemed to think I was being rude, but he didn't say anything. He just quietly repeated my response, probably so he wouldn't forget and could report it accurately, without missing anything, to his superiors.

They began to administer thinner needles in an effort to salvage my veins, but now the procedure is twice as long, and those bastards burst not only at the beginning of the whole process, but also in the middle of it.

Yesterday they took Ryzhy somewhere. First, an employee came and took him to someone for a conversation, then they came for his things. It's always like that in this camp: they take you away without saying where, then they collect your things after you so that no one can guess where you were transferred to.

But Ryzhy was most likely taken to one of the cells of the operative unit, Petrovka, so that he would cool off a little from his never-ending slanders and come to his senses. Gagarin killed himself flying, and Ryzhy will kill himself writing.

Yesterday I received some letters—about a dozen printed-out emails. They were mostly from some aggressive elderly women who attempted to intimidate me so that I would stop killing myself. There were also a couple of odd ducks, but the main thing was that I got a collective letter from my creative team, which was getting ready for the film adaptation of the play. They seemed to be working fine and getting along well with each other. I was very happy to read this! The auditions were already underway. And my friend, for whom I'd written the main role, successfully passed his audition. It was important to me that he earn the role and not just get it because he knew me. I've never liked having any dubious people involved with my work.

DAY ONE HUNDRED TWENTY-NINE

In my dream, I played soccer with some boys, then I helped my sick mother with household chores. After, I attended either a rally or a school assembly where everyone stood in formation with flags, and many of them had weapons. I also carried a rifle on my shoulder. While searching for familiar faces, I entered a store to buy groceries, but the saleswoman took so long to serve me that by the time I'd stepped out onto the street, the festive gathering had already dispersed. Back home, my father was sporting a beard like Hemingway's for some reason and was upset that I'd been gone for so long and hadn't helped him repair the pigsty. There was indeed a new iron fence, and a well-fed pig stood outside, gazing into my eyes. Just a typical night's delirium.

Yesterday, the prison was on standby for an important prosecutor for half the day, so they didn't even require the inmates to march in formation or follow the "One, two, one, two" rhythm. When I saw that silent crowd of prisoners through the window, I initially thought I was still asleep. But then the prosecutor never arrived, and after lunch, the usual muster resumed. In the evening, my blood pressure suddenly spiked, and my heart raced as if four people were chasing it, begging to be let out of my chest. It was the first time I'd experienced such a sensation. I've long ceased trying to understand my health and won't even attempt to analyze it. I'll live as I live.

Today, I briefly saw my doctor from a distance—he didn't come closer. He mentioned having a respiratory infection and being afraid of infecting me. Maybe it was true, or maybe there were other reasons they'd instructed him to maintain his distance from me.

In prison, trust in people eventually erodes entirely. It might be the same on the outside, but it's easier to pretend there. Though in terms of the ability to pretend, inmates can outdo anyone. The world I'm now immersed in is profoundly secretive and distrustful.

They brought me the complete works of Steinbeck from the library. It should keep me occupied for a while, though I've already read about half of them, judging by the titles. I started his first novel about Morgan the pirate; it's written in a childlike style but has interesting moments.

DAY ONE HUNDRED THIRTY

I lead a very predictable and monotonous life. Nothing eventful occurs, and I constantly feel unwell in the evenings. It seems like this has always been the case, already going on for an eternity and destined to continue indefinitely. The monotony of my current routine is what drains me the most. I wonder if my diary will ever leave these prison walls and find its way into the hands of publishers? If it does, they might read it and wonder, "Certainly, this is interesting, but can we really publish all this rambling?"

Ramis resides in the med point. He's survived this long because he's spent four out of his fifteen years in prison here, slowly nearing the end of his eighteen-year term. He's in the final stages of HIV, along with hepatitis and a host of other ailments. His leg is decaying, and he can barely move with the help of crutches. He experiences excruciating pain and is constantly on medication.

Ramis contracted HIV while in prison after getting a tattoo in unsanitary conditions. He applied for parole twice and was denied both times. This last denial came just this past week. The prosecutor uncovered five-year-old penalties in his record, and the judge cited them as a reason to reject his early release, despite his deteriorating health and being on his deathbed. The prison administration also did nothing to support his case.

He'd been a thief in his youth and spent most of his prison life as a *muzhik*. Now, in his forties, he only wishes for one thing: to die at home, surrounded by his family.

But he's not being given that chance. The local authorities only look out for their own interests—for those prisoners who embody the rules set by the *kozly*, those who cooperate with the prison administration. Ramis can only be released due to illness once he's on the brink of death, so his passing won't negatively impact the prison's mortality statistics. But he's afraid that by that time, he'll be too frail to transport and won't even make it back to his native village.

DAY ONE HUNDRED THIRTY-ONE

This morning, I woke up from a dream laughing. It's been a long time since that happened, and even in my waking life, laughter is a rare occurrence.

The weather has been exceptionally pleasant—no rain, no wind, no clouds. Just a blue sky and sunshine—a warm autumn tenderness. This kind of weather is unusual for the polar circle at this time of year.

I got a letter from my daughter. Apparently, she wrote to me several times over the summer, but none of those letters reached me. This time, she sent an email through my friends, and it finally got through. In her letter, she shared updates about her life, how she'd spent the summer, her plans for the future, and most importantly, her unwavering support, love, and her anticipation of my return. Her words were incredibly mature, coming from someone who not only resembled me, but also shared my values. It was the best day I'd had in a very long time.

They drew blood from my vein today, and it was a challenge to get it into the syringe. My blood appeared dark brown, almost black. The nurse advised me to inform the doctors that my blood was very thick. I knew it was a concerning sign, as I'd lately been feeling how hard it was for my heart to pump it through my body. But the doctors have been avoiding me like the plague, so I wasn't sure who to pass this information to.

The deputy chief of the colony paid me a visit, making feeble attempts to persuade me to end my hunger strike. Then, he shifted the conversation to my creative work, likely expecting me to inquire about the missing materials for the play. I revealed no curiosity about that matter. There seemed to have been quite an uproar on the outside, both due to this issue and because they cut my previous meeting with my lawyer short.

The deputy chief began not so much justifying himself as shifting all the blame for these mishaps onto my lawyer, detailing how many times he'd messed up and where. Though he did announce at the end of his monologue that the materials had been received and reviewed, and I would receive them either today or on Monday. I had no doubt it would happen today, so I didn't argue with him. As a farewell, he said, "You think you've caught a golden fish, but you'll remain by the broken trough." I didn't bother deciphering these cryptic words and simply thanked him for his concern and said goodbye.

Overall, today was a very good day.

DAY ONE HUNDRED THIRTY-TWO

Everything has been moving slowly and hesitantly, like a turtle that's laid its eggs and has embarked on making its way back to the sea.

I weigh seventy-one kilograms. I still don't have the details of my test results or EKG, as they've stopped sharing that information with me. But considering how I feel, I don't expect the news to be good.

As expected, the materials for the film adaptation that I'd been eagerly awaiting were delivered last night. It was a bit late, but alright . . . Later, I'll write my comments and advice for the team. Managing the creative process from a distance has been challenging, especially with the constant delays and interruptions both natural and artificial. I still have faith in my team, and I hope that the guidance I provide will be helpful and not too late.

I recently finished reading another work by Steinbeck, *The Pastures of Heaven*. It could be called a collection of stories set in a California valley or a novel broken into independent chapters. The specific format doesn't matter much. What's important is that it was a very well-written and engaging portrayal of people: truthful, funny, and poignant, much like life itself. I enjoyed reading it immensely, and it left me with a pleasant aftertaste. According to the author's biography, after this book, he found his distinctive style and main themes, launching his career to even greater heights.

Despite the worsening weather and my health last night, the sun has been shining brightly today. It warmed me as if bidding farewell before a long winter separation. Tomorrow could be uncertain in every sense, but today has been warm and delightful. Another good day. I even laughed in my dreams again.

DAY ONE HUNDRED THIRTY-THREE

The good days are behind me. The weather has turned freezing cold, with rain dripping down onto the concrete paths and creating a gloomy ambiance. My blood pressure and pulse have dropped significantly, leaving me feeling as if I've been struck on the head with a wooden club. Yesterday evening, I experienced sharp stomach pains, as if I'd swallowed a blade. Just what I needed. Maybe my stomach was reminiscing about the days when it had regular food to digest. By morning, things settled down a bit, as usual.

About twenty years ago, I went to Alushta with my future wife for a seaside vacation. There, I spotted a buoy in the sea—not the one marking the safe swimming area for vacationers but one much farther out. It appeared small and red, and by my estimation, it was about two or three kilometers away. I decided to swim to it. I've always been a good swimmer, and I particularly enjoy swimming with a purpose, like crossing a distance or reaching a specific destination. In that case, I had a clear goal in mind. The weather was overcast, not too hot, and the waves were manageable—ideal conditions for a swim. So, I began my journey.

I swam for an hour or two, taking short breaks and switching up my swimming styles. But the buoy didn't seem to get any closer, despite my efforts. I had miscalculated the distance by a factor of two. When I turned to look back at the shore, it was no longer visible, only the mountains behind the beach. By the middle of the third hour, having covered a distance of about five or six kilometers, I realized that I wouldn't reach the buoy. Even if I did, I wouldn't have had the strength to swim back. Though the buoy was just about two hundred meters away, a large red barrel used for mooring ships in the roadstead, I had to turn back, minutes away from what might have been a Pyrrhic victory. The wind had picked up, and the waves had grown, but strangely, it made swimming back easier. My only fear was getting a cramp, but fortunately, that didn't happen. An hour and a half later, I reached the shore and lay on a towel until evening, utterly exhausted.

It feels like I'm swimming toward that buoy again, only this time, the stakes are much higher: life versus freedom. I hope that this time, I won't have to turn back without reaching my goal.

DAY ONE HUNDRED THIRTY-FOUR

I dreamed about my mother, who looked relatively young in the dream. We were strolling around the lake formed in a former quarry near my village, accompanied by my Labrador. We unexpectedly encountered a German patrol unit as we ascended a hill in the fog. My dog barked at the soldiers, and a non-commissioned officer contemplated shooting her and, strangely, me as well. I urged him not to do so in English and demonstrated the dog's obedience by making her follow commands. Eventually, the Germans had mercy on us, and they didn't harm us. It was a memorable dream. My Labrador passed away two years ago and never had the chance to witness my release.

Last night, I paid a visit to Ramis. He resides in a separate, small room at the end of the corridor with another disabled person, and they have their own small TV, albeit one that functions poorly. We watched the week's news featuring Kiselyov. I managed to glean that in certain Russian regions, gubernatorial election results had been annulled due to falsifications, and in Syria, Assad's forces had accidentally downed a Russian reconnaissance aircraft with fifteen crew members aboard, blaming the incident, of course, on the Jews. I wasn't permitted to watch any further—the med point's head honcho came rushing in, fervently requesting that I not venture to other wards and stay in my room. Even on Sunday evenings, secret surveillance isn't relaxed around me.

Right after lights out, the deputy head of the colony popped in to inquire about my condition. Informants' watchful eyes and ears were always lurking around every corner.

My temperature, pulse, and blood pressure are monitored three times a day. Lately, my blood pressure has been extremely low. Yesterday, the nurse noticed it was seventy over fifty and offered me something to boost it, but I declined, despite the fact that they're constantly pumping me with drugs. The nurses, like geologists searching for petroleum, have continued to drill into the insides of my arms.

For the second day running, I've been experiencing a runny nose and a sore throat in addition to the usual hunger strike side effects. I can't pinpoint the cause since I don't consume cold water or venture outside where I might catch a chill—it's a mystery to me. Of course, I regularly ventilate the ward, but I've made an effort to avoid sitting in drafts. Getting sick now is not advisable because my weakened body is susceptible to any infection.

The view from the bathroom window encompasses a portion of the city and the nearby forest. The tree leaves have gone golden yellow, and it all appears remarkably beautiful in the dense morning fog, like a scene from a movie. Standing in the bathroom for an extended period and gazing out of a small window is too much though, even for a creative-minded prisoner.

DAY ONE HUNDRED THIRTY-FIVE

In my dream, I was drifting down a calm river with two friends. We each had our own boats, but the three of them were tied together. We had the idea of exploring the sea and crossing the bay. We headed toward the river's mouth but decided to make a pit stop near a store to buy some beer along the way. We pooled our money, and I went inside. Once inside, I realized that it would be windy and cold out on the bay, so it would be wiser to get something warmer, and I ordered brandy with a snack. Then, in my elementary school classroom, I played some tabletop game with my classmates while waiting for the teacher. When she finally arrived, I took until dawn to pack up the game.

In the morning, there was such thick fog that I couldn't see anything out of the bathroom window—no courtyard, no forest, just the roof of the neighboring barrack.

Yesterday, my doctor stopped by for just a minute. He looked lively, and it seemed he had recovered. When I asked how he was doing, he responded in his characteristic manner that he was doing better than me. My test results were terrible, and he predictably forecasted a decline for me in the near future. Not that it bothered me much—I've been hearing such unfavorable predictions for the past four months, even though I'm still alive.

I'm not so sure about my health anymore, though. I've been passing less urine than I've been taking in water, judging by my fluid balance. My weight has increased by almost a kilogram, and my face has started to swell. These are not good signs: they mean that my kidneys are gradually failing. Evenings are just as bad as usual, as if on schedule, but mornings are a bit easier.

I continue to read Steinbeck. I finished a collection of stories about a boy's life on a ranch, and I liked it—those who spend their childhood in nature are fortunate. Then, I made my way through a short novella, more like a screenplay or play—also about a ranch, and I liked it too, even though it was sad. It was about unfulfilled dreams, but that's essentially Steinbeck. Now, I'm reading *Cannery Row*, about the lives of the residents of a street in a small coastal town. So far, it's lively, enjoyable, and sad at the same time. Maybe that's why I like this author—and not just me.

DAY ONE HUNDRED THIRTY-SIX

A slow-moving autumn has settled in outside. The forest, obscured by fog for the past two days, has had time to absorb moisture, transitioning from a bright red hue to a deep brown. It's remarkable how quickly nature changes in the north during these transitional periods. A similar transformation occurred in June, when the forest transitioned from bare sticks to a lush green thicket in just two days. Now, the distant tundra has once again undergone a dramatic shift, adorned as it is in its autumn colors. Nature here appears to be in a rush to savor the brief summer warmth, like a sailor seeking fleeting pleasures during shore leave.

A recently returned nurse who had been on maternity leave came back to hone her skills on my veins. Today, she even managed to succeed on her fourth attempt, though the vein didn't hold up until the end of the procedure, swelling up like a stepped-on hose. But I didn't experience any nausea, and my sore throat subsided.

I've been struggling with a persistent feeling of breathlessness, as if I never have enough oxygen. I make sure to ventilate the room regularly, but the air that enters through the window carries the dampness of autumn.

Yesterday, the head operating officer visited and repeatedly inquired about my frequent intimate conversations with Ryzhy, which he believed justified removing Ryzhy from the med point. He playfully mused about what extremists and terrorists could have in common, seemingly hoping that I would find his question amusing. The suspicious police mind couldn't comprehend that our discussions might have revolved around topics like cinema.

I received letters yesterday, not many, but all positive. Progress was being made on the film adaptation of the play, with initial problems and misunderstandings seemingly resolved as the team continued to work together. We'll see what happens next, including potential new challenges. I also received more letters urging me to end the hunger strike, with the argument that some elements in the Ukrainian government might prefer my death over my release.

That's not going to happen! We're capable of fighting for a long time yet!

DAY ONE HUNDRED THIRTY-SEVEN

I started another notebook for my diary by sewing more white office-size sheets together. Already the sixth. I thought that the previous one would be the last, but no. This time I won't make any predictions or promises.

My doctor checked on me last night, and he also examined me in the afternoon, expressing concern about my appearance. He commented, "You look like you've risen from the dead." He had actually been sick, but was nearly recovered, though he still had a lingering cough. Even though my doctor was technically on vacation and had delegated the hospital's responsibilities to the Korean, he continued to make periodic visits to keep his finger on the pulse of what was happening, particularly my condition. He was about to leave for a few weeks on business elsewhere in Russia, so he wanted to conduct a proper examination before his departure.

What troubled him was my irregular pulse and low blood pressure. An EKG confirmed the issue: I had an arrhythmia, and my heart rate occasionally dropped to just thirty-four beats per minute. The doctor promptly initiated emergency measures, conducting tests and sending a messenger to the city hospital overnight with the results. Additionally, he performed local resuscitation procedures, administering certain injections and IV drips. Frustrated, my doctor even called his medical superiors in Moscow to ensure they were also notified of the fact that I was dying; he didn't want to shoulder this burden alone. We completed the IV drip after the lights went out. The test results arrived promptly. In short, the news was grim, and there was also a new concern: liver enzymes had emerged, indicating that my body was slowly breaking down my liver.

The doctor left during the night, feeling troubled, and I slept like a log until the morning thanks to the medication.

Over the past few days, I managed to shed an extra

kilogram of water weight, and my swollen face returned to its skeleton-like appearance.

My kidneys are still functioning, but it's evident that they're working inconsistently. I can feel their presence again. It's like walking on a tightrope over an abyss, and it's less frightening if you don't peer down into the depths. Yesterday I glanced down. It wasn't a pleasant sight. I'm now looking ahead once more, but the end of the tightrope isn't visible. It's shrouded in fog.

DAY ONE HUNDRED THIRTY-EIGHT

In my dream, I stormed a snow-covered mountain pass with a partner, hoping to find spring and warmth on the other side. Once we'd traversed it, we discovered that the winter cold awaited us there as well.

Conversely, it appeared that the colony administration deemed the weather outside to be too warm, leading to the heating being turned off. I've been relying on my small electric heater with a fan to keep warm. Even though I used it and wore socks to bed, the night was chilly.

The once-beautiful forest visible from the bathroom window has lost its appeal completely. Within a week, it transitioned from yellow-red to a dreary gray-black, resembling a fancy dress turned into a cleaning cloth.

The other day, I took the initiative to cut my hair and shave. A nurse noticed and commented that I "looked younger." I'm still struggling to come to terms with the fact that people see me as old now.

Patients at the med point have continued to gradually change, except for a few veterans, including me. There's no one to engage in meaningful conversations with, and there's not much to discuss either. I find myself missing Ryzhy a bit.

If someone like Ryzhy wishes to return to the med point, they know the way: a shard of a shaving razor or glass through the veins—a pricey ticket, but reliable.

It's a considerable challenge in prison to encounter someone with similar interests and beliefs. Typically, such intriguing people are only passing through, and it's not possible to communicate with them for very long.

The TV has been repaired, but it now only broadcasts Channel One, the state-controlled channel. When the others will be accessible continues to be uncertain, as the receiver was damaged.

I watched the news yesterday, and it felt like it was defined by a lackluster approach, reminiscent of the *Vremya* news program from the Soviet era. Nothing appears to have changed, not even the name.

The mail situation has improved slightly. I received a couple of letters, but there has been no progress on the matter of Ukrainian political prisoners. Everything appears to have come to a standstill. Unfortunately, this isn't the first time.

The prison has been anticipating the arrival of some important commission. Everyone has been bustling about the med point since the morning, tidying up everything they can. The Korean even ordered them to interrupt my IV drip in the middle of the process. How they were connected was beyond me. For some reason, the police have been quite reluctant to show me off while receiving treatment. They've frequently informed inspectors that I'm getting all the medical care I require, but God forbid they show it. It's challenging to discern meaning and logic in many police actions.

I've been feeling pretty awful since this morning.

DAY ONE HUNDRED THIRTY-NINE

Yesterday was an extremely busy and difficult day. The long-awaited commission turned out to consist of just one person, the woman from the Moscow headquarters who was my doctor's superior. She had called a couple of days ago and expressed her concerns about my condition. Her arrival was timely because, by lunchtime, I had deteriorated significantly. I was experiencing pain in almost every part of my body, but it was most pronounced in my heart and kidneys. Without waiting for the test results scheduled for today, the inspector decided to have me urgently transferred to the city hospital. She began by reprimanding the doctor for not paying enough attention to my condition, then she turned her attention to the Korean, who was officially responsible for me but had seemingly neglected me over the past few days. He mumbled that he'd been check-ing on me daily, but I didn't reveal this to the displeased Moscow colonel. We made our way to the hospital, with transportation and a swiftly arranged guard, but without the usual presence of dogs, machine guns, handcuffs, or even a full-body search. The priority was to get me to the hospital alive.

We arrived at the hospital, where a council of civilian doc-tors was convened, led by the same unforgettable resuscitator

I'd encountered before. This time, he was not angry but surprisingly polite. The first thing he said was, "Why did he come here on his own feet in such a condition? He should be lying down, transported on a gurney! His heart could stop at any moment; it's failing badly now." Other specialists examined me, conducted tests, and wheeled me on a gurney for a series of EKGs and ultrasounds. The conclusions were delivered about an hour later, and none of them were positive.

The findings indicated ischemic changes in my heart, an enlarged and deteriorating liver, clogged and drooping kidneys, gastrointestinal tract atrophy, a halted circulatory process, cerebral anemia, and more. The resuscitator, while acknowledging his support for my political stance—which caught the attention of the police present—declared that this was the point of no return. He wasn't certain which of these processes could still be reversed and which couldn't, but in my current condition, he could not release me. He ordered my transfer to the intensive care unit because neither medications nor nutritional formulas could save me—only feeding, and if necessary, force-feeding, could potentially make a difference.

Another hour was consumed by negotiations involving the inspector and others. My arguments about the European Court's prohibition on force-feeding and the potential violation of international law had no sway over the resuscitator. He emphasized that his primary role was that of a doctor, and I was his patient. He saw that I was dying right before his eyes, and he had a duty to intervene. He explained that he would call in a psychiatrist to evaluate whether I was still capable of making sound judgments about my condition and the current situation.

True, I could barely grasp or sense what was happening to me anymore, having grown accustomed to my perpetual pre-fainting condition. Yesterday, I seemed to slow down excessively and began to speak with a slur. It felt like déjà vu from July, when I'd initially agreed to commence the nutritional mixture. The question of ending my hunger strike came up sharply again. Eventually, I penned a consent letter for small-portion meals and opted out of hospitalization.

The resuscitator wasn't pleased; he understood that I was only writing this to elude his care, not to end the hunger strike. He concluded with a message to the police: "If he still doesn't start eating, then bring him back to us. He might last another week, provided he doesn't lapse into a coma first . . . "

DAY ONE HUNDRED FORTY

I had a bad dream, in which I moved into a wooden house with a neglected garden, along with some people who seemed like family but didn't recognize me, nor did I recognize them.

It's been a few nights since I slept well. My heart bothers me constantly, and now I have a new friend named Validol that I keep under my tongue.

My doctor and the Moscow inspector were frequently here at the med point over the weekend expressing concern and holding discussions about my condition. Today, the Korean also paid a visit and stayed for an hour while I was on an IV drip. He did most of the talking, as I haven't been very talkative lately. He talked about everything except for my condition. I appreciated the distraction. He's not a bad person, not unpleasant, but rather indifferent to those he considers to be beneath him.

They've been administering IV drips to me twice a day now, in the morning and in the evening. I can't quite tell if my condition is improving or deteriorating. I feel like I've been swaying, as if on a misty featherbed, even when lying down. During the night, an operational officer came to the med point, presumably looking for something.

Winter is drawing nearer outside, but the heating has been turned on, and the radiators provide comforting warmth. However, I still sense a slight chill within me and some twitching or tremors in my limbs. Or maybe they've been with me for a while now?

On a brighter note, they brought fresh letters and almost the entire September issues of *Novaya Gazeta*! I'm grateful to the kind people who managed to subscribe me to it from the outside, even having been told it was impossible. But as they say, people in uniforms can be quite untrustworthy.

Now I have something to occupy my time during these moments, though they no longer feel quite as bright as they once did—everything seems shrouded in a gray haze. I've started reading *Novaya Gazeta*, and I noticed they're still keeping a calendar of my hunger strike. It's impressive they haven't given up, just like many of my friends and comrades whom I don't even know yet.

My letters have become more regular, focusing on work and creative matters related to the film version of the play. Some were from acquaintances, while others were from strangers. I was also pleased to receive a letter from a fifteen-year-old boy seeking my advice because his girlfriend was moving to Europe.

DAY ONE HUNDRED FORTY-ONE

It got quite frosty at night, but in the morning, there was sunshine and clear skies. I still struggled to sleep well, perhaps due to the constant tightness in my chest or some underlying anxiety. I felt somewhat uneasy. It eased a bit during the day, with the help of IV drips and some medication, like Validol. I noticed that my face was puffy again this morning. I was practically comatose.

I've been reading *Novaya Gazeta*. There was a lot of interesting news. They covered the elections in Russia, which saw low voter turnout, but people had come out to protest against electoral fraud and pension reform. The police had used batons to suppress the protests, and unsurprisingly, there was no mention of this on TV. Local news reported the claim that the State Duma had unanimously voted for certain laws, showing a hundred percent consensus—just like North Korea.

Given the stark contrast between the will of the so-called "chosen ones" and the people themselves, there's still hope that this corrupt system will eventually crack open. Let's hope it doesn't result in bloodshed.

Another shocking piece of news was from one of the north Caucasus republics in Russia, where the city council nearly unanimously decided to rename Peace Street as Stalin Street— quite revealing to change a peaceful name to one associated with the devil.

A new inmate arrived at the med point, a young Tajik. He may not be the sharpest tool in the shed, but he's deeply rooted in the criminal subculture, aspiring to become a thief, the highest criminal authority. He rejects any form of authority, including wearing an inmate ID badge, security checks, and the like. Such individuals are rare in this camp, and they resist the most. He endured forty days of torture in a cell at the local operational unit, Petrovka, where I'd also spent time twice—a grim place. He didn't divulge many details about what he'd endured there, simply stating, "They had plenty of imagination." But I'm all too familiar with the torture and humiliation that happens here.

Having failed to break the Tajik physically, they allowed his injuries to heal, then transferred him to the barracks, where they initiated psychological pressure and tried to trap him into compromising and tarnishing his reputation.

To escape this vicious cycle, he cut his entire arm from elbow to hand, requiring forty-two stitches. Now he's resting and recuperating in the hospital, but he knows he'll have to face further challenges and they won't let him off easily.

Last night, the Moscow inspector left to report to her superiors. As she said goodbye, she shook my hand and mentioned something about an extraordinary reserve of health and fortitude. Today, my doctor also left for a couple of weeks, perhaps for vacation, work, or other reasons. A delegation of higher-ranking officials arrived in his place. They hinted that they could transfer me back to the hospital at any time and bypass the council, moving me directly to the intensive care unit. It seemed like they were backing me into a corner.

DAY ONE HUNDRED FORTY-TWO

After enduring long sleep deprivation, the night felt like a deep void. There was a cold fog outside the window in the morning, and I felt slightly chilled. I could sense my heart beating irregularly.

I've started noticing that at times, I need to re-read the same phrase multiple times because it's hard to concentrate.

I read about the so-called Penza terrorists, which was another high-profile case quite similar to ours: baseless accusations of preparing terrorist acts based on confessions obtained from the suspects under torture. Typical of the FSB. The individuals didn't give in. They refused to admit their guilt and spoke out about the torture they'd endured, but the pressure continued. The FSB agents even threatened one of the guys, saying he would be sent "up north to Sentsov" if he didn't confess. That's what my life has come to: they're already using me to frighten children . . .

The inmates in the TV room are constantly tuned in to the only available television channel at the med point. Besides the regular news, which portrays Russia as an idyllic place in stark contrast to the decaying and doomed west, they also broadcast police TV series and talk shows.

In the talk shows, which resemble the swirling muck of humanity, they eagerly air others' dirty laundry: who had affairs twenty years ago, whose children belong to whom, who is currently pregnant by whom, and even the details of certain legal cases, including those related to sexual assault. Young women argue with older women, drunkards, drug addicts, and other degenerates. Everyone shouts and seems ready to claw each other's eyes out. Russian television has plummeted to unimaginable depths, broadcasting nightly shows from hell itself. The inmates stare at the screen without blinking. I'd witnessed similarly fervent interest in another facility: there, a dozen teenage killers, who'd grown up in prison, eagerly watched . . . a new American cartoon.

My lawyer is expected to arrive this week. I have to decide something before they decide for me. I can feel my body starting to break down.

DAY ONE HUNDRED FORTY-THREE

My heart is no longer just skipping a beat; I'm experiencing occasional sharp chest pains. Not a good sign. I can tell it's not working as it should. This wasn't the case before, but expecting any improvement would be unrealistic.

I read in the newspaper about two Russian spies, posing as "tourists," who came to the U.K. to visit Salisbury Cathedral and, along the way, poisoned a former agent of Russia's Main Intelligence Directorate (GRU). Fortunately, they failed to kill the colonel and his daughter. They survived, but an unintended victim—a local resident—did not. British detectives tracked down the spies and presented photos and evidence to the world. Russia predictably denied their involvement, forcing these two incompetent fools to defend themselves on national television. Their story didn't seem very convincing. They had no well-crafted cover story. They resembled Lolek and Bolek, the two brothers from that Polish cartoon series of the 1960s–80s, with no believable background, as if they'd been created on a 3D printer at GRU just the day before.

Initially, when news of the assassination attempt first broke, I had my doubts: Could the Russian authorities really have acted so clumsily? It turned out they could—and that was just the start! This situation strongly resembled the crude polonium poisoning of Litvinenko, which British detectives were also able to fully uncover.

In summary: we've had enough of Max Otto von Stierlitz in Russia, and it turns out that Sherlock Holmes is still around in England.

I received mail yesterday in the morning and evening, just like at the best of times. There were many letters and postcards, filled with support, oddities, creativity, and business matters. I responded to the important ones, including a rather angry one to the producer of the play's film adaptation. I had already sworn off dealing with producers who wanted to dictate what I should do and how to do it. After the failure and disruption of my second film production, I decided to produce my future films myself. Due to the exceptional circumstances of prison life, I temporarily handed the reins back over to someone else. It was another unpleasant situation, but with a somewhat different twist.

In the previous case, it had dragged on for a year and a half, but here, on the contrary, they wanted to quickly cobble together the production in a month and a half. They were planning to submit it to various festivals, so my name would be associated with it. It was frustrating that I couldn't use profanity in my letters due to censorship, as I'd have liked to express my frustration even more strongly to make sure they understood me!

It's not easy to push me to the edge and make me boil over, but if someone manages to do so, they should be cautious—I'll respond fiercely! The letter made me so furious that for a while I couldn't seem to calm down, to such an extent that I even temporarily forgot about the hunger strike, both me and my subdued body. Though I know that after such stress, there will be consequences, and they won't be pleasant.

DAY ONE HUNDRED FORTY-FOUR

I can't tell if my condition is getting worse or staying the same. My heart is bothering me day and night, regardless of whether I'm sitting or lying down, no matter the position. Last night, I attempted to walk a bit in the corridor, but it didn't help.

It has been raining outside for two days straight. The Tajik has been arguing with the police recently about buying food. He wanted to go to the camp's shop to buy cigarettes at the very least. Yesterday, he was finally taken away, and he hasn't yet returned. They must be fulfilling his request somewhere at Petrovka.

The entire second half of yesterday was spent figuring out how many issues of *Novaya Gazeta* I had received. While I was reading the latest issue, which included a note from the editors wondering if I was receiving their newspaper, a policeman suddenly appeared with the same question. I told him I'd received the September issues and listed them. He nodded, went out, but returned five minutes later with a piece of paper for me to acknowledge it in writing. I wrote it down. The officer left, only to return again with more questions: Were there any more newspapers? I said no. After that, the policeman finally left.

Later, the Korean came—he had been summoned and asked the same question. I repeated my statement, then he left. Half an hour later, another officer came with a new list of issues I was supposed to have already received, and the questioning began again.

I get pretty irritated by the police's opacity and the inconsistency in their approaches: the Tajik is likely being handled roughly in Petrovka, and here they're trying to determine if I've received a few August issues of a newspaper. It's all just show and hypocrisy.

I remembered a letter from the last batch of mail that had struck me. It was from a young man in western Ukraine, around thirty-six years old, who worked as a van driver with BREAD inscribed on the side of the vehicle. He wrote that his birthday was coming up, but no one would come to see him because he had no friends. It was a sad and sincere letter from someone with obvious mental issues, but not malicious issues. It reminded me of Forrest Gump and my son, who still doesn't have any friends. I wanted to write something to this guy, to encourage him in some way, to be a distant but caring pen pal. But unfortunately, I ran out of stamps, so I couldn't.

They came and informed me that my transfer to the intensive care unit was scheduled for tomorrow. Therefore giving me another day to think, without any hint of menace.

DAY ONE HUNDRED FORTY-FIVE

I had bizarre dreams.

It's been raining non-stop.

My heart isn't bothering me for the first time in a long while—such a relief!

Yesterday, a supervising prosecutor visited with local authorities. He asked me many questions, and I answered with brief "Yes" or "No" responses. Then, they checked the cold radiators one by one, expressing their surprise and touching them repeatedly, but they never got warm. The discussion about hospitalization and force-feeding came up again.

They finally found the missing issues of *Novaya Gazeta* that the police were inexplicably searching for in my belongings. It turned out they'd had them all along and gave them back to me. The stack was quite large, but most of it was September reprints, with only a few August issues, which I already had. It seems like someone had subscribed me to the newspaper twice, or maybe two different people had. Life is like that—sometimes you get nothing, and at other times, everything comes at once.

To my surprise, I stumbled upon an interview with my mother in one of the August issues, along with a photo of her in our yard. It was a touching and heartfelt piece about me, my children, her life, and my childhood. It mentioned how her grandchildren feared she might disappear after my arrest, but they held on, supported each other, never gave up, and continued to believe and wait. I have an amazing mother and children. Thank you for being in my life because you are my life. I love you deeply.

I received a notification from the post office about two packages from the U.K. and one from Moscow in my name. The first two weighed just over a kilogram, and the last one was even lighter. I declined them all—I wasn't expecting anything from anyone.

Today marks exactly one year since I arrived in this camp.

When they moved me from the Yakutsk colony, they kept the destination a secret for a long time. It wasn't until closer to the final transfer that I accidentally found out where I was going. Fellow inmates started immediately offering their condolences—many knew it was a tough place. It all began after my departure from the police van, during what they called the "reception."

There were a bunch of policemen, masks, machine guns, barking dogs, darkness, and flashlights, and everyone was shouting and yelling. Inmates were forced to move quickly with their heavy bags in hand, which couldn't be left behind. They herded us from one officer to another in a circle: if you didn't introduce yourself correctly here or greet correctly there, you had to stand there, run, and then stand again.

They rushed the slow ones and often treated everyone the same way, with kicks and batons. That nightmarish ordeal seemed endless, a deliberately crafted performance to make sure you understood where you'd ended up. Then came the shakedown indoors, where all your clothes flew out of your bags toward the ceiling. In the end, you had to quickly collect them because every second, you were rushed and insulted. They kept inventing more crucibles to put you through. It was a very long night with one purpose—to humiliate, subjugate, and break the new arrivals. If someone dared to resist, there was no chance. They were immediately taken to a separate room "for roasting,", then a very thin, high-pitched sound would join the general cacophony, cutting through the noise and shouting. It was one of the most unpleasant nights of my life that I'd like to forget but never will.

Today will be a crucial day: either my lawyer will finally arrive, or I'll be taken to the intensive care unit by convoy. The wall clock in the corridor has stopped, and it feels like time has frozen in anticipation of a resolution.

Eventually, my lawyer came. I decided to take matters into my own hands. I wrote a statement to end the hunger strike starting tomorrow.

Inside, I still feel terrible, with a bitter taste of defeat in my mouth. This is how my chronicle of a hunger strike comes to its inglorious end.

Four and a Half Steps

STORIES

Four and a Half Steps

Prison has the creakiest doors, especially when they close behind you for the first time. Behind them is their airless world, filled with disenfranchised people, their common misfortune and suffering. You'd think it would be impossible to get used to it and survive here, but you do—though prison changes you forever.

The cell is small, with an iron bed along a concrete wall. Opposite the bed is a tiny iron table and bench welded into a single awkward structure. Near the door is a washbasin and a toilet. On the other side, a small and dusty window is covered by a thick, multi-layered grate, through which one cannot see the sky, the sun, or clouds, but only determine whether it is daytime or not. In this cramped and gloomy closet, there is only a narrow passage through the center down which one can walk. Four and a half steps to the door, then four and a half steps to the window. Four and a half steps there and four and a half steps back. There and back, there and back. There isn't much to do in solitary confinement except walk.

When a person lands in prison, he hopes for a miracle, thinking there's been some mistake, that they'll quickly work it all out, someone will make a call, and everything will be resolved. Especially since out there, behind the iron door that closed with such a disgusting screech, there is so much important and unfinished business, so many of your loved ones and friends. But with each new day in the slammer, the hope for a quick release melts away, and a person understands that this may well go on for quite a while. He plunges into the details of his case and begins to wait for the trial, thinking that it'll all get worked out there, based on truth and the facts. The period of detention before the start of the trial, six months or a year, seems huge and incomprehensible to him. This person is still living in the rhythm of a free life—he is used to thinking and acting differently. He does not imagine that he can spend a week or a month in this place, not to mention years of his life.

At first, the prison smell seems unbearable to him, sharply hitting his nose as soon as he crosses the threshold of the government building: a mixture of sweat, sewage, gruel, and cigarette smoke, which makes it impossible to breathe. But soon enough, a person ceases to notice this stench—he begins to have the same smell.

When a person tries prison food for the first time, picking up that eternally damp piece of bread, he thinks it's impossible to eat and get used to it. But a person can get used to anything—even prison. He is gradually drawn into this unhurried, monotonous rhythm of prison life. The days no longer seem so long, and the nights no longer sleepless. The smell of prison and the taste of gruel become almost familiar. Weeks pass by, followed by months. Time flows imperceptibly here, as if it didn't exist at all. Here, you live the same day over and over.

It's Groundhog Day: wake up, wash time, breakfast, roll call.

Going for a walk is the highlight of the day. While you are being led there, you can amble down the prison corridors a little, holding your hands behind your back and turning to face the wall at the guard's request as he opens the next door or grate, doing this several times before reaching the coveted walking yard. Sunlight is rare in this deep well, but you can see the sky through the grate that replaces the roof, and, most importantly, there is fresh air. Although these walking cages are hardly larger than a normal cell, you'll be lucky to get in six or even seven steps of length to pace in the yard due to their size. But the main thing is that, on a walk, you don't feel alone. Other people are walking in the neighboring yards, and you know this for sure, though you can't really hear them. Music is blaring from the speakers installed in each nook, and a security guard walks overhead, surveying the yard to ensure no one is talking. If they see an attempt to start a conversation, those prisoners will be deprived of exercise rights, which is why few people seek to communicate. Only by the sound of doors slamming can you determine that someone was in the yard adjacent to you.

Sounds are pretty much the main source of information in prison, especially in a "frozen" one,[*] where prisoners can't communicate with each other. The silence is striking when you first end up in this sort of prison, and the rare sounds from the corridor don't tell you anything. But gradually you learn to distinguish and identify them. They begin to make sense and carry

---

[*] A strict-regime, high-security prison.

the main thing missing in prison—information, including the time, as clocks are prohibited. The iron cart's wheels begin to rattle. It's carrying gruel, which means that dinnertime has come. In the adjacent cell, the "feeder," a small window for distributing food or communicating with guards, slams shut with a solitary thud. The prison guard briefly says something, then leaves. Not long after, the door in a neighboring cell opens with robotic precision, and the prisoner is taken somewhere, likely for interrogation or to his lawyer.

That's the sound of a woman's heels clicking down the hall, and one by one the feeders begin to clap open. It's the librarian, it's Thursday, and you can take two books from the list. In here, literature is salvation for those who love to read. Those who have never picked up a book in their lives begin to do so in prison. With them, you don't just have to pace from corner to corner all day long.

Then there's the sound of someone walking up to a cell door and placing a package by it. This quiet sound of a heavy burden pulled off the shoulder is barely audible. But the prisoner's sensitive hearing distinguishes it well—this is the sound of a delivery, what they call a "boar" or a "piglet." The name depends on the size and degree of expectation, but in any case, it brings you joy because it means normal food and attention from the outside world.

Somewhere in the distance down the prison corridor, several pairs of boots rush by and the door to someone's cell is abruptly opened. It's a raid, a shakedown. Always sudden and unpleasant. Now, they'll turn the whole cell upside down and rummage through that prisoner's things, destroying his already meager life and comfort. Sometimes they find and seize something—it's never any "contraband," like shiv knives, shanks, or pieces of glass, but some trifling, necessary household item, like empty plastic bottles, strings, or extra newspapers. Searches are carried out for internal reporting, as it were, but they often do a shake-up to disturb you and make a mess so that you have to clean up after them later. Even though you have plenty of time to kill in prison, such unceremonious visits always leave an unpleasant aftertaste. Every prisoner has his personal space, the little world he inhabits, and he does not like it when someone invades it, even though they technically have the right to do so because they're on duty. It's not for nothing that your cell is called a "hut" around here, and the prison is called a "house" where the prisoners live, and the guards only work.

Mail comes on weekdays in the late afternoon, and even then, only some days. Every prisoner is waiting for this time with the hope, albeit small, that he will receive a letter—get news from his relatives, learn something new about life in general, and, perhaps, about his future fate. The letters are handed out by an ordinary guard who moves in a peculiar way. You can hear in advance how he starts to walk from the far corner of the corridor, knocking at the "feeders," but he doesn't stop in front of every cell—only those of the lucky ones that have received something that day. It's a joy if your hatch happens to open, and a little sad if those footsteps pass you by. It's a kind of lottery, and you don't always win your coveted envelope.

In every prisoner's life, there's one day in the week that's guaranteed to be cheerful, or should I say clean. Bathhouse day. Of course, this word sounds a little excessive for what amounts to a ten-minute wash under a lukewarm shower, but the administration does not provide prisoners with another option for washing. On other days, a washbasin with cold water and a small basin are at your service—or personal initiative, if you will. Prisoners prepare for the bath in advance and look forward to it, because those ten minutes under the by no means hot water will warm you up for the whole week. After the bath comes a hot mug of *chifir*, an incredibly strong tea brewed in Russian prisons, or *kupchik*, the weaker version of this traditional jail brew.

Another monotonous day ends, and the prisoner waits for lights out as a temporary deliverance from this unbeloved world—to rest a little and embrace oblivion, especially if he can neither sit nor lie down on a hard bed for the whole day. A surveillance camera is filming you around the clock. In addition to that, a peephole opens in the door every five minutes for a "peek," and the guard looks to see if everything is in order, meaning that you haven't inadvertently hanged yourself or nefariously violated protocol by perching on the edge of the bed. The only place to sit is a small uncomfortable bench, which you can't sit on for a long time, so walking is the next best thing. Four and a half steps in one direction and four and a half in the other. Four and a half there and four and a half back. Back and forth. Back and forth. And you think—all day. By evening, your head is already beginning to swell from your thoughts, and you are waiting for the end of the day to rid yourself of consciousness.

Finally, the guard announces lights out, switching from the daytime light system to the slightly dimmer nighttime one. You can't cover this lamp, which irritates the eyes, but you can go to bed. Covering your head or turning to the wall for a long time is forbidden. They'll wake you up and check that you haven't attempted suicide.

The most vivid dreams occur in childhood and in prison. In your dreams you are still a free man—the subconscious hasn't yet had time to adapt to your new reality. As a result, the first dreams you have in prison put you in entirely different surroundings with good things that make you want to smile. But you have to wake up in captivity, and those first seconds of consciousness are the most unpleasant. You understand that you're not at home, the events of the last few days come back to you, and the gravity of the situation presses down like a tombstone. At first, the moment of awakening in prison is the most nauseating. But, gradually, prison penetrates deeper and deeper into you, finding its way into any dream. Even if you dream of being on a tropical island, you understand that a guard is about to arrive and take you back to your cell. But the deeper you're immersed into prison life, the easier it becomes to live with it, until it becomes basically normal. A person can get used to anything, and life under lock and key is no exception.

The days begin to blur into a gray faceless mass, like passengers in the subway, and the hour of judgment inevitably approaches. The prisoner understands that, most likely, there will be no acquittal. He has already been able to communicate with other prisoners, cellmates, or fellow travelers on rare trips in paddy wagons and heard all sorts of stories during the year of his imprisonment. He understands that the verdict will definitely be a guilty one. But, nevertheless, he is sure that he will be given a short sentence, and somewhere in the depths of his soul, he still hopes for an acquittal. Everyone considers himself to be special, and this is normal, so the sentence and the term announced for it plunges many into shock and hopelessness. Only one person in a thousand is acquitted in Russian courts. Not because only the guilty are arrested here—this system is set up for punishment. If you are accused, then you are already a criminal. Of course, not everyone is in prison with unfair sentences, but this does not mean that people agree with them. There are only two options for interpreting one's involvement in a case: "It wasn't me, bro, they pinned it on me . . . " or "Yes, it was me, but it wasn't like that and they dumped me in too deep . . . " You will not find a prisoner who says it's fair that he landed in prison.

Prisons can be very different: there are "frozen" ones, where you cannot meet with any other prisoner at all in a year, and there are those that are "on the go," where inmates are packed forty men to a "hut" and the law of the thieves, not the screws, dictates behavior. Most of the knowledge and skills acquired in the wild won't be helpful to you here. Almost everything you learn in prison will be useless to you on the outside. These are two very different worlds: in one, you live, and in the other, you survive. People are generally very clever and can adapt to living conditions, especially in prison. Where else but in prison do you gain the ability to cut a match in two to save money? Or brew tea in a plastic bag? What about making knives out of plastic toothbrush cases and sharpening them on a tile? Or sawing a bed with a "tooth"—a half-finger-sized piece of metal cloth, digging holes in concrete with an iron spoon, making a hiding place or "trigger" in a cell that even a whole pack of screws led by a service dog couldn't find? Why do you need the ability, with the help of a thread obtained from a loose sock and a disposable bag, to make a "parachute" to "catch on" or pass info via the air with the neighboring "hut"? Or, using the same thread and a "hedgehog" made of matches, make an "anchor" and dredge it through the sewer, where it will wind up with the same "anchor" from another chamber, creating a "wet" road where you can send each other notes and cargo? I don't think someone on the outside will need the ability to carry thieves' "runs"—criminal mail or mobile phones up their anus—past security, but this is a handy skill in prison. Prison teaches these and many other vital things. It teaches us to speak a language that few people understand on the outside. Although many prison words and expressions have long taken root among ordinary people, they often do not understand their original meaning and origin.

The prison world is cruel, but fair. There is a very clear division between what's personal and what's shared. The personal refers to the most precious things that no one has the right to encroach on, like your honor, dignity, family, and religion. If someone hurts or offends you in these matters, you have every right to deal with that person very harshly, up to the point of shedding blood. Everything else in prison is shared. The duty of every decent prisoner is to maintain this common good, to support and contribute to it. This matter concerns not only the essentials, like smoking or tea leaves, but above all something intangible, something even more important in prison—relationships, harmony, fraternity, unity, and mutual assistance. These are what unite prisoners. Yes, what's personal still includes the underpants that you wear, and no one dares to touch those either.

Prisoners have solid mutual support. Together, they are a force capable of resisting the police regime and lawlessness, but here, there's no such thing as friendship. Brotherhood and unity should not be empty words for the prisoner—they are driven by the need to stick together. For any careless word or deed, there can be very strict consequences. Depending on the degree of guilt, the prisoner can get a couple of slaps to the face or be beaten—not to death, but in a way they will certainly remember. Prison has its own scale of values, hierarchy, code of laws, and methods of applying them. Someone can be harshly criticized for the slightest trifle, but others are easily forgiven. It all depends on your position, your ability to explain your actions and words, and the ability to "hijack" an opponent—that is, verbally overpower him—if he comes across as weak. The rules on the other side of the fence are similar, with an established hierarchy system to maintain order, but with its own inequalities too. But "brotherhood and unity" exist only in name out there.

A lot of the guys who held prominent positions out in the wild, like lawmakers, officials, or businessmen, by no means always occupy the same position in prison, especially if the court confiscates those resources. Personal qualities are more valued here, and a person who knows how to present himself out there will be able to do it here. A person who knows how to get along with people out there will be able to do the same here. Because the most important thing you need to know about prison is that you'll find the same kind of people here as you do in everyday life, only here they're called "inmates." At the same time, it's not a given that a person who has achieved something in the world of inmates, who has comprehended it, settled down, and advanced in it, will also be able to settle down and advance on the outside—these are two very different worlds, after all. But the idealization of the criminal world is addictive to some men, and they cannot tear themselves away from it even after their release. Such a man leaves prison, but prison never leaves him, and it calls to him again and again—a vicious circle. But he no longer feels like a stranger here; he is at home.

Prison is a cursed mill of human destinies. It's impossible to talk about everyone and everything. For example: Shket's encounter with his abusive stepfather in prison. He remembered the torment he and his mother faced when he was a child and took revenge by killing him with an iron pipe, resulting in an extra sentence. Then, there's Hassan, who tries every day to write a letter to his wife but can't find the right words to explain that he's not the person she thought he was, can't say what he did twelve years ago and why he got arrested for it. What is Ivanych thinking about as he warms his stumps in the summer sun? Is he remembering how he lost his legs to frostbite after drunkenly stabbing a business partner to death and running off into the forest? When will Olya, who landed in prison pregnant at nineteen, see her daughter? Olya took the blame for her husband after he committed a murder, then he disappeared. Now, she's thirty, and there's no saying how long she'll be in prison, because she's always fighting with the guards, and that gets her a longer sentence. What will Polyana tell his mother about his return from the store where he went for vodka ten years ago with a knife, two drunken friends, and no money? How will Buzuk explain to his children why he couldn't pick them up after the matinee, having instead gone to court with the hope of a suspended sentence for possessing a small matchbox's worth of marijuana, only to be taken away under police escort with an eight-year sentence? How does one make sense of nineteen-year-old Komar, who stabbed a married couple for nothing after drinking with them and received a sentence longer than his years on Earth? What was Boris' encounter like with the father of the man he killed, who traveled from afar just to ask him, "Why?" One could write endlessly about these people's fates. However, any attempt to judge, justify, understand, or search for the truth will always be in vain.

A person who goes to prison ceases to believe in justice. A person who goes to prison ceases to believe in people. Most friends disappear in the first year of their sentence, the wife usually in the second, and only mothers wait until the end. As you read these lines, know that somewhere out there, people live in cramped and dirty cells behind thick walls and dull double-barred windows. They are the same as you—they've simply been dealt an unfortunate hand. When you read these lines, know that someone, right now, is splitting a match in half, brewing tea in a plastic bag, or measuring out their four and a half steps. Four and a half there, then four and a half back. Back and forth. Back and forth.

Robert

Robert's eye was gouged out during an assault. One of his fingers had been torn off even earlier, at about the same time his leg was dislocated. His body was covered with burns, inflicted at different times and in different places. In the shower, only those with a strong stomach could bear to look at him. But Robert remained unfazed. He carefully washed his long beard and the gray hair on his head, not thinking about his mutilations, just pulling his underpants above his belly button from time to time. Robert was a follower of Islam in its most extreme, radical, and, more precisely, fundamental form. According to his religion, a man should never show anyone his reproductive organs, not even his belly button. Washing in his underpants was not very comfortable, but Robert was unwavering in his beliefs.

Usually, when someone landed in prison they had a whole bunch of things with them, which they periodically moved from cell to cell. Robert had only a half-empty bag with him. No one would send him care packages. He ate only gruel and what his cellmates treated him to, but he easily managed without all that. If he didn't have tea, he drank plain hot water. If the prison food contained traces of meat, obviously not halal, then Robert refused it, chewing only bread. The bread had to be soaked in boiling water since he was missing teeth.

Robert did a very funny and accurate parody of Putin's walk, played chess well, and read newspapers through a plastic water bottle, which served as a magnifying glass. He had poor vision in his remaining eye and didn't have glasses. When compassionate human rights activists bought him a pair, he thanked them and continued to read through the bottle.

Robert was shy and quiet. He wasn't interested in anything but his religion, to which he had devoted his life, and was even willing to sacrifice others for it. For days on end, if he was not busy praying or offering praise to Allah, he studied the Koran, transcribed passages, and learned to recite passages in Arabic in a singsong voice, not always understanding the meaning of words, but always feeling the essence of these actions.

Robert considered himself a real Mujahideen, but that wasn't always so.

He was born a Tatar and lived in Bashkiria. He left to enter an institute for military engineers and graduated in the early eighties, served in the army for another ten years, got married, then had two daughters. They lived in a government-issued apartment in one of the many army bases spread across that vast country. They were an ordinary Soviet family—they even went on vacation to the seaside once. But the USSR soon collapsed, and Robert lost his position in the armed forces. He and his family returned to their native Bashkiria, where he got a job as an engineer at a factory. But the collapse was already in full swing, so he lost his job there too. Robert began to roam around looking for various jobs, everything from a taxi driver to a handyman at construction sites. Some were able to try their luck in the lawless years of the nineties, while others couldn't. Robert was one of those who couldn't.

Life somehow went on, his daughters gradually grew up, the family, at the very least, survived, and they even bought a car. Robert turned fifty, but happiness was nowhere to be found. He decided to try to look for it elsewhere, in religion's most radical form. It started with conversations with those already in that world, then came books, regular visits to the mosque, prayers, and a change in lifestyle and mindset. Soon enough, Robert became a different person: he let his beard grow and found peace and meaning, unlike his family, who were frightened by his metamorphosis. His wife and daughters sharply rejected his attempts to impose Sharia law in their household. It became problematic for Robert to get a new job—even at a construction site—as few employers were ready to coordinate the work schedule with a prayer schedule. Robert's new social circle, which consisted mainly of fundamentalists, experienced the same difficulties. Some of them had already left, and others were about to leave for Waziristan, a region in the mountains of Pakistan, where they could live according to Sharia law and obey no one but God—almost like heaven on earth, as Robert and his brothers saw it. So, he decided to leave too. His family, as expected, refused to join him. Robert sold the car to have money for the trip, then divorced his wife according to Muslim tradition by declaring "You are not my wife" three times in front of witnesses before heading to the promised land.

Robert didn't go alone, but with a group of like-minded fellow travelers. These semi-legal tourists took a not-very-popular one-way route. The Ahrisunnis, as they called themselves, got to their final destination by journeying through Turkey to Iran, followed by an illegal crossing over the Pakistani border, accompanied by local guides—sometimes on donkeys, sometimes on foot—moving toward the cherished Waziristan. This area was mountainous and inaccessible: where only Pashtun shepherds used to live in small villages, now Roberts gathered from all over the world. Under the guidance of gray-haired emirs, they were performing a holy feat. They were building paradise on earth and going to neighboring Afghanistan to commit jihad.

Life in paradise, however, turned out to be squalid and challenging. But Robert paid this no heed because he was finally among his own, living as expected: men with beards and no mustaches, women in chadors, stoning, whipping, and many other traditions that might have been better suited to the Middle Ages. There was no way to make a steady living there. Robert helped the community in any way he could, and his brothers in the faith fed him out of gratitude and sympathy—the Mujahideen's take on communism.

Like any devout Muslim, Robert had to get married and even made a serious attempt. A widow lived in their village. She was already over forty and had three children. The oldest son, a teenager, was present at this matchmaking as the head of the family. Negotiations took place, but agreeing on love and familial bliss was impossible. Robert was an aging bridegroom, not very attractive, and his possessions were limited to what he carried on him, so his marriage proposal was rejected. But Robert was not upset. He'd come to wage Ghazawat—a holy war against the infidels who oppress the true faith—not to start a family. He declared as much to the accursed Americans who'd invaded neighboring Afghanistan and did not allow his Muslim brothers to live how they wished, imposing their accursed democracy on them with weapons. That's why the indignant Waziristani brothers regularly went over the mountains to help their Afghan brothers do jihad. Robert tried to join them a couple of times, but since his health was poor and he was old, he did not become a warrior. They decided to leave him at the base, where a person with engineering skills was needed.

The Pakistani government was rather laid back regarding this uncontrolled land within its borders. The people of Waziristan tried not to start problems with the government and, by local standards, behaved quite well. They directed their sacred malice at infidels in the neighboring country, periodically killing the not-quite-orthodox Afghanis and those accursed Americans who prevented them from living their true faith. Everything would have been fine, but the situation didn't suit the Americans based in Afghanistan—they knew about this Taliban cell nestled in the mountains. They didn't like the radicals scurrying back and forth to kill as many Americans and American allies as possible or simply those who'd fallen beneath their righteous hand. The Pakistanis shrugged helplessly, claiming they could do nothing about this unrecognized mountainous republic. Besides, how can you tell a peaceful Pashtun from a non-peaceful Robert? They didn't even try, as the local shepherds and their families were closer aligned with the Pakistanis than the newly arrived Baptists. The Americans eventually ran out of patience: "Bomb the Taliban there and take them all out!" They didn't use strategic aviation since the Pakistanis would hardly have approved of them carpet bombing their territory, so they went with the tactic of pinpoint drone strikes. It was just as useless as the first option, but fewer extra victims were expected, and there, you see, a dozen or two Wahhabis could be taken out in one strike. That's what the Pentagon decided, then launched a swarm of drones at poor Waziristan: smaller observation drones and larger ones as direct punishment. As a result, the shepherds, their wives, children, and their elderly fled in terror upon seeing even a glimpse of a silent, white dot high in the sky, hiding in their cellars or underground in antici- pation of a missile attack.

Robert and his brothers were also forced to hide. There were no means to repel the small white dot, which often launched a deadly missile—the Mujahideen were mostly poor people and didn't have their own air defense forces. Then, one day, at a meeting of emir-commanders, they decided to start an anti-aircraft war with America. It was Robert who was entrusted with this task. He no longer needed to crawl through mountain gorges. Instead, he would wage jihad, using all his engineering knowledge and experience. Robert agreed happily. Despite the fact that he lacked experience in creating explo- sives or rockets, he opted to use a combination of both to shoot down American drones. Robert wanted to deliver real bene- fits to everyone and do more than indulge in free rye cakes and milk tea, so he decided to combine the power of the divine and the internet to achieve his goal. He started by offering prayers to the first, as was customary, and extensively googling on the second. Then, he converted a barn into a laboratory for just one person—himself.

The first experiment resulted in the laboratory's roof getting damaged and the inventor losing a finger. The emirs nodded their gray heads sympathetically, and the experiments continued. The next attempt relied on the lessons learned from the previous failure and advice gathered from others who had undergone similar experiences and survived to write about it on the internet with their remaining fingers. The tests took place in the open air before a crowd gathered at a prudent distance. The rocket did not take off this time, though it tried very hard, judging from the noise and smoke. Since then, Robert has limped heavily on one leg, and on the same side, his torso has resembled a medium-roasted barbecue. Nobody knows whether these experiments influenced the belligerent intentions of those accursed Americans. Still, even if they suspected a threat toward them, they did not show it and continued to attack the shepherds' clay dwellings with the methodicalness of a computer.

At the next meeting of the emirs, seeing how Robert was crippling himself more and more with his perseverance, they suspended the development of the third rocket experiment, reasonably believing that the inventor would not survive its launch. Knowing his indefatigable initiative had turned into devout fanaticism, and seeing the actual destructive result, they concluded that it would be more suitable to blow up living people than a small white dot in the sky. Once again, the emirs conferred and devised a new task for him: committing jihad in his homeland. Robert agreed happily. It wasn't that he wanted to return to Russia—he just wanted to help establish peace and justice on earth, even if peace and justice required blowing up a hundred or so infidels.

Having gathered a group of three brothers with Russian passports, the emirs equipped them with a couple of thousand dollars and extensive instructions, then sent them on a special mission, instructing them to backtrack the route that had brought them there. On foot and by donkey to Iran, by bus to Turkey, by plane to Russia, then to the station—Allahu Akbar! As the leading martyr, Robert was supposed to be responsible for the technical part of the project, the young commander for the organizational role, and the third one for something else and, if needed, to help the others. That was what they had decided.

Before leaving, Robert stopped by a family he knew; he'd come from Bashkiria to Waziristan with them. Even after her husband had been killed last year during the jihad in Afghanistan, he kept contact with the widow and her two children, especially the eldest boy. He was ten years old and went to the local religious school, the madrasah, because no others were operating under Sharia law. It was difficult for the boy there because everything was in Arabic, mainly about Islam, and it was very strict. Robert asked about his studies, and the boy told him with reluctance, but he recalled his old school back in Russia with greater joy. It was more fun there, and he could play with friends after class. He didn't have any friends here. Robert encouraged the boy and asked if he would avenge his murdered father when he grew up. After this question, the boy had tears in his eyes. He looked down and managed to say: "I will." Robert nodded contentedly and tousled his hair. When he came in for the last time to say goodbye before the long journey, the widow begged him to take her with him, but Robert refused and quickly left their house, once again convinced that Shaitan had created women, which was why they were weak in their faith.

Their group set off through the mountains the next day toward the Iranian border. This time, the journey was longer, more complicated, and more expensive. The young commander, tired or losing patience, decided to shorten their trip and fly straight from Tehran. Having bought tickets to Moscow with the last of their money, he confidently led his detachment to the Departures area, believing that he was more intelligent than the old and wise emirs, who had categorically forbidden them from doing such a thing. The emirs were old and wise, not only because they did not go on such risky business trips, but because they sent other Roberts in their place, knowing what would happen at the Tehran airport if they were caught poking their noses around there. As expected, the trio was detained at border control despite their freshly shaved beards and tickets on hand. The Iranian special services weren't fools, and it would be hard to fall for their story about a two-year visa delay due to enhanced religious education somewhere in the depths of Iran. After holding the Waziristan special forces for three weeks in a local prison and ensuring they hadn't pulled any dirty tricks on Iranian territory, the authorities decided to get rid of them. They were put on a regular flight to Moscow at the expense of the Iranian government, with a farewell deportation stamp and a ban on further entry. This option suited Robert's comrades, since they knew it was a one-way trip and were hurrying to become martyrs, knowing the houris were already waiting for them in paradise.

The Russian border guard at Sheremetyevo Airport carefully studied their passports with Iranian stamps, looked at the three suspiciously beardless individuals, then invited them to a separate room for a conversation. There, they were met by a man with an expressionless face, grayer than the color of his suit. He also carefully examined their faces against their documents and called for help from colleagues. The prospect of a Russian prison loomed before Robert. It was unlikely that people whose faces and suits looked like this would believe the old tale about the in-depth study of Islamic religious movements by three forgetful, overgrown students who were fifty, forty, and thirty years old. However, they did not detain them, and after a few hours, they were released. The group of Islamists guessed that they might be monitored, but they did not abandon their plans, believing that they would detect any surveillance on them and God would help them, as they'd come on a holy mission.

The Mujahideen landing force already had a brother-in-faith in the Moscow region with whom the gray-haired emirs had put them in contact. The Waziristanis set off to find him. Nobody knows if he was overjoyed or prepared for their visit, but he did not expel the brothers and persuaded a neighbor to rent an apartment to his three "relatives" who had appeared out of nowhere. He lived with his family and children on the first floor of the two-story building, into which his unexpected relatives moved. The newest member of this deadly puppet theater gave them some money to live on, and he paid for their rent—or at least he promised he would pay soon. The young commander got a job as a taxi driver since the Taliban dollars had long since run out, and he needed to eat and buy saltpeter for a bomb.

For a month, they lived on high alert, waiting for the manifestation of outside surveillance. When it seemed like nobody was monitoring them, Robert began to prepare his infernal machine by improvised means. Unfortunately—or fortunately—it suffered the same fate as the Waziristan missiles. The kitchen window frame broke, and Robert got unevenly burned on one side of his body. But even after this explosion in the house, the group of unfortunate terrorists did not change their place of deployment, relying on God-knows-what, apparently waiting to be detained by some rural cop from a 1970s Soviet film. The fourth Islamic brother from the Moscow region managed to more or less explain what had happened to the landlady and settle the situation, they inserted a new window frame, and Robert continued his work with trebled strength. But then, a new problem arose—the young commander disappeared. He went to work as usual in the morning and didn't answer his phone. With their leader's loss, the amateur Mujahideens' vanguard began to suspect something and stopped going outside altogether.

November was coming to an end, and the first light snow fell. On the third day of waiting, the *Spetsnaz* squad was tired of lurking in the cold and went in for their assault. They broke down the door and threw a few flash grenades as a bold statement, but did not go into the apartment itself, calling on everyone to turn themselves in. Robert could not give up, even if he wanted to. The grenade explosion gave him a small concussion and caused his eye to roll in the opposite direction, temporarily preventing him from taking part in what was happening. He lay in the corridor gasping while the other two brothers barricaded themselves in a room. The squad guys, deciding they'd been misunderstood the first time, threw two more flash grenades and one tear-gas grenade, then again called on whoever wanted to live to turn themselves in. Having come to his senses and choking on the gas, Robert crawled toward the voice in the direction of the exit and fresh air. They dragged him out onto the street, stripped him down to his underpants for some reason, laid him face down in the snow, then offered the rest of them a final chance to hand themselves in. Otherwise, they would proceed with an actual assault. Realizing this was their way out, the remaining brothers began to climb through the window. The security forces, thinking this was an attempt to break out, or maybe thinking nothing at all, shot one right in the window and the other right after he landed on the ground. The security forces threw some more grenades, continuing to call on them to surrender and seeing that this tactic was working. They finally ventured into the empty apartment to attack when no one else came out. They found no new terrorists, explosives, or weapons. They found Robert's partially completed products unconvincing, and, scratching their heads, they quietly planted a couple of Kalashnikovs of vague origin in the closet. Robert, who was peacefully cooling down in the snow all this time, was pulled away and taken to prison without noticing that his eye had remained somewhere in that snowdrift.

Robert saw his young commander a year later in court. He was pleased because he'd thought he was dead. But the joy was short-lived: the former emir had made a deal with the investigation team and received only seven years for the evidence needed by the FSB, and now he was a witness in the case against Robert. The one-eyed bearded man admitted his guilt but would not cooperate with the enemy. He did not renounce his beliefs and certainly not his religion, nor did he hide the ultimate goal of their voyage, for which he was given a total of seventeen years. But Robert did not pay attention to this: at the time of the verdict, the day's next prayer was already approaching, and he was thinking about something more important to him.

Anatoly

Anatoly was given a seven-year sentence in a medium-security prison for wanting to blow up the Israeli Embassy and its ambassador. It was difficult to understand exactly how the Jewish people had gotten on Anatoly's bad side. Maybe Moses hadn't been polite when asking Anatoly's ancestors for directions to the promised land? Still, although Anatoly was filled with burning hatred for Jews, he didn't admit his guilt in the assassination attempt. It wasn't so much his conviction that upset him as the fact that he wasn't put in a high-security prison, where, Anatoly believed, the real terrorists went. Terrorism, as a rule, is considered a serious crime that can earn you a strict sentence of life imprisonment, but for some reason the court decided to take pity on Anatoly. Either the criminal wasn't dangerous in the court's opinion or the evidence was inconclusive. Or maybe the leniency was due to the fact that, as the state of Israel apparently noted in clear terms in the accusation against him, there were no victims, no damage, and no demands.

Anatoly had been outed to the special services by a friend, who told them that Anatoly was planning to blow up the Israeli Embassy and its ambassador and had invited him to participate in this exciting event. The friend also handed over some explosives and a flash drive with recordings of his conversations with Anatoly. Anatoly was arrested. He didn't confess. The investigators checked the explosives for prints. There were some, but they belonged to Anatoly's comrade, not him. The investigators listened to the conversations on the flash drive and discerned some indistinct muttering that led them to make broad conclusions about Anatoly's fantasies, but there was nothing about preparing for an explosion. The only substantial evidence was his friend's testimony, although the friendship was unlikely to survive such a turn of events. In court, Anatoly pleaded not guilty but delivered a fiery speech about the threat of Zionism to the world. The judge gave him a seven-year sentence because you never knew what could happen.

Anatoly was well over fifty. He had a wife and three boys. After the arrest, the youngest son, who was seven, waited a long time for his father to return from his business trip. He watched the news on TV, wishing for a quick end to the war in Donbas, which he believed was the reason his father could not come home—because it had stopped the trains from running. As usually happens with these sorts of cases, it was difficult to find the extremist. The judge is sure that the investigators wouldn't just accuse anyone they came across, especially if the evidence is weak or nonexistent. The investigators work with the material that the field operatives have dug up, conferring on it an almost divine quality. The field operatives seize on any excuse to inflate the importance and existential necessity of their team. And this is how cases involving guys like Anatoly multiply all over Russia, while security forces receive orders and titles, TV channels scare their viewers with talk of terrorists, and the people shudder a little, but then sigh in gratitude that such vigilant special-services officers are there to protect them. No one cares that, somewhere, a little boy is waiting for the trains to bring his father home from a business trip. Such is the state's ruthless, repressive machine, which grinds up people's futures. Well, at least the Putin regime hasn't yet resorted to mass executions—unlike the Stalinist one, which made people disappear into the unknown by the millions. Things were done quietly and in secret then, and everyone tiptoed around in fear. Today's Russia prefers show trials, to make people terrified of becoming one of those highly publicized examples.

Anatoly was of medium height, lean, and athletic for his age. He tried to go to bed early, before lights out if possible. To ensure a good night's sleep, he'd plug his ears with red paraffin wax that he'd scraped off of cheese rinds. He also wore a homemade black eye mask to block out any interference from the duty light. In this state of sensory deprivation, he'd set off to visit Morpheus. In the morning, he rose long before sunrise. Having unsealed his ears and removed his Zorro mask, he washed with cold water at the sink and began his yoga. Each new cellmate, upon waking, was horrified to see the life-threatening positions into which Uncle Tolya contorted himself and rushed to save him. But there was no need for help: Anatoly unfurled himself with no aid. During his exercise time in the prison yard, he demonstrated how good he felt, raising his hands and greeting the sun with barely audible whispers, then racing around the cramped courtyard, practically running up the walls. When he was drenched with sweat, he would pause, still not out of breath, put on a special hat with a paper ball tied to it with string, and begin boxing furiously. Anatoly was a master of such homemade devices, and this was one of his most impressive. Even the guards, who had seen a lot in their lifetimes, would stop and watch from above, captivated, as Anatoly's ball twirled around. He did little actual boxing, but, judging by the way he relentlessly attacked and defended himself from the ubiquitous ball, it was clear that he had his own unique style.

Anatoly didn't smoke or have any vices, but he found a unique use for matches. He would burn bread crusts, using them to light or fumigate corners, even creating fire circles in harmless Zoroastrian rituals. Anatoly was also studying Farsi— an interest perhaps born of his desire to check the Ayatollah Khomeini Telegram channel for the celebratory news that the Israeli Embassy had been bombed. His progress was slow, but, as Anatoly himself would say, "The language is several thousand years old," so he was in no rush.

In many ways, Anatoly was a fairly typical inmate, but, as soon as the conversation shifted to the Jewish question, particularly when he himself redirected it there, his cell was filled with visions of Jewish Freemasons who controlled the world, weaving intricate plots and schemes with long-range goals beyond mere mortals' comprehension. The main question for Anatoly was: How can we fight all this? And the first answer that came to his mind involved explosives.

Anatoly was a seasoned ideological combatant, well-versed not only in the so-called Jewish world conspiracy but in the intricacies of Putin's regime. For many years, he'd followed a crazy colonel who intended to overthrow Putin with the help of a couple of divisions that were loyal to him, plus tanks, submarine mini boats in the Moscow River, and volunteers like Anatoly who belonged to a paramilitary organization named after Minin and Pozharsky. The uprising failed: either the tanks didn't arrive on schedule or the submarines surfaced in the wrong place. The colonel was imprisoned for a long time, but he continued to direct appeals to his supporters and shower curses on the heads of his enemies.

In his youth, Anatoly had served in Soviet military intelligence. He was sent to Afghanistan as part of a newly formed Muslim battalion. He did not take part in the Tajbeg Palace assault, but he performed other feats to protect the interests of the Soviet Union in a distant and barren land. Anatoly talked a lot about his service, the exhausting training, the long marches in full gear in forty-degree heat, his stupid fellow soldiers, the local life, the war. He described how he'd interrogated silent Mujahideen fighters by inserting an explosive with a Bickford fuse into their ears. While the fuse was burning, the gift of speech usually returned. The stoic ones had half their heads blown off. Every war has its laws, none of which can be called entirely fair. Anatoly did not like to describe what the Mujahideen did to the Soviet soldiers they captured.

He sincerely hated Putin for many reasons, including his attack on Ukraine, a country that Anatoly loved with all his heart and whose fate he now worried about from afar. It was not only because his wife was from there, or because they took a train there for a visit every summer, or because of the delicious food or the good people, and definitely not because of the freedom there after the Maidan Revolution, which he could not appreciate, sitting as he was in his cramped cell. He loved Ukraine because it was dearer to him than his own criminal country.

Once Anatoly had received his sentence, but had not yet been sent to the prison camp, he was allowed a short meeting with his wife in a booth where they were separated by a pane of glass. He returned, pale, to his cell, sat on the bed, and stared at the wall. Two of his best friends, former colleagues, had gone to Donbas to fight for Ukraine and had been burned alive in a damaged KamAZ truck. Anatoly spoke, as if to himself: "And my wife, silly woman, came all dressed up and happy. She says, 'It's good you're in prison, you old fool. Otherwise, you would have gone with them.'" Anatoly couldn't contain himself and started to cry. That evening, he burned even more matches than usual.

David

David was Armenian, had a beard without a mustache, thieves' stars on his shoulders, and Islam in his heart. Each of these things was not such a rarity, but the combination of them in one person was quite unusual.

David came from a wealthy family. True, when they moved from Yerevan to Moscow twenty-five years ago, that wasn't yet so. David was only a year old then, so he doesn't remember Armenia, unlike his older brother, who went to kindergarten there—he has some memories of a distant city in the mountains. The family also had an ordinary Armenian mother and an enterprising Armenian father, so things in their new place were slowly but surely going uphill. In fact, it is somewhat uncommon to meet a low-income Armenian family that has long left the boundaries of their historical homeland, especially in Moscow. In the nineties, David's dad opened his first restaurant and spent most of his time there, doing business, the primary consumer of his own food and drinks, and surrounded by many friends. But even with their joint efforts, they couldn't sink this business, and it thrived. Mom busied herself at home, managing the household, the kitchen table, and the children.

Dad periodically tried to raise his sons with a glass of cognac in hand, but basically, they were left to their own devices, especially David.

As a child, he attended computer clubs instead of school. In the first half of the day, he did it "unofficially," so to speak, and when the classes for the rest of the children ended, he went to play computer games again after having dinner at home and kissing his mother goodbye. By that time, Dad had already opened a third restaurant, so even when he regularly paid for his friends, David couldn't really lose all his pocket money. When his dad received persistent calls from school, he gave another useless scolding to his son and assigned his personal chauffeur to the boy, driving him to classes and monitoring his school attendance. David got out of the car, walked to the school building, waited for the car to leave, then headed in his usual direction to the computer club. However, David's grades in no way reflected his poor attendance, since Dad was one of the main sponsors of the school. Besides, the teachers were so used to free staff parties in Dad's restaurants at the end of each semester that they never gave David a grade of less than four out of five. Moreover, his older brother studied at the same school, was honest and calm, and received well-deserved A+'s, so the teachers observed a certain sense of justice.

In high school, David began to visit the gym in the evenings, studying martial arts there, and on weekends he circled his neighborhood with friends in search of opportunities to apply his acquired fighting skills. It was easy to win in such fights, as there were always more friends with David than enemies. In extreme cases, they were just passers-by, unless they met some serious sportsman who scattered their boyish gang. As a result of such an enchanting way of life, David's school years were full of various adventures of the same genre. Toward the end of his secondary education, David finally took a wrong turn, plunging into the romanticism of thieves, got a wind rose tattoo* on his shoulder as a hallmark of involvement in the criminal world, and began to consider himself an authority in the area.

After graduating from school, David successfully entered the commercial department of the Institute of Economics without taking entrance exams. His older brother had already studied there and done unsurprisingly well, and Dad was on the board of trustees, so their family name carried weight and David was enrolled as an add-on. As a student, his lifestyle didn't change much—computer games and fights were gradually, though not entirely, pushed aside for cars, girls, and booze. With such an abundance of interests, even a diligent student would not have had time to study, and David clearly wasn't one. But he still passed his classes, since by that time Dad had already engaged in large-scale wholesale trade in building tools, earning millions—first rubles, then dollars. The family had a wealth of apartments, cars, and other junk associated with prosperity. Dad had no time to call the institute before each session, so David dealt with this issue on his own, simply by buying good

---

* In the Russian criminal world, tattoos act as a visual marker of a criminal's history, including their rank, the amount of time served in prison, or their affiliations. The wind rose tattoo can appear on a criminal's shoulder or knees, indicating that they refuse to "kneel" to authority.

grades, because, according to his parents, a young guy from a good family should always have enough cash. Mom was very proud of her eldest son but loved her younger son more.

After five years of not attending the institute, David finally received his diploma, with which he successfully started working for his father. His older brother was already working there; having the same background as David, he'd graduated with honors and became a key employee of their enterprise, then their father's right-hand man. David worked approximately the same way he had studied. He wandered from one position to another, leaving behind a trail of chaos, problems, and conflicts. New clothes, entertainment, and high-level recreation in any part of the globe interested him more than honest work. Everyone has troubles, regardless of wealth, it's just that everyone is different: someone wonders where to borrow money before payday, and for someone else, the sea is too dirty in Bali and there's a scratch on his new Mercedes.

Despite their different personalities, the brothers got along well with each other. They got married at almost the same time, moved into separate apartments, had children, and grew fascinated with Islam. It happened so unexpectedly for their parents that, behind the everyday chores and problems that the global economic crisis had brought on, they didn't notice something important and irreversible happening to their children. Profits were falling while the dollar and expenses were rising, causing the "Titanic" of their family business, which was built on imports, to take a blow and start tilting heavily and irreversibly. The brothers, meanwhile, began to visit the mosque regularly. Although Dad had moved his headquarters from the restaurant to an office long ago, he did not part with his old habits and continued to lead, always keeping a glass of brandy in his hands. He rapidly developed cirrhosis of the liver, most likely due to this addiction or perhaps because of business problems and old age. But he ignored the pain, poured himself another drink, and continued like the captain of a doomed ship, trying to maintain turnover and a niche in the market, not really raising prices, working in the red, in the hope that the crisis would end, the dollar would fall, and things would get better again. But the crisis did not end, the dollar did not decline, and nothing improved. Debts began to appear, and then apartments, cars, and restaurants were sold to keep the main business afloat, but nothing helped him—he had already accumulated loads of problems. He could no longer move anywhere except down, dragging all his passengers with him. The brothers, meanwhile, began to introduce Sharia law into their families.

Mom, who started dyeing her gray hair quite early, rushed between her husband, sons, and already complaining daughters-in-law who did not want to become devout Muslim women. But she failed in strengthening the ties of this sprawling family. Their business had hit rock bottom, and their debts were only rising. The family had their last large apartment and penultimate car, Dad was being prepared for a liver transplant operation, and the brothers decided to go to Syria to fight the infidels because none of it worried them too much. They didn't tell anyone of their intentions—especially not their wives, who were not ready to wear a veil for them—not to mention the rifle ammunition magazines. By that time, the older brother already had two children from one wife. David also had two, but from different ones—he couldn't immediately do away with his former way of life. But having children didn't keep them from leaving.

The brothers packed their things and left without notifying anyone. In addition to his belongings, David also brought a woman who had agreed to go to war with him. She had not yet given birth to David's child, but she was already expecting, and most importantly, she shared his views on spreading their religion. The brothers informed their relatives about their departure once they'd already arrived at their destination.

For a year in Syria, the brothers did everything that people usually did in this war: they shot at other people and buried their own, struck with mortars and hid from bombardments, seized warehouses and houses, equipped themselves, took hostages and traded them, tortured and executed captives, sincerely believing that they were doing God's work. Five times a day, as should be so for faithful Muslims, they prayed, longing for only one thing—to reach paradise and, if necessary, to step over the corpses of millions of infidels to make it happen.

Sometimes they called Mom, but these were conversations with their past. It became more and more difficult for her to paint over her gray hairs. Meanwhile, her husband had a liver transplant but felt no better. They mortgaged the apartment, relations with David's second wife were better than with his first, their children were healthy, and most importantly for this simple Armenian mom, her sons were alive in this incomprehensible war. She took the news that David already had a third wife, and that she had again become a grandmother, rather easily. It was the least of her worries. When she asked them to change their minds and return home, the brothers hung up. She stopped asking them about it to be able to at least be able to communicate—it was better than living in ignorance, breaking all ties with her sons, as, for example, Dad had. Mothers will always stand by their children, no matter what they do.

Meanwhile, David's temperament and character turned out to be more in demand in military life than in peacetime. He quickly became a commander, with his quiet brother becoming his deputy. Both were already on the Russian federal wanted list, and it was only a matter of time before the case was filed with Interpol. At some point, David urgently needed a clean passport for his own purposes, perhaps an assignment. It turned out that making it in Ukraine was the cheapest and easiest option—there everyone from the president to the controller in the tram was corrupt. David remotely agreed on the price and method of obtaining it—all that remained was going to Kyiv and picking up the document so that he could flutter off like a free bird, not fearing any searches, including international ones.

He left his brother at the head of his detachment, kissed his child and wife, and departed for Ukraine as if on a diplomatic mission. And there, as luck would have it, it was the height of a revolution against the very corruption that David had wanted to take advantage of. If he had arrived a couple of months earlier when the spark of revolution was not yet in the air, everything would have gone well, but David ended up at the most unfortunate moment in history for him. The Yanukovych regime, fearing the invasion of foreign mercenaries, American special forces, and aliens, directly cooperated with the FSB, taking advantage of their databases, in which David was also listed in a place of honor. Caught in a trap set for others, Allah's warrior suffered from someone else's revolution, about which he was not particularly aware because he was completely occupied with his own war. Ukrainian border guards didn't let him into the country, put a deportation stamp in his passport, and sent him on a flight to Moscow.

David sat on this plane, following an initially unplanned route, upset that the deal with the passport had fallen through, but rejoicing that he would be able to see his mother and sick father, hoping they would not have time to inform the Russian special services about his arrival. But he was unaware of the level of interaction between the departments in the two neighboring states. As soon as he stepped off of the Ukrainian plane and onto the Russian air bridge, he was immediately tied up by people who descended upon him like spiders from the ceiling.

David was charged with participation in illegal paramilitary formations and also, terrorism. His video message had been circulating on the internet for a long time; in it, his face uncovered and in combat gear, he called on all Muslim brothers to start jihad, so it was pointless to deny it. David admitted his guilt and made a deal with the investigation—since the case involved only him, he didn't have to hand over anyone, and his conscience was clear. They promised to throw him a bone, and they would have if David, because of his character, had not quarreled with the investigators several times a day, either breaking or renewing the pre-trial agreement. As a result, he received five years in a general-security prison, which was still not much. He was one of the first people in Russia convicted for their participation in the Syrian war. His short sentence was because, at that time in Russia, the system wasn't quite sure what kind of punishment to deal out, as the FSB was practically buying tickets for such troublemakers to go there instead of stirring up trouble in the forests of the Caucuses. However, no one was waiting for them, so the returnees were punished. David was still lucky—later on, the courts began to give the same five years just for the idea of going there.

Mom finally saw her son in a Lefortovo court cell. At the age of twenty-four, David had already married three times. The first time to a Georgian woman, the second to an Armenian, and the third to a Dagestani. Each woman had birthed him one child, and they were all relatively close in age. However, he'd never been a polygamist. Only lovers of melodramatic TV shows could solve this logical puzzle, but David was not strong in puzzles or in movies—he just lived as best as he could. The children knew their father primarily through photographs or brief meetings through the glass aquarium in the courtroom. His third wife remained with their child in Syria for a while, not knowing what to do next, but she seemed to be looked after there.

Despite the financial crisis, Mom supplied David with lots of food in prison, even managing to get him homemade stuff. It seemed unrealistic in those harsh conditions, but Armenian mothers are capable of a lot, especially for the sake of their children. David himself was not very concerned with nutrition or the personal and financial problems of the family. He had one God, and he saw himself as only serving Him—it was this alone that gave him pleasure and peace. He prayed five times a day, observing the schedule clearly and up to the minute. He performed all other rites, remembrance, and praise and tried to read the Koran in its original language. He also strictly observed the rules of conduct, which he picked up from the available literature and also devised on his own. During prayer, the label of his bottle of olive oil was turned to the wall because it had the image of a girl on it. He caught and scolded himself for using obscene or even objectionable words. David always prayed very earnestly, often bringing himself to tears when giving thanks to Allah, which gave him large blisters on his knees and forehead. When David wasn't praying or conducting other religious rites, he would start talking with his cellmate, even if he had no particular desire to communicate or was busy with something. But this never stopped David—the Armenian spontaneity and sociability were thus awoken in him. In moments of communication, he forgot himself, joked, and laughed, but then he suddenly caught himself and abruptly interrupted himself, believing that he'd done something sinful. In subsequent prayers, he asked God for forgiveness.

David was rather dismissive toward Putin and his lot, as well as other people and things unrelated to his religion. On the eve of the trial, when the authorities came to him with a proposal to renounce fundamentalism, shave off his beard, and publicly repent in front of a television camera, he resolutely refused and, in anger, once again terminated the pre-trial agreement.

David often dreamed of his brother and the war. When he was told that his brother had been torn apart by an artillery shell and there was nothing to bury, he was not particularly surprised, as if he'd already learned about it, from his dreams or prayers, and was ready for this. According to his understanding, his brother was already in paradise, and David was only waiting in the wings to join him.

Mom did not believe in the death of her eldest son. She was still waiting for him, as well as for David's release, not realizing that neither of them would ever return to her.

Train Car

A certain type of train car can often be found at the station. Typically, the *Stolypin* is placed in a secure, dead-end area, and attached to the back of the train right before departure. It resembles an ordinary train car but has windows on just one side that are discreetly concealed behind a grid of thin bars. These windows can't be opened; they can only be lowered slightly to create thin openings for ventilation. The windows are almost always dirty, and you can hardly see anything through them, although none of the people boarding the train or seeing friends and loved ones off on the platform would ever try to look inside because the side of the train car is inscribed with the word "mail." What's interesting about the mail? Nothing. But real mail cars don't have windows. This train car isn't carrying letters and packages but living people—inmates, to be exact. Most of the people standing on the platform would have probably moved away if they knew that convicts were being transported in another train car because few people consider them to be human.

Ending up in such a train car isn't as difficult as you might think, and nobody is immune to this possibility. Consider a scenario: you're buying some weed with a friend, only to discover that friend is no friend at all but an undercover police officer. Suddenly, you find yourself branded an illegal drug distributor facing an eight-year prison sentence. Or maybe you quarrel with someone at a bar or club when you're drunk. There are a lot of people around, a fight breaks out, the situation gets chaotic, someone gets stabbed, and you're somehow implicated because there are traces of his blood on your clothes. He dies in the hospital, and you get slapped with ten years in a high-security prison because you refuse to admit your guilt, and the judges don't like that. Alternatively, the security forces might like your business, and you don't want to surrender it to them for pennies or share your earnings. In the blink of an eye, you become a big fraudster who stole from the state or your own funds.

Various paths can lead to the confines of this pseudo-mail car, where you, along with a bunch of other poor bastards, strain to catch glimpses of freedom and the human connections you've grown estranged from during your years of incarceration. After being immersed in a world of iron, concrete, bars, and enclosed spaces, watching people move peacefully around the station a few meters away from you becomes a unique experience and even a source of pleasure. Every detail can be appreciated—from the vibrant greenery of spring and summer, to the warmth of the sun and distant drifting clouds, houses, cars passing by, a woman selling small pies, a passenger carrying a suitcase, a girl calling someone on the phone, and a child meticulously eating ice cream.

The inmates chat about various car models, people's attire,

and phones from inside the train car. Some glimpse certain novelties on the platform as if they were prominently displayed on a podium. Others, seasoned train travelers, encounter plenty of unfamiliar sights. Their primary focus remains the people— after all, people continue to be the most compelling subjects. Someone attempts to spot familiar faces, thinking they've "seen that person somewhere." His brain fills in the details and vividly fantasizes, aiming to satisfy his hungry mind's craving for new experiences. "Look, look, what a chick! Over there, the one in the red tracksuit! An absolute knockout!" The girl is about fifty meters away. When she turns around, it becomes clear that she's actually a guy. Laughter and jokes ripple through the train car at the inmate's misplaced enthusiasm.

A disheveled and filthy-looking man of indeterminate age with that ever-drunken sort of gait walks by the train car, holding a bottle of beer in his hand. He catches the gaze of dozens of attentive eyes peering at him through the window cracks. The man turns around, smiles with a scruffy and toothless mouth, raises his hand with his fingers forming a "V," and shouts at the top of his voice, "Criminal code for life! Death to cops!" The whole car yells something in response. The angry guard on duty begins to forcefully close the windows all the way. The little man wraps his jacket around his slender, tattoo-covered chest. Satisfied and proud, he continues walking. It's clear he had ridden in such a car before, managing to find his way back to freedom. Many prisoners see in him a dim reflection of their own future.

The gateway to the outside world is abruptly slammed shut just as quickly as it appeared. The entertainment is over, and it's time for the train to depart. The windows may be opened later along the way. From there, you can gaze endlessly at the fields and forests passing by, which isn't too bad either. But, of course, it can't quite compare to the lively and interesting atmosphere of a train station.

The *Stolypin* prisoners' cars have changed a lot since Solzhenitsyn's time. They have seven compartment cells for convicted citizens. The back part of the car is separate—where the armed escort group stays in two compartments behind a door at the end of the corridor. Inside the cell, there are three wooden walls but no window. Instead of a fourth wall leading to the corridor, there's a strong lattice with a door and a feeding slot. Each cell has three levels of beds, like in a second-class train car. The only difference is that there are additional folding beds on the second level over the passage. There are a total of seven beds in total. If regular people were traveling, that number would be enough. But prisoners travel in these cars, so the norm is up to twelve people and, in reality, can go up to sixteen. That's the mathematical logic of the Russian state penitentiary system at work.

Each prisoner carries a bag or two. The overcrowding is terrible; they're penned in like cattle. Somehow, they manage to find some space. They take turns sleeping on the upper shelves, sit on each other, and place their bags underneath. Almost everyone smokes, even though it's not allowed. You can't control the convicts here. When the train is still, there's no air in the car, and it doesn't move often during its long journey.

A guard patrols the corridor, armed with just a club. The prisoners, despite being locked up, always need supervision—just in case. The rest of the escort group, around eight people, sit in the office, armed in case of need. More of them come into the corridor during hot water distribution or when prisoners go to the restroom. The feeder opens three times a day, with a guard pouring boiling water for everyone from a large kettle. The state provides dry rations for the journey, and the prisoners prepare their own porridge and tea in plastic containers. Three times a day, they're escorted to the restroom one by one, hands behind their backs. Walking along the corridor, you glimpse fellow travelers from other cells, with whom you could only communicate by voice before. In the restroom, you have to be quick—the whole car is waiting. Water is scarce, and the smell is best left unspoken.

A *Stolypin* takes four days to cover the distance that an ordinary car can in a day. At every station, the transit prison is unhitched from the other wagons and parked in a guarded area. Police vans with armed guards and dogs come, load or unload prisoners, and drive away. Then, the *Stolypin* waits for the next passing train. Sometimes, the wait can last all day or night, at various stops or intersections. But prisoners are used to sitting and waiting; it's part of prison life, and the prison car is no different. Inside the *Stolypin*, you stand most of the time, not moving much, but it's still more dynamic than regular prison life. The *Stolypin* is the closest thing to a free journey a prisoner gets in the penitentiary system. Prisoners often dream about travel, especially if they've never experienced it and might never do so. While in prison, they plan these dreams along with other things, like their new life after release: a life without alcohol, drugs, theft, or violence—the very things that landed them in prison. These dreams, like many others, are unlikely to ever come true, but, when available, TV programs about travel and distant lands are always popular in any prison cell.

When the car is cordoned off, all you can breathe is smoke and stench—what everyone else has been breathing. In winter, it's cold and stuffy, and in summer, it's hot and stuffy. On some routes, on which the *Stolypin* is stuck in extreme heat all day, a fire truck is called to pour water on this metal box of people. Otherwise, not everyone, including the armed escorts, would make it to the final station. It's hard to believe that even in the twenty-first century, people are transported like animals, but sadly, it's true. Yet, these people inside the *Stolypin* are the most interesting. They meet each other, talk, and share stories. They ask questions relating to where they're from, where they're going, and what's their sentence. And does anyone know what it's like at the final destination? Is it tough or bearable? Do they follow the convicts' rules or the cops' regime there? The conditions of the future lives of those traveling in these cages depend on this. Every person and their fate are unique.

Thirty-year-old Perets ("Pepper") looks more like a teenager and is facing his seventh prison term for theft. He shares with a lisp how he lost his front teeth in the last central prison and that the cops there sought revenge for some of his past actions against them. Like a child, Perets listens enthusiastically to stories about other countries and travels, looking into the narrator's eyes and smiling all funny with his sunken mouth.

Stories about Japan, crab fishing, the sea, storms, and dangers are told by Shoostry ("Nimble"), who took part in such trips twice and gained so many impressions that he's ready to share them to this day. Now, he is going somewhere to Siberia, and he doesn't expect to make it past his ten-year sentence because HIV and hepatitis are treated poorly in penal colonies. But Shoostry doesn't despair and laughs along with Perets. Death, whether it's someone else's or your own, is taken lightly here. It's not like a pack of tea or cigarettes, which take greater precedence.

Pasha the conscript is sitting nearby. He's a sergeant but hasn't been demobilized yet. A month before he was supposed to go home, he got a sentence because someone in his unit stole a machine gun. Now, he's headed back to serve his sentence in his hometown where his wife and two young children live. One of his kids was born after he was already locked up, so he hasn't even seen them yet. He's facing time in a penal colony and all the shame that comes with it.

Penal battalions don't exist anymore, so soldiers serve their sentences with everyone else. Pasha feels his humiliation deeply, unlike many others in the car. But like all of them, he hopes things will get better, that they'll sort it out, maybe even acquit him. After all, it wasn't his machine gun—it just can't be this unfair! Sadly, it can be, and sometimes, it's even worse.

A car with barred windows inscribed with the word "mail" on its side, full of people and injustice, rolls on through a huge gloomy country. Right by the bars, the old convict Chetvertak ("Quarter") sits. His nickname befits the sentence he's serving. He smokes a lot and talks little. He is forty-five years old, but his wrinkles add another fifteen years to his face. He ended up in prison at eighteen and has only been released once, for a couple of years. He still has seven years left to serve, and he won't get any better, younger, or smarter. The five people he killed won't be resurrected either. He got several of them when he was free, and he killed the others when he was already in the colony. No one here pities their victims. No one ever blames anyone for anything here. Here, everyone shares the same misery—prison.

In the depths of the cell, a kind-looking old man named Hottabych has settled in comfortably. He's definitely over seventy and speaks sparingly but always to the point, often with humor and attentiveness. He's a calm and kind long-term prisoner, displaying the quirks of an old man. He never started a family in his long life because he loved women and fighting too much. He mainly fought with a knife, which often seriously harmed his opponents' lives and health. Consequently, Hottabych found himself imprisoned multiple times, always for the same reason. Eventually, this fate led him to a nursing home in the twilight of his life. Even there, he managed to make an enemy—quite literally. During a TV show, a man blocked Hottabych's view. The arrogant man didn't realize the explosive nature of the elderly Hottabych and reacted dismissively, even rudely, to his request to move aside. By the time he'd understood who he was dealing with, it was already too late. A needle-point straight-blade knife landed deep in his belly. The person he argued with ended up in the hospital, then the morgue. Hottabych, unsurprisingly, was sent back to prison. Now, he happily shares stories with young inmates, occasionally sniffing a bar of soap one of them gave him. Conversations in prison never cease; there is always someone who's awake.

Prisoners in the *Stolypin* are divided according to regimes and lifestyles. The first division is dictated by the official rules for keeping prisoners, the second by unofficial, more practical ones. Besides the general and strict regimes, there is also a special one called *polosatiki,* or "striped," and for inmates sentenced to life, there is *pyzhiki,* literally, "fawns." The court decides based on the severity of the crime, but the "striped" regime is usually assigned to repeat offenders for committing the same type of crime repeatedly. A life sentence is given for a reason: each *pyzhik* almost always has a bunch of corpses to his name, although such a sentence can be received for killing a couple of policemen or one judge. They ride in the same *Stolypin,* but they always have a separate cell at the very end of the car along with a personal escort—they're even taken to the toilet in handcuffs. They have to pay a heavy price for the lives they've taken. The penal colonies for *pyzhiki* are the most cruel. No one really knows what happens in them. It's known that they often admit to other people's crimes to escape, even if temporarily, and find some respite in the central prison while the trial unfolds. During the trial, they confess to all crimes but prolong the process as much as possible. *Pyzhiki* usually don't talk much; there are things you can't speak of, things you prefer to keep silent about, and it's better to forget them altogether.

There are also the unconvicted and the colony-settlement prisoners among the travelers. As for the former ones, everything is clear with them—they haven't yet been given a final verdict. The guys who get sent to colony settlements typically have lighter sentences and are considered to be the lucky ones, including those avoiding alimony, DUI offenders who haven't harmed anyone yet, poachers, and other minor lawbreakers. They're given a year, maximum two. And, as often happens, it's precisely the person with such a short sentence who won't shut up. He's anxious and starts driving everyone as nuts as he is. If such a prisoner starts complaining too loudly about his relatively minor problems compared to others, he's told to be quiet and move to the upper bunk—the "palm tree"—and stay there until he's calmed down or reached the end of the trip.

In prison life, as in ordinary life, some rules are relative. All "regimes" must travel separately because the colonies are also different for everyone. The first-timers and the second-timers, under the general and strict regime, also serve their sentences separately, but not in the *Stolypin*. The head of the armed escort has a constant headache, even without them. He must organize everyone based on the rules, and it's essential to consider the convicts' own hierarchy, even though this isn't specified in any penal code. For the prisoners, this ranking matters more than any official categorization; it determines their fate. For example, the "former employees" are always placed separately. They're the convicted police officers, the FSB and the prosecutor's office employees, and other law enforcement officials. Judges also, in theory, belong to this group, but meeting a convicted judge in the *Stolypin* is more difficult than discovering Elvis Presley alive and well. The guards always keep them separate from the other prisoners; otherwise, prison justice is enacted and a lynching will occur right there.

The main part of the convicts are *muzhiki* of the "black suits" who live the life of a decent prisoner according to local concepts. They always try to stick together, and they are the backbone of the criminal world. They live like decent people but uphold thieves' traditions and codes. Their lives are on the right track. The opposite group, which decent prisoners despise, is that of the *krasnyye,* or *kozly*—those who cooperate with the administration and hold various positions in the colonies, from librarians to caretakers and foremen. Their goal is to get paroled, often by harassing other prisoners. The *krasnyye* usually keep to themselves—there is no sense of solidarity among their ranks. In prisons and colonies, *kozly* always sit and live separately, but in the *Stolypin* this isn't always possible, and they travel alongside the *muzhiki.* They travel quietly, and nobody bothers them unless someone holds a grudge against their way of life or the fate of prisoners.

The worst among the inmates are the sadists that willingly take part in tormenting others in disciplinary cells and strict-regime colonies. These individuals will show no mercy, and it can be challenging to identify them in the car during the transfer unless someone happens to recognize them. And nobody messes with the ordinary *krasnyye*—you demand nothing from prisoners for their way of life, they only need to be responsible for specific actions.

The third, most unprestigious group is the *obizhennyy,* who are sometimes also called *petukhi* ("roosters"), a caste of untouchables. They include mostly rapists, homosexuals, or victims of rape due to someone's malicious intent or their own negligence. These are the most despised prisoners, the lowest of the low. Washing toilets and providing sexual services is their eternal fate in the colonies. They always live separately, but, due to overcrowding in a car, they are often thrown into decent "human" cells. Nobody touches them either; they know their place: they quietly climb onto the top bunk, and you can't hear them until arrival. They are only allowed to go down to the restroom. Having *chifir* with the *obizhennyy* means to debase yourself and land in the roosters' coop. There is no return from there to a class of decent prisoners.

You can also encounter animals in the *Stolypin* who invoke hatred in every prisoner: pedophiles. These individuals always travel in a separate cell because the guards fear they might be slaughtered before reaching the prison. When such a person is escorted down the corridor, the entire car erupts with shouts and banging on the bars, like wild animals in a zoo. Nothing good is heard from the mouths of infuriated prisoners at the passing individual who has harmed a child. He walks with his head down, unaware that the promises others are making will soon become his harsh reality in the colony. And it'll even be much worse than that. The prisoner's world is tough, but just. Yet, like any prisoner, he hopes for the best, even though it will never come true.

Sometimes in the *Stolypin*, you can cross paths with a thief—the highest class of criminal circles—or a tramp, someone who aspires to, but has not yet been accepted into the thieves' world. This is the elite of the underworld—its leaders and authorities. Such a person is always transported in isolation, accompanied by a separate operative. But even in absentia, by voice alone, communication with such an "elder brother" means a lot for a simple prisoner. These godfathers are not only bearers of traditions and unwritten laws of the criminal environment, they are also the final authority in resolving disputes and conflicts between prisoners. But such a big fish is rare in the *Stolypin*.

The most frequent and most desirable companions for prisoners are, of course, women. They have their own colonies, and often prisons, or at least divisions within them. But here, in the car, they will be nearby, behind a thin, albeit firm, wall. Many prisoners haven't been with a woman for a very long time. The presence of these young ladies always adds a special charm to the transfer, setting it apart from the ones without them. Men attempt to swear less or discreetly pass goods like cigarettes or sweets to the women through the guards. If the guards refuse, the men find ways, even passing small bundles carefully through the bars from one cell to another and through the entire car. The women notice this extra attention and shamelessly exploit it, responding with promises and flirtation in exchange for packages. After the initial exchange of goods, a sign of promising future relationships, small personal notes start passing between them. Friendships form, communication improves, and the prison mail operates smoothly. The seasoned male and female inmates don't engage in these activities; such car flirtations are mainly a game among the younger inmates.

The next day of a joint journey, the relationship of couples who accidentally joined here develops into a stormy romance, with quivering glances, just a glimpse on the way to the restroom, with passionate finger touches through the grating on the way back. The lovers quickly move from nicknames to names, then to swearing their love and promising to wait for each other's release. This Shakespearean drama unfolds before dozens of unwilling onlookers, yet it doesn't deter or embarrass anyone. The longing for something warm and bright is so powerful, especially in prison where such things are scarce. Of course, young Caucasians demonstrate passion most of all, insisting that despite their language mistakes in Russian, they can woo any woman. Women periodically switch to their own fights, which turn into screaming, insults, spitting, and tearing out hair. Women don't follow the rules of decent prisoner behavior that prohibit swearing and assault. They have their own internal laws, or rather, total lack of them.

Women in prison are the most unnatural and alien phenomenon that can be found here. When a prisoner sees a woman being escorted down the corridor, his mind inevitably conjures his mother, wife, sister, or daughter in her place, and he understands that prison is one of the vilest inventions of civilization. A human being should not be in prison, a woman even less so. But there will continue to be prisons for as long as there are people willing to work in them.

Night. The car continues to live its own life, carrying people who are sitting together. The train gradually begins to slow down as it approaches the next station. Maybe, you'll get lucky again, and the escort soldier will crack the window open.

Lyokha-Leshch

Lyokha found himself in the intermediary state between being a perpetual thief and continuing his thieving ways—in other words, he was in prison. Despite being thirty-five years old, he looked much younger and behaved younger too. He was swift and nimble, and perhaps that's why he'd acquired the nickname "Leshch," a type of bream fish. Being cheerful and audacious—not to mention the life of the party—Lyokha was one of those inmates who effortlessly secured the prime bunk next to the window, far away from the entrance. He also had a knack for swiftly finding someone to carry his suitcase or brew him *chifir*. Moreover, he was a true criminal—a thief, a person who lived only through theft. This is generally one of the most respected professions in the criminal world, alongside robbers and burglars. Thieves are held in the highest regard because they have a stable income from their activities with minimal risks and short sentences in case of failure—one year, maybe two at most, even if caught multiple times. But if you've been to prison for theft for the seventh time, someone might smirk and say, "Hey, maybe it's just not your thing?"

Good thieves get caught rarely—they are cautious and meticulous, preferring to work solo. If they do team up for a job, it's usually with a trusted partner, ensuring that only one of them takes the fall in case they get captured. By doing so, they not only protect their accomplice, but they also get a shorter term. Group crimes can receive double the punishment. Professional thieves always look down on the majority of inmates who ended up in prison by accident, like the victors of drunken brawls who fatally stabbed their drinking buddies, the heroin addicts who destroyed themselves, the drug couriers and dealers, or the run-of-the-mill drug-thrill-seekers that fill Russian prisons. While those losers serve their seven to ten years, the skilled thief manages to come and go freely, pulling off multiple successful endeavors and relishing a vibrant existence. Lyokha happened to be one of those fortunate and skilled thieves who had a keen eye for spotting opportunities.

Prior to this stint, he had only been in prison once. And even then, he wouldn't have ended up there if he'd conducted himself as composedly in court as he had during the investigation. He and his partner were apprehended in the stairwell of the building they had just finished burgling. Spotting the police, they managed to discard their loot down the garbage chute. As they were being caught on the landing, they quickly agreed to stick to their story that they were not involved, just passing by. At the local police station, they were put in different rooms and beaten for three days, with brief breaks for the operatives to rest. But the guys stood firm, and from their swollen mouths, only one phrase could be heard: "We weren't there. We don't know. Why are you hitting us?" There was no evidence against them in the case—no keys or lock picks were found on them. The loot they'd disposed of through the garbage chute disappeared. Maybe someone had picked it up, or maybe they simply couldn't find that particular bag. After all, it's not forbidden to roam this country wearing leather gloves and getting confused in apartment buildings. The detectives were certain it was them, and Lyokha and his friend knew that they knew, so the game of cat and mouse continued—a waiting game to see who would lose patience or their teeth first.

The police eventually found themselves in a time crunch: they couldn't hold them forever, so they brought Lyokha and his accomplice to court to formalize their arrest, citing the injuries on the suspects' faces as evidence of resistance during apprehension. The judge listened indifferently to the testimonies of the two thieves—the fabricated one about the burglary and the true one about the police station—and sentenced them to two months of detention. The accomplice, perhaps wiser or rendered speechless, remained silent in response. However, Lyokha couldn't contain himself and uttered unnecessary remarks to the representative of Lady Justice. He boasted about how many times and in what various places he would stab her, first with his leather stiletto—that is, his dick—then with a real one when he caught her in a dark place. Offended, the judge proceeded to charge Lyokha with theft, sentencing him to two years for threats against the court. The silent accomplice, lacking evidence, was subsequently released.

The term, which he received for no particular reason, naturally upset Lyokha. That was only half the trouble, though. He'd been sent to prison with a *tochkovka*, a mark in his case papers indicating that he was a threat. The judge also seemed intent on making Lyokha's life difficult, as he never made it to the camp. Instead, he was sent to a provincial federal remand and correctional institution—something like a transit prison. Usually, inmates don't stay there for long, but Lyokha was kept there for the entire term of his sentence because it had a strict regime, and it was precisely there that they could "roast" him, according to the *tochkovka*. Immediately after the initial transit search, they locked him up in punitive confinement. It's a very small cell with nothing in it except a bed attached to the wall during the day, a small iron table with a chair bolted to the floor, and a washbasin where water drains through a pipe into the *alyonka*. That's one of the nicknames in prison for toilets, but calling it a toilet is too fancy. It's basically just a hole in the floor that is covered by a plug made from breadcrumbs placed into a plastic bag attached to a string. With this homemade plug, you can diminish the smell of the sewage, and with some skill, it even allows you to dispose of waste from your daily activities, since the *alyonka* doesn't have a built-in tank.

At 9:00 PM, the vertical bar is lowered, and a mattress with a blanket and pillow is handed out, signaling bedtime. At 5:00 AM, it's wake-up time: the bedding is collected, and the bed is once again attached to the wall. There's a check, a one-hour walk, meals are brought on a tray three times a day, then that's it. Inmates are forbidden from having any personal belongings, food, cigarettes, tea, and any form of minor household items. Except for the robe you wear and basic toiletries, nothing else is allowed in the punitive isolation cell, not even books or notebooks—only double bars on the window and a lamp that burns round the clock. A razor is only provided upon request, and you have to shave under the watchful eye of the guard, who makes sure you don't get any ideas and harm yourself. You get to bathe once a week and take a warm ten-minute shower.

In the punitive isolation cell, there are usually two people, but especially dangerous individuals—which, according to the administration, included Lyokha—could be held there alone. According to the rules, isolation can only last for a maximum of fifteen days. So after this stint came to an end, Lyokha was transferred to a regular but empty "hut," only to be placed back in isolation the next day. After the second stint, he would spend one day in a regular cell, then return for another fifteen days, repeating this cycle. Such a funhouse ride is reserved only for the chosen few. Lyokha got incredibly lucky—they gave him a season ticket for the entire two-year term. But he didn't despair or lose hope. The radio played a crucial role in boosting his spirits. They turned it up to maximum volume right outside Lyokha's door, blaring pop music of the lowest quality from morning until night after playing the Russian national anthem. Over the course of two years, Lyokha memorized all these songs and the names of Russian performers, along with their biographies, and planned a mass extermination of pop artists daily. Whether this torment was intentionally inflicted to drive the inmate crazy or it was a protective measure to prevent him from communicating with his neighbors remained unclear. In this system, not all the harm inflicted upon prisoners is a result of the guards' malicious intent. It often stems from their indifference, and this is par for the course. However, no inmate will acknowledge this; instead, he will grumble about every little thing, saying, "This is deliberate torment!"

Prisoners are a resilient group of people who can adapt to any conditions. Lyokha was particularly skilled at navigating such situations. He would ask the guard for a pen to write some trivial statement addressed to the administration. Then he would jot it down on the provided sheet and return it, while also managing to slip in a couple of small requests for necessities. During his outdoor exercise time, Lyokha would distribute these short notes into various small hiding spots in the exercise yard, which experienced inmates used everywhere. After a couple of days, if his "little messages" were discovered by inmates going to the same yard who understood the needs of others, one could find a few cigarettes with a couple of matches, a Snickers bar, or a handful of candy drops in their place. Lyokha would consume these items immediately, as it was risky to bring such prohibited items back to his cell. The next day, he would write new messages expressing his gratitude and new requests. In times of need, it's not embarrassing to ask for support from other prisoners. It's actually embarrassing not to help someone in need. For some reason, it is believed that prisoners are very mean and aggressive, ready to stab anyone with a shiv knife over any trifling matter. But that's not the case. The prison world is strict, but it has its own unwritten set of rules and mutual aid, and without either of them, survival would be impossible.

Like any seasoned prisoner, Lyokha was skilled at faking illness—an ability that develops quickly when one is locked up—to get transferred to the infirmary and take a short break from that exhausting mattress marathon. After trying various ways to exacerbate his chronic conditions and constantly acquiring new ones, Lyokha visited the local infirmary a couple of times but was not satisfied with it. It was just the same prison cell, the same meal, only with slightly better conditions, and still the same isolation. Upon hearing that the central prison hospital offered better conditions, he decided to make a trip there. By the way, prisoners don't say, "They were taken to court" or "Vasya was brought from the central prison." Inmates use different wording: "They were transferred" or "Vasya arrived from the *kicha*."* The difference may seem small, but it creates an illusion of freedom in deciding their own movement rather than being forcibly escorted. But in this case, the decision to go, or rather the actions leading to that result, were indeed made by Lyokha. His perpetually sickly appearance as a supposedly healthy prisoner prevented him from going beyond the neighboring corridor of the local infirmary. So, he decided to fake madness to secure a guaranteed three weeks of examinations and rest with better meals. Lyokha started acting crazy and "performing," then, in the end, he was sent to the prison psychiatric hospital.

He was content, but not for long. The thought of being placed with real psychos hadn't occurred to Lyokha. He'd hoped to meet fellow fakers there and have a good time together. He actually did have a good time, but the food fell short of his expectations. The ward in this prison hospital differed little from a regular cell, except that it was slightly more civilized and spacious. It was clean and quiet, and a female guard worked her way down the corridor. Compared to the cell where Lyokha was forcefully subjected to Russian pop music

---

* "Kicha" is slang for the main/central prison.

from morning till night for the past year, any other cell seemed a peaceful mansion to him. The ward had a two-person cell, and his cellmate seemed quiet and not very talkative. He avoided responding to questions about why he was serving time and what he was being treated for. Lyokha immediately recognized that he was a bit dazed, but he still had yet to experience the full effects of what delirium tremens does to people. As Lyokha received his lunch tray and took the plates through the hatch, simultaneously striking up a conversation with the corridor female guard, the neighbor managed to spill hot soup not only on himself but also on Lyokha's neck down the collar. Lyokha lightly tapped the psycho on the ear. The cellmate straightened up, held his hand out in front of him, and said in a sober voice, "Lyuba, I understand everything!" Lyokha wiped off the vegetable soup and thought it would end there, but in reality, this was only the beginning.

For the next three weeks, that retired alcoholic got on his nerves. Lyokha would go for some examinations, and his cellmate would turn everything upside down in their "hut." It turns out he was searching for where his wife had hidden the last bottle. A slap on the face, and "Lyuba, I understand everything now!" No sooner had Lyokha dozed off after a sleepless night cleaning up after Lyuba's husband, who had drowned himself in phantom booze, when the man stuffed two bags full of Lyokha's belongings and started banging on the door to be let out because the train was coming soon. Two solid blows and the double "Lyuba, I understand everything!" like a spell to ward off all troubles. Lyokha was already counting down the days until he would return to his beloved cozy isolation cell.

But shortly before this blissful moment, the deranged alcoholic was unexpectedly transferred. Lyokha was so exhausted by his company that he'd paid little attention to the new cellmate, who wrapped a blanket around his head and methodically smeared his own shit on the wall while reading poetry.

After the epic journey to the house of prison sorrow, the remainder of Lyokha's term passed quickly and, one could say, without incident. When he was released, he immediately returned to his old, familiar, and beloved ways. In memory of his solitary confinement, he tattooed the standard convict mark on his knuckles: five dots arranged like dice, symbolizing "one in four walls."

The first year after his release went well, then there was another setback after a certain incident, and Lyokha was declared wanted by federal authorities. After learning about it, he suddenly yearned for his disliked aunt who lived somewhere down south, whom he had seen only once in his childhood and had always dreamed of visiting again. Lyokha made a run for it but was apprehended at some passport control. "Purely by chance, bro!" Now he was heading back to his own city, on a long journey through Moscow along with a group of detainees being transported to the famous Koshkin House for a forensic psychiatric examination. There weren't any particularly rowdy individuals among them, although there were enough "loopy" ones, but Lyokha, with his experience in mental institutions, easily handled this squad. He talked a lot, humorously recounted stories from his life, lounging on the lower bunk near the window, sipping tea brewed by his fellow traveler, and engaged in a friendly competition of magic tricks with a fly, which, at his command, would either pull a match out of the box or put it back in.

Lyokha, like most criminals, was indifferent to politics, the ruling power, and Putin. He was a staunch opponent of the state because he didn't expect anything from it except for a new prison term. He didn't care at all about the specific regime currently governing his country, whether money was being stolen by the truckload or just in copy-paper boxes. Lyokha would steal his own share without their involvement. Like any inmate, any political changes in the country interested him in relation to only one question: "Will I get amnesty?"

When they were loaded onto the transport, Lyokha put on his branded clothes, shouted at Vaska,* who had grabbed his own bag but forgotten Lyokha's, then led the whole gang toward the exit, calculating along the way who among its members had the most supplies left and who would therefore have the honor of riding next to him in the carriage.

---

* A further diminutive of "Vasya."

Maga

Maga killed one Dagestani prosecutor. He never denied it—he was even proud of it. He was only given twelve years, though he could have been locked up for life for such a crime, since the Russian state didn't really like it when someone did something like this with one of its faithful servants. But Maga was lucky. Despite the fact that he emptied half of a Kalashnikov magazine into the prosecutor, they gave him a relatively short sentence. The thing was that he cooperated with the police—he confessed and even voluntarily surrendered to the authorities.

It's not that Maga felt deeply compelled to go to the police, he just had no other choice. He'd committed murder cleanly and walked away leaving no evidence. But the organizer of the assassination, and part-time driver who'd driven Maga directly to the scene, was soon detained. He confessed to everything and handed over his accomplice with all the details and addresses. But they failed to apprehend Maga—he was an experienced predator and went to the mountains, closer to his relatives.

He was wanted by the federal authorities for six months, with police dogs searching for him throughout Dagestan. Maga was hiding in different places, mostly with his relatives among the Avars of the Northeast Caucasus. He couldn't leave the republic secretly, but it was also impossible to hide forever, considering that they were searching for him on a grand scale—the prosecutor whom he'd shot hadn't been just any ordinary guy. Security forces blocked a village suspected of sheltering a fugitive. Armored personnel carriers and Ural trucks arrived, and special forces visited each house, questioning residents about Maga. This process frightened women and children, while men were occasionally taken for intense interrogations regarding their missing relatives. After these interrogations, some were released if they were still able to walk, while others were simply cast away. But not everyone returned home. That couldn't continue forever, and therefore, the elders asked Maga to surrender. He agreed and made arrangements through intermediaries given certain conditions, guarantees, and an approximate sentence. When everything was decided, the highlander moved from his lair to the central prison of Makhachkala.

During the investigation, Maga sincerely tried to describe where he'd tossed the assault rifle. They searched for it diligently for weeks, combing through the ravine and neighboring ones, even using an excavator to scoop up sand along with seawater. They found rusty pistols, a partial skeleton, and an empty safe, but these were traces of different stories in the restless Caucasian region. The coveted "Kalash" seemed to have vanished without a trace. Everyone was interested in finding it, including Maga himself, since the voluntary surrender of a weapon used during a crime was a good argument for the court. The investigation team regularly took Maga on the excursions to the area of the assault rifle excavation, including to the site of that epic, Xerxes-style digging-up of the sea with excavators. Maga sincerely tried to recall the place where he'd hastily dropped the rifle that night, constantly offering new locations for digging pits, but the weapon was in no hurry to give up, unlike its owner.

The investigators thought that Maga was mocking them, so they beat him. He was beaten quite often. They beat him right after the arrest because they couldn't find him for a long time. They beat him while they were looking for the assault rifle, and even harder when they realized it would never be found. They also beat him in prison, regularly and for no reason, not because he'd violated some rule, but because it was customary there. Maga finally asked the investigator, "Why are they constantly beating me? I've already confessed to everything, haven't I?" The investigator thought for a moment, then scratched his head. The beatings became a little less frequent after that.

The prosecutor who Maga executed had been some big shot. Shortly before, he'd returned from Moscow where the chief commander awarded him with a personal pistol and another state decoration. As it turned out, the latter would be awarded posthumously, since right upon his arrival, he was met by Maga with a Kalash at the entrance to his house. Whenever Maga retold this episode, he always jerked the imaginary bolt of the assault rifle and said, "As-salamu alaykum!" while slightly shaking from the virtual recoil.

Though Maga approached the case with a smile, it was a high-profile one even in his perpetually turbulent republic. While the performer and organizer were detained and confessed, the person who ordered the murder remained elusive.

OLEH SENTSOV

In Russia, especially in Dagestan, the norm was to pursue whoever seemed most useful or suitable as the main instigator of contract killings. Truth seldom mattered, even in minor cases, let alone in such significant ones. Maga and his accomplice belonged to the same Dagestani clan, a group connected more by shared interests in money and power than by family or national ties. Life's logic suggested looking for the instigator at the top of Maga's group. However, due to the political situation in the republic, authorities began detaining individuals from another competing clan, attempting to link them to the case, seemingly for different reasons.

The main goal of this plan was to snatch up the mayor of Makhachkala, the most powerful and influential figure in Dagestan. Considering himself untouchable, the mayor did as he pleased, accustomed to everyone bowing down. However, he overlooked the fact that only one person in Russia could truly be untouchable—the one sitting in the Kremlin, not the Makhachkala City Council. Eventually, the mayor, nicknamed "Bloody Roosevelt" due to his disability from an assassination attempt that left him wheelchair-bound—his tough character had been shaped during the criminal conflicts of the '90s—was outmaneuvered. He was airlifted, wheelchair and all, to the primary Russian prison for such special cases.

While on trial for allegedly attempting to shoot down a competitor's passenger plane from his wheelchair using a portable air defense system, another case involving the murder of the prosecutor emerged. Six individuals had already testified that the mayor instructed them to locate Maga's accomplice so that he could find Maga himself. The final witness, armed with an assault rifle, declared "As-salamu alaykum!" Maga, however, wasn't forced to identify anyone, as the individuals had accused each other multiple times without his involvement. Maga, seeing the main initiator on wheels for the first time, harbored doubts. The six, who didn't immediately confess, faced some beatings and extensive torture—mainly with electric shocks. The wires were wrapped around their fingers, hands, or genitals, then connected to the outlet. Some started to sign everything once they heard screams from neighboring cells, but they were tortured later anyway—just in case—because it was customary for them. They were willing to say anything to stop the torture. Maga's accomplices were fortunate that their case involved a criminal investigation, albeit with some political aspects. The key was that authorities didn't spend time on actual terrorists in the North Caucasus. These guys called themselves "wolves of the forest" and, when they were captured, they would get a tube inserted into the anus and a barbed wire would be pushed into it half a meter inward and the same length outward. Then the tube was pulled out, and the barbed wire remained, and the torturee was thrown into the cell like that: "Well, since you're a wolf, here is your tail!"

Six months later, after confessions were beaten out of them and a case against the all-powerful invalid was cooked up, a helicopter arrived to rescue the six from the Dagestan Gestapo. Initially disoriented in the capital's prison for state criminals, they couldn't believe they were no longer being tortured, and guards greeted them with a "Good morning." Realizing they had moved from hell to heaven, they unanimously disavowed the testimonies obtained under duress. Despite showing scars and describing torture, the judges leaned toward previous protocol pages. It seemed the case arbitrators had no alternative, given the unforgiving system that necessarily did away with any part challenging it. Consequently, those uninvolved in the assassination attempt and prosecutor's demise received sentences ranging from fifteen years to life, including the wheelchair-bound leader, who showed no emotion at his verdict. Maga received a twelve-year sentence for his actions, but the others harbored no resentment toward him. They understood he hadn't dragged them into the situation; they were simply connected to him and his case.

Maga had ten brothers, all wild highlanders like him. Once, three of them went to a restaurant where some other Dagestanis made inappropriate remarks as they passed by their table. Things escalated quickly, with everyone spilling into the street, pulling out pistols, and shooting at each other. Maga's relatives turned out to be better shots, sending their opponents to the cemetery. After this incident, the brothers' paths diverged: one to the intensive care unit, another to prison, and the third onto the wanted list. Fortunately, things calmed down before they could reach their cars and grab assault rifles. They were in Dagestan, after all, not Somalia, which meant that well-mannered people didn't bring Kalashnikovs to restaurants; they kept them in their car trunks.

Maga had a girlfriend whom he considered his bride, though it was uncertain if she saw it the same way. Her grandmother, of Ukrainian origin, had been kidnapped by a spirited highlander during Soviet times and brought to his village. Surprisingly, she adapted quickly and, as a young woman, rose to power both within her new family and on the entire street. As a grandmother, she held the whole village in fear. One of her granddaughters inherited her assertiveness, which was likely what had captivated Maga. His heart remained faithful to her despite his prison hardships. However, there was a problem—Grandma didn't approve of Maga. She was familiar with such men, as many in their village were similar. Consequently, the beloved granddaughter was sent away from the daring highlanders to Moscow to establish a new life and pursue a career as a supermarket seller. It seemed the bride herself was none too thrilled with Maga, as otherwise, she wouldn't have followed her grandmother's advice over her heart, explaining her silence to Maga's letters and calls from prison. Maga couldn't really comprehend her way of refusing him. After one of his unsuccessful attempts to get through to her—the last one, as it turned out—Maga returned to the cell silent and angry. He tore all the old letters, photographs, addresses, and contacts to pieces, then, with particular cruelty, carried out an imagined "point bombardment" of some street in a small town near Moscow, saying at the same time: "Shave her head and pour iodine on her, shave her head and pour iodine ... and let her walk through the streets like that ... "

Maga enjoyed playing backgammon, but he wasn't great at it. He easily got nervous, struggled to admit mistakes, and didn't know when to step back or retreat. He always believed his game pieces were in the right place—it was just the dice not cooperating, and he couldn't have miscalculated. After the board slammed shut, signaling the premature end of the game, dice and pieces scattered across the cell amid Avar curses. Maga proudly abstained from helping to search for them or engaging with his, in his view, defeated cellmate.

Maga's unusual fondness for watching repetitive Russian TV series about the tough lives of agricultural workers puzzled others in prison. When such a show aired, he adamantly refused to change the channel, much to the annoyance of fellow inmates. Arguing with Maga was problematic; he'd had a lot of experience boxing in his youth. Despite claiming to have taken his fair share of beatings, he took pleasure in showcasing his old boxing skills to anyone who doubted him. Maga considered himself a Muslim, but he observed namaz prayers irregularly, and his periods of religious zeal alternated with apathy—when he simply lay on the bunk and stared into space. He never read books.

Maga loved watching TV news, especially when it dealt with global events. He had a routine of discussing each country mentioned on the news, pointing out the challenges they faced. According to him, Russia was the only place that thrived in the world of information. The density of his criticisms intensified as soon as it came to gays or, God forbid, their marriages. In such cases, all that was left of Europe was the Mercedes factory—generously left intact by Maga's calls to bomb the continent solely because of his devotion to this old brand-name. America had long since become a radioactive wasteland, and Israel had been reduced to a smoking crater. Maga believed he was fighting against global imperialism, but ongoing concerns about the gays and the Jews kept him awake at night, leading to frequent trips to the toilet. One could hear constant comments from there about how he was about to get Frau Merkel to quench her thirst or feed something unpleasant to Mr. Obama, depending on the purpose of his visit. Maga's sense of humor was quite something. On the contrary, he respected Putin very much because he looked like a person who could start bombing those damned *pindosy** for real. When Putin shifted to bombing Muslims in Syria, Maga grew contemplative. He chose not to comment on those reports, acting as if they didn't exist. Based on the news, it seemed unlikely to ignite anti-Semitism in Putin's heart. Maga held on to a glimmer of hope that, at the very least, the Russian president disapproved of the gays, the "tolerant ones," as Maga liked to refer to them. Attempts to explain to him the correct meaning of this word always ended in failure and could incur terrible suspicions of sympathy for homosexuals. Like many Russian citizens, Maga preferred not to notice the domestic problems of the country, which he faced firsthand, especially in the run-up to the invasion of Americans, gays, and Jews. Maga absolutely refused to connect the lawlessness that was happening in his native North Caucasus with the actions of his idol and the system he'd built, believing that only Obama and too many still-living prosecutors were to blame.

---

* A pejorative term Russians use for Americans.

Sasha

Sasha couldn't see well in his left eye. It wasn't some condition that he was born with—it was something that typically happened with old age, but whether old age was the culprit here remained a question. It was pretty noticeable that Sasha's eye didn't work well, since he had a cataract and the eye always moved in the wrong direction. His eye had gotten like that after Sasha had been hit with an arrow. And when I say "hit" I don't want to suggest that it happened on purpose. It happened accidentally, but he did bear some of the blame for having gotten into such a mess.

When an arrow is flying straight toward your eye, your vision doesn't perceive it as an arrow. You only see a rapidly approaching black dot. Then—bam!—you have one eye different from the other, if it remains in its place at all. When such a dot approaches, you need to act quickly; otherwise, you'll have to get several surgeries and spend many years applying drops from various vials three times a day to regain even a tiny bit of vision.

When Sasha noticed the flying dot, he also tried to do something, but couldn't. The thing was, at that time, he was standing among the ranks of heavily armed infantry of the old Russian army, holding a shield and a spear in close proximity to his comrades. Suddenly, there was a black dot—bam! After that, three cheerfully colored vials were always by his side. The arrow whistled into Sasha's eye, not intentionally, but not accidentally either—it was trained to do so. More precisely, a poorly trained girl was trying to shoot from a bow at a well-trained formation of warriors—presumably for another campaign to Tsargrad.

The girl was not supposed to hit Sasha's eye specifically, but she had. Sasha was supposed to dodge it, but he hadn't. Pharmaceutical companies producing colored vials were sponsors of the next historical reenactment tournament.

"And that's how it's always been," Sasha shrugged, telling the story as if he were talking about a carton of sour kefir or a September rain. Sasha made a dismissive gesture with his left hand, which also had its issues. While the fingers were all there, he had some problems with his skin, which meant that his hand was always slightly clenched and wrinkled, like a bird's claw. He'd left his original skin, given to him by nature, hanging on some rusty fence back in his childhood. That's when the doctors sewed on a replacement, and apparently, without much searching, they'd cut out a large patch from the same arm, from the bicep area. It wasn't their finest operation, although it could have been a lot worse. As a result, Sasha looked more or less fine on the right side, but the left side didn't quite work out for him. In tough times in a bustling crowd in an underpass, with a certain degree of exposure and from certain angles, he'd manage. But Sasha probably wouldn't have reached that point anyway, since he came from a good family.

In school, Sasha excelled academically, participated in numerous clubs and activities, and didn't have any harmful habits, except for his tendency to encase himself in armor and sword fight with other reckless enthusiasts. Later, he enrolled in university, majoring in physics and mathematics. His parents had every reason to be proud of him. Despite this, Sasha wasn't a complete bookworm or nerd. He enjoyed drinking beer, hanging out with friends, and going on dates with girls. Despite his less-than-presentable appearance, girls were attracted to him, which probably meant that external qualities weren't as important to them as his open and kind character.

He was locked up during his final year. After three years passed, Sasha could only vaguely explain why he, along with two accomplices, had attempted to detonate a bomb targeting the head of the local migration service. At the time, it must have seemed very important to him. The assassination attempt failed, even though they had already planted the bomb under the unsuspecting official's car. It could have been because Sasha made errors during assembly, or the explosives were unexpectedly discovered before the intended time, or they'd simply fallen off, unable to cling onto the dirty undercarriage with Scotch tape. In the world of terrorists, even more significant blunders could happen due to minor details. For Sasha and his group of fellow would-be bombers, a small SIM card in a cell phone played a crucial role in their discovery. It had been inserted into a cheap mobile phone that served as the triggering mechanism for the revenge weapon they had manufactured.

The Avengers, for reasons unknown, hoped that this SIM card would be destroyed along with the other components during the explosion. But it didn't work out that way. In such situations, some find themselves betrayed by their own partners, while others are compromised by a tiny piece of plastic. It was precisely this seemingly silent object that had betrayed Sasha. It couldn't speak, but in the depths of its memory, it stored a lot of information, including details about their group. All the intelligence agencies had to do was use this list to identify those involved, which was already a matter of technique. When they were arrested a week later, they immediately confessed. There was no need for torture because resisting would have been foolish. The evidence piled up from all sides: fingerprints on the internal device of the bomb, footage from surveillance cameras, wiretapped conversations after the failed attempt, and various additional materials discovered during police searches. As the device maker, Sasha received a ten-year sentence, while the other direct participants in the terrorist plot received longer terms. Sasha didn't like to delve into who was to blame for everything, nor did he enjoy recalling why he got involved in the first place. He habitually waved away these events with his bird-like hand, as if they were foolish dreams from the past.

After the verdict, Sasha wasn't sent to a penal colony. At that time, another group of young extremists was found with the exact same literature of malicious content as Sasha had. As a result, Sasha's transfer was delayed, and he was held either as a witness or as a suspect in this new case. "They won't give me much time." Sasha waved his hand, dismissing the annoying fly. "At most, they'll add six months." Stuck between two proceedings, he had been living peacefully in the small FSB prison of his southern hometown for three years. Sasha had become a seasoned resident there, and the prison guards treated him as their own. The grim bearded men transported in batches from the Caucasus for similar charges were treated completely differently.

Sasha proudly showed photos of his family to anyone interested. It was your typical ordinary family. His mother, a middle-ranking civil servant in her fifties with dyed blonde hair, was a lifelong supporter of the United Russia political party. His father, a regular hard-working man in his pre-retirement years, had the look of someone whose son was in prison. His older sister and her husband were successful, well-off bank employees with an adorable little child. There were many photographs and letters. In addition to his relatives, Sasha maintained extensive correspondence with a bunch of other people—his acquaintances and girlfriends. While prison often led to severed connections with the outside world, Sasha's situation was the opposite. Sasha had already served three years for the morally questionable actions for which he'd been incarcerated, but he received frequent and abundant letters. He eagerly replied, spending a couple of hours each day on them, most of that time thinking about what else to write; however, after three years of correspondence from a place where nothing much happens, he often struggled to come up with new things to write about. Sasha had a whole box of new holiday greeting cards, with greetings that included "Happy New Year!" and "Congratulations to the Newlyweds!" He never disclosed the circumstances of how he had acquired such an impressive collection or why it consisted of just two types of cards. But he sent them to anyone and everyone throughout the year, on any occasion—even without a specific reason.

Sasha loved buckwheat, saving tea bags to reuse them later, fantasy, esoterica, and arguing. In fact, he enjoyed arguing more than anything else. He could argue about anything, and the initial side he took in an argument was not as important to him as the process of arguing itself. Despite being well-read and knowledgeable, Sasha's perspective on the world was influenced by elves and reptilians. They had shaped his views, allowing him to see things from a distinct angle, using his remaining first eye and newly awakened third eye. The theory that humanity was created by extraterrestrials in an attempt to grow obedient slaves left no doubt in Sasha's mind. And when they'd realized there was too much hassle with us and little benefit, they flew away, leaving us to our own devices. Since then, for the past ten thousand years, we had been fumbling along without coming up with anything substantial, except for the wheel, gunpowder, and sophisticated ways to kill each other. While our ancestors managed to snatch first- and second-generation technologies from the wreckage of the alien ship, the third was purely a human invention, diversified over the centuries through all means available to our wild and one-sided nature. A hundred years ago, the extraterrestrials returned and found that the human civilization they had birthed had produced certain results. At the very least, people had universally learned to wear clothes, stopped eating each other, and even managed to devise a secret government to which they willingly submitted, unaware of its existence. The aliens immediately made contact with this council of three hundred, exerting pressure and threatening until they took control, slowly feeding some of the oldest technologies through their influence agents to bring humanity into the light, so to speak. This explained the rapid progress in scientific development in recent decades. However, our creators from other worlds periodically thinned out Earth's population through artificial wars, disasters, and diseases—like thinning out a carrot patch—to prevent us from growing excessively, overdeveloping, then rebelling. They continued to nurture our race for some mission, but Sasha didn't yet know what that mission was. Additionally, the extraterrestrials possessed technology for direct mind control, and Sasha himself was a shining example of its effectiveness.

Half of the books that made up the prison library collection were sent by Sasha's friends. He would initially read them in bulk, then pass them on to the administration for other inmates. The selection was specific: knights and dragons, aliens and the Illuminati, underground gnomes, one hundred ways to build Egyptian pyramids, and everything written by Mikhail Veller. Sasha held great respect for Veller as the only true Russian author and simply as a person with whom he agreed on many things. Veller, if he met Sasha, would have probably not agreed with him on anything. It was a one-sided connection, but Sasha, as a faithful apprentice of Veller, was fine with it. He regularly received printouts of Veller's latest statements, and Sasha passionately agreed with him, always reading them aloud. Veller was the only person Sasha didn't argue with.

Sasha liked to have the television on all the time, even if it was playing quietly in the background while he wasn't watching. It made him feel less alone. Like most Russians, he respected Putin for his foreign policies but criticized him for his domestic ones. The love for the former overshadowed the flaws in the latter. It was difficult to explain and understand, but many Russian citizens lived harmoniously with this feeling, and Sasha was among them. But there was one noticeable difference: Sasha believed there were seven Putins. He couldn't always distinguish them by sight when watching the news or reading the newspaper, but he claimed to have a collection of photos at home with a comparative analysis of their ears, necks, and botoxed cheeks. According to him, he could accurately identify which body double was being presented to the people. Sometimes Sasha suspected that he had been imprisoned precisely for exposing this state secret, and the failed explosion was just an excuse.

Sasha was sleeping in the same position as when he was watching TV, so it was difficult to tell if he was still here or already on his way to Rivendell in the dim evening light. Visual identification was challenging, and one had to rely more on the sound of his light snoring. Without computer games, Sasha played chess in prison, but he didn't try too hard. He rushed through the game and sometimes ended up losing. But he always fought until the end, and even when he was left with only one king against the entire enemy army, he demanded a checkmate from his opponent. It was clear that Sasha was a resilient person, and in case of retreat, he could be trusted to blow up a bridge.

Spetsblok[*]

A mini-play of a day of life in one spetsblok of one of the central prisons.

Characters:
Cell 90: Magas, a forty-one-year-old man, Ingush, charged with terrorism, serving two life sentences.
Cell 91: Valei, a twenty-eight-year-old man, Ossetian, "orderly officer of the republic," serving fifteen years for political banditry.
Cell 92: Amazon, a forty-seven-year-old woman, Russian, charged with robbery, shooting of policemen, serving a twenty-one-year term.
Cell 93: Rashid, a thirty-five-year-old man, Tajik, wanted to go to Syria, received seven years in prison.
Cell 94: Azamat, a thirty-two-year-old man, Dagestani, charged with illegal arms possession, serving twelve years in prison.
Cell 9: Artur, a thirty-eight-year-old man, Ossetian, accomplice

---

[*] A unit within a colony for holding inmates deemed a higher security risk.

of Valei, serving sixteen years in prison for giving someone a ride to the wrong place.

The duty officer, the chief, the *balander*.

The stage is a replica of a prison's spetsblok corridor. It features six cell doors in a row numbered 90 to 9; they have feeders, peepholes, and small lattice ventilation windows above them. On the left side, there's an entrance door to the spetsblok, while a security camera is positioned on the right at door number 9. Dim light fixtures are suspended above. Instead of walls, the corridor has partitions between cells, providing a view of the basic interiors—iron beds, tables and chairs, washbasins, and toilet bowls—within each cell.

The nightlight is switched on, and the Azan—the call to prayer—resounds. Subdued muttering in Arabic follows. In cells 90, 91, and 93, people are seen performing morning prayers on makeshift rugs, sheets, and oilcloths. The prayer concludes.

Daylight floods in, accompanied by the brief wail of a siren. Footsteps echo on the stairs. The door to the spetsblok opens with a key, and the chief, wielding a large wooden hammer, and the duty officer, carrying a set of keys, enter the corridor. The Russian Federation anthem plays. Both the chief and the duty officer are overweight, dressed in the blue-and-black-spotted uniforms of the Federal Penitentiary Service. The chief is notably fatter.

The prisoners wear a variety of clothes: tracksuits, house pants, shorts, T-shirts, tank tops, flip-flops, and slippers. They don't have uniforms at the moment; they'll receive them once they're in the colony.

The duty officer (loudly): Wake up! Get ready for the morning check!

The duty officer walks up to the first cell, peeks through the peephole, then opens the door. The prisoner steps into the corridor, stands facing an imaginary wall with legs apart and palms out against the wall. The duty officer hesitantly pats the prisoner down, searching thoroughly. During this, the prisoner provides information about himself: full name, birth year, charges, prison term, and the strict regime applied to everyone.

The chief enters the cell and begins tapping his hammer loudly on iron objects, checking for structural integrity and simultaneously inspecting under the table and bed. He carries out the examination with minimal movements, then calmly exits.

Chief: Complaints? Statements?
Prisoner: No.
The duty officer: You can go back.

The prisoner goes into his cell, and the duty officer shuts the door with a loud clang, glancing through the peephole once more. The chief and the duty officer move on to the next door, repeating the process with a new prisoner. Everything happens routinely and calmly, without unnecessary commotion or cruelty.

This begins with cell number 90 and goes to cell number 9. Once it's over, the chief and the duty officer leave.

Artur stands on his bed to reach the ventilation window and shouts into it. Many prisoners do this, as it makes their voices easily heard through the corridor and doors.

95: Good morning, spetsblok!

A dissonant echo of voices from still half-asleep prisoners comes back to him. Some approach their doors, others attempt to peek through the peephole, gently opening it with their fingers, and a few even pull themselves up to the ventilation.

95: Nine one! Nine one!

91: Speak!

95: Valiko, how are you, brother? Do you need anything?

91: No, Arturio! From the bottom of my heart, bro! I have enough of everything for now!

95: Well, you can make some noise[*] if you need anything. I'll push[†] as much as possible.

91: Sounds good.

95: What's that?

91: I said *sounds good*!

95: Got it . . . Any news about crude oil prices yet, Valiko?

91: I dunno. I haven't turned on the news yet.

---

[*] Prison slang for "let us know."
[†] Prison slang for "send, provide."

95: Understood. Well, keep us informed.

91: Uh-huh. (*Moves away from the ventilation window.*)

95: Azamat, my brother, do you need anything?

94: Push sausages.

95: No sausage!

94: Then, some lard—half a kilo!

95: The lard is also gone. Magas ate all the lard.

90: What are you talking about! I don't eat human flesh!

Everyone laughs.

95: Magas, my brother, how are you?

90: I'm fine.

95: I heard that you're going to live two lives, is that true?

90: Ha-ha. Yes! I got the second life sentence yesterday.

93: Subhan Allah!

90: Don't worry, Rashid! Everything is in the hands of the Almighty!

93: Inshallah!

95: Magas! Nine zero!

90: Speak.

95: Magas, how many children do you have?

90: Five. For now. (*Laughs.*)

95: Magas, what a handsome bastard, he never loses hope that he'll outlive all his tormentors.

90: Hang 'em all!

94: Definitely!

95: Nine three! Rashid!

93 (*replies in Russian with a strong Tajik accent*): Speak!

95: Have you recited your prayer?

93: Of course, of course! I already did it this morning.

95: So, you can eat some lard then?

93: Pork?

95: What do you mean? It's not human!

93 (*frowning*): Then I won't.

95: And what about *kurdyuk**? It's lamb. (*pronounced in a mocking Tajik accent.*) Fresh and tender.

93 (*overjoyed*): Then I will!

95: But there is no tail fat! (*laughs, but already alone—not all of his jokes land.*)

Footsteps and the clatter of an iron cart echo on the stairs. The duty officer, carrying keys, enters, and behind him comes the balander, wearing a white and greasy tunic and a hat. He pushes a cart with two large food containers and a ladle in each.

The duty officer: Get ready to eat!

The duty officer and the balander go to the end of the corridor, beginning breakfast service from cell 95. The duty officer opens the feeder, and the prisoner puts their empty aluminum bowl on it. The balander ladles gruel into the bowl, the prisoner takes it, and the duty officer closes the feeder with a thud.

95 (*looking out through the feeder*): Boss, let's pass some boiling water to 90.

---

* Tail fat.

The duty officer: Not allowed.

The duty officer closes the feeder, and he and the balander move on.

91: Artur! I'll push! I already boiled it.
The duty officer: Not allowed.
94: Duty officer! He doesn't have an outlet in there!
The duty officer: Exactly. There are no outlets in the punishment cell.

The duty officer closes the feeder of cell 94, and he and the balander move on.

93: Brother Magas shouldn't be in the punishment cell!
The duty officer (*mocking the Tajik's accent*): Shouldn't, shouldn't. (*Slams the feeder.*)

Amazon from cell 92 receives her ration in silence. The balander pours it for her a little more carefully than for the others. They approach cell 91.

91: He's in the cell because you don't have any vacant chambers. His bed isn't even secured to the wall.

Valiko takes his portion and then puts down a small plastic bowl with steaming water in it.

91: Boss, please pass it on. He's serving two life sentences; he has a lot of suffering in store. (*Puts a pack of cigarettes next to the bowl.*)

In his usual manner, the duty officer swipes the pack into his pocket and signals to the balander. The balander takes the bowl in his hands, the duty officer closes the feeder, then they move on to cell 90.

The duty officer (*muttering quietly to himself*): It begins.
91: Thank you, boss!
The duty officer: Corruption starts with a pack of cigarettes.

The duty officer opens the feeder of cell 90. The balander silently pushes forward the bowl with boiling water into it and pours the gruel into a bowl. The duty officer slams the feeder; stomping and rattling, he and the balander go out with the cart while the door to the spetsblok is left ajar.

91: Did you get it, Magas?
90: Yes. Thanks, from the bottom of my heart, Valei.
91: Well, you know it yourself!

For some time, there's silence in the spetsblok, only the clang of spoons on bowls is heard. Then the water starts gurgling as the prisoners wash their dishes after breakfast. Some do their business, small and large, on the toilet; it is fenced off by a small partition, by the slonik, so their actions are only partially visible. The TV is turned on in cell 91, the only one where TV is available, and the*

---

* Literally "small elephant," slang for the toilet partition in a cell.

OLEH SENTSOV

news begins to murmur indistinctly. The TV is old, with a room antenna, so the signal is bad and noisy.

95: Valiko! Nine one!

91: Speak!

95: What's up with the price of crude oil?

91: Wait! (*After a pause.*) Thirty-five a barrel!

93: Wai-wai!*

95: Great!

91: Will Putin be taken out soon?

95: Coming soon!

91: Will they let us all out?

95: Yes! Everyone! Even Magas!

Everyone laughs.

90: Hang 'em all!

Cautiously, almost tiptoeing, squeezing through the door to the spetsblok, the duty officer enters and begins to eavesdrop at each of the doors.

95 (*after a pause*): Valiko, what else do they say?

91: All sorts of stuff. Nothing special.

95 (*after a pause*): Valiko!

91: Speak!

95: Listen, why do you deserve to be the only one with a TV?

---

* The Caucasus ethnic groups' equivalent of English "wow!"

91 (*laughs*): I dunno! Some Ukrainian spy was here before me—they brought it here for him, but they haven't taken it away from me yet.

95: And what did he do to deserve a TV?

91: He confessed that he'd killed forty people in the Donbas in one night.

93: Wai-wai!

94: He killed forty people in just one night?

93: Where did he kill them?

95: Rashid, you should also confess that you whacked forty people, then you'll see—you'll definitely get one too.

Laughter.

93: Nope! Rashid wouldn't have killed that many!

95: Well, at least twenty! Maybe that's enough to earn a radio! You'll know when to start praying.

94 (*interrupting*): Valei! How much did they give him for so many people murdered?

95: Three life sentences!

Laughter.

91: No. Seven years.

94: Seven years!

93: Subhan Allah! Seven years for forty corpses!

91: No. He only confessed to killing forty, but at the trial, he retracted his testimony. He said that he'd been tortured.

94: We were all tortured, so what? If they gave me seven, I'd confess to a hundred!

90: Sounds like he gave up early, on the very first night.

95: Magas!

90: What?

95: How long were you tortured?

90 (*after a pause*): For three months.

94: And you confessed?

91: Nobody lasts long. No man can ...

90: I only confessed to what I did. And only at the end.

94: You see! And here, he confessed to forty on the first night.

91: The first night is the hardest ...

90: They all should be hanged.

95: And what about the spy, Valei?

91: I told you—they gave him seven years!

95: For what?

91: For stealing a car! How can they let him out!

The whole corridor begins to laugh out loud. It is only Rashid who understood little of the conversation.

93: Subhan Allah! Seven years for forty people! What kind of a country is this, and why did Rashidka come here!

95: What do you mean why?! He wanted to get married!

94: To the FSB girl!

95: Then take her to the Islamic State!

Everyone starts laughing even harder again, even Rashid and the duty officer who has relaxed his vigilance.

94: Shush! Looks like this rat is eavesdropping again.

Silence fills the spetsblok, and the duty officer stands frozen, hesitant to take a step. A person attempts to peer through the peephole, pushing back the iron curtain with a finger. Azamat forcefully strikes his door, startling the duty officer. He steps back, and his retreat is audible. Someone whistles after him.

Life in the cells resumes. Valei watches TV in his cell. Magas engages in exercises—push-ups, abs, and shadow boxing. Someone paces back and forth, another lies on a bunk, someone is immersed in a book, and someone brews tea, tinkering with a mug and a boiler.

91: Thirty-three a barrel! Putin is done soon!

95: Yeah, not long to wait! (*Laughs.*)

93: Inshallah!

94 (*speaking with Abdullah's intonation as if demanding Gulchitai to bring some water*[*]): Nine two. (*Pause.*) Nine two.

92: Yes . . .

94: Come closer to the ventilation.

Both Azamat and Amazon pull themselves up to the ventilation and start whispering about something slowly and indistinctly. Artur is also pressing his ear close to the vent, but he can't really make out anything they're saying. He goes down to the peephole and opens it from the inside with his finger.

---

[*] A reference to the characters Abdullah and Gulchitai in the famous Soviet movie *White Sun of the Desert* (1970).

OLEH SENTSOV

Rashid is sitting and reading a big book.

95: Nine three. Nine three. (*In a loud whisper.*) Rashid!
93: Huh? Who is this?
95: Are you acting dumb or what? It's me, Artur.
93: Ah! What? I'm reading the Quran.
95: Wait. Try to listen to what they're talking about.
93: Who?
95: Well, those two.
93: Ah! Azamat and Amazon?
95: Shush, you. Yes, them.
93 (*listens, but not for long*): I don't know. Unclear. They speak
quietly.

There is silence in the cell corridor.

92 (*barely audible*): . . . I only saw you once and even then, it
was through a crack . . . when you went for a walk . . .
95: Rashid! What has she just said?
93 (*not particularly listening and continuing to read the book,
moving his lips*): I don't know. I can't hear. It's not decent.
95: It's not decent? You mean like, "I'm throwing you on the
bed, tearing your robe, looking for you in your gray curls,
it's like a jungle in there!"? (*Laughs, once again alone.*)

*Rashid grumbles discontentedly and buries himself deeper into the
book.*

95: Nine one! Valiko!

91: Speak!

95: What's with the price of crude oil?

91: I don't know.

95: What?

91: I don't know. I'm watching a movie!

95: About what?

91: It's not clear yet . . .

95: About what? About love? You're lucky! Love is the only thing I can listen to here . . .

The whispering between Azamat and the Amazon has ceased, and they both settle down, going about their tasks. The Amazon is inspecting her poorly dyed and untidy blonde hair, while Azamat simply paces back and forth in the cell.

95: Nine one!

91: Speak!

95: How's the movie, Valiko?

91: Not that interesting; I switched to a different channel.

95: And crude oil?

91: Wait . . . (*Pause.*) It's thirty-one.

95: Oh! So it won't be long!

93: Long until what?

95: Until lunchtime!

93: Ah! What about prayer?

90: There's still time. I'll tell you brother!

Magas has finished doing his physical exercises and is now freshening up over the washbasin.

93: Sounds good, brother!

Magas wipes himself with a towel and walks up to the door.

90: Valei! Nine one. (*He speaks in a low voice, so even the neighbor doesn't hear him right away.*)

91: Speak, Magas!

90: You, brother, why do you watch this haram all day long from morning to evening? Is this what a Muslim is supposed to do? Prayer is coming soon.

91: Magas, I . . .

90: We already talked about this. Come on, get closer to the ventilation.

Valei switches off the TV and approaches the ventilation window. Magas does the same, and they begin talking quietly. Afterward, both come down. Magas sings the Azan—a loud, melodious call to prayer. Valei and Rashid then perform a purification ritual, Wudu, over the washbasin.

90: It's time, brothers!

Magas, Valei, and Rashid begin praying almost simultaneously in their cells. Artur is bored in his cell; he cannot live without communication for a long time.

95: Nine four!

94: Speak.

95: Azamat, how are you doing there?

94: What do you mean?

95: *Whaddyamean?* Are you that serious there?

94: Of course!

95 (*after a pause*): And what will you do with her husband?

94: He's not her husband.

95: Then who?

94: Nobody. Consider him a nobody.

95: Ah . . . Well then, I see, that changes a lot. Amazon! Is it true, they say, that you and your husband shot five policemen?

Artur listens attentively, but the Amazon is silent.

94: You know she doesn't talk to anyone.

95: Ha-ha! Only our Azamat, the mountain eagle, was able to pick up the keys to this um . . . safe and her iron heart. We're not him, not even close—just a bunch of half-educated tilers!

94: Can you be quiet there!

95: Wah-wah, I'm so scared. Azamat is the real thing! He's the fearless one among us—he's not afraid of any monsters.

94: Artur! I warned you!

95: It's fine, all fine, brother, don't lose your cool! A prisoner's feelings are sacred! Tell me, how can I help you?

94: How can one really help me here?

95: Well, you know . . . Maybe try to talk to the duty officer so that he takes you to the bath together on Thursday.

94: Try it! It may work, why not? You seem to be getting along fine with him!

95: I'm good with everyone! I didn't promise to stab him in the corridor!

94: It's just I couldn't hold on. He knows how to drive a person
mad, you see . . .

95: I know. Just tell me, do you really need this? Are you sure
you'll get it up for that old crocodile?

94: Ha-ha! Don't doubt me! I can even get a hard-on for a table!

95: How's that???

94: Well, I simply start thinking that it's bent over on all fours!

Both start laughing like crazy.

95: Deal, bro; I'll give it a try, but I won't make any promises.

94: Don't promise—just do it!

95: Cool! It'll be done.

*Amazon listened to all this dialogue through a half-open peephole,
and in the end, with force and a thud, she slammed it shut.*

94: Shush! The rat came to eavesdrop again.

95: Rashid, is that you?

93: What?

95: Nothing, sleep!

93: No, I'm not sleeping, I just prayed.

*Azamat, realizing what was happening, reached for the ventilation
to call his princess.*

94: Nine two. Nine two . . .

But there was no answer this time.

The duty officer and the balander with a cart enter, announcing their approach with steps and rattling beforehand.

The duty officer: Get ready for the meal.

The duty officer and the balander are handing out lunch in the same manner as they did for breakfast. Artur subtly attempts to engage the duty officer at his door. Instead of closing his feeder, he opens the next one for the balander's distribution, then goes back to cell 95 and resumes whispering with its occupant. They are engaged in a hushed argument about something.

95 *(quietly)*: Bring it on now.
The duty officer: Corruption starts with a pack . . .

Artur places five packs of cigarettes on the feeder. The duty officer quickly stuffs them into his pockets, slams the feeder shut, and hurries over to the waiting balander. The food distribution continues, with the duty officer prompting the balander. Once done, they depart. Lunch spoons clink, and then faucets babble. Some prisoners settle onto their beds, others go about their activities, and Valei switches on the TV once again.

91: Arturio! Nine five!
95: What do you want, Valiko?
91: Thirty a barrel!
95: That's it, then! They'll release us tomorrow!
91: Praise the Lord, the ruler of worlds!
95: Nine zero! Magas!

90: Speak!

95: I wrote a poem just for you. Do you want to listen?

90: Go ahead, burn rubber.*

95: Father Athanasius bought a phonograph
and decided loud music was his new path.
The neighbors were disturbed by such loud sounds,
no one wanted to endure that torment around.
The neighbors yelled and loudly cursed,
They tried to take away the phonograph first . . .
To end this chaos and bring calm,
Father Athanasius embraced Islam.
Now silence and peace in the neighborhood reign,
Only the call to prayer is heard on the balcony each day . . .

91: Arturio, I didn't know you were a poet!

Everyone starts laughing and one can hear giggling even from cell 92.

95: Bro, there's a lot more you don't know about me!

The duty officer enters again—cautiously and quietly, holding a chair this time. He silently approaches cell 95 and almost silently opens the feeder, a surprising contrast to his usual noisy handling of the inmates. Artur, unsurprised by the duty officer's presence, promptly spreads a newspaper on the slot in the door and begins arranging modest snacks on this improvised table. The duty officer takes a seat on a chair facing the rest of the corridor and produces a

---

* Slang for "do it."

liter bottle of clear liquid. Artur places two aluminum mugs on the table, the duty officer fills them, and they start drinking and eating. They consume quickly, almost hurriedly, and quickly become intoxicated. Artur, leaning toward his drinking companion, points at the video camera hanging above. The duty officer dismisses it with a wave of his hand.

The duty officer (*chewing, quietly*): It doesn't work . . .

Artur laughs softly; the duty officer laughs too.

91: Arturio! Arturio!
95: What's up there, Valiko?
91: Twenty-nine! (*Pause.*) Have you heard, Artur? Twenty-nine!
95 (*chewing*): Yes, yes. In the evening, they'll release us—get your bag ready.
91: Twenty-nine! Fuck you, Putin, I swear on my mom's life.

The duty officer listens in surprise, then looks at Artur. He waves his hand and twists his finger at his temple. Both drink. Both scrunch up their faces.

95: It's strong today, huh?

The duty officer grunts, takes a bite, then nods his head.

94: Nine two . . . Nine two . . .
92: What?

94: Come closer to the ventilation, please. (*Pause.*) I beg you.

Amazon follows Azamat to the ventilation, and they start a sub-dued but intense argument. The duty officer, chewing away, attempts to eavesdrop on their conversation, but the mumbling is indistinct. They're either speaking too softly, or he's already quite drunk.

Artur, also in a similar state, listens out of habit. Then, as if recalling something, he pulls the duty officer's head closer to the feeder and tries to explain something in his ear. However, the duty officer firmly shakes his head in disagreement.

The duty officer: Are you out of your mind? And what about the camera on the stairs? And the guard?
95: Well, then not in the bathhouse!
The duty officer: No . . .

The duty officer vigorously shakes his head, and it's clear that the liter of moonshine has already taken its toll.

95: Then during a walk—take them to the same courtyard. Or here, in the cell . . .
The duty officer: No, I've already told you! (*Hiccups.*)
95: Well, just consider it. She's already over fifty, though I believe that's already a discounted rate. They gave her more than twenty—that also counts as a discount. How much is it?

Artur bends his fingers wryly, presenting his arguments, and tries to count something else, but he isn't entirely sure of the answer himself.

95: She'll be seventy when she's free . . . maybe even eighty! Consider this her last chance to have a man. And what a man!

The duty officer: No.

95: A carton of cigarettes.

The duty officer (*sharply*): No.

95: Two cartons.

The duty officer: No-o-ope.

95: Two and a half.

The duty officer (*scratches his head*): I need to think about it . . .

Artur pours the remaining moonshine into glasses, then, clinking their glasses, both of them finish this rather large portion, which gets them even tipsier. The duty officer leans back in his chair, as if contemplating a Russian campaign like Napoleon, reflexively tapping his hand on his knee. Hearing movement in the corridor, Amazon and Azamat pause their conversation and step away from the ventilation.

94: Artur. Nine five.

91: Thirty-one again! Fuck 'em all!

95 (*moving his tongue slowly*): What?

94: That rat seems to be roaming around somewhere again. Do you have it there?

The duty officer wakes up and shakes his head negatively. Artur mimics the same movement.

95: I'll take a look.

93: The duty officer's dried up* somewhere . . .

94: Yeah. I've gotta scare him away from the door constantly.

90: He definitely needs to get burnt!

91: I heard that he picks up the moonshine during shakedowns in other cells, then sells it for cigarettes in others.

94: Yeah—and the phones too.

The duty officer sleeps peacefully on a chair in the pose of Napoleon, tired after his Russian campaign.

91: Nine five!

95 (*leaning against the feeder, under his breath*): Uh-huh . . .

91: Artur! Look for the duty officer there, at your place.

95 (*quietly*): Yeah . . .

94: He's hiding around here somewhere. Duty officer!

The entire cell corridor erupts with banging doors and shouts for the duty officer. Startled, the duty officer wakes up in a daze, momentarily unsure of his surroundings and the cause of the commotion. He jumps up, runs along the corridor, stumbles, falls, and settles on the floor. Meanwhile, Artur, awakened by the noise, attempts to close the feeder from inside his cell. It takes a moment, and he also ends up falling in his cell.

After these chaotic moments, the screams and noise suddenly quiet down, and the inmates in the special block try to make sense of the situation. A brief moment of silence ensues.

---

* Slang for "hid himself."

Suddenly, a siren blares, and footsteps on the stairs signal the arrival of the alarmed chief and the balander. *Confused, they look around, then proceed to drag the unconscious duty officer toward the exit. The duty officer briefly regains consciousness and lets out a loud scream.*

The duty officer: Lights out!

They go away. Silence. The TV plays quietly. Everyone is trying to look through their peepholes.

91 (*quietly*): Nine five! Nine five! Arturio! How are you? Are you sleeping? Twenty-nine a barrel again! Everything'll be fine! I know it!

94: Nine two . . . Nine two . . . Good night . . . (*Pause.*)

92: Good night, my love.

93: Nine zero. Nine zero. Magas.

90: Speak.

93: Magas, where are they taking you to serve your sentence now, what do you think?

90: They said they're sending me to the Polar Owl.*

93: Wai-wai! That sucks!

90: We're in Russia, everywhere sucks.

The lights go out, leaving only the emergency light. The TV sound cuts out along with bright lights. A quiet Muslim prayer begins to float above the spetsblok.

---

* A colony for strict-regime convicts and those serving life sentences located on the bank of the Sob River near the Polar Urals.

Kutuz

Kutuz loved freedom dearly, which was why he'd ended up in prison. In his childhood, he'd enjoyed wandering and running away from home. For that, he was painfully and frequently beaten by his mother and first stepfather. Later, it was his mother and his second stepfather, who replaced the first but differed from him very little. His biological father had perished during his second fifteen-year sentence, leaving Kutuz to his mother and his own genes to Kutuz.

All that Kutuz remembered from his early childhood was standing on buckwheat in the corner as punishment, either on his knees or along the lines between tiles; scalding hot baths that almost boiled off his skin; and being dragged across the floor by his leg, resulting in bloody scrapes. Kutuz still had scars on his legs from the clothesline they would use to tie him up for extended periods of time. These scars served as a reminder of a time in his life when he faced beatings for the smallest reasons. He'd certainly provided them with plenty of reasons for it. The number of broken windows, broken vases, and ruined furniture and decor had, in his mother's opinion, exceeded all imaginable limits. In a family in which she struggled fiercely to maintain a cozy home, her own son became a cursed outcast. It was also during that time that Kutuz lost one of his front teeth, which his mother had knocked out because smoking was bad. Apparently, hitting a child with a pointer was a much lesser sin.

They lived a relatively comfortable life but never bought anything for Kutuz—especially not sweets, because he didn't do well in school and behaved even worse. His stepbrother, the son of his second stepfather, was not subjected to the same restrictions. Maybe it was because he excelled in his studies, or maybe he was just the favorite child. They also lived with Kutuz's grandfather. The old man had difficulty speaking and moving, but he owned a shotgun. Naturally, it was kept in a safe, and Kutuz knew where the key was.

Then, on an unsuspecting day that would bring about yet another calamity, the stars aligned for Kutuz: his grandfather's shotgun, the absence of sweets, his criminal inclinations, two friends slightly older, but even more rebellious, and a kiosk on the neighboring street. The three of them embarked on a robbery, armed with the shotgun. Their loot consisted of chewing gum and chocolate bars. At the age of ten, these were their prized possessions. Meanwhile, the kiosk managed to catch fire. Kutuz didn't remember whether they had set it ablaze or if it caught fire on its own—his poor memory might have been due to shame over what had happened, or perhaps it was simply due to the heat. None of these versions convinced his parents, who interrogated their child as if conducting a professional investigation no less stringent than operatives would. In the end, Kutuz partially admitted his guilt and turned over his share of the stolen goods, but this didn't save the kiosk, which had completely burned down. Kutuz's parents paid out for it and, since their patience had already run out, sent their under-age offspring to a specialized detention center for juvenile offenders. It was a cell where you had to sit on wooden benches the entire day. For a change, they could only sit on the floor, and at night, they were allowed to sleep. A prison for children. There was hardly anything more terrifying.

At first, Kutuz spent three months in that place. It didn't change him, so he was sent there more than once afterward. Kutuz never had his own bicycle, so he rode other people's bikes. He didn't have a game console either, so he played others'. He never had money or sweets, so he took them from others. He took without asking, took forcibly, relying on his agility or strength. The final destination of his adventures was always the same: the detention center. This continued until Kutuz reached the age of twelve, when he could finally be "conscientiously" transferred to a full-fledged boarding school for troubled teenagers. There was no mother there, but there were drunken guards who would beat the minors on their legs or backs with batons or simply kick them. When asked about the bruises, they would explain that the children fought among themselves. For the boys' safety, surveillance cameras were installed in the isolation cells, but by that time, the boys didn't trust anyone anymore and broke them, along with everything else that could be broken. Once, as a punishment, they wanted to make Kutuz clean the toilets. He broke them all, and from then on, the boarding school had to use outdoor restrooms, even in winter. Other boys, especially those who were older and stronger, would also beat Kutuz. Not because they were mean and he was considered bad. It was just that they would beat any-one younger and weaker. Boys whom they could take meatballs and candies from during lunch, then torment afterward. Kutuz resisted as best he could, and the number of scars on his head only increased. And when he grew up and became stronger, he could not only fight others, but also take meatballs and candies from them. Not because he was mean and the younger ones were considered bad. It was just the way things were there.

At the age of fifteen, Kutuz returned home. He still didn't listen to anyone, but now no one in the family could lay a hand on him. Not because they didn't try, but simply because they couldn't—he could stand up to anyone and disregard any authority, even if he had none. Kutuz started attending a tech-nical school during the day and went to the gym in the eve-nings, but he didn't stop getting into trouble. He was naturally strong, and sports benefited him. Kutuz even managed to par-ticipate in some competitions and win a couple of certificates and a tin cup. He didn't rush to move out of his house, not because he missed his mother so much, but because of the home-cooked meals.

The first time he was expelled from the technical school was when he threw a practice grenade into the classroom, causing it to roll under the front desks. Many didn't under-stand what had happened at the time, but those who did would remember that day forever. His relatives somehow managed to get him reinstated. They realized it was better to keep Kutuz in the technical school than in prison, which would have ruined the boy completely. The reasons for his subsequent expulsions were no less spectacular, but with his family's collective efforts,

Kutuz managed to complete the educational institution just before the annual fall military conscription began. To the great relief of his entire family, Kutuz joined the army at the age of eighteen.

There was a common misconception that marine infantry was solely focused on practicing ground assaults or close-quarter combat techniques. But Kutuz and his comrades mainly trained by gathering mushrooms while fully equipped. The norm was to collect a trailer load of mushrooms per marine squad per day. At night, instead of sleeping, they often conducted fire drills. This involved the entire unit rushing out to the training ground, holding mattresses, bedside tables, clothing, and other easily flammable and cumbersome items. Occasionally, as an alternative to mushroom gathering, they would set up large military tents on the same concrete training ground. The process, which only involved using entrenching tools, was considered by the superiors to be not only entertaining—for them—but long-lasting. The day after such exercises was dedicated to meticulously filling in the holes left by the soldiers. Everyone participated in this lively hustle and bustle: fresh concrete was mixed in the courtyard, and they had to run two hundred meters in full gear, swiftly carrying a trowel and a bucket of mortar. Apparently, all of this was vital for enhancing the country's defense capabilities. These maneuvers, varying in degrees of absurdity, proceeded relatively calmly when the military unit commander was sober. However, if such soldierly fortune was absent, an assault rifle would find its way into his hands, and the exercise environment would immediately become combat-like, as neither the weapon nor its owner would remain silent. The commander's favorite expression was, "You are not marines, you're a bunch of faggots piled on top of each other." The commander's favorite pastime was demonstrating how the bolt of the Kalashnikov could be pulled back forcefully by striking a rifle butt against the chest of a soldier wearing a bulletproof vest. The rifle was almost always reloaded, and the soldier rarely remained on his feet. Then, after such an ordeal, they still had to spend the whole day collecting mushrooms . . . Kutuz preferred not to remember the month when, before the general formation, he had attached the flag to the flagpole upside down, or what the commander had done to him for it. Kutuz somehow managed to complete the training, avoid ending up in a punishment battalion, and become not just a marine, but a sapper. He knew how to probe the ground to search for training mines, as well as to stack expired ammunition into massive piles and detonate them from cover. He was paid sixty kopeks for each round. At the end of his year of service, the Defense Ministry transferred two hundred and fifty rubles to his account, and the day after his demobilization, Kutuz bought himself a car.

After returning from military service, Kutuz started living on his own, got married, and drove around in his newly purchased used car. He quickly got into an accident and wrecked it, but he didn't have money for repairs. The remaining earnings on his card had been successfully spent, just like any other money that came into Kutuz's hands before and after that. He repaired the car himself, teaching himself bodywork in the process. Kutuz enjoyed the process of making repairs and the result. It seemed that after breaking and destroying so much in his life, he now wanted to fix something. He opened a small auto workshop with his friend, and the business slowly began to thrive.

Kutuz didn't stop drinking, fighting, or stealing while working in the garage, which was left unattended or wasn't guarded well. One day, he and his partner managed to steal an entire container of children's gifts and sweets. But since they still had the sponsor's branding on them, it was difficult to sell them. The friends ate as much as they could and distributed the rest, including to an orphanage. Soon after, they both got involved in another shady business venture. Kutuz took the blame upon himself because his friend had a wife and child, whereas he only had a wife. Kutuz was lucky; he received a two-year suspended sentence, and life continued in the same rhythm. On his way back from another job, thinking he was escaping pursuit, Kutuz ended up completely wrecking his car. There was no police chase at the time, but what didn't seem like a chase to a drunk person?

His wife eventually got fed up and left, but Kutuz wasn't too bothered by it because he already had a new love interest who was an old acquaintance. She was older than him, had a teenage child, owned a dog-grooming salon, and had a pet chihuahua. But most importantly, they were happy together. His new relatives were well-off, and his mother-in-law even gifted Kutuz a new car for their wedding. It was a good reason to start a new life, but Kutuz preferred the old one, and the gift ended up smashed against a wall that appeared on his path even before the end of their honeymoon. It was a serious accident, and not even having his own body-repair workshop could save him. Kutuz loved to drive drunk, strictly adhering to the direct correlation between his blood alcohol level and speed. Poles, fences, and ditches became the best friends of his cars. But eventually Kutuz ran out of vehicles, his wife wouldn't give him the keys to hers, and his mother-in-law had no intention of buying a new one or ever interacting with that idiot. So, he started driving other people's cars. The condition was the same as when he drove his own: habit became second nature, and Kutuz, following the famous advice of psychologists, never went against his desires. The police chased him so many times, setting up roadblocks and shooting at his wheels, that it could have provided material for a short crime series. The plot, however, would have become somewhat monotonous. When the police finally caught the fugitive, they couldn't even take away his driver's license because Kutuz had never had one, and the car didn't belong to him.

After one of his thrilling boozed-up joyrides in a car he took without permission from a friend, and a minor—by Kutuz's standards—accident, it turned out that the vehicle belonged not to his friend but to someone entirely different who had no knowledge of Kutuz and reported it stolen. He was taken to court. Taking into account his previous unfinished suspended sentence, Kutuz received a total of three years, which, in principle, wasn't too long—but it was an actual sentence, not a suspended one. He didn't serve it in a full-fledged prison camp, but in a colony settlement. The settlement was neither a strict zone nor one of complete freedom; it was something in between. At night, you slept under supervision in barracks behind a fence, and during the day, you could officially work in the city—also under supervision. It wasn't about a convoy or a restricted area with barbed wire; they simply checked for your presence several times a day.

As a sentenced settler, Kutuz found a job at a car wash. The conditions were good, and there was under-the-table income and the opportunity to show off in other people's cars. The main thing was not to miss any checks; otherwise, he'd have to wear a prison tunic and move to a neighboring general-regime colony. After six months of this dull life, Kutuz's rebellious spirit finally couldn't take it anymore, and he escaped, taking his weak-willed body with him. You see, Kutuz's wife had remained in his home-town, while he was taken to a different place, to the colony. And one day, despite occasional meetings and frequent phone calls, Kutuz suspected her of infidelity. More precisely, he suspected that someone was mistreating her or causing her harm in some way. He urgently had to go and figure everything out. This noble thought, of course, would never occur to Kutuz in a sober state of mind, but when he was drunk, he was ready for any heroic feat, especially rescuing a princess. Drinking, just like leaving the colony, was a gross violation of the conditions of his con-finement and posed an immediate transfer to a different regime, but such trivial matters didn't concern Kutuz much when his love was in danger. If this surge of romanticism had occurred during the day, he would naturally have taken any car he could get his hands on at the car wash. Since romantic heroes usually find themselves in trouble at night, Kutuz embarked on his jour-ney by taxi, covering a thousand kilometers, taking with him all the money he'd earned, both honestly and not so honestly, at the car wash—for fuel and a bottle of vodka to sustain himself.

It wasn't clear whether he managed to save his beloved from all the imagined and real enemies, but after a week of not-quite-sober adventures back in his hometown, Kutuz was surprised to find himself on television in the "Wanted" section. Surrendering to the authorities was not in his principles, so he decided to keep running as the noose was tightening. Kutuz asked for help and money from a friend whom he'd saved during his first sentence, as the late-night taxi ride and subsequent loud partying had depleted his financial resources to just a couple of Snickers bars and a loaf of bread. The friend refused to come down to where Kutuz was standing and instead spoke cautiously, peering out from the balcony. The conversation didn't go well and revolved around words like "wife" and "child." Now, Kutuz had a wife and a child too, albeit not his own, but still. The conversation didn't progress. The two friends found themselves in different circumstances again: one stood with a backpack below, while the one who wasn't shown on television as being a wanted convict hid behind a curtain somewhere upstairs.

In the end, Kutuz set off into the unknown, on foot and without any possessions or former friendships, but with love in his heart, departing from his hometown's harbor. He had to make his way through the Siberian expanses, mostly through forests and sparsely populated areas. Kutuz avoided roads and encounters not only with the police, but also their voluntary assistants—vigilant television viewers. He preferred to sleep in trees, fastened to the trunk with a belt. It was safer and warmer than on the ground. He was wary of forest animals, not realizing that they preferred to avoid him as well, and soon enough,

Kutuz would differ very little from them. Fortunately, it was summer, so he mainly relied on forest berries for sustenance, while mosquitoes feasted on him. Once, he even attempted to catch fish in small lakes with a homemade net, without, however, too much success. The fish took offense at Kutuz's opinion of their primitive mental abilities and scorned his crooked net.

Sometimes, he would come across small villages along the way where he could find temporary work, eat, and spend the night. In the mornings, some grandmother would always prepare a little bag for Kutuz with bread, milk, and a tomato. By that time, Kutuz had stopped stealing and fought much less. The work and love of recent years had worked their positive influence.

The simple and unpretentious life on the land in the village suited this wandering city dweller so well that, eventually, after several weeks of wandering, he decided to settle in one of the remote settlements deep in the taiga. He wanted to live, wait things out, and see what would come next. Kutuz wasn't skilled at planning his life too far in advance; at most, he would think until lunchtime, as he knew planning was futile—each evening could bring anything imaginable.

Kutuz turned out to be a very sociable and hardworking guy, attracting people to him just as he was drawn to them. He settled in well in his new surroundings, finding work as a lumber truck driver where neither licenses nor personal backgrounds were questioned. Kutuz often lent a helping hand to the locals, whether it was for food or simply out of kindness. Money wasn't a significant currency there; instead, genuine and honest relationships held value. Digging up two sacks of potatoes for a neighbor and one for himself became a regular and gratifying task. He didn't quit drinking entirely, but moderated his consumption, no longer driving under the influence. Now, he differed little from the local workers, including occasional drunken brawls, as there were no theaters in the village.

Mobile connectivity was poor in the settlement, so Kutuz would find spots on the road or elevated areas to maintain communication with his beloved. It was through this connection that they eventually tracked down Kutuz. A capture team arrived and took him back to prison.

At the court, luck was on his side again. Despite an unfinished first term and an escape attempt during the second, he was sentenced to only four years, but under strict conditions, with half of the time already considered served. During transportation, while handcuffed, Kutuz somehow found himself in a scuffle with the convoy guards, fueled by either joy or some other intense emotion. They didn't pursue the matter, but as a result, Kutuz arrived at the camp not only with a battered face, he was also labeled as a persistent violator prone to escape and assaulting staff members. With such a record, he of course wasn't assigned to the residential area but was kept "under the roof" in a prison within the colony. But Kutuz didn't lose hope. He had less than two years to serve, which was nothing compared to any of his cellmates. He spent his time corresponding and eagerly anticipating a meeting with his beloved wife, stepson, and their dog. His wife awaited him in heart-felt fashion, sending passionate letters in return. To make sure their meeting wouldn't be disrupted or delayed, Kutuz engaged in daily self-training, repeating to himself, "Just don't cause any more trouble. Just don't cause any more trouble . . . "

In prison, Kutuz grew a beautiful beard, which, combined with his youthful face and innocent blue eyes, made him look like a country priest. If it weren't for the numerous scars on his face and on the back of his head, as well as his missing front tooth, it would be difficult to believe his story.

Lately, Kutuz had developed a love for drawing. Though nobody quite understood the meaning behind his ballpoint pen sketches, it didn't bother him much. The newfound passion for painting within him was too strong. For the New Year, Kutuz dreamed of receiving colored pencils as a gift.

Vasya

Vasya knew how to cook delicious pilaf, and he loved classical music, weapons, and burning people's remains in barrels. And if the law didn't pay much attention to his first three hobbies, it for some reason reacted with extreme disapproval to the last one.

Vasya grew up in an intelligent family: his mother had been the director of a music school, his grandfather an orchestra conductor, and his father a prosecutor. Vasya remembered little of his childhood. His grandfather was almost a celebrity. Mom, of course, didn't reach his level, but she was also an important lady, who, naturally, placed great hopes on her Vasenka. Dad wasn't at home that often: his work demanded a lot of him, and he was often called in even when he was at the Sunday dinner table. But he took a lot of work home in order to spend more time with the family. The cases of the accused lay in huge piles in various rooms of their large apartment. Little Vasya sometimes played with them, but he always did so nicely as Dad asked him to be careful—someone's fate lay in those folders. Vasya used to anxiously untie the white ribbons on the cardboard cases, but he never found any fates inside—only records, protocols, and sometimes photographs. He preferred the ones with naked dead women. Dad forbade him from look-ing at those ones, but Vasya did so anyway. Then one day, they bought Vasya a gun that shot plastic bullets, and he lost interest in those folders. The same affliction appeared to strike his dad, who had a heavy workload but got around to less and less of it. The cases gathered dust sitting in the corners of their apart-ment for a long time, and Mom would swear at him, begging him to take those criminal cases away from her house. Vasya didn't yet know where the owners of the names indicated on the folders were, and his dad didn't say anything.

Vasya received a good secondary and higher education as well as an education in art at home, but his teachers managed to overlook something important. It so happened that Vasya fell in love not only with knives and firearms, but also with violence as a way of life. When you are raised in a respectable environ-ment while harboring something like that inside, you inevita-bly have to adapt and maneuver, something Vasya learned to do with finesse even as a child. Maybe that's why he chose to study and pursue a career in law—seeing it as the practical manifesta-tion of violence in life as well as a way of earning money. Things turned out very well for Vasya, and this allowed him to have his own lifestyle independent from his parents. He rented a place and was later able to buy an apartment for himself, going through several cars and even more women.

Vasya was not attractive and didn't have a strong body or a tender heart, so he had a peculiar relationship with the oppo-site sex. He chose his partners to match—cynical and empty—always surprising them with the fact that someone could be even more cynical and empty than themselves. Of course, restaurants and trinkets also did their job, but Vasya still needed feelings, albeit rather ambiguous ones: he wiped his feet on his women, they hated him for it, but they didn't leave him either.

Vasya's clients were also quite odious, arising from the depths of his criminal city. At the beginning of his career, Vasya didn't go to work in any respectable office and didn't open his own small office, preferring to work from home. During the day, Vasya slept, waking up at best after dinner, paid his tribute to the computer and the internet, then went to the city to eat, drink, carouse, get chicks, and work at the same time. Vasya liked this way of life. Moreover, his main clients were those who also didn't sleep at night and got into various messes, shootings included. Having gotten into such a mess, while everything could still be resolved quickly, they called Vasya in the first few hours, and he hurried to help. Vasya's strong grasp of the law, his understanding of weapon-related procedures, his connections with government agencies—thanks to his dad—and his smooth way of talking enabled him to handle cases successfully. His ties to the underworld also provided him with the excitement he craved.

Vasya could not only explain every weapon model and the laws relating to them in detail, but could also recognize classical symphonies just by listening to them. He had wide-ranging cultural and intellectual knowledge. By reading various books, both specialized and fiction, learning foreign languages, traveling abroad, and having diverse contacts, Vasya experienced rapid personal growth and received opportunities for higher achievements. During the elections, he worked as a legal adviser at the headquarters of a government candidate and participated in some political talk shows and television programs. The dirty trough of politics attracted him as if it were his own, and his future prospects sparkled somewhere very close already, as if he were going up on a lift to the heights of the Swiss Alps—if not for one "but."

A person could realize his passion for music by listening to it, his love for books by reading them, and his weakness for women through a string of relationships, with or without pre-payment. Even his craving for firearms could be released at a shooting range, firing at targets without restraint. But what if he thought some people were beneath him? Or that he was better than others? So much so that it was expressed not in the desire to turn his nose up at the matter, but something more? What if he thought that this issue needed to be addressed more rad-ically? What if he thought that certain living creatures deserve nothing but death, just because they had a different skin color or eye shape, or they spoke a language he didn't understand that was unpleasant for him to hear? What if he were sure that they were all stupid and dirty, that they were the ones whose presence was like litter not only in his city, but the whole coun-try, the whole planet? They were the only ones who committed theft and robbery, killed and raped his white race. He celebrated Hitler's birthday and affectionately called him grandfather, see-ing only positive aspects in National Socialism. In such matters, neither theory nor a shooting range, nor, moreover, computers, could ever be enough. Realization of one's beliefs and aspira-tions required practice—especially if the objects of your hatred were so near and there were many like you, and you loved to deftly use knives to solve interethnic issues. It was very hard to hold back. And Vasya didn't hold back.

It took the investigation several years to figure out how many participants were in Vasya's gang, who played the role of leader, as well as how many people they'd managed to kill, dismember, burn, or simply bury. The prosecution spoke of about seventeen victims and said around seven had been whacked by Vasya himself, but even in those cases, he was just a kind of observer there. His experience as a lawyer as well as his almost innate ability to dodge trouble in any situation were very useful to him in this case. The court couldn't prove Vasya's leading role, especially since they had one dead accomplice on whom they could hang everything. Of the dozen surviving former associates involved in the case, most chose a pre-trial agreement and began vying to rat on each other, mostly on Vasya. He also concluded a pre-trial agreement and began to hand everyone over, pitting them against each other, and most importantly, causing them to quarrel with the investigator. The last one finally reached a dead end and, as a result, having broken agreements with everyone, kicked the case to court. The court trial went on for a long time. The accomplices were kept in the same hall, but in different cages so that they wouldn't attack each other. The principle of racial superiority that used to unite them earlier gave way to another: every man for himself. Some lived to see the verdict, some did not, some went on to serve a life sentence, some got shorter terms. Vasya was also facing a life sentence, but he managed to get off with twenty-two years, which he was incredibly happy about. Vasya was sure that he would be able to gradually bite off pieces of his term and eventually get out on parole in ten to twelve years. Every prisoner hoped for the best, but Vasya definitely had reasons for this. His father-prosecutor, though he was not eager to communicate with such a son after all this, probably used his influence to help the outcome of his case just before retiring.

Vasya had a wife and two small children on the outside. But he was not particularly interested in them, neither before this nor after. They responded with the same lack of interest in kind. The children hadn't yet realized that they had a father, and his wife didn't want anything to do with him anymore. He married her shortly before their children's birth, though he'd lived with her for quite a long time. Or rather, she had already been living in his house for a long time, but like a dog or a washing machine. Vasya treated her accordingly. He said that he'd picked her up on the street so she wouldn't die there. He threw it in her face along with confessions of his numerous cheatings and perversions, not really considering them to be such. She was silent, as befitted home appliances—she washed clothes, cooked, and cleaned. When the children appeared, Vasya completely stopped coming home, as crying and diapers weren't for him. He preferred to hang out with his mistresses. As a result, the response to such behavior in the family caught up with him behind bars. His wife divorced him, removed his name from the joint apartment ownership documents and stripped him of his parental rights. That didn't upset Vasya at all, and he was sure that he would be able to shake her out of his apartment along with the little rugrats in time. His mother was the only one who didn't turn away from Vasya. But mothers almost always stayed with their children until the end. Even in spite of all the shame, when everyone admitted that he was a murderer—even he did!—she still believed and waited. Letters and parcels, hope and love. A mother's heart was boundless in devotion to her child.

Throughout the long-term investigation, Vasya was in a very bad prison in his hometown. And the point was not that he spent almost all the time at the spetsblok in solitary confinement, where there was practically no daylight. Nor was it that those in uniform reacted extremely badly to Vasya's past actions and would beat him regularly and cruelly, with or without reason. In that prison, it was not the police who ruled, but the sadistic convicts used by the prison administration for beatings, torturing, and raping other convicts in specifically arranged cells called "press huts," which were meant to break inmates.

And though they beat, insulted, and humiliated you, these were not the worst things that could happen in those sad places. You could also be left tied up in a bag for a whole week with only your head stuck out of it for receiving a drink once a day. Sitting soaked in your own urine and feces was not the most pleasant pastime, but the main thing was that you hoped nobody pissed on your head. If they did, you wouldn't be able to avoid the "rooster coop," the cell for prisoners that got raped. All this limitless terror was conducted by convicts who, due to various circumstances, went against the prisoner's way of life and were now cooperating with the police for their own safety and better conditions in prison.

As a sign of gratitude for this, they tortured other prisoners at the instigation of the administration or the operatives from the outside if some person under investigation didn't want to confess. Those who agreed to do such work were usually the people who themselves liked to torture and humiliate people, especially if the deed went unpunished. The most zealous sadists were singled out by the *muzhiki*, and lists with their names circulated around the central prisons and colonies by way of the prisoner's mail. When encountering such individuals, any decent prisoner was obliged to "deal" with them—to beat them, preferably to death. But in practice, not all of them were punished for their deeds—there were few willing to risk extending their sentence for the sake of avenging others' suffering.

In a detached building on the colony territory where Vasya was kept during the investigation, the convicts not only beat and humiliated the prisoners mercilessly, but also raped them with all possible cruelty. They threw a mattress on the floor right in the corridor, and on top of it, they threw down a victim targeted by the administration or chosen at their discretion. One person sat on the victim's head while the others held him firm, then they took turns raping him. The screams reverberated throughout the corridor, terrifying the already intimidated prisoners. The prisoner was thrown into the "rooster coop," and everyone waited in horror for the next session of sexual torture, which could happen to each of them at any moment. Having been humiliated in this or that, the prisoners spent all their free time standing upright—"legs together"—with their heads lowered down near their perfectly and evenly tucked prison beds, addressing the sadist who looked into their cell by name and patronymic. If a prisoner stumbled, in the literal or figurative sense of the word, and the sadist broke him for that right there in the cell, he knew that he'd gotten off lightly because he could have ended up in the corridor on the mattress. When they weren't busy humiliating other prisoners, these sadists would spend time in the gym, watching movies, playing on the console, and eating other people's parcels of food. They didn't want to think about what retribution might be in store for them after their release, living here and now, even if each of them had at least three death sentences declared against them by the criminal world.

The police didn't meddle in this building. There was only a lone guard on duty at the entrance, and even he was considered to be standing on the lookout. The main sadist would run daily to the operation officers in the administration with a report and to receive new instructions. If a commission suddenly came to check up on things, then everything would immediately start working according to the rules—the sadists would take off their tracksuits, put back on their prison uniforms, and stand next to the rest of the prisoners who would nod in unison, saying that they were absolutely fine, they had no complaints. When the doors were closed behind the inspectors, the humiliation conveyor was turned on again. Nobody ever thought of complaining or "falling out": if such a thing were ever done, everyone knew that finding themselves on a mattress in the corridor was only the first step into their personal hell. According to Vasya, he was beaten only for the first six months, and even that was done only by the police. He immediately tried to level with the sadists by saying that he had people on the outside and if something happened to him, those guilty would be punished once he left the prison. They didn't touch him, but they did try to frighten him. They even offered for him to periodically participate in the fun on the corridor mattress—in an active role—but Vasya refused, well aware of how precarious his position was and that he could end up playing a passive role at any moment.

It was only in the fifth year of his incarceration, when his sentence finally took legal effect, that Vasya was able to escape from this separate two-story purgatory thanks to his connections. He arrived at another colony with a sunken face; he had hand tics, and at first, it took him a long time to adapt to normal conditions. But even later, judging by his twitchy gait and the way he would sometimes freeze standing against the wall or when sitting on the bunk—he was looking into nowhere with a strange smile on his lips—one could understand that he'd gone through a lot. It became especially uncomfortable if a person suddenly discovered that Vasya was looking at him, carefully studying him, as if figuring out how many car tires should be put under a barrel with his body so that even his bones would burn. Most of Vasya's jokes were about forced sodomy, and this was noticed by those around him who suspected it originated from some sort of trauma. Vasya replied to their insinuations about his involvement in such actions that he'd simply seen a lot, and he had heard a lot of the sounds and screams that accompanied them in the corridor of his former prison. You had to believe him because no one could prove otherwise. In the world of prisoners, there was no doubt about the words of a decent prisoner, a *muzhik*, but if another prisoner was caught lying, he was beaten mercilessly and there would be no more faith in him. Vasya knew how to speak beautifully and clearly, explaining all of his actions. But it was one thing when you did it on the outside, and a completely different thing in prison, even more so in a colony.

Prison tested you with isolation, loneliness, and strict rules, which hit you especially hard at the beginning, right after losing your freedom. In the colony, where prisoners go after legal processes, the challenge was more about living with others. There were many people, sometimes too many; you were never alone. You were allowed to do a little more there, awarded more opportunities, but there was also a completely different atmosphere. There, everything was in sight. You couldn't hide. You wouldn't be able to pretend to be someone else and live with a mask for a long time. There, your real character would show itself in time and, if things went unplanned, it might well let you down. There, all your actions or words became immediately known to everyone, so you needed to be very careful with them as they could greatly affect your life in the colony and even your fate. For a cigarette taken without asking, you could be declared a rat for stealing from your own. They treated such people harshly, beat them unconscious, and then threw them out of the mass of decent prisoners. You could go look for your own in the *krasnyye,* unsure if they would even accept you. Or you could be deemed an untouchable, one of those who lived on their own, without specific rights and with a stigma attached to them for the whole term. There were quite a lot of such non-prestigious marks you could collect during your imprisonment. There were serious moments that determined your fate. A name was worth a lot on the outside, but in prison it often had a decisive meaning.

Vasya wasn't very neat in everyday life, and this was not welcome among the prisoners. For some reason, people think prisoners live in dirt and squalor. This has never been true. Any respectable convict paid attention to his appearance, which was like his business card, and maintained order and cleanliness in the prison facility he now called home, whether it was a cell or a barracks. The police didn't force him to do this; people organized themselves so that there was no mess or tuberculosis; they observed cleanliness in clothes, food, and everyday life. He who didn't understand this was taught quickly and cruelly. First with words, then, if necessary, with slaps.

Judging by films, prisoners did nothing but fight and stab each other with shivs, dropping bloody bodies onto the dirty floor. This wasn't so in reality. The floor of the prisoners' spaces was always clean. In the colony, this was being taken care of by the *obizhennyy*, and in the prison "huts" as well as at the *kichas*, the *muzhiki* did it themselves, since the *obizhennyy* lived in different cells. In order to raise a hand, or even a knife, against a decent prisoner, you had to have a very weighty reason, and it was usually related to the fact that your honor, dignity, life, or fate depended on it. But even in that case, you still needed to "explain" yourself within reason. Otherwise, you could be beaten to a pulp or become an outcast. That was why convicts tried not to bring disputes and conflicts to the point of assault and resolve everything with words—with conversation. These conversations had to take place in a calm and respectful manner, but this didn't always come to pass. In verbal skirmishes, the art of mastering prison language was of the utmost importance, as well as knowledge of unwritten laws and traditions, the ability not only to explain one's words and actions, but also the ability to unravel or convince your opponent. Convicts were very experienced and hardened people, and they couldn't be really "tricked" into something or "told" something—passing off black as gray, then as white.

Vasya, with his over-the-top selfishness and constant inability to admit a mistake, even in an absolutely clear situation, sparked only hostility and neglect. This applied to everything, whether it was the number of people he killed, leaving socks lying around, or not washing a mug on time. People soon understood Vasya and his habits, and they dealt with him accordingly. He would often be corrected for his mistakes, big or small, and face consequences, sometimes even physical ones.

Depending on the purpose of the conversation and the interlocutor's position, Vasya either completely denied his participation in murders or, on the contrary, hinted that the seventeen corpses were only those that they'd managed to find. Though it didn't matter at all—in places of deprivation of liberty, none of the prisoners could pump you for anything or present anything for your case, with some exceptions. Your business was your business. But there were bits of background information that inmates not only inquired about but also used to assess your place in life . . . Rapists, especially pedophiles, were broken in such a way that they were not able to start walking immediately afterward and did so with difficulty. They were doomed to live in a separate section with their own kind until the end of their term, in a "rooster coop," spending time washing floors and toilets. Drug dealers who sold their conscience for money also faced restrictions within the prison community. They were required to provide money or cigarettes to respectable prisoners throughout the course of their sentence. Hard drugs, apart from naturally grown marijuana, were strictly prohibited in camps and colonies. This ban was enforced by the criminals themselves, who understood how many lives these substances had ruined, even within the prison system. And, finally, there were the people without limits, those who'd killed a child, a woman, or an old man on the outside—basically, anybody helpless. Such people were strictly interrogated and restricted from general prison activities.

Vasya was considered a *bespredelshchik*—a lawless man— although he called himself a bandit, apparently sincerely believing this himself, unlike those around him. Vasya's frail and twitchy frame, along with his round, bald head, didn't make much of an impression on others. What truly stood out were his vacant, almost insane-looking eyes. Though he didn't see himself as a maniac: he believed that attacking defenseless migrants in dark alleys was genuine banditry. No one challenged his views in the prison. One's identity didn't hold much weight around here. The prison operated like a pack of wolves, where only the strong endured, and the weak were pushed aside. Mental strength mattered as much as physical strength in this environment. Education, culture, or upbringing wouldn't protect you here. Your age didn't matter much; the time you served was more crucial. It didn't matter who you were on the outside; what mattered was who you were in the prison. While Vasya might have seen himself as significant before, it didn't count for much in the colony. He helped other prisoners write letters to the courts and was thanked for this with tea and cigarettes, as was customary, because the word "attention" among prisoners has an absolutely physical embodiment. You could always talk with Vasya about various topics—he loved cooking and was good at it, he knew a lot about humor and could joke nicely—and not just about other people's asses. Sometimes, it seemed that all those corpses attributed to him, in fact, were not his and he'd stood by at most, until you accidentally caught his gaze, directed somehow *through* you. And all of a sudden, you felt the cold emanating from someone else's grave.

Arturik

Arturik lived with the *obizhennyy*, the lowest and most rejected caste of prisoners in the camp. Their living quarters, called the "rooster coop," were separated from the main mass and located at the beginning of the barracks, closer to the toilets, which they were responsible for cleaning. In addition to cleaning toilets, the *petukhi* swept the floors, took out the trash, and performed many other dirty and unpleasant tasks. They also ate separately, using their own dishes instead of the communal ones. To eat from one of their bowls or drink from their mugs meant to debase oneself—then such a person would have to go and live among them.

Taking their belongings or even touching them also meant unpleasant consequences. If a *petukh* dared to ask for someone's old, unwanted clothes, a cigarette, or even a match, the giver tried not to touch them with their fingers, either placing it on something or simply laying it down for the *petukh* to pick up. The *obizhennyy* were not allowed to enjoy the few comforts that a regular inmate in the zone had, like sitting with everyone

---

* "Rooster" in Russian, a pejorative term meaning "faggot."

in the mess hall at the same table, watching television, going to the sports area, or simply having a conversation with someone outside their circle of untouchables. All the free time they had from their unclean work was spent mainly on their beds or sitting on a separate bench in the corner of the local area in front of the barracks away from others. They were often not even allowed to walk in the *lokalka*, the specially designated area for walks, so that their presence wouldn't disturb the other prisoners. The *petukhi* always entered last, and they were obligated to let all other prisoners go ahead of them, while looking down at the ground.

The *obizhennyy* led an extremely dismal life in the prison camp, but they were not awarded this status without reason. Typically, rapists and pedophiles ended up in the "rooster coop." In the past, upon arrival in the prison zone, they would be brutally beaten to the point of death, then subjected to sexual assault, then finally, they'd be placed in the group, where they would endure their miserable existence until the end of their sentence, which included beatings, humiliations, cleaning toilets, and continued sexual violence.

However, times had changed; they were still beaten, but no longer subjected to sexual assault; this form of punishment was no longer practiced due to a prohibition imposed by the *muzhiki*. Instead, the *petukhi* engaged in sexual relationships—voluntarily, so to speak—and they were referred to as "workers." They received "attention" for this, such as a pack of tea, cigarettes, or food, but often this contact remained somewhat coerced. Some *petukhi* willingly involved themselves and entered into unnatural relationships; there were plenty of latent and open homosexuals among their population. A convict caught in passive homosexuality immediately joined the ranks of the *obizhennyy*. This was called a "loosening." By doing so they were added to the ranks of *petukhi*, those who worked not with their hands but with another part of their body. Shaking hands with such an individual was unacceptable, but inserting a penis into him was permissible. Hygiene rules in prison often took on a ritualistic character.

A certain portion of the wayward inmates ended up in the rooster coop not for sexual actions, but due to their lifestyle. Any seasoned prisoner was very careful and meticulous about their hygiene and cleanliness. If you didn't wash, didn't take care of yourself, and wore dirty and untidy clothes, you might be labeled a misfit—a slob. But mockery on this account was just part of the problem. If you washed your feet where everyone washed their face, or if you got soiled by someone else's feces or urine, even if you simply touched the things used to clean the toilet, you might be put "under question" regarding cleanliness, or you might immediately be given a place in the rooster coop.

Arturik was one of those people. He hadn't harmed anyone, but his peculiar lifestyle of being a slob eventually led him to join the *obizhennyy*. Even among them, Arturik stood out with his untidiness and smell. Usually, *petukhi* didn't look very present-able, and it was immediately noticeable, including their perpet-ually troubled gaze. But Arturik stood out even among them in the worst way possible and became an outcast among outcasts.

Decent inmates would beat him up because he was a slob and slow-witted. The *petukhi* would do the same, just with one difference. The *muzhiki* used to beat Arturik with sticks or boots so as not to "degrade" themselves, while the *petukhi* did so with anything they could find. There was always something to punish him for, even though he often did things out of ignorance. Arturik sometimes extended his hand to greet a newcomer inmate, a "newbie," and unknowingly got him downgraded. He sometimes went and told the guards about what was happening in the barracks, when snitching was probably one of the worst deeds a prisoner could commit. Or he sometimes simply annoyed many with his appearance and manners. Arturik was a slob and slow-witted, and he snitched not because he wanted to harm anyone, but because he didn't always understand what he was doing.

The thing was, Arturik had intellectual disabilities. Not so severe that he couldn't go to school or be declared mentally unfit for trial, but enough to prevent him from completing school and fitting in with the rest of the inmates—something that wasn't difficult for an ordinary person. Living like everyone else was not easy for him.

Arturik constantly did everything wrong, although he wasn't allowed to do much in the first place. He wasn't even permitted to do the regular tasks assigned to the *petukhi*. The maximum responsibility entrusted to Arturik was collecting cigarette butts and other trash in the barracks; even then, someone had to supervise him. However, he struggled and made mistakes with that task too. Then, Arturik would be beaten yet again. If he managed to get through a day without being hit on the head or other body parts, it was like a celebration for him. Though such days were rare, as most days were hardly distinguishable from one another.

In the morning, he was kicked out of the barracks early along with his smelly mattress, and he spent the whole day sitting on a bench near the enclosure of trash bins, begging everyone passing by for cigarette butts to spare. Sometimes, he was lucky, and someone would give him a whole cigarette. In return, he was often asked to sing. Arturik had absolutely no vocal ability and couldn't remember more than four lines of any song. His repertoire was limited, but he sang regularly. Often, his performances were in vain, as he might not receive the promised cigarette, with the excuse that his singing was bad. Then he would start repeating the same monotonous lines again, but the person who'd thrown the cigarette butt would have already left, not waiting for the song to end. Arturik would stop singing and start searching for a discarded cigarette butt. If it was still smoking, he managed to take a couple of greedy, short drags.

If he found a used cigarette butt that had gone out, a new problem arose—how to light it, as Arturik never had matches. And again, he had to either ask for a light, or sing, often both. In the mess hall, like all the other *obizhennyy*, Arturik brought his own utensils, but he was made to sit on a separate stool away even from the other *petukhi* and eat separately. It was tough to live without anyone close to you in the camp, even among a rejected caste, especially if you were a bit mentally challenged.

Arturik sat on a small bench for the *obizhennyy* all day long. Nobody allowed him to wander around, even within the small confines of the area or the camp itself, as he might well cause trouble for himself or others. Although his situation couldn't get any worse, as he was already resting at the bottom of the dirty world of prisoners.

Arturik sat on his bench, be it in rain, heat, or snow. Sometimes, he could walk along it, but only a couple of steps to the left and right; he wasn't allowed to move any further, or else he would be punished with a stick again. He could only go to the toilet or bathhouse when accompanied by someone from the other *petukhi*. There were few among the *obizhennyy* who wanted to deal with him, but plenty who were ready to taunt him whenever the opportunity arose.

Only in heavy rain or blizzard was he allowed to enter the barracks during the day. Usually, he had to wait alone until it got dark, and only before lights out would he sneak into the barracks with his perpetually damp mattress, crawl onto the second tier of the bunk, and hide there until morning.

Any of his unnecessary movements, even just turning from one side to another in his sleep, irritated his unfortunate neighbors. During these brief movements around the barracks, mostly toward the toilet, everyone considered it their duty to hasten him with a kick or a harsh word. The main instigator only shook his head low and tried to do everything better and faster, but he never succeeded.

The police treated Arturik with condescension and would have gladly gotten rid of him, since he regularly caused them problems too. Whenever he was left unsupervised, Arturik would always manage to disappear somewhere. It was good if they realized it immediately, and not during the evening roll call; in that case, the search could drag on until morning. The police would search the far corners of the camp with flashlights, then they would make the *obizhennyy* look under the barracks, built on piles, where escapees liked to hide. They would invariably find him in some dirty corner and escort him back to the group under guard, where, of course, nothing good awaited him.

The colony administration was willing to release Arturik early, just so he wouldn't be a nuisance to them, but he still had several years left until he was eligible for conditional release. They couldn't expedite his release based on health grounds since he wasn't completely mentally disabled.

Arturik was permitted to skip joining everyone on the square during the camp-wide roll call twice a day. He would observe the squads' formations from his bench. Sometimes, with a couple of cigarettes in hand, Arturik would approach the fence of the local area and from there, not very loudly or clearly, perform a few of his favorite hits upon request, always dancing along. Arturik's dancing was on a similar level as his singing, but his performance always brought some variety to the routine and long inspections. Occasionally, when in the mood, he would sit on a white swan made of painted car tires and attempt to take off with a run. On such a day, the inspection certainly became far from boring—prisoners sometimes need little reason to have a laugh. In general, inmates are a cheerful bunch, often joking and laughing; without it, life here would be entirely grim, though they smile very rarely.

Some inmates believed that Arturik was actually faking it, pretending to be ill to be taken to the hospital. But Arturik wasn't pretending; he was genuinely sick. True, occasionally, he experienced something unusual: his neck would get stiff, his eye wouldn't open, or saliva would keep flowing without end, just hanging there. But this was an even more pitiful sight—a fool trying to seem even more foolish.

Arturik went to the hospital frequently. It was located in another large camp and served as a place for seriously ill prisoners from all prisons of the penitentiary administration to be transported. Conditions were slightly better there, with better food, and regular inmates lived in wards, while individuals like Arturik were kept in a cage, as they were considered to be unruly. Some say that he was sometimes allowed to take a stroll outside the hospital, but despite this, Arturik enjoyed being there, so he constantly sought to go back. Apparently, life in the animal-like cage suited him better than being around people in the camp.

As soon as he returned to his home zone, Arturik would start planning to go back after just a week. But they often couldn't take him there since he wasn't ill. Treating him was considered useless, and there was little that could be done. There were no medications for mental illness, not only in prison, but also in the outside world. So, he continued to sit on his bench, begging for cigarettes and pestering everyone passing by with the question, "Do you know when I'll be able to go back to the hospital?"

After about a month, no longer satisfied with answers like "tomorrow" or "soon," he took matters into his own hands, consumed by a burning desire to return to the hospital cage. He ran to the duty station, grabbing a bag with his belongings. Of course, in response to this outburst, the police didn't take Arturik anywhere, but sent him back to the barracks. He wasn't in a hurry to go there, so he just sat on the steps of the duty station until lights out.

Sometimes, instead of thinking about the hospital, Arturik would start planning to go home to his mother. Then, the question to anyone passing by the barrack would shift to: "Do you know when they'll release me? I need to go home to my mother in Pokrovsk!" Arturik didn't understand that he wasn't particularly needed by his mother either. She visited him only once during his entire sentence, and his father didn't come at all—he had an auto-repair shop and was too busy. A couple of times, his mother sent him a package. On those days, nobody would beat him, as if it were his birthday, and he suddenly had many friends drawn to his *obizhennyy* lifestyle. Together, they would devour all the goods in a single sitting, and Arturik would join them eagerly, as if it were his last meal.

After sharing some of the cigarettes from the package with his neighbors in the rooster coop, Arturik would sit on his bench and start smoking them one by one, even if he'd received three whole packs. He didn't respond to advice about saving some for tomorrow; there was no tomorrow in his life, and he knew this with absolute certainty.

When Arturik wasn't asking for cigarettes, singing songs, or getting ready for a hospital transfer, he would sit in his usual spot, sketching figures in the mud or snow with a stick, murmuring something to himself quietly. He would grumble at someone, argue with someone else, or tell stories, occasionally laughing at something. All his communication revolved around this internal monologue or dialogue with himself, as Arturik didn't expect anything good from interactions with others. He particularly disliked questions about his grandmother and would always fall silent if someone intentionally brought up that topic, since Arturik was serving time for clubbing her to death with an iron bath ladle. She'd refused to give him her pension money for vodka. The pension had been small, the grandmother old, and the ladle heavy.

Fyodor

Fyodor didn't notice the man when he entered the cell. He lay in his spot, arms folded, staring out the window. Because Fyodor didn't move, the man didn't immediately realize he wasn't alone. The cell was incredibly small, but they weren't cramped in. The man was used to such confined spaces, and Fyodor, even though he was there by chance, didn't complain.

The window offered a clear view of freedom through a large grid. This fact both surprised and delighted the man—the pleasure of standing and looking out the window is not usually provided for in a *spetsblok*. Having recently seen nothing but iron bars and concrete walls, he now occupied himself for a long time by just standing and looking out the window. Below lay a dirty street, along which cars and people were tirelessly scurrying back and forth; there was a row of rickety wooden houses fenced off with the same rickety fences on the other side of it; behind them was a field with the road's barely distinguishable line, then a large overflowing river with steamers and barges slowly floating off somewhere, and already quite far, beyond the river, at the very horizon, an endless brown tundra spread forth. The man seemed to be ready to look at this living picture forever. He didn't obstruct Fyodor's view, as Fyodor, uninterested by earthly matters, only gazed at the sky—as if he'd forgotten something important there.

Fyodor didn't speak much, he was rather silent, or more precisely, he didn't say anything at all. The man didn't hear a single word out of him. To begin with, the man wasn't very talkative, and the silence suited him. Even though it was pretty strange the two of them kept silent right from the very beginning and not after several months of joint isolation, having already spoken about everything pertaining to themselves and quarreling several times over. Although he was an obvious newcomer to the prison, Fyodor didn't go around with stories about his past life, about how he'd gotten here and whom he'd left on the other side of the wall. The man was grateful to him for that. Lately, he'd grown tired of hearing repetitive tales of human sorrow. His soul felt saturated by them, like the lingering smell of nicotine on a smoker's hands. New strangers' stories didn't affect him much anymore. He wasn't accustomed to delving into others' souls, and he was glad Fyodor felt the same.

Fyodor didn't go for walks, and the man walked alone. But heading back through the echoey prison corridors, he knew that "at home," in the cell, a kindred spirit was waiting for him, and a smile appeared on his face. The man preferred to eat and drink alone, including sipping his *chifir*. Offering for Fyodor to join him in this prison tradition would have seemed strange. They didn't wish each other good night or good morning, but this typically happens even if there are only two of you in the cell; there is no good morning in prison.

The man knew that he wouldn't stay in this cell for a long time as his path lay further, beyond the surveillance-raked sand strip between the barbed wire fencing that could be seen a little ways off, to the colony which was a disastrous place, according to the stories of those who'd already served their term there. However, the man had already been in many similar establishments. This particular one was still very different from the previous ones, and not at all for the better. The very location of the colony was inhospitable—right in the Arctic Circle, from where it was a stone's throw to the icy northern sea, which was so different from the warm southern one to which he was accustomed. It was already the middle of autumn, and winter weather hadn't yet begun. But in the North, with a chilly wind and slanting cold rain accompanied by the occasional frozen snowflake that looked like tiny ice floes, there were signs that it was already close.

The man, standing as usual by the window, looked out into the drizzling street and studied his neighbor. Fyodor was right there, nearby, at the windowsill, between the first and second bars, right by the windowpane. He lay on his back, resting on his large, bright red-and-black wings, with his two pairs of front legs crossed over his chest. Fyodor was a butterfly, his small head adorned with antennae, and his glassy pin-like eyes forever fixed in that serene gaze. Fyodor was a dead butterfly. The man did not doubt the fact that his neighbor was a male. It was clear not only because of his large and richly decorated tattooed body, but also because of the air of importance and even arrogance with which Fyodor rested on his pedestal. It would be unthinkable to compare him to some feeble and weak character after such a sight. But Fyodor looked more like a dried-up Pharaoh's mummy, considering both his posture with his arms folded across his chest and the dignity with which he lay on the lid of the windowsill sarcophagus.

The reason Fyodor, clearly not native to the harsh northern lands, had ended up in prison was a mystery. Maybe he was carried so far away by a strong wind, or even more powerful forces that picked up both this insect and this person and threw them so far into the same cell. The man was not an entomologist, but he wanted to consider Fyodor a swallowtail. Though he knew that this was certainly not the case. But any person not well-versed in butterflies, upon seeing such a bright specimen, would have thought that it was a swallowtail. And Fyodor himself would certainly have liked it if he had known the thoughts of his cellmate. But he had no idea about his status, which had grown so much after death, even if in the eyes of only one person. Maybe butterflies lack vanity, focusing on more significant matters, like the sky that Fyodor continued to gaze at even after his fragile body had ceased to live. His unblinking eyes seemed to dream of returning there even in death. He appeared more asleep than dead, and only his still posture, unusual for insects, revealed that this slumber was eternal. "Just like people," the man thought, recalling how many he'd had to bury.

The next day, the man was told to pack his things. At first, he even wanted to take Fyodor with him and carry him in the small box, into which he put souvenirs for his loved ones, hoping to see them someday, but then he changed his mind. Everyone has their own path, and here, their paths diverged. Fyodor had already come to a rest at his final stop, and the

OLEH SENTSOV

train called life still had a few more stops for the man to travel. Besides, the tiny corpse of a butterfly would certainly have been taken away at the next search—prisoners are forbidden to have animals with them, including dead ones.

When the cell doors opened and the perpetually dissatisfied guard, jingling his keys, began to rush him out, the man on the threshold turned and looked at Fyodor for one last time. In parting, either by choice or because of the draft, he turned on his side and slightly moved one of his long antennae. The man smiled back at him and silently walked away. As he was going down the stairs, accompanied by an escort, he was thinking about what Fyodor dreamed of at night and whether butterflies, especially dead ones, have dreams at all. The man was sure that they had. Because there was no death, there was only heaven.

Luntik

Luntik sat on a stool, keeping an eye on the order in the barracks' sleeping area. The room had two rows of neatly made bunk beds with perfectly arranged bedding—a characteristic feature of a strict-regime prison camp. If anyone didn't make their bed properly or hung their towel unevenly, Luntik would approach them, point out the issue, and ask them to fix it. That was his job. If an inmate entered the area before 6:00 PM and stayed near their bed for too long, Luntik would remind them that this wasn't allowed during the day, asking them to leave and standing next to them until they did. This was also part of his job.

Whenever a staff member from the colony's administration visited during their regular rounds, Luntik would quickly get up and walk alongside them, accompanying them just in case a police officer needed something. Sometimes, the staff member would ask him to call a specific inmate for a planned search, and Luntik would hurry around the barracks looking for that person. Occasionally, the staff member would mess up someone's bedding or flip their mattress, "blow it up," just to bother a prisoner they didn't like or following orders from higher-ups to punish a defiant individual. It was a form of minor police harassment.

Since people in the barracks were frequently moved from one bed to another without clear reasons, to save time, the inspector would simply ask Luntik where a particular prisoner slept. With pleasure and ahead of the staff member, Luntik would point to a neatly made bed, which seconds later turned into a mess. After the inspection, Luntik would find those whose beds were "blown up" and ask them to remake their sleeping place. That was also his job, and he did it with a sense of some satisfaction.

Luntik was a *krasnyy*, a *kozel*, and an orderly. There are many names for these people, but the essence is the same. They were the prisoners who collaborated with the administration, helping to maintain order in the camp. All decent inmates— the *muzhiki*, the general population—disliked the *kozly*. Some were hated more, some less, but they were all despised. In the black zones where inmates set the rules, the *krasnyye* served the *muzhiki*, afraid to raise their heads or their voices. In the strict-regime camps, the *krasnyye* were the ones calling the shots. Not everyone, just the chief custodians and other important "activists" in powerful positions, forming the peak of the local hierarchy. Others, like Luntik, worked at the bottom, scurrying around.

The *muzhiki* were not at all integrated into this system— for them, working for the administration was considered disgraceful. That's why the police, with the help of the *kozly*, kept them under control so that they couldn't revolt, unite, or break the system. To achieve this, the colony's administration imposed an extremely strict regime in such camps. The ones who suffered the most from it were mainly the *muzhiki*—those who didn't break, didn't crawl on their knees to the prison staff to tie in with the so-called activists. The *kozly* assisted the police in maintaining this order of things because it gave them bonuses and privileges, and the higher you sat on this pyramid, the more you received—by local standards, of course.

Luntik was a small fry who simply did his job as an orderly, never hitting or trying to scare anyone. And how could a scrawny twenty-year-old drug addict scare a forty-year-old gangster who'd received his fifteen-year sentence for a series of audacious robberies, shootouts, and dead bodies? The burly criminal, living as a *muzhik* by his own code of honor that prohibited any concessions to the police, had to reluctantly adjust his white towel under the constant watchful eye of Luntik, who pointed out its improper placement. He could have beaten Luntik to death right there, but that would have been considered a sheer incitement and slapped an additional ten years onto his sentence. He could've roughed him up a bit, but just one sucker punch was enough to add only a couple more years to his sentence. For every feeble *kozel* like Luntik, there would be another one replacing him in no time, as there were many willing to work as an orderly for the rewards and a possible early release.

As another option, the gangster could have slapped him, just brushed him off, or ignored him. But then, Luntik would immediately run to the custodian, who would promptly call the duty officer or, in extreme cases, press the emergency button. Then, the boots of the response team would clatter down the concrete path, and their batons would rattle against handcuffs. The offender would be dragged to the duty unit, where the boots and batons would extract unpleasant sounds from him. This kind of prisoner would only return to the barracks closer to evening, limping, angry, and silent. If he'd repeated this behavior before, after the duty unit, he would be sent on a brief vacation to the operating unit, where they might not beat him but leave him to rest for a few days, either tucked into his mattress or locked in a small locker-like compartment. They would emerge from there in complete silence, only uttering the phrase, "Yes, Citizen Officer!" That's why the former gangster would straighten his towel without a word, then leave, quietly muttering to himself.

Throughout the day, Luntik had to document all incidents, events, and violations in the barracks. If he heard or saw anything forbidden or even just thought he did, he would take out a small piece of paper—an informant report—and jot down a brief note about it. This, too, was part of his job. All the *krasnyye* in the barracks did the same without exception. In the evening, the papers had to be handed over to the custodian. Anyone who failed to do so received a slap on the face for their lack of diligence. Luntik tried his best, sometimes submitting two or three notes at once. The custodian would compile the daily written reports, writing his own summary and submitting one copy to the head *kozel* of the camp and another to the authorities.

This comprehensive system of round-the-clock surveillance and informing on others was a part of the broader system aimed at suppressing and subjugating inmates. In the barracks, there was no video surveillance system. It'd been replaced by thirty pairs of attentive eyes and ears. Moreover, the *krasnyye* didn't just watch the *muzhiki*—they also kept an eye on each other, reporting and plotting against their own guys and strangers alike. They tried to excel and climb higher on this pyramid of filth—by any means, willing to push anyone down to achieve their goal.

The barracks were filled with an atmosphere of decay and human cruelty. Strangely, Luntik didn't seem to notice it. He found satisfaction in his work and strived to do it well.

The barrack where Luntik lived was small, housing about sixty people. Nearly half of them were *kozly*, representing various levels of betrayal. There were two dozen *muzhiki* of different degrees of decency, which was challenging to maintain in such a vile place. The rest were a mix of *obizhennyy*—the untouchables—and other types, including former so-called activists who'd been expelled from their work for misconduct or dereliction of duty, along with volunteers who willingly took on extra work, mainly clearing snow. This barrack was one of the smallest in the camp, while others housed up to two hundred or even three hundred people. Despite having two or three Luntiks in each section of the larger barracks, the percentage ratio of the "types" of inmates remained roughly the same.

There were a lot of *krasnyye* in the camp, and Luntik knew where they came from very well. He hadn't experienced the terrible inductions of previous years, where they went through all the stages of initiation, and blood pooled in the quarantine area as an ever-flowing puddle. He had heard about them when he was on his way here during his trip in the *Stolypin*, the train car transporting prisoners. He'd also heard stories about having to greet the police dog or even kiss a wooden phallus. Luntik had no intention of suffering for unclear prisoner principles. So, he willingly joined the *krasnyye,* especially since almost everyone did the same. Those who believed they were tough were beaten until they agreed to become one of them. If someone seemed resistant, they were taken to the detention unit and returned three days later as a completely different person—quiet and compliant, signing anything and accepting everything.

According to statistics, only one out of ten prisoners remain principled and strong-willed until the end. For this kind of principled person, they were periodically toughened and grilled for several months after entering the residential zone of the camp before they were left relatively untouched, the focus having been shifted to another non-compliant individual. And just when such a fighter, thinking that this hellish experience would never be repeated, started to relax at a table with the *muzhiki* who shook his hand and patted his back, saying, "Well done, brother, you got through it," groups of Luntiks with their informant reports began circling around. These reports listed the perceived flaws of the individual, such as poorly hung towels, unbuttoned buttons, or walking unevenly in formation—the possibilities were endless.

Luntik had a gentle nature and an even kinder face: open, childlike, with protruding ears. It was this resemblance to an animated character that earned him his prison nickname and his notoriety. Luntik seemed no worse than other *kozly,* doing what he was told and telling others what to do, but everyone in the barrack, including his fellow informants, despised him. And he couldn't understand why. After all, he was just trying to do his job well.

When the *krasnyye* became too much of a nuisance for the *muzhiki,* the latter could revolt, as occasionally happened. At that point, the cry would go out, "Beat the *kozly*!" and a handful of desperate prisoners would chase the so-called activists around the barrack, striking them with fists and stools. The *krasnyye* would cower in all corners, seeking shelter under bunks, praying for the police to come quickly to their aid. Luntik had heard about such incidents and already had a small crevice in mind where he could hide in case of such turmoil, knowing he would be one of the first people to be targeted.

Luntik had been born and raised in a small village near Odesa. His family life was far from happy. His mother hadn't loved him, and he'd felt the same way about her. He kept running away from home as far back as he could remember; he couldn't even count how many times he'd done it. The destination didn't matter; escaping from a loveless home was all that he wanted. But Luntik was always caught, then beaten mercilessly.

His mother and stepfather competed in mistreating him, each trying to be more cruel than the other. Their other children didn't face the same level of abuse as Luntik. They were younger, less rebellious, and more loved. When Luntik grew old enough, he escaped to his aunt in a nearby district, deciding to live with her. Life there wasn't easy either, but at least his aunt didn't beat him or drive him away. She only scolded him for eating her bread and said he should live in the barn.

Having struggled to the end of ninth grade, Luntik then enrolled in a boarding school, leaving behind his aunt's barn and stale bread. The new place seemed promising: he had his own bed, regular meals, and a vocational education. In three years, he would earn a diploma as a cook. Yet, survival was tough because they'd beat him in the boarding house too. Not a day had passed before the first time they beat him even worse than his parents had. Some students became embittered after such ordeals, channeling their pain into sports or strength. For Luntik, this meant adapting rather than resisting. He gave up his food, washed senior students' socks, and ran errands for them, like running to the store for beer. After finishing school, Luntik couldn't find work in his field, not due to lack of interest but because, even as a cook, jobs required connections. Homeless, he considered going back to school, hoping they wouldn't mistreat him immediately, but they didn't accept former students.

After a year of wandering like an ill-fated knight, Luntik, armed with his culinary diploma, landed a job as a janitor in Kyiv. While some might view it as unglamorous or dirty, he didn't mind. Having his own apartment, even if it came with the job, was far better than a shanty house. The work only took a few hours each day, though early in the morning. It had its challenges like fallen leaves, snow, garbage bins, and homeless people. But Luntik faced it all bravely and diligently. Most importantly, he now had both free time and money.

If he'd had plenty of time before, it was mostly spent on two thoughts: "What will I eat?" and "Where will I sleep?" Now, with his own place and money, he could spend his hours on pleasure. He read books, strolled around the city, bought and cooked his own food, got a mobile phone with a big screen, and even attempted to pursue girls. He'd faced rejection before with local girls from his village, and Luntik found it even more challenging with Kyiv girls. But he didn't give up. He continued to practice his skills with different girls, at least through internet videos available to him.

Things were going well, and Luntik even considered saving up for a computer. But this venture didn't work out so well for him—getting a phone on credit turned out to be much easier. Luntik was already a hardened drug user by then. He'd gotten addicted to weed back during his school days, often trading it with someone for a joint or a couple of drugs. Thankfully, the southern steppes of his homeland were full of this important plant in young Luntik's life. He wasn't a botanist or a nerd, he just had a craving for cannabis. Dried, preferably just the buds, and preferably already rolled into cigarette paper.

But that was during the days of his early youth. As he became an adult, or rather an adult in his own eyes, Luntik, upon arriving in the big city and starting to earn some money, moved on to something heavier and more potent—synthetic marijuana, also known as "spice." There were different types of spice, ranging from ones that hit you hard with a single drag to those that kept you high for two days straight. Luntik tried them all. With plenty of free time and even more spice available for sale, his money only covered essential food and payment for his phone. There was no money left for a computer or any other enticing things that the city's temptations offered in abundance.

Luntik began searching for additional income and quickly found an opportunity thanks to his phone and the internet— it turned out that besides nude girls, it offered some pretty vital information. Real earnings! Very good money! Huge, especially compared to a janitor's salary. But there was a catch. He needed to go to Russia, and Luntik didn't have the money for a ticket to visit his mom, let alone for a trip to another country. Truth be told, he didn't have much desire to see his mother either, and it seemed she felt the same way. They hadn't seen or spoken to each other for about five years.

But he had a strong desire to go to Russia and earn money. Unfortunately, there was no possibility of this, and he honestly explained this to the distant employers in his response. Miraculously, they replied that it wasn't a problem, and the company would cover the transport expenses for such a valuable employee. He could pay it back when he started earning money. They were confident that he would do so quickly and earn a lot. Luntik shared their confidence.

Only at the very end did he inquire about the job's nature. "Sales representative, courier," was the response. "Well, that's close to what I do," thought Luntik. In his mind, a salesman stood somewhere between a chef and a janitor. They sent him an electronic ticket, and off he went. He didn't quit his job, just took a vacation in case things didn't work out; at least he would have something to return to.

Luntik was already an experienced and seasoned guy, or so he believed. When he arrived at his destination, it turned out he had to trade drugs, namely the ever-familiar spice. He was even happy about this—it was his thing, and why pretend otherwise? He would've come anyway, maybe even faster. The job seemed easy: pick up a packet in one place and drop it off in another. Instructions came on his phone through the internet, where all previous communication had taken place, without any face-to-face meetings. Luntik understood that this was for the sake of secrecy, as the business was not entirely legal. But he believed that in the future, when the earnings started rolling in, he would be able to meet and possibly become friends with his mysterious employers. Once they saw how efficient and good he was at his job . . .

Luntik was caught during his very first deal. He couldn't understand or believe how absurdly it all turned out, couldn't understand where he'd gone wrong. He spoke openly and honestly with the police officers. They didn't beat him up too much because of that. Luntik showed his Ukrainian passport, hoping that this, along with his sincere cooperation with the investigation, would result in a conditional sentence or a small fine. Instead, he received eight years. Shocked, Luntik realized in prison that he wasn't the only one. A large portion of inmates in Russia were there for drug-related offenses. Not everyone sold drugs—most were users—but they were charged for it, as the police needed to show good progress in the fight against drug trafficking.

At first, the sentence spanning nearly half his life seemed unreal and endless to Luntik, but it turned out to be just the beginning of his ordeal. Some received sentences of ten, fifteen, or even more years. A few luckier ones got around five years, but only by betraying someone. Luntik would have done it willingly, but he had no one to betray. His online friends, his failed accomplices, had disappeared into the depths of the internet. Despite Luntik's insistence that they were the ones responsible, the police weren't in any rush to find them.

During his time in prison, Luntik realized that many other one-time fools from Ukraine had fallen into the same trap, enticed by the promise of easy money. The pattern was always the same: they looked for jobs online and got invited to Russia, either traveling on their own or funded by recruiters. One or two drug stashes later, they were caught red-handed. The court. The charges. The sentencing. The metaphorical prison boot.

When Luntik arrived at the camp, there were already dozens of such clones from Ukraine, and that was in just one colony. If Luntik had a propensity for analysis and generalizations, he would have realized that he'd become an involuntary participant and victim of a massive provocation, for which considerable resources and efforts had been expended. The goal was not merely to fill Russian prisons with young, naive Luntiks, but to demonstrate to everyone: "Look, it's actually Ukrainians who are selling drugs in Russia." And such a large-scale operation wouldn't have been possible without the patronage of Russian law enforcement and intelligence agencies. The command for it came from the top, with the sole purpose of discrediting Ukraine at any cost during this post-Crimean period of confrontation between the two countries.

Luntik, like other young Ukrainian men seeking easy money and landing themselves in the northern colony, did this without considering the implications. They came to the aggressor country and tried to play their hand at selling drugs that bring nothing but death and sorrow. But their actions weren't politically motivated—they were simply driven by the desire to make money. They didn't concern themselves with how many of their compatriots and peers were losing their lives in the trenches of Donbas while they did it.

When Luntik arrived at the colony, he first asked for an international envelope and wrote a letter to his mother. In the letter, he admitted his mistakes, explaining that her wayward son had ended up in prison and needed help in the form of packages, money, and just simply keeping in touch. He emphasized that they were still family, and he hoped that they still cared for each other. He'd already sent a couple of similar letters from the central detention facility but never received a response. Undeterred, Luntik continued bombarding his mother with pitiful messages month after month, now from the colony. Still, there was no reply.

Gradually, he adapted to life in this new environment. Every day, he sat on his stool, monitoring the circumstances in the section until the evening, at which point another orderly took over the post, and Luntik could attend to his own affairs. He didn't have many tasks to do: he didn't write letters to his mother every day. He played chess, read, or watched television. At any moment, some higher-ranking *kozel* could call on him and give him a task. Mostly, Luntik moved along the service lane, as they say, voluntarily performing chores. He brewed tea and carried it to the custodian's office, where the tougher *kozly* often gathered. He washed their cups and plates, made their beds, changed their linens, and carried clothes to the laundry. He didn't wash socks—that was someone else's job, someone even lower in the hierarchy than Luntik. For his "swiftness," the activists would sometimes slip him some tea or sweets, and at other times, a slap on the back of his head. They didn't give him cigarettes because the kid was a drug addict, had never smoked cigarettes, and didn't even start smoking in prison. Maybe he would have started, but he never had his own, and others didn't share theirs with him.

The days went by, and nothing in Luntik's life changed. He'd been in prison for less than a year, and under the best circumstances, he had four more years to go, even more if he misbehaved and was kicked out of the activist group. Several more years of such a monotonous, despised existence, then the same thing, but on the other side of the fence.

Luntik marched with everyone in formation to the mess hall or the bathhouse, attended lectures at the club, and went through daily inspections. The life of an ordinary *kozel* standing on the lower rungs of the pyramid was hardly different from that of a regular inmate. In this camp, the Groundhog Day effect was particularly strong, and it was impossible to distinguish Monday from Friday. Only a couple of visits a year, one phone call per month, or at the very least a letter could somehow diversify the gray life of the prisoners. But no one came to see Luntik, he had no one to call, and he no longer expected any mail.

He had no friends, and no one wanted to socialize with him, not even from his own kind, the *krasnyye*. It was unclear what he thought about while sitting on his stool. But he clearly pondered something from time to time, furrowing his brow with his eyebrows twitching as he chewed the words inside his mouth. Luntik didn't yet know that tomorrow would be a celebration—that he'd receive a letter from his mother.

Kalyna

Kalyna glanced at his watch—he still had time before heading to church. The Orthodox church in the colony held services twice a week, and Kalyna never missed one. He couldn't recall when he became so devoted, but it felt like it had always been a part of him.

Kalyna said a brief prayer, crossed himself thrice, and bowed to the small icons in the room's corner. After this ritual, he checked his surroundings. Kalyna lived in a small two-story building. On the second floor, there were three offices where colony workers spent their days, while the first floor housed two cells for prisoners and a closet where he stayed. Kalyna was a convict, but he wasn't any ordinary one. Unlike the others, he had keys to cells and *lokalki*, the fenced sectors. Regular convicts followed the strict rules established by the colony administration, marching in formation and standing for hours on end during lengthy checks. Kalyna, however, enjoyed a number of privileges. He could move freely, sleep whenever, receive extra parcels and phone calls, along with other small comforts that made prison life more bearable. Most importantly, his cooperation earned him official praise and a positive record, greatly improving his chances for parole as a completely reformed person. Kalyna was known as a *kozel*, an "activist." They were different names that meant the same thing: he cooperated closely with the administration, specifically the influential operational unit.

When Kalyna first arrived at the harsh prison colony ten years ago, he'd gone through a brutal initiation process. Upon arrival from a long-distance transfer, newcomers were beaten and humiliated for hours to make them realize the harsh reality of their new environment. The message was clear: obey unquestioningly, never object, complain, or resist. Many newcomers yielded under the pressure, immediately cooperating with the prison administration. At first, Kalyna refused to disconnect from the decent prisoners and become a part of the submissive mass that flocked to the despicable *kozly*. He endured beatings, objecting to such prolonged humiliation. But observing the better treatment of the "activists," Kalyna eventually joined them voluntarily, though he had to compete with others for his place among them.

At first, Kalyna, because of his strong physique, cruel character, and terrible-looking physiognomy with his broken nose, was accepted. If they'd beaten him earlier, now, together with other *kozly*, wearing balaclavas on their heads and taking wooden sticks in their hands, he met the newcomers. After that, when Kalyna earned the trust of the police, he was transferred to a cleaner job. He held various unofficial positions in the colony, from a *kaptyor*—a prisoner who handed out clothes, bed linen, soap, etc.—to supply manager, until he found himself in a small two-story building, the worst in this already sad zone.

His role was quite straightforward: maintaining order in the room and keeping an eye on the guilty prisoners occasionally confined in the lower cells. These tasks had a hidden agenda: delving into the prisoners' minds, extracting information, and reporting to the higher-ups. Kalyna didn't directly participate in the tortures and humiliations orchestrated by the operatives. Instead, he acted as an assistant and a listener. He was responsible for playing louder music to drown out any screams, ensuring they remained out of earshot. When it was all over, he had to make sure that those who had been raped washed their blood off the floor. Kalyna himself didn't lift anything heavier than a spoon or keys. His status in the colony, even among *kozly*, was very high—the operatives didn't trust just anyone.

Kalyna's decade-long service to "activism" wasn't without its setbacks. A few years ago, there was a change in the power structure within the prison. This kind of shift was common, with staff competing for positions and influence, often relying on the *kozly* and using underhanded tactics. These internal power struggles didn't directly impact regular prisoners, but made their situation worse. In the last power struggle, Kalyna had sided with the wrong group and ended up losing. His handlers had to quit, and Kalyna got himself into more serious trouble. He was given six months of the strictest incarceration conditions and taken to a neighboring colony, even tougher, where he'd suffered to the fullest for his slip-up. But in the end, he was forgiven and brought back. Kalyna immediately "fastened himself" to the new owners in uniform and began to serve them even more zealously. A year later, Kalyna faced a deadline to apply for parole. He didn't want to miss the opportunity to escape the wretched prison, even though he didn't really have a home to return to.

Before prison, Kalyna had lived the simple life of a laborer in a small northern town. He had a wife and a little daughter, and he worked hard driving a car all day. Their life had seemed normal, like everyone else's. He used to drink—mostly on weekends—like all drivers. He would argue with his wife, but no more than others did. He would beat his wife, but no more than others did. Unexpectedly, his wife went on a drinking spree and decided to leave Kalyna for her new lover. In fact, she'd brought the new man home and kicked Kalyna out. When Kalyna returned from work and found another man in his place, he'd tried to object, but the new man was stronger and threw him out, breaking his nose in the process. Kalyna, looking at his belongings strewn on the street, realized that his family life had been shattered. He spiraled into a destructive lifestyle, found himself some slut, quit his job, and turned to heavy drinking. He hadn't exactly been part of the town's high society before, but after this incident, he sank even lower, finding companionship among heavy drinkers. It was an environment where people were united by one common interest: vodka. And it was during one of those drinking parties that things took a turn.

Kalyna never spoke about the details of his case, but the facts were clear. Late at night, a fire broke out in a family's apartment. Firefighters quickly arrived and put out the flames. The bodies of a married couple were found in one room. It didn't look like an accident because their severed heads were found on the table, on plates. Their tongues, noses, and ears cut off, their eyes gouged out. Only Kalyna and his girlfriend had been with those people the night before, so there was no one else to suspect. Denying their involvement seemed pointless, as there was strong evidence against them. If they'd denied it during the trial, they could have been sentenced to life in prison. In the end, Kalyna received seventeen years, and his girlfriend got thirteen years. The motive behind their actions remained unclear. It must have been a drinking conflict that escalated into a knife fight before pivoting to desecration and mutilation of corpses. It was impossible to justify it, but it wasn't hard to believe. One thing, however, wasn't clear—there had been a child. The family had a child, a four-year-old girl. She was there and had seen everything. Kalyna couldn't leave the witness, even though she was so small. But she was already speaking and aware of everything. Still, he couldn't raise his hand against a child. They did worse. They tied her up, gagged her, and threw her on an open balcony. Outside, it was a ruthless northern winter, and the girl, dressed in nothing more than house clothes, probably would have frozen to death before morning.

After their night-time crime, Kalyna and his accomplice, fueled by alcohol, thought they needed to destroy the evidence. They returned to the scene and set fire to the apartment. In their drunken haze, they forgot about the child on the balcony. Firefighters arrived quickly and managed to control the fire, preventing complete destruction of the apartment and saving the balcony. However, the girl wasn't immediately found. While she wasn't burned, her arms and legs suffered frostbite and had to be amputated later. Losing both parents and limbs on one tragic night, the child was placed in a special boarding school.

Like any other prisoner, Kalyna didn't believe he was guilty. He thought he'd received excessive punishment for defending his woman against a wrongdoer. He claimed he attended church not to atone for sins, but out of genuine faith. Kalyna read only the Bible and religious texts, observed fasting, and respected Orthodox traditions and holidays. He wasn't ashamed of his actions in the colony, even those that harmed others. He did what he could to survive and adapt, regardless of the cost to others.

Once, Kalyna watched a TV program about Nazi death camps where thousands of Jews had been tragically burned up in crematoriums. The program revealed that only prisoners involved in camp work survived—those who served the mass extermination process passively. Kalyna empathized with those people, *kozly* of a different era, understanding how they'd clung to their positions as a means to survive, even if that meant pushing someone else into the maw of the merciless monster instead of them. The program didn't explicitly mention this moral dilemma, but Kalyna grasped it. Although he wasn't in a concentration camp like Auschwitz and his situation wasn't life or death, he still wanted to get out as soon as possible, just like any other prisoner.

Kalyna's thoughts were consumed by the prospect of his upcoming release and the chance to reunite with his daughter. They hadn't met once in the past ten years and had only exchanged letters at the beginning when she was in elementary school. Now, she was in college, but Kalyna was confident they could build a good relationship once he was free. Still, there was at least another year to wait. Fortunately, he'd received plenty of appreciation and support from the colony's administration. His past mistakes were forgiven by the new management, giving him a strong possibility of being granted parole as someone genuinely committed to change. Kalyna tried his best not to dwell on his past victims or the harsh words spoken about him during the trial, like that person who said, "I don't regret that we don't have the death penalty, I regret that we don't have drawing and quartering."

Kalyna heard a gentle ringing, a homemade bell by the temple calling the prisoners to the church service. He quickly put on his prison jacket and cap, locked the door, and hurried to the church, walking across the crisp snow in the cold. Kalyna wanted to find a seat in the front row, near the altar. He believed that being closer to God would bring him solace.

Oleh Sentsov is an award-winning Ukrainian filmmaker and writer from Crimea. He was unjustly imprisoned by Russian authorities for opposing the occupation of Crimea in 2014 and spent five years in prison, during which he went on a hunger strike. In 2019, he was freed during a prisoner exchange. Since the start of the full-scale Russian invasion in 2022, Sentsov has been serving in the Ukrainian Armed Forces.

Dmytro Kyyan is a Ukrainian-American writer, editor, and translator from Kharkiv. From the 1990s to the early aughts he was the editor-in-chief of *Foto & Video Magazine*, and under his direction, it became the leading publication in photography throughout Eastern Europe.

Kate Tsurkan is a writer, editor, and translator. Her work has appeared in the *New Yorker*, *Vanity Fair*, *Harper's*, the *Los Angeles Review of Books*, the *Washington Post*, the *Guardian*, and elsewhere. She is the founding editor of *Apofenie Magazine*.